A General Equilibrium Analysis of US Foreign Trade Policy

A General Equilibrium Analysis of US Foreign Trade Policy

Jaime de Melo
David Tarr

The MIT Press
Cambridge, Massachusetts
London, England

This book was set in Palatino by Asco Trade Typesetting Ltd., Hong Kong and was printed and bound in the United States of America.

Library of Congress Cataloging-in-Publication Data

De Melo, Jaime.
A general equilibrium analysis of US foreign trade policy / Jaime de Melo, David Tarr.
p. cm.
Includes bibliographical references and index.
ISBN 978-0-262-51213-8
1. Import quotas—United States—Econometric models. 2. Foreign trade and employment—United States—Econometric models. 3. Labor market—United States—Econometric models. 4. Textile workers—United States—Supply and demand—Econometric models. 5. Automobile industry and trade—United States—Supply and demand—Econometric models. 6. Iron and steel workers—United States—Supply and demand—Econometric models. I. Tarr, David G. II. Title.
HF1757.D43 1992
382'.3'0973—dc20 91-3989
CIP

To Rosemary and Nano

To my wife Linda Haas Tarr and
our sons Michael and Adam

Contents

List of Tables xi
List of Figures xv
Preface xvii

1 Recent Issues in US Foreign Trade Policy 1
1.1 Policy Issues 3
1.2 Why a General Equilibrium Model? 6
1.3 Previous Studies of the Cost of Protection 7
1.4 Plan of the Book 10

2 Trade Policy Analysis in a One-Sector General Equilibrium Model with Product Differentiation 15
2.1 Product Differentiation and Specialization 16
2.2 A One-Sector Model with Differentiated Trade 18
2.3 Comparative Statics: A Graphical Analysis of Terms-of-Trade, Transfer, and Tariff Changes 24
2.4 A Digression: Choice of Numéraire and the Real Exchange Rate 29
2.5 Costs of Protection in the One-Sector Model 31
2.6 Trade Policy and Resource Shifts in the Presence of Product Differentiation 34
2.7 Conclusion 39

3 The Basic General Equilibrium Trade Model 41
3.1 Overview of the Model 41
3.2 Equations of the Basic Trade Model 46
3.3 Modeling of Quantitative Restrictions 56
3.4 Welfare Measure 58
3.5 Conclusion 59

Appendix 3A Definition of the Welfare Measure 59
Appendix 3B The Real Exchange Rate 62

4 Quota Premium Rates and Rent Capture 65
4.1 Who Captures the Quota Rents? 65
4.2 Quota Rent Estimates in Textiles and Apparel 69
4.3 Quota Rent Estimates for Automobiles from Japan and Europe 78
4.4 Voluntary Export Restraints on Steel 83

5 Welfare Costs of US Quotas in Textiles and Apparel, Automobiles, and Steel in the Basic Model 85
5.1 Elasticity Specification 87
5.2 Removing Quotas on Textiles and Apparel 89
5.3 Removing Voluntary Export Restraints on Japanese Automobiles 93
5.4 Imposing Voluntary Export Restraints on Steel 96
5.5 Joint Removal of Quotas in the Three Sectors 98
5.6 Introducing Terms-of-Trade Effects 103
5.7 Comparisons with Earlier Estimates 105
Appendix 5A Liberalization with Endogenous Quota Premia and Sectoral Rationing of Steel 107

6 Welfare Costs of Quantitative Restrictions under Different Factor Market Assumptions 111
6.1 Labor-Leisure Choice 112
6.2 Welfare Costs of Quotas in Steel and Automobiles in the Presence of Wage Distortions 115
6.3 Modeling Labor Unions in the Automobile and Steel Sectors 123
6.4 Short-Run Welfare Costs of Quotas in Textiles and Apparel, Automobiles, and Steel 130
6.5 Welfare Costs of Quotas with International Capital Mobility 134
6.6 Conclusion 138
Appendix 6A The Welfare Measure and Labor-Leisure Trade-off 139
Appendix 6B Derivation of Labor Union Wage Differential 142

7 Welfare Costs of Quantitative Restrictions with Imperfect Competition in Automobiles and Steel 145
7.1 Evidence on Economies of Scale and Pricing Rules in Steel and Automobiles 146

7.2 Modifications to the Basic Model to Accommodate Imperfect Competition 150
7.3 Welfare Costs of Quantitative Restrictions with Imperfect Competition 156
7.4 Conclusion 166
Appendix 7A Derivation of the Price Elasticity of Demand 167

8 Revenue-Raising Taxes: Evaluation of Alternative Strategies for Taxing Petroleum Industries 173
8.1 Recent Proposals for Taxing Petroleum Industries 174
8.2 Adaptation of the Basic Model to the Energy Sector 175
8.3 Revenue and Welfare Effects of Tax Proposals 178
8.4 Efficient Taxation of Petroleum Industries 184
8.5 Conclusion 189

9 Conclusions 191
9.1 Summary of Results 192
9.2 Costs per Job Protected by Quota Protection 196
9.3 Estimated Costs of All Quantitative Restrictions 199
9.4 Computation of Tariffs with a Welfare Cost Equivalent to That of Quotas 199
9.5 Directions for Future Research 200

Appendixes
A Data Set Construction and Model Calibration 203
B Elasticity Specification and Data Sources 229

Notes 241
References 261
Name Index 277
Subject Index 281

List of Tables

1.1 Partial equilibrium estimates of the costs of protection in the textile and apparel, automobile, and steel industries 9

2.1 A one-sector small-country model with differentiated trade 19

2.2 Welfare and real exchange rate calculations for an increase in transfers 31

2.3 Welfare gain from a foreign transfer 32

2.4 Welfare costs of protection 33

2.5 Degree of trade dependence as trade substitution elasticity varies 37

3.1 Model equations 47

3.2 Definition of endogenous variables 49

3.3 Definition of exogenous variables and parameters 50

5.1 Elasticity specifications 88

5.2 Production and demand structure in textiles and apparel, automobiles, and steel 89

5.3 Welfare gain and employment effects of removing quotas in textiles and apparel 90

5.4 Welfare gains and employment effects of removing voluntary export restraints in automobiles 94

5.5 Welfare costs and employment effects of imposing voluntary export restraints in steel 97

5.6 Changes in welfare, real wages, and the real exchange rate from the joint removal of quotas and elimination of all tariffs 99

5.7 Sectoral changes in employment from removing quotas in textiles and apparel, automobiles, and steel separately and together and from removing all tariffs: central elasticity case 100

5.8 Sectoral changes in exports and imports as a result of simultaneously eliminating quotas in textiles and apparel, automobiles, and steel: central elasticity case 101

5.9 Welfare effects of quotas with large-country assumption: central elasticity case 103

5A.1 Welfare changes from removing quotas and tariffs with endogenous premia in other sectors: central elasticity case 108

5A.2 Welfare costs of rationing steel by sector 110

6.1 Welfare costs of quotas with labor-leisure choice: central elasticity case 114

6.2 Employment effects of removing quotas on textiles and apparel, automobiles, and steel with labor-leisure choice: central elasticity case 115

6.3 International comparisons of hourly compensation costs for production workers in iron and steel and motor vehicles and equipment, 1984 117

6.4 Welfare effects of removing wage distortions in automobiles and steel, separately and together: central elasticity case 120

6.5 Employment effects of removing wage distortions in automobiles and steel, separately and together: central elasticity case 121

6.6 Welfare costs of quotas in the presence of wage distortions in automobiles and steel: central elasticity case 122

6.7 Employment effects of removing quotas separately and together in the presence of wage distortions in automobiles and steel: central elasticity case 123

6.8 Welfare costs of quotas in the presence of endogenous wage distortions in automobiles and steel: central elasticity case 129

6.9 Welfare effects of removing quotas and tariffs with fixed capital stocks in each sector: central elasticity case 131

6.10 Employment effects of quotas with fixed capital stocks in each sector: central elasticity case 132

6.11 Welfare and employment effects of removing quotas in the presence of internationally mobile capital 136

7.1 Profits in the US automobile industry, 1979–84 149

7.2 Welfare costs of quotas on steel under different pricing rules: central elasticity case 159

7.3 Welfare costs of voluntary export restraints on Japanese automobiles under different pricing rules: central elasticity case 160

7.4 Combined welfare costs of quotas in automobiles and steel under imperfectly competitive behavior in both industries: central elasticity case 164

8.1 Production and demand structure and elasticities in US petroleum industries 177

8.2 Revenue, welfare, and employment effects of tariffs and excise taxes in the petroleum industry: central elasticity case 179

8.3 Relative efficiency of tariffs and excise taxes in the petroleum industry: low and high elasticity cases 181

8.4 Optimal excise tax and tariff rates for raising $20 billion in government revenue: central elasticity case 185

9.1 Welfare cost comparisons with earlier studies 192

9.2 Net benefits from quota removal: central elasticity case 198

9.3 Tariff structures yielding costs equal to those of quotas: central elasticity estimates 200

A.1 Mapping of eighty-sector input-output (I/O) matrix into twelve sectors 205

A.2 Mapping of National Income and Product Accounts (NIPA) value-added data into the twelve-sector aggregation 207

A.3 Mapping of Standard International Trade Classification (SITC) data into the twelve-sector model 209

A.4 Twelve-sector interindustry flow matrix for the United States for 1984: intermediate flows 212

A.5 US civilian employment by sector in 1984 214

A.6 A Social Accounting Matrix 216

A.7 Accounting identities underlying table A.6 217

A.8 A US Social Accounting Matrix for 1984 219

B.1 Elasticities of substitution: imports for domestic goods in intermediate production 231

B.2 Elasticities of substitution: capital for labor in production 232

B.3 Elasticities of transformation in production: domestic goods and exports 233

B.4 Elasticity of final demand for composite goods: price and income 235

B.5 Foreign direct investment in the US automobile industry, 1982–88 238

B.6 Foreign direct investment above $50 million in US automobile assembly plants, 1979–88 239

List of Figures

2.1 Equilibrium in the small-country case 21

2.2 Equilibrium with constant foreign demand elasticity 23

2.3 Terms-of-trade improvement 25

2.4 Increase in foreign transfers 27

2.5 Imposing a tariff 28

3.1 Model structure: (a) allocation of production; (b) consumer demand 45

3.2 The elasticity of substitution and cost minimization in intermediate demand 51

3.3 The elasticity of transformation and revenue maximization between domestic and export sales 52

3.4 Import price determination with rationing: (a) example of preexisting rationing for consumer good; (b) example of imposing rationing on intermediate good 57

3.5 Hicksian equivalent and compensating variations: (a) welfare measure (EV); (b) welfare measure (CV) 60

4.1 Quota rents 66

4.2 Determination of marginal textile supplier 75

4.3 Quality upgrading under a VER 79

5.1 Distortionary cost of QRs under different elasticities of import demand for final goods with and without quota 91

5.2 Distortionary cost of imposing QRs under different elasticities of import demand for intermediate goods 98

6.1 Extended utility choice 113

6.2 Distortions from interindustry wage differentials 119

6.3 Employment determination with passive firm 125

6.4 Employment determination through negotiation 126

6.5 The union-firm contract curve 127

6.6 Benefits of tariff removal depending on supply elasticity homogeneous product 133

6.7 Benefits of quota removal depending on supply elasticity for differentiated product 133

7.1 Calibration with initial profits in automobiles 156

8.1 Import demand elasticity and welfare loss 182

8.2 Welfare impact on domestic petroleum products of a tariff on imported petroleum products given an excise tax on crude oil 187

A.1 Benchmarking 204

Preface

This book uses applied general equilibrium methods to analyze recent issues debated about the conduct of US foreign trade policy. In many respects, the general equilibrium approach is superior to the more traditional partial equilibrium approach. But the general equilibrium approach is often criticized for the opaqueness surrounding model-generated results. Our aim is to remove this opaqueness by carefully giving the economic intuition behind each result—at the risk, no doubt, of sometimes appearing pedantic. We hope that, on balance, the reader will be convinced that thoroughness is worthwhile and that applied general equilibrium analysis is a valuable and sensible tool for analyzing trade policy.

We owe thanks to many for their help. Our greatest debt is to those who provided immediate logistic support. Julie Stanton and Alex Pfaff worked long hours in assisting us, with both great insight and humor. Ghislaine Bayard accurately and patiently typed numerous drafts of the chapters, sometimes from barely decipherable manuscripts. Meta de Coquereaumont greatly improved the presentation through her editing.

We thank Morris Morkre for reading the entire manuscript in several different drafts and for his many helpful comments and corrections. We also thank Drusilla Brown, Ann Harrison, Paul Pautler, David Roland-Holst, Wendy Takacs, and John Whalley for commenting on early versions of the manuscript. Sherman Robinson provided the input-output table, advice on a number of aspects of modeling, and, along with Ken Hansen, Mylo Peterson, Mark Planting, Bob Rabinowitz, and Eleanor Uzzelle helped with data reconciliation issues. Tony Brooke, Alex Meeraus, and Soren Nielsen provided advice regardings GAMS programming questions. We would also like to thank Tim Condon, Shantayan Devarajan, Elias Dinopoulos, Riccardo Faini, Rob Feenstra, Mike Finger, Gene Grossman, Carl Hamilton, Glen Harrison, Ron Jones, Kala Krishna, James Levinsohn,

Arvind Panagariya, Dani Rodrik, Clint Shiells, Tom Rutherford, Susan Vroman, and Alan Winters for helpful discussions.

Of course, any remaining errors are our responsibility. The views expressed are ours and do not necessarily reflect those of our affiliations. We would especially like to express our gratitude to our families for their understanding and support during the preparation of this book.

A General Equilibrium Analysis of US Foreign Trade Policy

1 Recent Issues in US Foreign Trade Policy

Along with the rising US trade deficit in recent years has come rising pressure for increased protection.[1] During recent presidential campaigns, proposals were put forth urging that the United States protect high-skill sectors to keep real wages up.[2] Pressure for increased protection has also gained momentum among those who would like to use a revenue-increasing tariff on crude oil imports to improve the fiscal deficit. Despite the debacle of the Smoot-Hawley tariff, which gave protectionism a bad name in the United States, the benefits of free trade are now being seriously questioned.[3] Other observers have been alarmed by the increase in protection and argue that it should be lowered. They note that the spread of nontariff barriers in recent years has canceled many of the benefits that were gained through the painstaking efforts of twenty years of multilateral trade negotiations from the Dillon to Tokyo rounds.[4]

In the popular discussion of trade protection, two themes are especially prevalent. One is that the succession of multilateral trade negotiations has reduced barriers to trade to insignificant levels. To the informed international economist, this statement is clearly false. Today trade faces myriad costly import restrictions whose impact is no less severe simply because they have been negotiated with exporters or take a legal form that is not barred by the General Agreement on Tariffs and Trade (GATT). The other theme, which surfaces in US presidential politics, is that "unfair foreign trade practices" must be counteracted. For example, as pointed out in Finger (1990), while the first draft of President Reagan's fall 1987 trade speech might have been a free trade speech, the draft he delivered was a fair trade speech.

As is often the case with policy debates, information is lacking or, when available, sometimes manipulated to support a particular position. The purpose of this book is to analyze the relative merits of the various positions in this debate. Along with countervailing duties and antidumping measures, import quotas and voluntary export restraints are the primary instruments of current US protection. Our main focus in this book is on the costs of protection from the quotas on textiles and steel and the export restraints on automobiles that were in effect between 1981 and 1985. We also assess the merits of alternative taxation schemes in the US petroleum products sectors, in terms of their revenue-raising potential and their efficiency.

The method of analysis is counterfactual simulation. This means that we never test *directly* for the validity of the underlying behavioral assumptions. For example, when we assume that the automobile industry is characterized by oligopolistic Cournot behavior or when we assume that the steelworkers union sets the wage rate in the steel industry, we do not know to what extent this assumption is representative of actual behavior. But we do test indirectly for most major behavioral assumptions by looking at the sensitivity of our results to changes in behavioral rules. We are also fortunate that considerable empirical work is available on supply and demand elasticities for a great number of industries, as well as evidence on the importance of economies of scale and of union influence in wage determination. This allows us to establish ranges of estimates by carrying out simulations for high, medium, and low sets of demand and supply elasticities. As a result of this accumulated evidence, we are fairly confident in the estimates in this book and of our success in addressing the major criticisms raised against counterfactual simulation analysis.

Against the disadvantage of not yielding confidence interval estimates is the advantage that counterfactual simulation analysis based on a clearly defined structural model simplifies the task of identifying the role of assumptions in determining the outcome of simulations. For example, we are able to isolate precisely the influence of labor union behavior or of collusive behavior on the magnitude of the costs of protection. We are also able to assess the importance of induced "terms-of-trade" losses in mitigating the estimates of the costs of protection. We take advantage of this transparency of counterfactual simulation analysis to carefully disentangle the relative importance of each of these effects in our estimates. We also hope that this approach will help readers form their own judgments about the role of varying behavioral assumptions.

In some cases we devote considerable space to explaining why two simulations with different behavioral assumptions (or based on different elasticities) give different results, even though both results are of the same order of magnitude. Our emphasis is deliberate. Throughout the book we make a point of explaining the mechanisms that affect estimates so that the reader can judge the validity of the underlying behavioral and elasticity specifications. We hope that the reader will not be left with an impression that general equilibrium modeling is a black box.

This chapter is organized as follows: Section 1.1 summarizes the recent debates on US protectionism, both in the broad policy arena and among academics. Section 1.2 provides examples that justify our general equilibrium approach to the study of US trade policy. Section 1.3 summarizes results from previous studies of US trade policies. Finally, section 1.4 outlines the book.

1.1 Policy Issues

This book focuses on the allocative and efficiency implications of US trade policies with respect to industry. Since voluntary export restraints (VERs) and quantitative restrictions (QRs) are the most costly trade restrictions, we look closely at the implications of these nontariff barriers to trade.[5] Accordingly we survey the policy issues in the narrower context of industrial trade policy, bypassing issues of trade in services and of US agricultural trade policy. Analysis of these other issues would require either a different approach (in the case of trade in services) or a different focus (in the case of agricultural trade) involving the interaction of domestic policies (e.g., supports) and trade policies. The following paragraphs briefly summarize some of the major issues in the trade policy debate that are examined in this book.

Efficiency costs of quotas. For those who have followed the rise in US protectionism, it is apparent that the increase in nontariff barriers has had high efficiency costs for the US economy. Just how costly have the quotas in automobiles, steel, and textiles been for the US economy? If these quotas are more costly than tariff protection, then bilateral protectionism through VERs or QRs threatens the efficiency gains achieved through successive multilateral trade negotiations.

The capture of quota rents. Does the United States capture the quota rents associated with nontariff barriers? We argue at length in chapter 4 that the US method of allocating quota rights allows foreign countries to capture the quota rents. That is, the difference between the nonquota price of imported articles and their higher price under the quota goes to the exporting nation, not the United States. Alternative methods of allocating quota rights exist that would allow the United States to capture the quota rents. These methods include raising the tariff rate, allocating quota rights to domestic citizens, or auctioning the quota rights.[6] Australia and New

Zealand have successfully auctioned quota rights, and the US International Trade Commission recently recommended that the president impose an auction quota in the footwear industry.[7]

But can the United States actually capture the quota rents by auctioning the quota rights? If imports are supplied monopolistically, auctions will not capture the rents from foreigners (see Krishna 1989a, 1990). While there is probably much competition among suppliers of imported textiles and apparel products or steel, this may not be the case in automobiles, which are highly differentiated products.

Quotas as facilitating practices. The US auto industry is dominated by three firms. In 1984, when the VER on Japanese auto imports was most binding, the US auto industry made abnormally high profits. Evidence summarized in chapter 7 suggests that profits in the industry were abnormally high in 1984, due in part to the lack of foreign competition because of the VER on Japanese autos. Negotiation of the VER in autos is likely to have allowed the US auto industry to restrict output below the levels that would have been produced under more competitive conditions. These quotas act as a "facilitating practice" for monopoly power (Krishna 1985).

Employment. Much of the debate on protection concerns its effects on employment. Protection is often regarded as a mechanism for preserving jobs in the protected industries. But what is the impact on jobs in industries that are not receiving protection? How many people would have to change jobs if protection were removed? Although many economists do not believe that protection is capable of generating employment, the large rise in the US deficit has generated fears of widespread unemployment. Yet this large increase in the trade deficit has been associated with a decline in the unemployment rate. Although economists would not suggest a causal relationship, an awareness of these numbers has given pause to those who argue that protection is needed to preserve US jobs. Because the employment effects of protection are such an important issue in the debate on US trade policy, we need economywide and individual sector estimates of the employment effects of protection.

Capital mobility. Between 1984 and 1988 the share of the US capital stock owned by foreigners increased fourfold, reaching 4 percent. As world capital markets have become increasingly integrated, foreign direct investment has responded strongly to trade policy changes. How important is this effect? Will allowing for international capital mobility in response to trade policy changes significantly affect estimates of the costs of protection?

Wage distortions. Wages in the steel and automobile sectors are considerably higher than the average wage for US manufacturing. Furthermore the ratio of wages in steel and automobiles to the average manufacturing wage is much higher in the United States than in other industrial countries that produce steel and autos. Many have argued that these high wages have made it difficult for US auto and steel products to compete with foreign products. Would these two industries be more competitive internationally if these wage distortions were removed? Are the benefits of trade liberalization substantially less in the auto and steel sectors because of these distortions?

Interactions between product and factor market distortions. It has been argued that the unusually high wages in the auto and steel sectors owe much to the monopoly power of the United Autoworkers and the United Steelworkers Unions. If so, the situation is more complex since any change in trade policy will affect the wage demanded by the labor unions, which in turn will affect the costs of protection in these sectors. Are these effects important, and how should they alter our approach to trade policy in sectors in which labor unions play an important role?

Costs of protection under imperfect competition. For sectors in which there is evidence of economies of scale, such as automobiles and steel, assessing the efficiency effects of protection becomes complicated by the interactions of two opposing effects. On the one hand, according to the traditional arguments for freer trade, these sectors should probably contract because of the distortionary production and consumption costs of protection. On the other hand, with unexploited economies of scale, there is potential cost saving through expansion, provided there is not excessive entry. Which of the two effects dominates?

In automobiles there is evidence of pure profits and evidence that these profits were greatest at the height of the VER on Japanese auto exports to the United States. How does this affect the costs of protection?

Revenue-raising protection. Recently several proposals have been made to increase taxes or tariffs in the energy sector. The most notable proposals have suggested (1) an increase in crude oil tariffs of $5 or $10 per barrel and (2) an increase in taxes on final petroleum products of 5 to 25 cents a gallon. How efficient would such increases be in raising government revenue? Which of these proposals is least costly to the US taxpayer? Which combination of excise taxes and import tariffs in the petroleum product sectors would be the least costly way to reduce the fiscal deficit?

1.2 Why a General Equilibrium Model?

Because most of the questions raised in the preceding section have economywide implications, this book assesses the consequences of protection using a computable general equilibrium (CGE) model for the US economy with a trade policy focus. The usefulness of a general equilibrium approach is illustrated by the following examples.

Tariffs have been progressively lowered through multilateral negotiations, but the use of nontariff barriers has risen. How have these offsetting changes affected the welfare of the United States? What is the average economywide level of tariff protection that would yield the same welfare loss as do the quotas in textiles, autos, and steel? Partial equilibrium estimates may yield accurate estimates in particular sectors, but estimates of the aggregate costs of trade restrictions across sectors require a general equilibrium model to account for economywide budget and resource constraints.

Other examples of the usefulness of a general equilibrium approach arise out of second-best situations. One concerns the recent controversy regarding trade and industrial policy in sectors with wage distortions. The second-best evaluation of the movement of labor across sectors in response to trade liberalization is a general equilibrium evaluation of the relative valuation of labor. Another example is the surge in foreign direct investment in US automobiles by Japanese automakers, which raises the possibility of welfare- reducing capital import in the presence of protection in several sectors. Only a general equilibrium valuation of the imported capital can answer the question of whether capital import reduces welfare.

Consider the case of the removal of protection in the steel and auto sectors, two sectors that have received special nontariff protection. Removing protection in the steel industry will cause a loss of jobs in that industry, but the auto industry will be able to purchase steel at a lower price than before. Will the automobile industry then expand despite the removal of its own protection? If so, then auto and steel workers would not share a common interest in protection. Interindustry linkages, like the obvious one between the steel and auto sectors, or between the crude oil and petroleum products sectors, are best captured in a general equilibrium framework.

Or take as another example the debate about the relative merits of an import tax on oil versus an excise tax on the sale of petroleum products for reducing the fiscal and trade deficits. What is the least costly (in terms of welfare) combination of excise taxes and import tariffs that would raise a specified amount of tax revenue? Again, because of interindustry linkages, the answer to this question is best obtained in a general equilibrium setting.

A general equilibrium model that explicitly models labor supply is also helpful for assessing the economywide employment effects of QRs, which are at the heart of the US trade policy debate. For example, should farmers lobby for free trade under the assumption that agriculture would expand if nontariff protection were removed?

Or take the issue of whether, as many argue, the United States has monopoly power in exporting or monopsony power in importing. If this is the case, trade expansion will take place at a lower unit export price and a higher unit import price. However, import supply and export demand elasticities are not independent because of the balance of trade constraint. Again, a general equilibrium model is the better way to assess the relative importance of terms-of-trade effects on estimates of the costs of protection.

As a final example, consider the costs of relocating workers if protection is removed. We have estimates of the time it takes a worker to find a new job. The issue, then, is how many workers would have to relocate if quotas in textiles, steel, and automobiles were removed. Here again, because of interindustry linkages, it is preferable to obtain estimates of labor displacement in a general equilibrium setting rather than to add the costs of relocation for displaced workers across all sectors and then subtract them from the overall benefits of removing protection.

While a general equilibrium model has many advantages for our purposes here, econometric estimates representing different sectors have considerable value as well. Such estimates are especially useful for industry studies, and we rely on these estimates in some of our modeling work, particularly for the auto industry. The two approaches should be viewed as complementary since it is probably neither feasible nor desirable to estimate as a system of simultaneous equations the full set of equations describing a multisector economywide model like the one in this book.

1.3 Previous Studies of the Cost of Protection

In view of the concerns about the costs of protection, it would be useful to know the costs of nontariff protection individually for the auto, steel, and textile and apparel industries as well as the combined costs. Several studies have analyzed the effects of quotas on these three (and other) industries separately. Tarr and Morkre (1984), Hickock (1985), Hufbauer, Berliner, and Elliot (1986), and Cline (1987) have estimated the costs for textiles and apparel. The welfare effects of the auto VER have been estimated by

Feenstra (1984, 1985), Tarr and Morkre (1984), Hickock (1985), Hufbauer, Berliner, and Elliot (1986), Winston and associates (1987), and Dinopoulos and Kreinin (1988). In steel, the effects of VERs have been estimated by Tarr and Morkre (1984), and Hufbauer, Berliner, and Elliot (1986).

Table 1.1 surveys the results of these studies. Many of the differences in results within industries are explained by differences in coverage and years of the estimates. For example, in the case of automobiles Tarr and Morkre (1984) and Feenstra (1984) who estimate the costs of protection for 1981, a recession year, obtain low estimates. The other estimates, which are for 1984, are higher and are probably more representative of the costs of protection in automobiles. Among these estimates that of Dinopoulos and Kreinin is the most comprehensive because they recognize and estimate the impact of the VER with Japan on the prices of European cars. (How these interactions are estimated and incorporated in our model is discussed in detail in chapter 4.)

Underlying model assumptions are yet another source of difference in estimates. For example, Winston and associates estimate that monopoly power allowed the domestic auto industry to restrict output and employment following negotiation of the VER. For textiles and apparel the Tarr and Morkre estimates consider only the costs of quotas for imports from Hong Kong, whereas the other estimates reported in table 1.1 include the costs of quotas (and tariffs) for all textile and apparel imports.

All the studies listed in table 1.1 are partial equilibrium studies. While often they were able to model detailed features of an industry, they could not endogenously determine feedback effects from the rest of the economy of a policy change in the sector because of the underlying partial equilibrium assumptions. By contrast, the general equilibrium approach used in this book determines these feedback effects endogenously.

None of the studies reported in table 1.1 estimates the economywide employment effects of protection. Also, as we show in chapter 5, partial equilibrium estimates misestimate the effects of protection because they do not properly account for budget constraints (in particular, the balance of trade constraint). Not accounting for this constraint yields an overestimate of the costs of QR protection in automobiles, steel, and textiles and apparel of about one-third. Moreover income transfers to or from the rest of the world are more properly accounted for in a general equilibrium model. Thus a trade policy change that has an income effect on the United States will induce shifts in demand curves that are accounted for in a general equilibrium model but ignored in a partial equilibrium model. For example, a partial equilibrium analysis might predict that capturing quota rents

Table 1.1
Partial equilibrium estimates of the costs of protection in the textile and apparel, automobile, and steel industries

Industry/study	Year of estimate	Welfare costs (billions of $)	Consumer costs (billions of $)[a]	Jobs protected (thousands)	Welfare costs per job (thousands of $)
Textiles and apparel					
Tarr and Morkre (1984)	1980	0.37	0.38	8.9	43
Hickock (1985)	1984	na	8.5–11.0	na	na
Hufbauer, Berliner, and Elliot (1986)	1984	6.65	27.0	640.0	42[b]
Cline (1987)	1986	8.13	20.34	234.9	87
Automobiles					
Feenstra (1984)	1981	0.33	na	11.0	30
Tarr and Morkre (1984)	1981	0.99	1.1	4.6	216
Hickock (1985)	1984	na	4.5	na	na
Hufbauer, Berliner, and Elliot (1986)	1984	1.4	5.8	55.0	105[b]
Winston and associates (1987)	1984	5.0	14.0	−31.7	∞
Dinopoulos and Kreinin (1988)	1984	5.86	na	22.0[c]	181
Steel					
Tarr and Morkre (1984)	1985	0.80	1.1	10.0	81
Hickock (1985)	1985	na	1.0	na	na
Hufbauer, Berliner, and Elliot (1988)	1985	1.3	6.8	9.0	750[b]

Source: Compiled by the authors from sources listed in table.
a. Estimates of costs to consumers exceed welfare cost estimates because estimates of consumer costs assume that consumers do not receive payments from firms or the government.
b. Indicates consumer costs per job.
c. Job estimates are for 1981.

would have no resource allocation effect, which is not necessarily the case, as our general equilibrium analysis shows. Moreover protection can generate changes in the real exchange rate and the real wage that affect all sectors, including sectors receiving protection.

A few general equilibrium estimates of the cost of US protection are available. Prominent among these are the studies by Whalley (1985) and Deardorff and Stern (1986), which estimate the effects of a unilateral removal of protection in a multiregion model. The multilateral approach has the advantage of allowing for a study of the effects of multilateral trade liberalization, such as that emerging from the recent Tokyo round or the ongoing Uruguay round. However, the results of these studies cannot really be compared with the partial equilibrium estimates presented in table 1.1 because the level of aggregation is dictated by patterns of worldwide protection rather than by the pattern of sectoral protection in the United States. Furthermore, for reasons discussed at length in chapter 5, we believe that the general equilibrium estimates of multicountry models overestimate the terms-of-trade effects induced by a unilateral reduction in protection. For these reasons, we discuss these estimates, which usually show welfare losses from the unilateral removal of protection, in chapter 5 and contrast them with our estimates.

In summary, then, inaccuracy develops in a partial equilibrium model to the extent that changes are occurring in the variables that are being held constant for the analysis. As the magnitude of the policy changes becomes large, so does the inaccuracy. Partly for this reason, most of the studies listed in table 1.1 have not attempted to aggregate the costs to the economy of all the trade restrictions.[8] Adding up separate partial equilibrium estimates does not yield reliable global estimates. Several examples of this kind of aggregation bias are provided throughout this book.

Finally, as a prelude to the forthcoming chapters, we note that our estimates (for 1984) of the welfare cost of QR protection in automobiles, textiles and apparel, and steel exceed the partial equilibrium estimates in table 1.1 and, to an even greater extent, the earlier general equilibrium estimates alluded to above.

1.4 Plan of the Book

We wrote this book with two objectives in mind. First, we have attempted as much as possible to make our modeling assumptions transparent. We believe that we have been largely successful in this endeavor—perhaps occasionally at the expense of some overlap or repetition—by progressing sequentially from the simpler to the more complicated models. For example, we start with a simple neoclassical general equilibrium specification, then one by one we relax the restrictive assumptions about factor and product market behavior. Every extension is compared to the "basic" model, so it is easy to see where differences arise. In addition to its pedagogical advantages, this approach enables the reader to weigh the relative importance of relaxing various assumptions about competitive behavior in product markets or factor markets.

Second, we have placed more emphasis on parameter search than on modeling refinements. We believe this emphasis is well-placed for an exercise on the US economy, since the relative abundance of econometric estimates makes such a search rewarding. In particular, we devote an entire chapter (chapter 4) to justifying our choice of the magnitude of QR-induced premia in the textile and apparel and auto sectors. We are confident that the search was rewarding.

The remainder of the book is organized as follows. In chapters 2 and 3 we lay out the modeling assumptions for our specification of foreign trade and the consequences of these assumptions for our efficiency estimates. While the assumption of product differentiation on the import side is common in applied general equilibrium trade modeling, the symmetric assumption of product differentiation on the export side is less common. In chapter 2 we explore graphically, analytically, and numerically the implications of this assumption first in a one-sector general equilibrium formulation and then in a multisector partial equilibrium analysis.

In chapter 3 we present the full specification of the multisector model. We start with a nontechnical description of the model, followed by a more complete description of the full set of equations for the reader who is interested in modeling specifications. The chapter closes with a discussion of how we model rationing and with a brief presentation of our selected welfare measure, which is defined in detail in appendix 3A. Appendix 3B briefly discusses the real exchange rate for our multisector model.

Chapter 4 is devoted to the estimation of quota premia in automobiles and in textiles and apparel in 1984, the year for which we implemented the model numerically. First, we discuss how market structure in importing and exporting will affect whether the exporting or the importing country gets the quota rents. Then we give evidence suggesting that in the case of automobiles and textiles and apparel, foreign countries capture most of the rents, not the United States. Finally, we estimate the premium rates themselves; first for textiles and apparel, where we deal with the issue of estimating the marginal supplier under the complicated Multifiber Arrangement (MFA), and then for automobiles, where we control for quality upgrading induced by VERs.

Chapter 5 presents the core estimates of the welfare and employment consequences of QRs in textiles and apparel, automobiles, and steel. The chapter also derives estimates of the costs of protection from remaining tariffs. A comparison of the distortionary costs of QRs in the three sectors with the distortionary costs of the remaining tariff protection reveals that the costs of QRs are about ten times larger than the costs of tariffs. Because of the size of these costs of QRs, we subject our estimates to several sets of elasticities and compare the results from removing QRs individually with the results of removing QRs jointly in the three sectors. Several interesting general equilibrium results emerge, among them the biases from an aggregation of individual estimates to derive total estimates of the costs of QRs in the three sectors and the biases from partial equilibrium estimates. The appendix to chapter 5 further explores the sensitivity of our results to the way steel rationing is modeled and to trade liberalization in the presence of remaining QRs.

Chapter 6 analyzes the sensitivity of the results presented in chapter 5 to the specification of factor market behavior. First, we introduce an endogenous labor supply into the model by incorporating labor-leisure choice into the utility function. With this expanded opportunity set, the welfare costs of protection are marginally lower, and removing QRs reduces the supply of labor. Next, we give evidence suggesting that wages in the US auto and steel sectors are abnormally high by both US and international standards and are distortionary. This implies that the removal of QRs in these sectors starts from a second-best situation. We show that the numerical importance of second-best effects is not important. However, when the possibility of wage setting by the steelworkers and autoworkers unions is considered, our previous results of the welfare and employment effects of QRs in steel are substantially affected. Finally, we close the chapter with estimates under different assumptions about capital mobility. We start with the assumption that capital stocks are sector specific, and then we allow for international capital mobility.

In chapter 7 we explore the implications of imperfect competition in automobiles and steel because the evidence suggests some unexploited economies of scale in these sectors. The results in this chapter are more tentative because the evidence on economies of scale and on pricing can be interpreted in various ways. We explore three possibilities: (1) a contestable-markets pricing rule, which gives similar results to those for the competitive pricing rule under constant returns to scale; (2) conjectural variation pricing with and without firm entry and exit to allow for short-run profits and losses; and (3) departure from average cost pricing because of barriers to entry in the auto industry created by the VERs on Japanese autos. In the estimates of this chapter, the distortionary cost component of protection varies greatly because of the variety of model closures. Estimates are lower when protection allows firms to reap the benefits of scale economies. Estimates are higher when quotas are modeled as a "facilitating practice" to achieve monopoly power in the automobile industry.

In chapter 8 we shift the focus to the use of trade and tax policy as a means of raising government revenue to reduce the fiscal deficit. While a model with a more complete specification of the government sector and the government budget constraint would be more suitable for such an exercise, we are nonetheless able to illustrate and quantify several tradeoffs involved in the recent proposals to tax the oil and gas and petroleum products sectors to raise government revenue. Among the results we show that tariffs on imports of crude oil would be very inefficient (in the sense of a high welfare cost per dollar of government revenue raised). We also show that sales taxes, which do not discriminate by source, would be a more efficient instrument. Finally, while recognizing that optimal taxation principles are unlikely to be achieved in practice, we derive estimates of the optimal combination of taxes, tariffs, and subsidies in the oil and gas and petroleum products sectors that will raise a target amount of government revenue at the lowest welfare cost.

Chapter 9 summarizes the main empirical results in the book. It also provides calculations of the welfare cost per job protected in textiles and apparel, automobiles, and steel by discounting from our calculated benefits of QR removal the relocation cost incurred by workers who would have to change jobs if QRs were removed. Finally, we report on further simulation results indicating what tariff structure would yield the same welfare costs as those imputed to QRs in the three sectors. It turns out that, in terms of protection costs, QRs are taking us back to the days before multilateral tariff negotiations, especially if one includes the rent transfer element.

2 Trade Policy Analysis in a One-Sector General Equilibrium Model with Product Differentiation

This chapter is somewhat more technical than the rest of the book and may be skipped without loss of continuity. It explores, in as simple a structure as possible, the important qualitative properties that drive most of the results obtained with the multisector model presented in chapter 3. This exploration has three parts. First, we present a one-sector model with product differentiation for both imports and exports, yielding a one-sector, three-goods model. Although this model lacks a number of important features captured in the multisector model, it captures the most essential features. Also the model is simple enough to be analyzed graphically. For example, we illustrate graphically the effects of several changes that occur as a result of the policy experiments conducted in later chapters in the book—a change in the terms of trade, a transfer payment from abroad, and monopoly power in exporting. Second, we use the one-sector model to explore the impacts of changing "closure" rules on the calculated value of the real exchange rate, of trade elasticities (product differentiation) on estimates of the cost of protection, and of trade elasticities on the benefits of a foreign transfer. Third, we analyze systematically in a partial equilibrium framework the implications of product differentiation for resource allocation.

The chapter is organized as follows: Section 2.1 briefly covers the motivation for assuming product differentiation, an assumption often made in applied general equilibrium analysis. In section 2.2 we lay out the structure of the one-sector model, showing the links between import demand and export supply when product differentiation is assumed for both exports and imports. A graphical solution of equilibrium is shown for the small- and large-country cases. In section 2.3 the qualitative properties of the model are examined in several comparative statics exercises. We show the implications for the shape of the offer curve of product differentiation in *both* imports and exports. In section 2.4 we discuss the interpretation of the real exchange rate—the relative price of traded to nontraded goods—and the choice of numéraire. (This section provides a practical justification for the choice of numéraire in chapter 3.) Numerical exercises with the model in section 2.5 show the sensitivity of policy changes to variations in the elasticities describing import demand and supply response. For example, we compute the welfare costs of an array of tariffs in two stylized versions, one with and one without intermediate imports.

Finally, in section 2.6 we turn to a partial equilibrium analysis of the implications of product differentiation for the effects of trade policy changes on resource allocation. The analysis derives conditions under which the removal of protection can have the unexpected result of increasing demand and supply for the domestic competing good. This analysis helps to explain the effects of the removal of quotas on industries that compete directly with the commodities previously subject to quotas.

2.1 Product Differentiation and Specialization

Most recent multisector computable general equilibrium (CGE) models assume national product differentiation. Under a constant-returns-to-scale technology and perfect competition, these models rely on the assumption that domestically and foreign-produced goods are imperfect substitutes in use to overcome the "specialization" problem. (See Shoven and Whalley 1984 and de Melo 1988 for surveys of models using the assumption of imperfect substitution.) The specialization problem arises because CGE models with a foreign trade focus are usually designed to estimate the welfare cost of trade distortions, which requires a fair degree of sectoral disaggregation in order to capture the costs of tariff rate dispersion across sectors. (That the costs of protection are a function not only of average tariff levels but also of their dispersion is well known; see Johnson 1960.) The assumption of imperfect substitution is needed because sectoral disaggregation in the presence of few primary factors of production would lead to extreme specialization if domestically and foreign-produced goods were perfect substitutes.[1]

Those working with CGE trade models have long been aware of this specialization problem. Usually modelers have overcome the problem by dropping the law of one price—that is, by allowing domestically produced and foreign produced goods to be imperfect substitutes in use. This assumption of national product differentiation has often been referred to as the "Armington" assumption since Armington (1969) first explored the nature of import demand functions when domestically produced and imported goods are imperfect substitutes in use. In virtually all applications an interindustry table is used, and intermediates from different sectors usually enter with a fixed-coefficient (Leontief) technology. This choice of functional forms has the great practical advantage of reducing considerably the number of parameters necessary for implementing the models. However, these modeling assumptions, while defensible, are not innocuous. As this chapter shows, the result is a reduced scope for substitution possibilities.

Empirical evidence by Isard (1977) and Kravis and Lipsey (1971) justifies the practice followed by modelers. Isard's results for the United States indicate that for the most narrowly defined domestic and foreign goods for which prices can be matched (four- and five-digit Standard Industrial Trade Classification [SITC] categories), disparities between the common currency prices of goods from different countries are systematically correlated with exchange rates rather than randomly fluctuating over time. Moreover these relative price effects, indicating the presence of a wedge between domestic and import prices, were found to persist for several years. More recently Dornbusch (1987) offers several explanations for the departure of import prices from exchange rate movements during the period of significant change in the value of the dollar (1982–87). In one explanation he shows that in a perfectly competitive environment with product differentiation, the relative prices of domestic and imported goods (of the same sectoral classification) will diverge if import prices follow exchange rate movements. Finally, two-way trade has been observed in trade statistics at an extremely disaggregated level of coverage, a principal justification for assuming product differentiation.[2]

There are, however, other reasons for two-way trade in differentiated products. First, product differentiation at the firm level is likely to be prevalent in manufacturing. Second, in imperfectly competitive industries one may observe two-way trade in homogeneous products if, for instance, the market structure is Cournot. In recent theoretical work on imperfect competition, cross-hauling is usually the outcome of firm product differentiation in a monopolistically competitive market structure (e.g., see Krugman 1979). This justification for product differentiation is an alternative to the more common justification of perfect competition with national product differentiation made here. It has been used in recent modeling exercises under imperfect competition by Brown and Stern (1989). Since this alternative is only relevant in the context of increasing returns to scale, we discuss it again in chapter 7. We note, however, that in steel, one of our sectors with increasing returns to scale, Jondrow, Chase, and Gamble (1981) have provided strong evidence of the presence of national product differentiation. United States buyers of steel were found to be willing to pay a 15 to 20 percent premium for domestic steel without physical differences from foreign steel. Slightly over half the premium was due to the perception that domestic sources of supply were more secure.

2.2 A One-Sector Model with Differentiated Trade

In this section we introduce a skeletal version of the multisector model developed in chapter 3.[3] To ease the transition between the two, we assume the same behavioral assumptions with respect to foreign trade but eliminate factor markets, intermediate demand, and other details. We concentrate on the effects of different "external closures," beginning with a small-country assumption on world markets, then allowing for monopoly power in exports.

We adopt the following assumptions:

1. Domestically produced and imported goods are imperfect substitutes —the Armington assumption.
2. Domestically produced goods sold on the domestic market differ from domestically produced goods sold on the export market.
3. The economy can purchase or sell unlimited quantities of imports and exports at constant world prices—the small-country assumption.
4. Aggregate production is fixed.
5. There is a balance of trade constraint.

2.2.1 Model Equations

Equations are described briefly in this chapter and in more detail in chapter 3. (Equations are summarized in table 2.1, which links these equations with analogous equations in table 3.1 of chapter 3.) Equations 1 and 2 in table 2.1 give the trade aggregation functions. Equation 1 is a constant elasticity of substitution (CES) function, following Armington, and equation 2 is a constant elasticity of transformation (CET) function.[4] For the analysis here, we require only that $F(-)$ be convex, that $G(-)$ be concave, and that both be homogeneous of degree one in their arguments. Given the assumption of fixed output, $G(-)$ represents a production possibility frontier delineating the trade-offs between exports and domestic supply.

Equations 3 and 4 translate foreign prices into domestic prices using a conversion factor r, which we refer to for now as the exchange rate. As discussed below, this conversion factor is not a financial exchange rate

Table 2.1
A one-sector small-country model with differentiated trade

(1)	$Q = F(M, D^d)$	Import aggregation (utility) function (21)
(2)	$\bar{X} = G(E, D^s)$	Export transformation function (9)
(3)	$P^m = r\bar{\pi}^m$	Import price (17)
(4)	$P^e = r\bar{\pi}^e$	Export price (15)
(5)	$P^q = f_1(P^m, P^d)$	Consumer price (13)
(6)	$P^x = g_1(P^e, P^d)$	Producer price (11)
(7)	$\frac{M}{D^d} = f_2(P^m, P^d)$	Import demand equation (22)
(8)	$\frac{E}{D^s} = g_2(P^e, P^d)$	Export supply equation (10)
(9)	$\bar{\pi}^m M - \bar{\pi}^e E = \bar{B}$	Balance of trade constraint (30)
(10)	$D^d - D^s = 0$	Domestic demand-supply equilibrium (32)

where
M, E = imports, exports
D^d, D^s = demand and supply of the domestic good
Q = composite consumer good
$\bar{X}$ = composite production
$\bar{\pi}^m$ = world price of imports
$\bar{\pi}^e$ = world price of exports
r = conversion factor, "nominal" exchange rate
P^m = domestic price of imports M
P^e = domestic price of exports E
P^d = domestic price of domestic sales D
P^q = domestic price of composite consumer good Q
P^x = domestic price of composite output X
$\bar{B}$ = exogenous balance of trade or net foreign capital inflow (or outflow for negative B).

Note: The number following the equation description is the corresponding equation in table 3.1 in chapter 3. A bar denotes an exogenous variable.

variable. Though often referred to as "the" exchange rate, we refer to it as the "nominal" exchange rate to avoid confusing it with the real exchange rate—the relative price of traded goods to the domestic good—which is determined by the model. Indeed, the model could be written without reference to r—as is common in trade theory—by implicitly choosing it as the numéraire. Although we use this approach below in section 2.4, we maintain r in our formulation because we wish to consider alternative choices for the numéraire.[5]

We assume that producers maximize profits and that demanders minimize the cost of purchasing a given quantity of composite good Q.[6] These assumptions lead to equations 5 through 8 in table 2.1. Equations 5 and 6 define composite good prices and are effectively dual unit cost functions. They are homogeneous of degree one in prices. Equations 7 and 8 give the demand for imports and the supply of exports arising from the first-order conditions.

Because agents are profit maximizers or cost minimizers, the functions describing the model are homogeneous of degree zero in prices. To set the absolute price level, select $r \equiv 1$ as numéraire. Equation 9 gives the equilibrium condition for the balance of trade, namely, that in foreign units (expressed in terms of the numéraire) the value of imports equals the value of exports plus $\bar{B}$. Finally, equation 10 is the equilibrium condition for the supply and demand for the domestic good. Overall, the model has ten equations and ten endogenous variables: Q, M, D^d, D^s, E, P^m, P^e, P^d, P^q, and P^x. Using the linear homogeneity of equations 1 and 2, one may verify that the system satisfies Walras' law by writing out the aggregate income and expenditure equations:

$$P^x\bar{X} + r\bar{B} \qquad \text{(total income)},$$

$$P^x\bar{X} = P^eE + P^dD^s \qquad \text{(value of production, or GDP)},$$

$$P^qQ = P^mM + P^dD^d \qquad \text{(total expenditure or absorption)}.$$

Given the equilibrium conditions in equations 9 and 10, it follows that income always equals expenditure. The variable $\bar{B}$ in equation 9, denominated in foreign units, can be thought of as net transfers. It represents an increase (or decrease) in real income measured in terms of net imports.

2.2.2 A Graphical Presentation

This model is simple enough for its properties to be shown graphically. Figure 2.1 presents a four-quadrant diagram that captures the essential

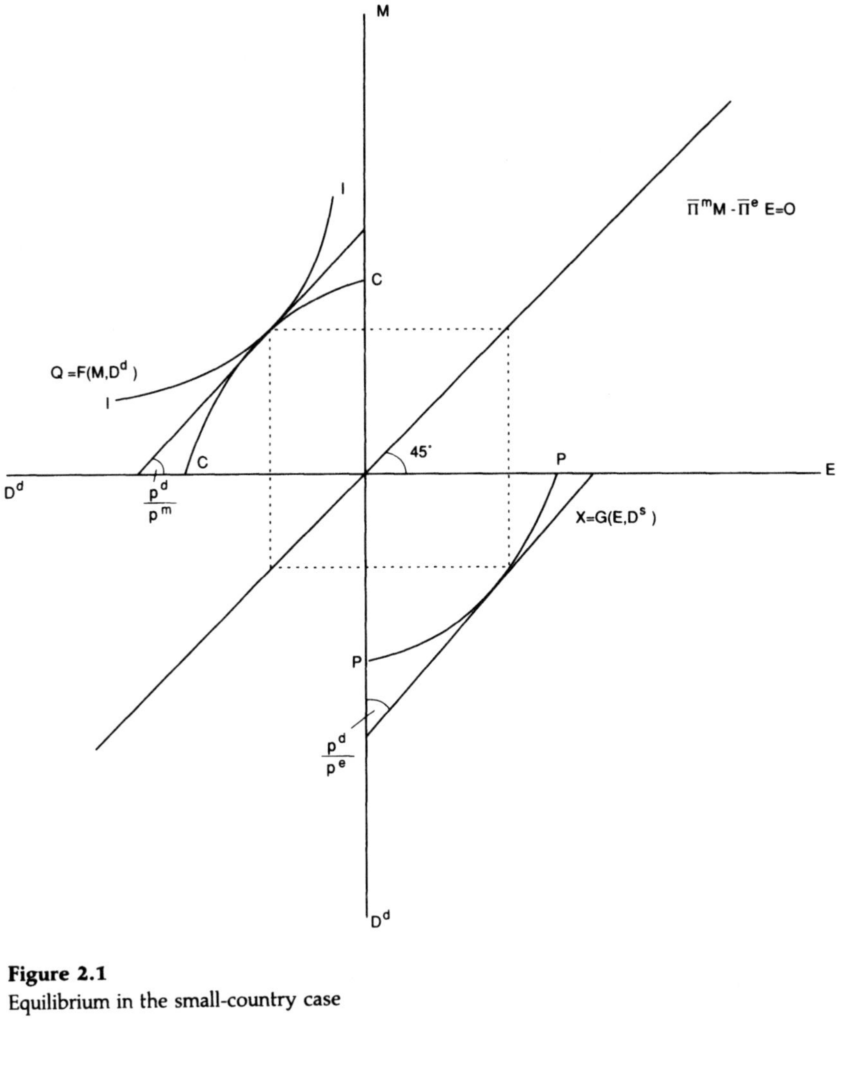

Figure 2.1
Equilibrium in the small-country case

features. For convenience we choose units so that the exogenous world prices for both exports and imports equal one. Also we set r as the numéraire and initially assume that $\bar{B} = 0$. In this case the balance of trade equation defines the foreign offer curve and graphs as a 45-degree line in the northeast quadrant. The production possibility frontier PP (equation 2) is graphed in the southeast quadrant. The southwest quadrant has a 45-degree line that simply indicates that domestic goods D, which are supplied to the domestic market, are available for demand, defining equilibrium in the domestic goods market. The concave (to the origin) curve CC in the northwest quadrant is the consumption possibility frontier, which is the locus of points that simultaneously satisfy the balance of trade constraint in the northeast quadrant and the production possibility frontier in the southeast quadrant. Since the balance of trade is a 45-degree line through the origin, the consumption possibility frontier in the northwest quadrant is a mirror image of the production possibility frontier PP in the southeast quadrant.

In the northwest quadrant the import aggregation function (equation 1) generates a series of "iso-good" curves II analogous to indifference curves.[7] Equilibrium is achieved at the point of tangency with the consumption possibility frontier. At this point the equilibrium price ratios, P^d/P^m and P^d/P^e, equal the slope of the tangents in the northwest and southeast quadrants, which are derived from the first-order conditions in equations 7 and 8, and the two ratios are equal.[8] Thus the relative price of the (one) domestic good D to either traded good M or traded good E is the same. Consequently one can unambiguously refer to the relative price of tradables to nontradables as $P^e/P^d = P^m/P^d = 1/P^d$. Thus selecting r as numéraire is convenient since it allows us to interpret $1/P^d$ as the real exchange rate.

Consider the limiting Ricardian case when PP becomes a straight line, which in turn implies a straight line consumption possibility curve under the small-country assumption. The real exchange rate is now fixed and, as in a Ricardian world, is determined by technology. Imperfect substitution in demand precludes complete specialization, which usually occurs in Ricardian models with homogeneous goods.[9]

2.2.3 The Large-Country Case

Consider now the large-country case, which corresponds to some of the external closures adopted in the applied chapters in this book. We adopt a specification with product differentiation on the import side and less than infinitely elastic foreign export demand. In this case the model would include an extra equation,

$$\pi^e = \left[\frac{E}{E_0}\right]^{-1/\zeta} \tag{2.1}$$

where $\zeta > 1$ is the constant price elasticity of foreign export demand and π^e is endogenous. Now the foreign offer curve is given by[10]

$$M = E_0^{1/\zeta}E^{\alpha}, \qquad \alpha \equiv 1 - 1/\zeta, \qquad 0 < \alpha < 1, \tag{2.2}$$

which is derived by substituting the expression for π^e of equation 2.1 into the balance of trade constraint. This case is depicted in figure 2.2, where C_0^*

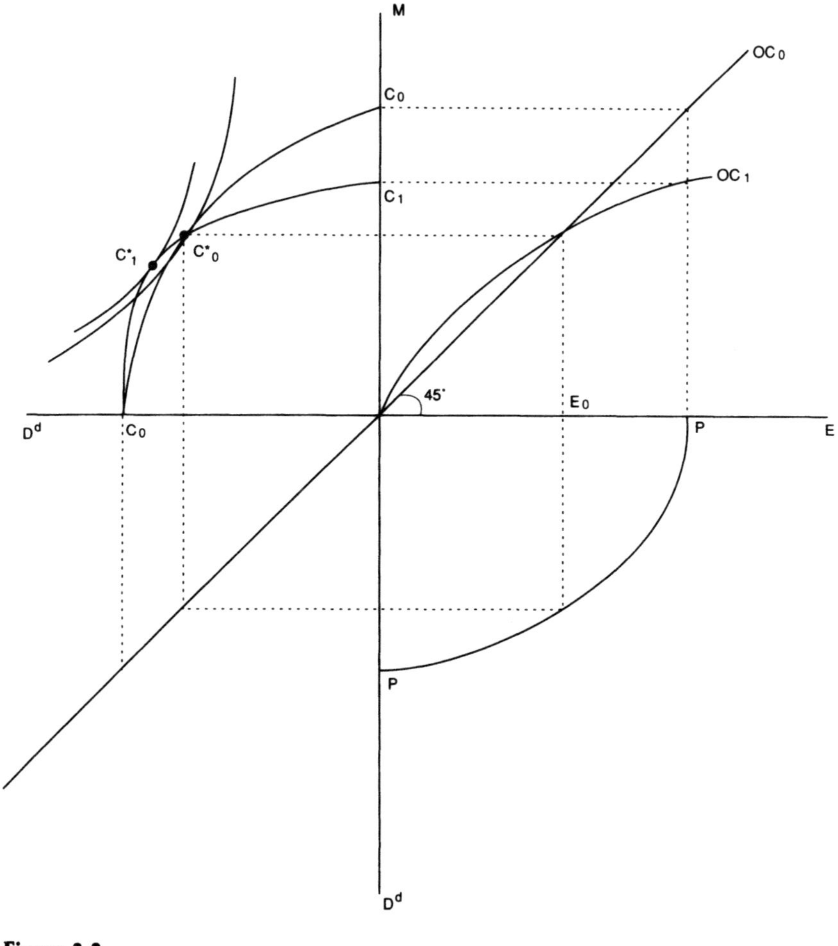

Figure 2.2
Equilibrium with constant foreign demand elasticity

is the equilibrium under the large-country assumption (i.e., $\alpha < 1$). With market power the foreign offer curve becomes equation 2.2, which is concave since $\alpha < 1$ and is graphed as OC_1 (northeast quadrant). Because of the assumption of market power, the foreign offer curve lies above OC_0 for $E < E_0$ but below OC_0 for $E > E_0$. Correspondingly the new consumption possibility curve C_0C_1 in the northwest quadrant is above C_0C_0 for $E < E_0$ and below C_0C_0 for $E < E_0$. Clearly, the optimum consumption bundle for the economy moves from C_0^* to C_1^*. In general, however, the economy will not achieve C_1^* without the use of an instrument such as an export tax. This is because the marginal gain to the economy of selling an additional unit of exports is less than its price, and small exporters choose sales based on price.

The presence of monopoly power complicates the assessment of the welfare costs of US trade restrictions since free trade is no longer optimal. Throughout this book we ignore the possibility of foreign retaliation, which would further complicate the analysis.[11] To facilitate the interpretation of results, in all cases we first report the results of our experiments in the absence of monopoly power in foreign trade and then with monopoly power. This allows us to isolate clearly the effects of terms-of-trade changes induced by the removal of protection.

2.3 Comparative Statics: A Graphical Analysis of Terms-of-Trade, Transfer, and Tariff Changes

In chapter 5 we ask, What are the welfare costs to the United States of quantitative restrictions in the textile and apparel, auto, and steel sectors? The welfare cost has two components. One cost component is the quota rents that are captured by foreigners. A second cost component is the distortionary costs in production and consumption arising from quotas. Both effects can be easily handled within the graphical apparatus developed here. The effects of a terms-of-trade change, which occurs with a large-country external closure, can also be shown in this way. All three exercises are illustrated here, starting with the effects of a terms-of-trade change.

2.3.1 Terms-of-Trade Changes

Consider the effect of an improvement in the terms of trade that occurs, for example, as a result of a decrease in production capability among competing export suppliers in the rest of the world. Figure 2.3 shows the effect on equilibrium of an improvement in the terms of trade (TOT_0 to TOT_1)

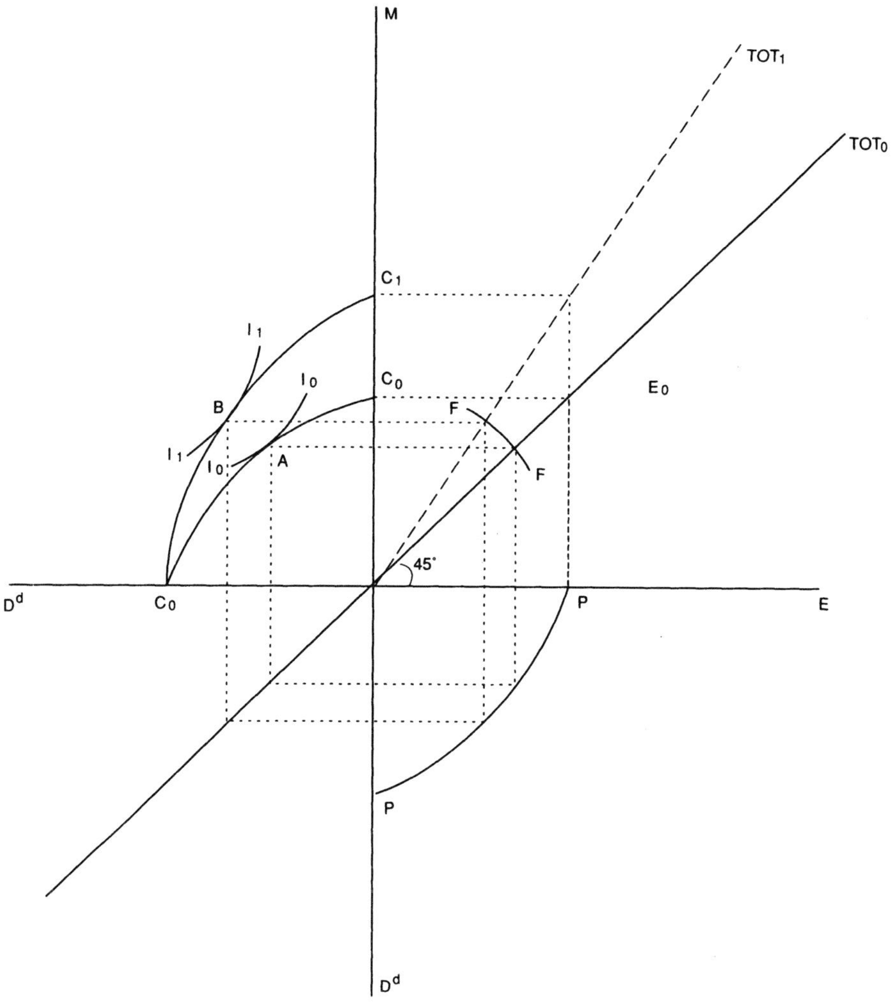

Figure 2.3
Terms-of-trade improvement

corresponding to an increase in π^e, such that $d\pi^e > 0$. This terms-of-trade change shifts out the consumption possibility schedule to C_0C_1 (northwest quadrant). Will the economy supply a larger volume of exports under this improved terms of trade? The result depends on the shape of the domestic offer curve.[12] As it is drawn in figure 2.3, exports fall. Since the economy responds to an improvement in the terms of trade with fewer exports, it is in the inelastic portion of the domestic offer curve *FF*.[13]

2.3.2 Capturing Foreign Quota Rents

In chapter 4 we show that with the system of import quota arrangements in force between the United States and foreign exporters, foreigners capture most of the quota rents. Here, ignoring for now the distortionary cost component, we consider the quota rents that would be captured by the United States if, for example, quotas were auctioned off to US importers.

Figure 2.4 shows the effect on equilibrium of capturing foreign quota rents. This effect is equivalent to an increase in $\overline{B}$, which implies an upward parallel shift of the external budget constraint to O_1O_1 and of the consumption possibility curve to C_1C_1. Will capturing these rents lead to appreciation of the real exchange rate, as one would expect in a model in which the domestic good is consumed? Yes, if the domestic good is not inferior in consumption, which is the case drawn in figure 2.4 and is guaranteed for the CES function used in applied work. Domestic consumption of D increases, exports fall, and imports rise. From the southeast quadrant we see that P^e/P^d will fall. Since optimization by consumers and producers implies that $P^m/P^d = P^e/P^d$, the real exchange rate will appreciate.

2.3.3 Imposing a Tariff

The effects of imposing a tariff (equivalent to the distortionary cost component of a QR) are shown in figure 2.5. Under free trade the economy produces at P^* and consumes at C^*. Under this allocation pair the usual conditions of Pareto optimality are satisfied since the marginal rate of substitution (*MRS*) in consumption and the domestic marginal rate of transformation in production (*MRT*) are both equal to the rate at which the economy can trade its export good for the import good, or the foreign rate of transformation through trade (*FRT*). By choice of units, initially all three ratios are equal to negative one.

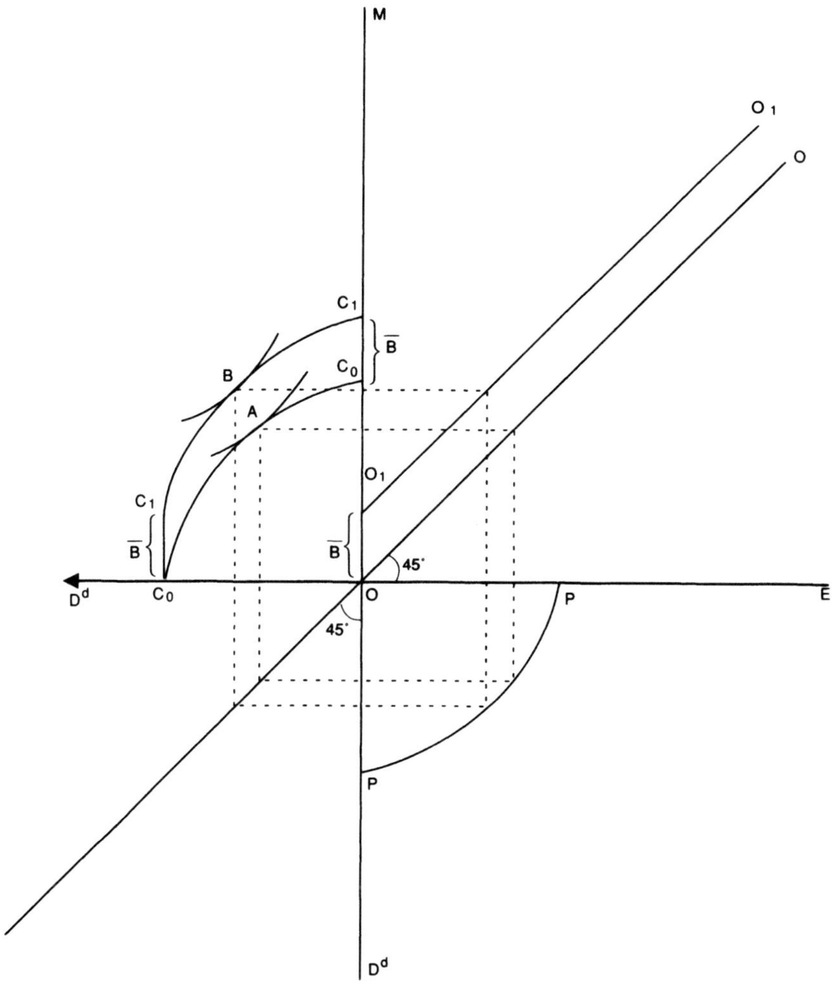

Figure 2.4
Increase in foreign transfers

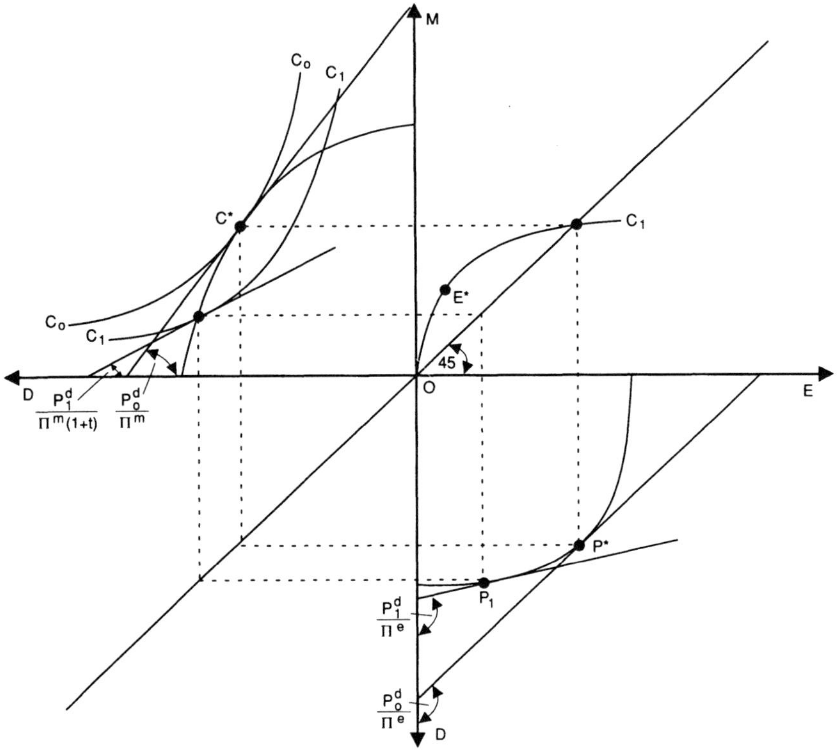

Figure 2.5
Imposing a tariff

Suppose a tariff is imposed at an ad valorem rate t (or a binding quota at premium rate t); this will lead to a nonoptimal pair (P_1, C_1). The FRT, which is defined by world markets, is unchanged. As a result of the tariff, consumers, who are faced with a budget constraint in which the relative price of the import good has risen, will optimize by altering their purchases such that a unit of the import good is valued relatively more highly than a unit of the domestic good, that is, $-MRS = P_1^d/\bar{\pi}^m(1 + t)$. But since the export price of producers remains undistorted, producers will optimize their production decision where $-MRT = P_1^d$. This implies that a reallocation of resources can increase welfare.[14]

Figure 2.5 can also be used to illustrate Lerner (1936) symmetry. An effect similar to that of tariff protection could be achieved with an export tax at the rate t.

As shown in figure 2.2, if the economy is large in international markets, the foreign offer curve is no longer a straight line. Then removing a tariff may lead to a welfare loss. This case is illustrated in the northeast quadrant of figure 2.5, where OC_1 is the foreign curve under the large-country assumption. The corresponding consumption possibility frontier is not drawn, but the optimal degree of trade restriction is denoted by E^*. In the case shown here, any reduction in protection will lead to a welfare loss since production for the domestic market at P_1 is already less than the optimal level implied by E^*.

In the experiments reported in chapter 5, the foreign offer curve is usually close to a straight line for the case of a departure from the small-country assumption. This is because monopoly or monopsony power is considered for only a few sectors. Then there is a welfare gain from reducing protection, albeit a smaller gain than under the pure small-country assumption. It is only when we introduce across-the-board monopoly and monopsony power (section 5.6) that removal of tariff protection leads to a welfare loss in some cases. This is the case shown in figure 2.5.

2.4 A Digression: Choice of Numéraire and the Real Exchange Rate

In some of the results presented in later chapters, we report on the real exchange rate change that would result from a policy change. As we show below with a numerical example with trade shares close to those in our multisector US model, the choice of weights entering the aggregator for the domestic price index will affect the computed value for the real exchange rate. Since this issue is somewhat technical and of greatest interest to the modeler, the reader with a general interest may wish to skip this section.

If we assume that the import aggregation function is CES and the export transformation is CET, then equations 1 and 2 in table 2.1 are given by

$$Q = \bar{A}_1[\beta M^\rho + (1 - \beta)D^\rho]^{1/\rho}, \quad \sigma = \frac{1}{1-\rho}, \qquad \rho < 1, \tag{2.3}$$

$$\bar{X} = \bar{A}_2[\alpha E^h + (1 - \alpha)D^h]^{1/h}, \quad \Omega = \frac{1}{h-1}, \qquad h > 1, \tag{2.4}$$

where a bar denotes an exogenous variable and σ and Ω are elasticities of substitution and transformation, respectively. Following the calibration procedure common in CGE models, we choose units of the goods such that prices are initially unity. In this one-sector model we have three goods (the import, export, and domestic good) for which units of measurement must be defined. This allows us to define $P^m = P^e = P^d = 1$. From this it follows that $P^q = P^x = 1$. We may also arbitrarily choose $r = 1$ initially. Without trade distortions, it follows that the world prices $\bar{\pi}^m = \bar{\pi}^e = 1$ as well. If we were to introduce trade distortions into equations 3 and 4 of table 2.1, as we do in our multisector model, the world prices would differ from unity in our initial calibration. We next choose ρ and h to be consistent with elasticity values. Finally, we choose $\bar{A}_1$ and $\bar{A}_2$ to replicate an initial equilibrium, which we take here to be $\bar{X} = 100$, $E = 25$, $M = 25$, and $\bar{B} = 0$.[15]

First note that the model in table 2.1 yields an unambiguous definition of the real exchange rate. With fixed terms of trade ($\bar{\pi}^m = \bar{\pi}^e = 1$), the real exchange rate is $P^x/P^d = P^m/P^d = r/P^d$. If trade distortions are introduced, the real exchange rate will depend on weights.

Table 2.2 shows the effects on welfare (column 3) and on the real exchange rate (column 4) of setting transfers equal to 10 (i.e., to 10 percent of initial GDP) under different values of the elasticities of import substitution and export transformation. In this section only we use Q/P^q (real national income) as a welfare measure. Note that in the limit the increase in welfare is equal to the transfer itself. This result occurs when the marginal rate of transformation of production between sales to the domestic market and sales to the export market is infinite (i.e., in the Ricardian case discussed above). As expected, the adjustment in the real exchange rate required to absorb the transfer is an increasing function of the curvature of the CES and CET functions.

In this example the numéraire is $P^q \equiv 1$. Had we selected another numéraire, such as fixing the value of the GDP deflator with base-year

Table 2.2
Welfare and real exchange rate calculations for an increase in transfers

σ[a] (1)	Ω[b] (2)	Q/P^q (3)	r/P^d (4)	r (5)	r/P^x (6)
0.2	0.2	106.9	0.38	0.46	0.45
0.5	0.5	108.7	0.68	0.75	0.74
2.0	2.0	109.6	0.91	0.93	0.93
5.0	5.0	109.9	0.96	0.97	0.97
5.0	∞	110.0	1.00	1.00	1.00

Note: Transfers ($\bar{B}$) are set equal to 10; $\bar{X} = 100$.
a. Elasticity of substitution in CES (equation 1 in table 2.1, and equation 2.3 in text).
b. Elasticity of transformation in CET (equation 2 in table 2.2, and equation 2.4 in text).

quantity weights (i.e., setting $P^x \equiv 1$), then the equilibrium values of the nominal exchange rate (or conversion factor) in column 5 would have been replaced by the values in column 6. Likewise, with $P^d \equiv 1$ as the numéraire, the equilibrium values for the nominal exchange rate would have been given by the values in column 4. And with $r \equiv 1$ as the numéraire, the equilibrium value of $1/p^d$ appearing in column 4 would have corresponded to the equilibrium value of the real exchange rate. Regardless of the choice of numéraire, the equilibrium values of the relative price indices appearing in columns 4 and 6 of table 2.2 remain unaltered.

Consequently, in this version of the one-sector model, there is no ambiguity with respect to the appropriate definition of the real exchange rate, r/p^d. In applied work, however, two problems arise. In multisector CGE applications, if one is interested in the equilibrium value of the real exchange rate, one must select the weights entering the aggregator for the domestic price index, and the choice of weights will affect the computed values for the equilibrium real exchange rate. However, the equilibrating mechanism working through changes in the real exchange rate is the same, no matter what price is chosen as numéraire.[16]

In chapter 3 we choose as numéraire a weighted sum of all domestic prices p^d, using base gross output quantities as weights. We fix this value at unity because then the change in the endogenously determined value of r is the change in the real exchange rate. (For details, see appendix 3B.)

2.5 Costs of Protection in the One-Sector Model

We close the discussion of the one-sector model with illustrative welfare calculations derived from a one-sector model representing an aggregation of the disaggregated ten-sector model of the US economy used in later

Table 2.3
Welfare gain from a foreign transfer

Transfer[a] ($\bar{B}$)	$\sigma = 0.5$ $\Omega = 0.5$	$\sigma = 1.2$ $\Omega = 0.5$	$\sigma = 0.5$ $\Omega = 1.2$	$\sigma = 1.2$ $\Omega = 1.2$	$\sigma = 2$ $\Omega = 2$
2	1.8	1.9	1.9	1.9	2.0
4	3.4	3.6	3.6	3.7	3.8
6	4.6	5.1	5.1	5.4	5.6
8	5.7	6.4	6.4	6.9	7.3
10	6.7	7.6	7.6	8.4	9.0

Note: Welfare gain is given by the equivalent variation (EV) measure, expressed as a percentage of initial GDP. (For an exact definition of EV, see appendix 3A in chapter 3.) Initial values are $\bar{X} = 100$; $E = M = 10$. σ is the income-compensated price elasticity of demand for imports; Ω is the income-compensated price elasticity of export supply.
a. Transfer is expressed as a percentage of initial GDP.

chapters. The model in chapter 3 is explained extensively, and that explanation is not repeated here. The one-sector model does, however, have several simplifications compared with the multisector version. The one-sector version does not include factor markets. Also, in the multisector model, the utility function is Stone-Geary between sectors with a nested CES within sectors, whereas the one-sector version has only the CES portion. Finally, there are no intermediates in the version reported in table 2.2; intermediates are introduced in the version reported in table 2.4. Otherwise, the functional forms representing this model are those of table 3.1.

As discussed in more detail in chapter 4, the US system of QRs results in two component costs: (1) a rent transfer component that arises from the nature of the quota allocation system applied, which ensures that the quota rents go primarily to exporting countries, and (2) a distortionary cost component comprising the familiar production and consumption costs. Tables 2.3 and 2.4 show the effect of varying trade elasticities on the welfare effects of a rent transfer and a distortionary cost, respectively.

In table 2.3 we show the impact of varying the trade elasticities on the welfare gain from a transfer, as could be done, for example, by capturing the quota rents accruing to exporters through auctioning import quota rights to US importers. (As noted in chapter 3 and further explained in appendix A at the end of this book, σ is the income-compensated price elasticity of demand for imports and Ω is the income-compensated price elasticity of export supply.) This exercise serves as an introduction to the systematic sensitivity analysis of these parameters reported in later chapters, particularly in chapter 5.

Table 2.4
Welfare costs of protection

Tariff rate (%)	$\sigma = 0.5$ $\Omega = 0.5$	$\sigma = 1.2$ $\Omega = 0.5$	$\sigma = 0.5$ $\Omega = 1.2$	$\sigma = 1.2$ $\Omega = 1.2$	$\sigma = 2$ $\Omega = 2$
5	0.054	0.074	0.078	0.125	0.199
	(0.057)	(0.077)	(0.081)	(0.130)	(0.206)
50	0.175	0.231	0.253	0.389	0.593
	(0.183)	(0.240)	(0.265)	(0.404)	(0.611)
75	0.327	0.421	0.476	0.705	1.038
	(0.342)	(0.436)	(0.499)	(0.730)	(1.065)

Note: Welfare costs are measured by the equivalent variation (EV) measure (negative sign omitted). For an exact definition of the EV measure, see appendix 3A in chapter 3. For figures not in parenthesis, initial values are $Y = \bar{X} = 100$, $M = E = 10$. For figures in parenthesis, initial values are $Y = 94$, $\bar{X} = 185$, intermediate imports $(VM) = 6$; final imports $(CM) = 4$. σ is the income-compensated price elasticity of demand for imports; Ω is the income-compensated price elasticity of export supply.

Two results are apparent. First, for a given level of transfer, the greater the value of the trade substitution elasticities, the greater is the welfare gain. It should be noted, however, that since GDP is fixed and we do not model factor markets, these estimates are not strictly comparable with the corresponding estimates reported in chapter 5. Second, for a given set of trade substitution elasticities, the percentage increase in welfare is a decreasing function of the amount transferred. This is so because the marginal utility of the extra income is a decreasing function of the level of income.

Table 2.4 presents illustrative calculations of the costs of protection. Of course these calculations are lower-bound estimates because, by construction, there is no variance in protection across sectors in a one-sector model. We consider two cases. In the first case the economy has no intermediate production, so gross output is equal to value added; the benchmarking is the same as in table 2.3. These results are presented in the first row of figures for each tariff rate in table 2.4. The second case is based on a modified model with intermediates. This modification recognizes that much of production is for intermediate use. (In 1984 the value added to gross output ratio in the United States was about 54 percent, and about 60 percent of the volume of imports was for intermediate use.) The results reflecting these initial conditions are presented in parentheses for each tariff rate. These calculations take into account the additional distortionary costs of higher-cost imported intermediate inputs when a tariff is levied on both final and intermediate imports.

The distortionary costs of tariff protection are less than 1 percent of GDP, except at the tariff rate of 75 percent and the set of elasticities

$\Omega = \sigma = 2$. Thus the distortionary costs of protection are small both because there is no variance in tariffs and because only 10 percent of GDP is traded. The distortionary costs of protection rise more than proportionately with protection (as measured by the distortion wedge) in part because, with nonlinear demand and supply curves, distortionary costs rise more than proportionately with the distortion wedge, and in part because, if the distortion wedge increases, then with no change in elasticity, the quantity change also increases which acts multiplicatively on the distortion wedge in calculating welfare change. This result also shows up in the multisector version of the model in chapter 5. Moreover, as the price elasticities of import demand (σ) and export supply (Ω) rise, so do the costs of imposing a tariff. The intuition for these results (with respect to σ and Ω) is explained in partial equilibrium terms in chapters 5 and 6, respectively. For most elasticities in the disaggregated model, comparisons are made between low, middle, and high elasticities, with the high elasticities being up to four times larger in absolute value than the low elasticities. The results in table 2.4 allow us to assess the expected variation in the distortionary cost component of protection.

2.6 Trade Policy and Resource Shifts in the Presence of Product Differentiation

When the price of an import good is lowered because of, say, the removal of a tariff or a quota, will the demand for the domestic competitive product decrease?[17] Normally, but not always. The reason is that there is a trade-off between two effects. Take steel as an example. As discussed in chapter 3, we assume weak separability and two-stage budgeting so that in the first stage the buyer chooses a composite amount (domestic plus foreign production) of steel to purchase. In the second stage the buyer optimizes steel purchases, subject to the predetermined expenditure limit on steel. When the price of imported steel falls, the first-stage effect is a lowering of the price of composite imported and domestic steel, which induces an increase in the quantity demanded of composite steel. As a result of this effect alone, the quantity demanded of domestic steel increases.

The second effect of the decrease in the price of imported steel is that the buyer substitutes imported for domestic steel, subject to the predetermined expenditure limit on steel derived from the first-stage maximization. This second-stage effect reduces the quantity of domestic steel demanded. Which of the two effects dominates defines whether the goods are gross substitutes or complements. In the limiting case, where the goods are perfect complements in production (i.e., in the Leontief case, where the elasticity of substitution is zero in the second stage), any increase in the quantity demanded of composite steel results in an equiproportionate increase in the quantity demanded of domestic and imported steel.

So for imported and domestic goods in a sector to be gross substitutes, we see from this discussion that the elasticity of substitution in the second stage must be sufficiently large relative to the elasticity of composite demand. We establish this fact more formally here by developing the precise relationship between these elasticities (and the share of imports) that shows whether the goods are gross substitutes or complements and, more generally, how much of a resource shift we should expect from a fall in the price of imports. The derivation is carried out in partial equilibrium analysis since income is held constant and the calculus techniques imply that the derived relationships are valid for local changes. These relationships will be helpful in assessing the magnitude of the resource shift that occurs in the multisector model in response to a change in protection.

2.6.1 Product Differentiation and Imperfect Substitution on the Import Side

The demand for the domestically produced good D is a function both of the domestic price of that good and of the import price of the foreign-produced good of the same category. The supply S of the domestic good is a function of its own price. (We reintroduce the price of exports in the supply function below.) Thus

$$D = D(P^d, P^m) \tag{2.5}$$

and

$$S = S(P^d). \tag{2.6}$$

The equilibrium condition in the market for the domestically produced good is

$$D = S. \tag{2.7}$$

We now investigate the determinants of the degree of trade dependence by asking how the domestic price is affected by a policy-induced change in the import price, such as that resulting from a change in the tariff. The domestic price system is said to be trade dependent if a given percentage change in the tariff is reflected in a large percentage change in the price of the domestically produced competing good. If the resulting change is small, the domestic price system is said to be independent. To get an expression for the degree of trade dependence, we differentiate totally the equilibrium condition (equation 2.7), which yields

$$\frac{dP^d}{dP^m} = \frac{\partial D/\partial P^m}{\partial S/\partial P^d - \partial D/\partial P^d}. \tag{2.8}$$

Equation 2.8 can be rewritten in terms of elasticities, using the following definitions:

$$E \equiv \frac{dP^d}{dP^m}\frac{P^m}{P^d} \equiv \frac{E^{d,m}}{\varepsilon^s - \varepsilon^d},$$

where

$$E^{d,m} \equiv \frac{\partial D}{\partial P^m}\frac{P^m}{D},$$

$$\varepsilon^s \equiv \frac{\partial S}{\partial P^d}\frac{P^d}{D} > 0,$$

$$\varepsilon^d \equiv \frac{\partial D}{\partial P^d}\frac{P^d}{D} < 0.$$

It turns out that the sign of E, the domestic price response elasticity, is ambiguous. Assume that the functional form aggregating M and D at the lower level is CES with elasticity of substitution σ (i.e., equation 2.3, with $\bar{A} = 1$). Let ε^q denote the elasticity of demand for the composite good Q with respect to its composite price P,

$$\varepsilon^q = -\frac{\partial Q}{\partial P}\frac{P}{Q} > 0.$$

As explained in appendix 7A in chapter 7, we may rewrite equation 2.5 as $D = D(P^d, P^m) = H[P^d, P, Q]$. From the techniques presented in appendix 7A, it can be shown after some manipulation that at the initial equilibrium

$$E^{d,m} = (\sigma - \varepsilon^q)S^m \tag{2.9}$$

and

$$-\varepsilon^d = \varepsilon^q + S^m(\sigma - \varepsilon^q). \tag{2.10}$$

It therefore follows that

Table 2.5
Degree of trade dependence as trade substitution elasticity varies

σ	$S^m = 0.1$	$S^m = 0.5$	$S^m = 0.9$
0.5	−0.03	−0.14	−0.29
1.0	0.00	0.00	0.00
2.0	0.05	0.20	0.31
5.0	0.16	0.50	0.64
10.0	0.31	0.69	0.80
20.0	0.49	0.83	0.90
50.0	0.59	0.93	0.96
100.0	0.83	0.96	0.98

Note: The entries are tabulations of equation 2.11, with $\varepsilon^q = \varepsilon^s = 1$. σ is the trade-substitution elasticity, and S^m is the import share (in value) of total supply.

$$E = \frac{(\sigma - \varepsilon^q)S^m}{\varepsilon^s + \varepsilon^q + (\sigma - \varepsilon^q)S^m} = \frac{E^{d,m}}{\varepsilon^s + \varepsilon^q + E^{d,m}}, \tag{2.11}$$

where $S^m = P^m M/PQ$. We can see from the definition of E (or equation 2.11, because with $S^m < 1$ the denominator is positive) that a necessary and sufficient condition for the domestic price (and so domestic supply) to increase as a result of a decrease in protection is that domestic and imported products be gross complements ($E^{d,m} < 0$). From equation 2.9 we have $E^{d,m} < 0$ if and only if $\sigma < \varepsilon^q$. Based on appendix 7A, one can show that the expression is somewhat more complicated when intermediates are included, but the main result carries through, namely, that a low value of σ relative to the price elasticity of demand ε^q for the composite good Q will lead to complementarity. It turns out, however, that for the range of elasticities in our model, it is usually the case that $\sigma > \varepsilon^q$.

Table 2.5 gives the value of E for various values of initial trade shares and trade-substitution elasticities. It is especially interesting that when the import share is low, E is very low, even when the trade-substitution elasticity is as high as 5. Also, when the import share is very high (90 percent), a trade-substitution elasticity of 20 yields a value for E of 0.90, which is still less than the value of 1 that applies to perfect substitutes. These results emphasize the importance of import shares and of the share parameter in the CES trade-aggregation functions. Standard trade theory, with perfect substitution between domestic goods and imports, would predict that, for large countries in which import shares are relatively low, changes in world prices would exert a strong pull on domestic prices. On the contrary, the specification with imperfect substitution implies that a country with a low trade share will have substantial autonomy in its domestic price system even if trade-substitution elasticities are very high.

As the trade-substitution elasticity approaches infinity, E approaches 1, and we are back in the world of perfect substitutes and the law of one price.[18] As the import share tends toward 0, we approach the case of a pure nontraded good. The degree of autonomy of domestic prices is also sensitive to conditions of supply and demand in the domestic market. The higher the elasticity of domestic supply, the lower is E. If the trade-substitution elasticity equals the price elasticity of demand for the composite good, then $E = 0$. In this special case any change in import price leads to a change in composite price and to a change in demand for the composite good such that demand for the domestic good remains unchanged. Given the typical range of parameters assumed in most studies, this possibility should be kept in mind when interpreting the results of exercises involving single tariff cuts.

2.6.2 Introduction of Exports

The other important determinants of the domestic price elasticity to a trade policy change are the share of exports in domestic production, $S^e = P^eE/PQ$, and the elasticity of transformation Ω. To incorporate the impact of exports on domestic production, we adopt the CET function (equation 2.4, with $\bar{A}_2 = 1$). Then equation 2.6 becomes

$$S_d = S_d(P^d, P^e) = F(P^d, P^x, X), \tag{2.12}$$

where S_d is the supply of the domestic variety. Define

$$\varepsilon^s \equiv \frac{\partial S_d}{\partial P^d}\frac{P^d}{S_d} \quad \text{and} \quad \varepsilon^x \equiv \frac{\partial x}{\partial P^x}\frac{P^x}{X} > 0,$$

where we interpret ε^x as the industrywide elasticity of supply.

By differentiating equation 2.12 along the lines presented in appendix 7A, it can be shown that

$$\varepsilon^s = S^e\Omega + (1 - S^e)\varepsilon^x. \tag{2.13}$$

Substituting equation 2.13 into equation 2.11 yields the generalization of equation 2.11, which incorporates the impact of exports on the elasticity of supply:

$$E^m = \frac{(\sigma - \varepsilon^q)S^m}{S^e\Omega + (1 - S^e)\varepsilon^x + \varepsilon^q + S^m(\sigma - \varepsilon^q)}. \tag{2.14}$$

The corresponding expression for the elasticity of domestic price with respect to a change in the price of exports is

$$E^e = \frac{(\Omega - \varepsilon^x)S^e}{S^e\Omega + (1 - S^e)\varepsilon^x + \varepsilon^q + S^m(\sigma - \varepsilon^q)}, \qquad (2.15)$$

which is symmetrical to E^m. In particular, for a fixed level of composite output, if the price of exports increases, the firm will substitute away from production for the domestic market. However, the increased price of exports implies an increase in the composite price of output P^x and an increase in composite output X. This effect, which induces an increased supply of domestic output, could dominate the other effect (substitution away from domestic production) and produce the surprising result that domestic output and its price both increase. This will occur if and only if $\Omega < \varepsilon^x$. This condition is analogous to the one derived in section 2.6.1. Here an export subsidy will lead to an increase in output of the domestic variety of the good if the domestic and export varieties are gross complements. With the small-country assumption, P^d is now linked to the (fixed) prices of imports and exports through the two aggregation functions.[19]

The implication of these expressions and of the numerical examples in table 2.5 is that even with high price elasticities (e.g., high values of σ and Ω), the link between world and domestic prices is rather weak and depends significantly on import and export shares as well as on demand and supply conditions in the domestic market. The evidence cited at the beginning of this section suggests that this modeling assumption is not at odds with the empirical evidence. At the level of aggregation common in most economy-wide modeling exercises, the assumption of product differentiation certainly appears reasonable, even though the discussion here suggests that it may give too much autonomy to the domestic price system.

2.7 Conclusion

This chapter introduced a skeletal version of the model that is used in the empirical chapters of this book. We have discussed the main properties of the model and shown how the specification of trade in the model relates to the more standard perfect substitution assumption usually adopted in trade theory textbooks. The presentation shows that the introduction of product differentiation adds greater flexibility to the description of how domestic sectors compete in the world economy. In chapter 3 we turn to a description of the full model and of how we model trade barriers.

3 The Basic General Equilibrium Trade Model

This chapter presents the multisector general equilibrium trade model used for the analysis in this book. Although most of the properties of the model are those of the simplified theoretical one-sector model presented in chapter 2, this model is more complex because of interindustry linkages, the specification of factor markets, and the treatment of protection in the textiles and apparel, auto, and steel sectors. Yet the model is relatively simple and closely follows neoclassical theory. In this chapter we present what we refer to as the "basic" model, leaving refinements for subsequent chapters which introduce various other behavioral assumptions individually. Thus all modifications in later chapters allude to the basic model presented here.

Section 3.1 gives an overview of the model, discussing aggregation and functional forms. A more detailed description of the model follows in section 3.2, which may be skipped by readers uninterested in modeling details. The algebraic description of the model is presented in a dual (cost minimization) rather than primal (profit maximization) form, to simplify the introduction of increasing returns to scale and noncompetitive behavior in chapter 7. Section 3.3 describes briefly how the model is calibrated to the benchmark year, 1984, in particular with respect to the treatment of quantitative restrictions (QRs) in the textile and apparel and auto sectors.

3.1 Overview of the Model

Since we are interested in estimating the effects of trade policies and are not concerned with policy issues related to investment decisions, we avoid unnecessary complication by not modeling the investment decision. Similarly we do not model consumption decisions by the US government. Thus we treat all final domestic demand for the output of a sector as private consumption demand. Total domestic demand for the output of a sector is the sum of domestic intermediate demand plus domestic consumption demand. We assume that all consumers have identical preferences so that their behavior is modeled by a "representative" consumer.

The government collects tariffs and taxes (and possibly quota rents at auction). Given that our interest is limited to trade policy experiments, we confine the government's role to collection and distribution of trade-related revenues. The government's budget surplus, however, is distributed to the consumer as a lump-sum payment; similarly any deficit is adjusted through lump-sum tax payments from the consumer. Thus the government is treated as though it operates under a balanced budget in which lump-sum distributions of taxes compensate for any residual of taxes over spending. We do not attempt to assess the impact of costly rent-seeking activities associated with efforts to erect or preserve barriers to imports (on this, see Krueger 1974). Nor do we address issues relating to the political economy of protection. That is, we do not explain why one industry obtains protection from the government over another (on this, see Baldwin 1984a).

As explained in chapter 2, the real exchange rate is assumed to adjust to maintain the current account position, expressed in foreign units, unchanged as a result of a policy simulation. Thus any exogenously given current account deficit that exists in the year for which the model is benchmarked will continue to prevail after the policy simulation. This guarantees that there will be no permanent free lunches, either taken from or given to the rest of the world in the policy simulations. This assumption makes welfare analysis of changes in restrictions more meaningful and transparent.

The basic model is designed for a range of trade policy experiments. In chapter 5 we use the basic model to analyze the long-run effects of removing preexisting quotas in the base year data, given exogenous estimates of preexisting quota premia. Also, given the importance of who captures the quota rents, for the reasons explained in chapter 4 we generally assume that foreign firms capture the rents from import quotas or from voluntary export restraints (VERs). Under these institutional arrangements we use the model to simulate the long-run effects of a US recapture of these rents through an auction quota or similar mechanism.

The model is a general equilibrium model in the sense characterized by Arrow and Debreu (1954). Producers maximize profits subject to a constant-returns-to-scale (*CRTS*) technology. Given technology and output and input prices, the representative firm in each industry purchases primary factors and domestic and foreign intermediate inputs so as to minimize the costs of producing any level of output. The single representative consumer purchases domestic and foreign goods and maximizes utility, given income and prices. The consumer's income is determined endogenously. Consumer demand functions are continuous, nonnegative, and homogeneous of degree zero (in absolute prices). At any set of prices, consumer expenditures on commodities equal consumer money income inclusive of transfers. The latter property means that the model satisfies Walras' law. Given the prices that firms face in the export and domestic markets and their production allocation possibilities described in chapter 2, firms allocate their output between the domestic and foreign markets so as to maximize profits. This, together with the homogeneity of degree zero of the demand functions, implies that only relative prices are of significance for domestic agents.

A general equilibrium results when all industries are in equilibrium, all product and factor markets clear, and the balance of trade expressed in world prices equals its initial value. Given the properties discussed in the previous paragraph, a general equilibrium is known to exist. Since preferences are reduced to a single representative consumer, the resulting equilibrium is unique (e.g., see Arrow and Hahn 1971). Finally, the model is required to replicate a historical data set (in our case, that for 1984) as an equilibrium. Determining the parameter values that, together with the observed data set, lead to an equilibrium of the model is known as benchmarking (or calibrating) the model. How this is done is described briefly in section 3.3 and in more detail in appendix A.

3.1.1 Aggregation

For analyzing the costs of protection, the economy is aggregated into ten sectors: agriculture, food, mining, textiles and apparel, autos, iron and steel, other consumer goods, other manufactures, traded services, and construction and nontraded services. We chose this aggregation because it enables us to isolate as separate industries in the model most of the significant industries that frequently petition and obtain trade protection in the United States, while treating other industries in a more aggregegated manner. However, for the analysis of efficient tax schemes in US petroleum sectors in chapter 8, we disaggregate the model further to twelve sectors, adding two more policy- relevant sectors: petroleum products and crude oil and natural gas.

Since both the average level of protection and the dispersion of protection across sectors contribute to the cost of protection, in principle it is always preferable to disaggregate further. However, disaggregation is difficult in an economywide context for two reasons. First, as our exhaustive search for elasticities in appendix B shows, it is often difficult to obtain reliable elasticity estimates even for a ten-sector model of the US economy. Second, computational difficulties arise when disaggregation is pushed too far, especially when one is looking for efficient combinations of tax instruments, as we are in chapter 8. For assessing the costs of protection in the auto, steel, and textile sectors, however, our aggregation is fully adequate because these sectors remain as isolated sectors in the ten-sector model.[1]

3.1.2 Elasticity Specification

The functional forms used in the ten-sector model are summarized in figure 3.1. Starting with foreign trade, we treat the products produced by the United States and the rest of the world as differentiated, for reasons explained in chapter 2. Functional forms for import demand and export supply are the CES and CET aggregation functions introduced in chapter 2.

Figure 3.1 indicates that we parameterize production substitution possibilities by assuming CES functions for value-added and Leontief functions between intermediates and value added and across intermediates. However, within each intermediate sector, a CES function describes substitution possibilities between the domestically produced intermediate and the competing foreign-produced intermediate. To give an example, no substitution is allowed between steel and other manufacturing, but substitution is allowed between domestically produced and foreign-produced steel. The substitution possibilities are given by a CES function. The CES and CET functional specifications could, of course, be relaxed to include second-order approximations, as in the flexible functional forms proposed in the production and consumer choice literature (e.g., translog functions).[2] However, such specifications would unnecessarily complicate our parameterization of the model since many more cross-elasticities (which are difficult to estimate precisely) would be needed. These second-order approximations would not add any further insight to our estimates of the welfare costs of protection.

For consumption demand a linear expenditure system (*LES*) allows for cross-price effects in demand. Substitution possibilities between domestically and foreign-produced goods of the same category (e.g., between domestic and imported autos) are represented by nested CES functions. The choice of the *LES* demand system is convenient because, as discussed in appendix B, fairly extensive estimates of its parameters exist. (See appendix 3A for a discussion of welfare analysis based on this demand system.)

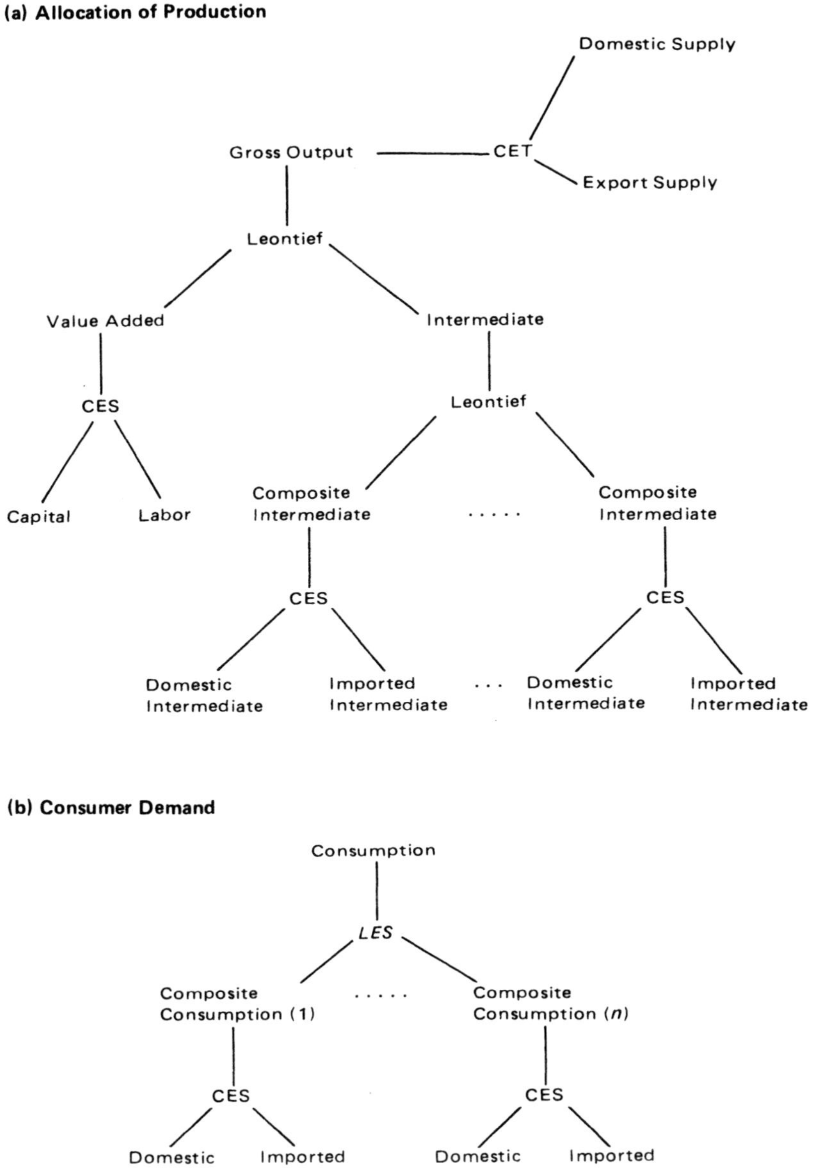

Figure 3.1
Model structure: (a) allocation of production; (b) consumer demand

A final issue is whether the United States would face fixed terms of trade for the trade policy changes presented here. Our view is that in most instances the small-country assumption for the United States in world markets is a good first-order approximation. Indeed, this is the assumption made in most of the single-country partial equilibrium estimates surveyed in section 1.3. We also argue, however, that differences in standards as well as the size of the US market may result in a noninfinite foreign supply elasticity for autos. Also, when we consider the simultaneous removal of all discriminatory protection, we assume that the United States would face a noninfinite elasticity of demand for its agricultural exports. Furthermore, because of the controversy raised by the strong terms-of-trade effects recorded in global general equilibrium simulation analyses (see the discussion in section 5.7.2 of chapter 5), we explore systematically the sensitivity of our welfare estimates to across-the-board monopoly and monopsony power in section 5.6.

3.2 Equations of the Basic Trade Model

3.2.1 Notation

The complete set of equations describing the basic model is given in table 3.1. Definitions of endogenous variables and of exogenous variables and parameters are given in tables 3.2 and 3.3, respectively. Variable subscripts indicate sectors. If double subscripts are employed, the first subscript denotes the sector of origin, the second the sector of destination. Uppercase letters are reserved for endogenous variables, unless they have a bar, in which case they are exogenous variables or normalization constants. Parameters and policy variables are denoted by Greek or lowercase Latin letters. There are $i, j = 1, \ldots, n$ sectors, of which $k = 1, \ldots, l$ are traded and the remainder ($m = l + 1, \ldots, n$) are nontraded. The index k is reserved for traded sectors, and m for nontraded sectors. NT refers to the set of nontradables sectors; T refers to the set of tradables sectors; N refers to the set of all sectors. NT and T are nonintersecting sets whose union equals N.

3.2.2 Equation Description

Production is characterized by two-level nesting (see figure 3.1). At the first level is a Leontief input-output production function. At this level firms use a composite of primary factors of production and n composite intermediate inputs (one for each sector). Since the composite primary factor cannot be

Table 3.1
Model equations

1. Cost

$CV_i \equiv PVC_i + INTC_i$

$$CV_i = X_i \overline{AX}_i^{-1}[\alpha_i^{\sigma_i} W^{1-\sigma_i} + (1-\alpha_i)^{\sigma_i} R^{1-\sigma_i}]^{1/(1-\sigma_i)} + \sum_{j=1}^{n} a_{ji} X_i PV_{ji}, \qquad i \in N \qquad (1)$$

2. Factor markets

$$K_i = \left(\frac{X_i}{\overline{AX}_i}\right)^{(1-\sigma_i)} \left[PVC_i \times \frac{1-\alpha_i}{R}\right]^{\sigma_i}, \qquad i \in N \qquad (2)$$

$$L_i = \left(\frac{X_i}{\overline{AX}_i}\right)^{(1-\sigma_i)} \left[PVC_i \times \frac{\alpha_i}{W}\right]^{\sigma_i}, \qquad i \in N \qquad (3)$$

$$\sum_{i \in N} L_i = \overline{LS}, \quad \sum_{i \in N} K_i = \overline{KS} \qquad (4)$$

3. Intermediate products demand

$$V_{ji} = \overline{AV}_{ji}[\delta_j VM_{ji}^{\rho v_j} + (1-\delta_j) VD_{ji}^{\rho v_j}]^{1/\rho v_j}, \qquad \rho v_j < 1, j \in T, i \in N \qquad (5)$$

$$\frac{VD_{ji}}{VM_{ji}} = \left[\left(\frac{1-\delta_j}{\delta_j}\right)\left(\frac{PMI_j^v}{PD_j}\right)\right]^{\sigma v_j}, \qquad j \in T, i \in N \qquad (6)$$

$$\sigma v_j = \frac{1}{(1-\rho v_j)}$$

$$VM_{ji} = 0, \quad V_{ji} = VD_{ji}, \qquad j \in NT, i \in N \qquad (7)$$

$$V_{ji} = a_{ji} X_i, \qquad i, j \in N \qquad (8)$$

4. Output allocation for tradables

$$X_i = \overline{AT}_i[\gamma_i E_i^{\rho t_i} + (1-\gamma_i) D_i^{\rho t_i}]^{1/\rho t_i}, \qquad \rho t_i > 1, i \in T \qquad (9)$$

$$X_i = D_i, \quad E_i = 0, \qquad i \in NT$$

$$\frac{D_i}{E_i} = \left[\left(\frac{1-\gamma_i}{\gamma_i}\right)\left(\frac{PE_i}{PD_i}\right)\right]^{-\sigma t_i}, \qquad i \in T \qquad (10)$$

$$\sigma t_i = \frac{1}{\rho t_i - 1}$$

5. Unit cost and revenue prices

$$PX_i = \overline{AT}_i^{-1}[\gamma_i^{-\sigma t_i} PE_i^{1+\sigma t_i} + (1-\gamma_i)^{-\sigma t_i} PD_i^{1+\sigma t_i}]^{1/(1+\sigma t_i)}, \qquad i \in T \qquad (11)$$

$$PV_{ij} = \overline{AV}_{ij}^{-1}[\delta_i^{\sigma v_i} PMI_i^{v\,1-\sigma v_i} + (1-\delta_i)^{\sigma v_i} PD_i^{1-\sigma v_i}]^{1/(1-\sigma v_i)}, \qquad i \in T, j \in N \qquad (12)$$

$$PC_i = \overline{AC}_i^{-1}[v_i^{\sigma c_i} PM_i^{v\,1-\sigma c_i} + (1-v_i)^{\sigma c_i} PD_i^{1-\sigma c_i}]^{1/(1-\sigma c_i)}, \qquad i \in T \qquad (13)$$

$$PN_i = PX_i - \sum_j a_{ji} PV_{ji}, \qquad i \in N \qquad (14)$$

6. Definition of internal prices of traded goods

$$PE_i = PWE_i ER, \qquad i \in T \qquad (15)$$

$$PMI_i^v = PWI_i(1+tm_i)(1+pri_i)ER, \qquad i \in T \qquad (16)$$

$$PM_i^v = PWM_i(1+tm_i)(1+prc_i)ER, \qquad i \in T \qquad (17)$$

7. Import supply and export demand

$$PWE_i = \overline{PWE}_i \quad \text{or} \quad E_i = \overline{E}_i(PWE_i)^{-\pi_i}, \qquad \pi_i > 0, \qquad i \in T \qquad (18)$$

Table 3.1 (continued)

$$PWM_i = \overline{PWM}_i \quad \text{or} \quad CM_i = \overline{CM}_i(PWM_i)^{\psi_i}, \qquad \psi_i > 0, \qquad i \in T \tag{19}$$

$\pi_i < \infty$ for agriculture, $\psi_i < \infty$ for autos

8. Consumer and Intermediate Demand

$$C_i = \lambda_i + \left(\frac{\beta_i}{PC_i}\right)(Y - \text{COMIT}), \qquad i \in N \tag{20}$$

where $\text{COMIT} = \sum_{j \in N} \lambda_j PC_j, \quad \sum_{j \in N} \beta_i \equiv 1, \beta_i > 0$

$$C_i = \overline{AC}_i(v_i CM_i^{\rho c_i} + (1 - v_i)CD_i^{\rho c_i})^{1/\rho c_i}, \qquad \rho c_i < 1, i \in T \tag{21}$$

$$C_i = CD_i, \quad CM_i = 0, \qquad i \in NT$$

$$\frac{CD_i}{CM_i} = \left[\left(\frac{1 - v_i}{v_i}\right)\left(\frac{PM_i^v}{PD_i}\right)\right]^{\sigma c_i} \qquad i \in T \tag{22}$$

$$\sigma c_i = \frac{1}{1 - \rho c_i}$$

$$VTD_i = \sum_{j \in N} VD_{ij}, \qquad i \in N \tag{23}$$

$$VTM_i = \sum_{j \in N} VM_{ij}, \qquad i \in T$$

$$D_i = VTD_i + CD_i, \qquad i \in N \tag{24}$$

9. Rationing

$$\overline{VTM}_i^1 < VTM_i^0 \Rightarrow PMI_i^v = PWI_i(1 + tm_i)(1 + PRI_i)ER, \qquad i \in T \tag{25}$$

$$\overline{CM}_i^1 < CM_i^0 \Rightarrow PM_i^v = PWM_i(1 + tm_i)(1 + PRC_i)ER, \qquad i \in T \tag{26}$$

10. Rents in rationed sectors

$$\text{RENT}C_i = \left[\left(\frac{PM_i^v}{1 + tm_i}\right) - PWM_i ER\right] CM_i, \qquad i \in T \tag{27}$$

$$\text{RENT}I_i = \sum_{j \in N} \left[\left(\frac{PMI_i^v}{1 + tm_i}\right) - PWI_i ER\right] VM_{ij}, \qquad i \in T \tag{28}$$

11. Government revenue (GR), trade balance constraint ($\overline{B}$), and income definition (Y)

$$GR = \sum_{k \in T} \left[PM_k^v - \left(\frac{PM_k^v}{1 + tm_k}\right)\right] CM_k + \sum_{k \in T} \sum_{j \in N} \left[PMI_k^v - \left(\frac{PMI_k^v}{1 + tm_k}\right)\right] VM_{kj} \tag{29}$$

$$\overline{B} = \sum_{k \in T} (PWE_k E_k - PWM_k CM_k - PWI_k VTM_k) - \sum_{k \in T} \frac{\theta_k(\text{RENT}C_k + \text{RENT}I_k)}{ER} \tag{30}$$

$$Y = W\overline{LS} + R\overline{KS} + GR + \sum_{k \in T} (1 - \theta_k)(\text{RENT}C_k + \text{RENT}I_k) - \overline{B}ER \tag{31}$$

12. Market equilibrium

$$PX_i = \frac{CV_i}{X_i}, \qquad i \in N \tag{32}$$

13. Numéraire

$$1 = \frac{\sum_{j=1}^n PD_j D_j^0}{\sum_{j=1}^n PD_j^0 D_j^0} \tag{33}$$

Table 3.2
Definition of endogenous variables

Variable	Definition	Number of variables
CV_i	Unit costs	n
K_i	Sectoral capital stocks	n
L_i	Sectoral employment	n
V_{ji}	Composite intermediate purchases of sector i from sector j	n^2
C_i	Composite final consumption of sectors	n
VD_{ji}	Domestic intermediate purchases of sector i from sector j	n^2
VM_{ji}	Imported intermediate purchases of sector i from sector j	$n(n-1)$
X_i	Gross output of sector i	n
D_i	Supply for domestic sales	n
E_k	Supply for export sales	m
PX_k	Unit price of composite domestically produced traded goods	m
PD_i	Unit price of domestically sold goods	n
PV_{ij}	Unit price of composite intermediate product of sector i sold to sector j	n^2
PC_i	Unit price of composite consumption of sector i	n
PN_i	Value-added price of sector i	n
PE_k, PWE_k	Domestic and border price of exports from sector k (PWE_k are mostly exogenous)	$2m$
PM_k^v, PWM_k	Premium-inclusive and border price of consumer imports of sector k (PWM_k are mostly exogenous)	$2m$
PMI_k^v, PWI_k	Premium-inclusive and border price of intermediate imports of sector k (PWI_k are mostly exogenous)	$2m$
$RENTC_k$, $RENTI_k$	Rents on consumer and intermediate imports	$2m$
VTD_i, $VTM_k(PRI_k)$	Demands for domestic and imported intermediates (premium on imported intermediates)	$2m+n$
CM_k, $CD_i(PRC_k)$	Consumer demand for imports and domestically produced goods (premium on imported consumption goods)	$m+n$
GR, Y, ER	Government revenue from tariff collection, disposable income net of transfers, and real exchange rate	3
W, R	Wage and rental rates	2
	Total number of variables	$3n^2+n(n-1)+11n+13m+5$

Note: The number of endogenous variables varies according to model closure (see text).

Table 3.3
Definition of exogenous variables and parameters

Variable/parameter	Definition
$\overline{LS}$, $\overline{KS}$	Supply of labor and capital
$\overline{AX}_i$, $\overline{AC}_i$, $\overline{AT}_k$, $\overline{AV}_{ij}$	Normalizing constants (see appendix A)
λ_i, β_i	Parameters of the linear expenditure system
α_i, δ_k, δ_j, ν_k	Quasi-share parameters of various CES and CET functions
σc_i, σt_i, σ_i, σv_i	Elasticities of substitution in final demand (CES) and transformation (CET), capital and labor in value-added functions, and substitution in intermediate demand
ρc_j, ρt_i, ρ_i, ρv_i	Parameters corresponding to the just mentioned elasticities. In particular, $\sigma = 1/(1 - \rho)$ except for $\sigma t = 1/(\rho t - 1)$
tm_k	Ad valorem tariff on imports of intermediates and consumer goods of sector k
$pri_k = prc_k$	Premium rate on imports of intermediate and final goods
π_k, ψ_k	Foreign elasticity of demand for exports and of supply of imports
$\overline{B}$	Exogenous component of the current account expressed in foreign units
θ_k	Share of quota premia accruing abroad

substituted for the composite intermediate, nor can intermediates of one sector be substituted for intermediates of another, the production function at level one is strongly separable (see Blackorby, Primont, and Russell 1978 or Phlips 1974). At the second level each of the composite functions is defined. The primary factor of production is a composite of two primary factors, capital and labor. Primary factors of production substitute smoothly for each other through CES value-added functions (or as a special case, a Cobb-Douglas function). The parameters of the CES vary across sectors. Each sector uses intermediate inputs, and except for nontraded goods, these inputs come from both domestic and foreign sources. Intermediate inputs from a given sector are a composite of domestic and foreign intermediate inputs. Firms smoothly substitute domestic and foreign intermediate inputs in a given sector through a CES aggregator function defined by equation 5 in table 3.1. These assumptions are reflected in the first-level Leontief production function:

$$X_i = \min\left[F_i(K_i, L_i), \frac{V_{1i}}{a_{1i}}, \cdots, \frac{V_{ni}}{a_{ni}}\right], \tag{3.1}$$

where X_i is gross output of sector i. The functions $F_i(K_i, L_i)$ are the CES value-added functions in labor and capital.

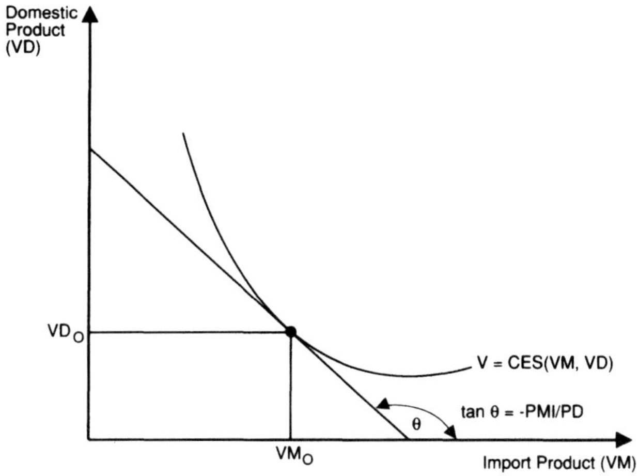

Figure 3.2
The elasticity of substitution and cost minimization in intermediate demand

The cost function CV_i in equation 1 of table 3.1, which is composed of primary costs (PVC_i) and intermediate costs ($INTC_i$), is the result of cost minimization by the representative firm with respect to its variable inputs—capital, labor, and intermediates—subject to the technology described by equation 3.1.[3] The Leontief assumption in technology implies that the cost function is additively separable in its primary and intermediate cost components.

Factor demands are given by equations 2 to 3. Factor demands are obtained from Shephard's lemma, that is by taking partial derivatives of the cost function with respect to the relevant factor price. The assumption of fixed factor endowments is reflected in equation 4.

Equations 5–8 describe the choice between domestically and foreign-produced intermediates. As with primary factors, demands for intermediate products are the result of cost minimization by the representative firm with respect to its intermediate inputs, subject to the technology described by equation 3.1. Equation 8 describes the demand for intermediate purchases by sector i from sector j resulting from the Leontief technology assumption in equation 3.1. In turn equation 6 describes the cost-minimizing choice of domestic and foreign purchases from sector j, subject to the constraint that substitution possibilities between domestic and imported intermediates in production are characterized by equation 5. The firm's cost-minimizing choice of domestic and imported intermediate inputs is depicted in figure 3.2.

Equation 9 is the constant elasticity of transformation (CET) function introduced by Powell and Gruen (1968). It allows us to extend to exports naturally and symmetrically the idea of product differentiation so commonly used for imports in general equilibrium models. Equation 9 reflects substitution possibilities in production between the domestic and the export product. As the elasticity of transformation increases, goods for sales on the domestic and export markets become homogeneous.[4] The curvature of the CET function reflects the view that initially a producer can shift resources from domestic to export production, and vice versa, with almost no loss in production efficiency. As larger shifts in product mix are desired, however, increasing production of the variety that is expanding its share will require a reliance on labor and capital that are relatively less efficient at producing the expanding variety. Thus the CET curve is concave. The allocation of a given output between domestic and export sales described by equation 10 is the result of revenue maximization subject to the CET function (equation 9) and is depicted in figure 3.3.

Equations 11, 12, and 13 define price indices of the corresponding composite good. In all cases the price indices are the unit cost functions that are dual to the corresponding unit quantity aggregator functions. Equation 12, for example, is the unit cost function that is dual to equation 5, with $V_{ji} = 1$. Since the quantity aggregator function (equation 5) is linear homogeneous, the total costs of V_{ji} may be written as $PV_{ji} V_{ji}$, where PV_{ji}

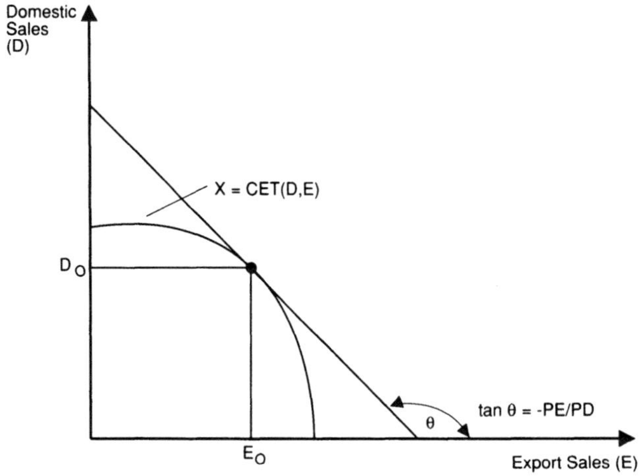

Figure 3.3
The elasticity of transformation and revenue maximization between domestic and export sales

is the unit cost function (equation 12) (Varian 1984, 28). This implies that the average costs of V_{ji}, when purchased at minimum cost, are independent of the number of units purchased, so the unit cost function is an acceptable price index. An entirely analogous argument justifies the use of equations 11 and 13 as the price indices for the firm's composite output (equation 11) and the consumer's composite final consumption (equation 21, discussed below), respectively. Clearly equation 11 is a unit revenue function.

Equation 14 is the value added or net price per unit of output. It follows clearly from the unit revenue function (equation 11) and the cost function (equation 1).

The relation between border (or world) prices and internal prices is given in equations 15 to 17. Since there is no money metric in the model, all prices are relative prices defined in terms of the selected numéraire. In equation 15, PE_i is the number of units of the numéraire good that the firm receives for one unit of the export variety of the output of sector i, and PWE_i is the border or world price of the same good relative to the numéraire. The variable ER converts the world price of goods in any sector into the price received by firms. As shown in appendix 3B, given our choice of numéraire, ER is the price of tradable goods relative to nontradable goods, or the real exchange rate.

Equations 16 and 17 deal with imports and are analogous to equation 15. However, in addition to tariffs, they allow for rationing in the base year, in which case the premia rates pri_k and prc_k are positive. For sectors with no rationing, $pri_k = prc_k = 0$. (How the premia are determined is discussed further in section 3.3 and in chapter 4.)

Premium-inclusive intermediate and final import prices, which are introduced in equations 16 and 17, respectively, are denoted by the superscript v. This superscript denotes the "virtual" price that sector i must pay for imported intermediates from sector j. The concept of a virtual price was introduced by Neary and Roberts (1980), who used duality theory to show how to derive constrained demands when the quota is allocated or rationed in some way other than by market-clearing prices. An obvious reason for nonclearing prices would be government price controls. Neary and Roberts call the virtual price that price that would result in a user purchasing the same amounts when unrationed as when rationed. Although it is common in developing countries to forbid the transfer of quota rights received under import allocation schemes (resulting in non-market-clearing prices), the practices allowed in the United States generally result in market-clearing prices of goods imported under a quota. Thus in our simulations the virtual price reduces to the ordinary market price under a quota. Our specification, however, allows for a generalization to the case where the market does not clear.

Equations 18 and 19 define the extent of monopoly or monopsony power the United States has on world markets. The left-hand side sets of equations 18 and 19 reflect the small-country assumption in which the United States is unable to influence the price of its exports or imports of sector *i*. If the United States is assumed to have monopoly power in its export or monopsony power in its import market in sector *i*, the right-side sets of equations 18 and 19 are used.[5] In general, we drop the small-country assumption for agricultural exports and auto imports.

Equations 20, 21, 22, and 13 describe consumer demand equations. The consumer maximizes a Stone-Geary utility function of all final commodities (both imported and domestic) subject to consumer income given by equation 31. We assume that imported and domestic commodities in a given sector substitute in the consumer's utility function in a CES nest given by equation 21. This implies that the top-level Stone-Geary utility function is weakly separable in the composite final commodities of the model (equation 3A.1 in appendix 3A).[6] Moreover, as discussed above, because the commodity aggregator is linear homogeneous, the price index of the composite commodity can be represented by the unit cost function (equation 13) that is dual to the commodity aggregator (equation 21). Weak separability combined with the existence of the price index of composite commodities implies that the consumer's decision problem may be decomposed into "two-stage budgeting."[7] Thus in the first stage (or the top level) the consumer maximizes the separable Stone-Geary utility function of composite commodities, given income (equation 31) and composite prices. Equation 20 follows from this maximization. In the second stage the consumer maximizes each of the subutility functions (equation 21) subject to expenditure allocated to consumption of the *i*th commodity from the first-stage maximization. (Further details are provided in appendix 3A.)

The model includes a balance of trade constraint in equation 30 so that trade policy changes are not financed by a free lunch from the rest of the world. That is, without a balance of trade constraint, import liberalization, which results in increased imports in the liberalizing sector, will not have to be offset by increased exports or decreased imports elsewhere. This is an unrealistic assumption, which implies a permanent increase in capital inflow from the rest of the world. We show in chapter 5 that it leads to a severe overestimate of the benefits of trade liberalization.

Note, however, that the value of quota rents accruing to foreigners is subtracted from foreign earnings and that the trade deficit prevailing in the base year is unaffected by changes in trade policy. Moreover the balance of trade constraint is expressed in foreign units because otherwise the balance of trade would be variable.

Prices are determined by average costs (equation 32). Until the introduction of economies of scale (chapter 7), it is evident from equation 1 that average and marginal costs are equal, so equation 32 is the zero-profit equilibrium condition.

The reader can verify that a proportionate change in all prices (including factor prices) does not change any demand or supply function; that is, the system is homogeneous of degree zero in prices. Since this implies that only relative prices matter, one must choose a numéraire to determine prices. An exceptionally convenient numéraire for our purposes is a weighted average of all domestic goods, expressed as in equation 33. We show in appendix 3B that as a result of this numéraire selection, the percent change in the variable *ER* is the percent change in real exchange rate.

Finally, equation 31 is the income-expenditure identity, which states that the consumer's income derives from factor income, government lump-sum distributions, and domestically captured quota rents less the trade deficit. Given that all agents in the model (firms, consumers, and the government) satisfy a budget constraint, it is well known that the sum of the excess demands for all goods is zero; that is, Walras' law holds. Consequently there is a functional dependence among the equations of the model, and one equation is redundant. For our system of equations, this may be verified directly, as was done explicitly in chapter 2, by showing that equation 31 is implied by the other equations of the model.

In this dual formulation output is determined by demand and sectoral equilibrium is determined (in equation 32) by the condition that unit price equals unit cost. Given that export price is determined by equation 15, equation 32 determines the domestic market price PD_i.

Had the model been formulated in the primal, several other changes would have occurred in the equations. Total output X_i would have been supply determined (by replacing equation 1 with the corresponding CES equation for gross output), equation 30 would have been dropped along with unit marginal cost (CV_i), and sectoral equilibrium would have been determined by equation 24. In the primal formulation, factor demands would have been determined by the first-order conditions for profit maximization, with output levels appearing in equations 2 and 3 and net price PN_i being substituted for unit primary cost PVC_i. It can be shown that in equilibrium $PVC_i = PN_i$ because of course the primal and dual formulations give the same result, a fact verified numerically for a large set of simulations with a primal formulation of the model. However, as stated in the introduction, we have chosen to formulate the model in the dual rather than in the more familiar primal formulation because we introduce increasing returns to scale and several pricing rules in chapter 7 that are better handled with a formulation of the model in dual form.

In the application with infinite trade elasticities, the model reduces to a system of $[3n^2 + n(n-1) + 9n + 13m + 5] - 3m$ simultaneous equations.

3.3 Modeling of Quantitative Restrictions

Finally, we have to deal with QRs. This section explains equations 16, 17, and 25–28 in detail and establishes that quota premium rates and quota rents are residually determined from the tariff-ridden inverse demand curve. Readers familiar with these propositions may skip this section.

A superscript 0 denotes the initial situation and a superscript 1 the new equilibrium. We start with the case of binding QRs in the base year (i.e., the case in textiles and apparel and autos). Figure 3.4a shows how the premium-inclusive price is determined under the assumption of an infinitely elastic import supply of autos. For illustration we assume that all imports are for final demand, which can be written as

$$CM_k = D(PM_k^v). \tag{3.2}$$

In the initial equilibrium imports are restricted by VERs to CM_k^0. Since PM_k^v is the price actually paid by consumers, it includes both the unit tariff paid and the premium resulting from the restriction of auto imports to CM_k^0 in the base year. By choice of units, we choose the premium-inclusive price in the base year to be equal to 1.

The price paid by consumers exclusive of the unit tariff is denoted by PM_k^t, which is the unit amount received by private agents in domestic units. Then the inverse demand curve is

$$PM_k^v = PM_k^t(1 + tm_k) = d(CM_k), \tag{3.3}$$

where d is the inverse function of D and tm_k is the ad valorem tariff rate. The tariff-ridden inverse demand curve is

$$PM_k^t = \frac{d(CM_k)}{1 + tm_k}. \tag{3.4}$$

From equation 3.3 we know that the tariff- and non-tariff-ridden inverse demand curves intersect the quantity axis at the same point, but the

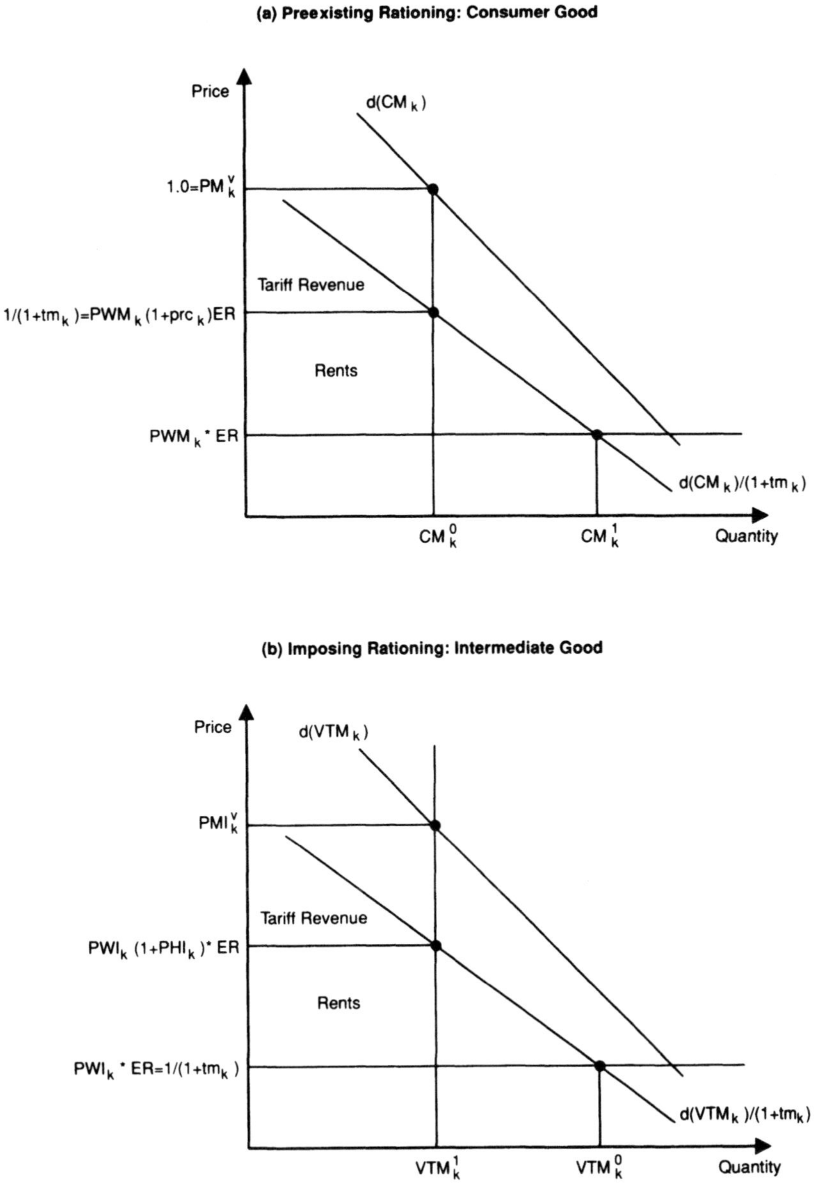

Figure 3.4
Import price determination with rationing: (a) example of preexisting rationing for consumer good; (b) example of imposing rationing on intermediate good

tariff-ridden curve is flatter. Also $d(CM_k)$ passes through the point (CM_k^0, 1.0) where by choice of units $PM_k^v = 1.0$ in the initial equilibrium. In our illustration foreigners are willing to supply the product at $PWM_k \times ER$. Thus initial per unit rents are

$$\frac{PM_k^v}{1 + tm_k} - PWM_k \times ER = \frac{RENTC_k}{CM_k}, \tag{3.5}$$

which is equation 27, where all variables take their values in the initial equilibrium. We define prc_i as the premia or rental rates on imports. As depicted in figure 3.4a, we have

$$\frac{PM_k^v}{1 + tm_k} = PWM_k(1 + prc_k)ER, \tag{3.6}$$

which is equation 17. The estimates of prc_k are crucial and are discussed extensively in chapter 4.

Next we consider the case of an unrationed sector in the base year (i.e., steel, an intermediate product that was predominantly free of quantitative restrictions in the base year). We ration, or impose quotas, by setting $\overline{VTM}_k^1 < VTM_k^0$. This induces a price increase and generates an endogenously determined amount of rents and premium rate PHI_k on imports. This case is illustrated in figure 3.4b, where the curves are defined analogously to those in figure 3.4a. It follows from this discussion that equations 25 and 26 characterize the determination of price and endogenous premium rates. Equations 27 and 28 characterize rents in rationed sectors for both exogenously and endogenously determined premium rates.

Figures 3.4a and 3.4b indicate that an increase in the ad valorem tariff rate will flatten out the tariff-ridden inverse demand curve. This will have the effect of reducing the "rents" rectangle and the premium rate on quota-restrained imports. So an increase in the tariff is one instrument available to the government to "capture quota rents." (Quota rents are discussed further in chapter 4, and the effect of increasing the tariff rate when quotas are in effect is illustrated in appendix 5A.)

3.4 Welfare Measure

We measure the change in welfare induced by trade policy by the Hicksian equivalent variation (EV). The exact measure of EV and of the Hicksian compensating variation (CV) is developed in appendix 3A and is extended to the case of labor-leisure choice in appendix 6A. A brief intuitive presentation and rationale for the measure is provided here.

How we measure welfare depends on whether we use initial prices (P^0) or new prices (P^1) to measure utility (superscript 0 denotes the initial equilibrium and superscript 1 the equilibrium that prevails after the policy change). The *EV* measure is based on initial prices and the *CV* measure on new prices. The difference between the two measures is illustrated graphically in figure 3.5. Our numerical experience, however, conforms with that of Willig (1976), who found very little difference between the two measures. Therefore we report only one measure.

In the welfare results reported in this book, welfare changes are not always measured from the same base. For example, when we measure the welfare costs of imposing quotas in steel (chapter 5), the base is an equilibrium without quotas on steel, whereas when we measure the welfare costs of combined QRs in autos, steel, and textiles and apparel, the corresponding base is an equilibrium with quotas on steel.

3.5 Conclusion

This chapter has introduced the basic trade model used in the simulations of chapter 5. The model is relatively simple and transparent in structure, as it is a direct extension of the simpler one-sector model presented in chapter 2. The model yields results that are straightforward to interpret. In chapter 6 we add complexity to the model by introducing labor-leisure choice and (endogenous) union behavior affecting wage distortions in autos and steel and by adopting a range of assumptions about international and intersectoral capital mobility. In chapter 7 we allow for economies of scale and imperfect competition. In all cases the results obtained with the more complicated structures are compared to the results obtained in chapter 5 with the basic model. This helps in interpreting the numerical results. The next chapter explains at length how we obtained the premium estimates, which are crucial for determining the magnitude of the costs of QR protection reported in chapters 5, 6, and 7.

Appendix 3A: Definition of the Welfare Measure

As discussed in the text, our functional forms for consumer behavior are sufficient to allow two-stage budgeting. Consequently we may base our welfare measure on the expenditure function associated with the top-level utility function, which is a Stone-Geary function. To simplify notation, we denote the composite final good price of sector i (equation 13) as P_i, and denote $COMIT = \sum_{j=1}^{n} \lambda_j P_j = \mu$. The top-level Stone-Geary utility func-

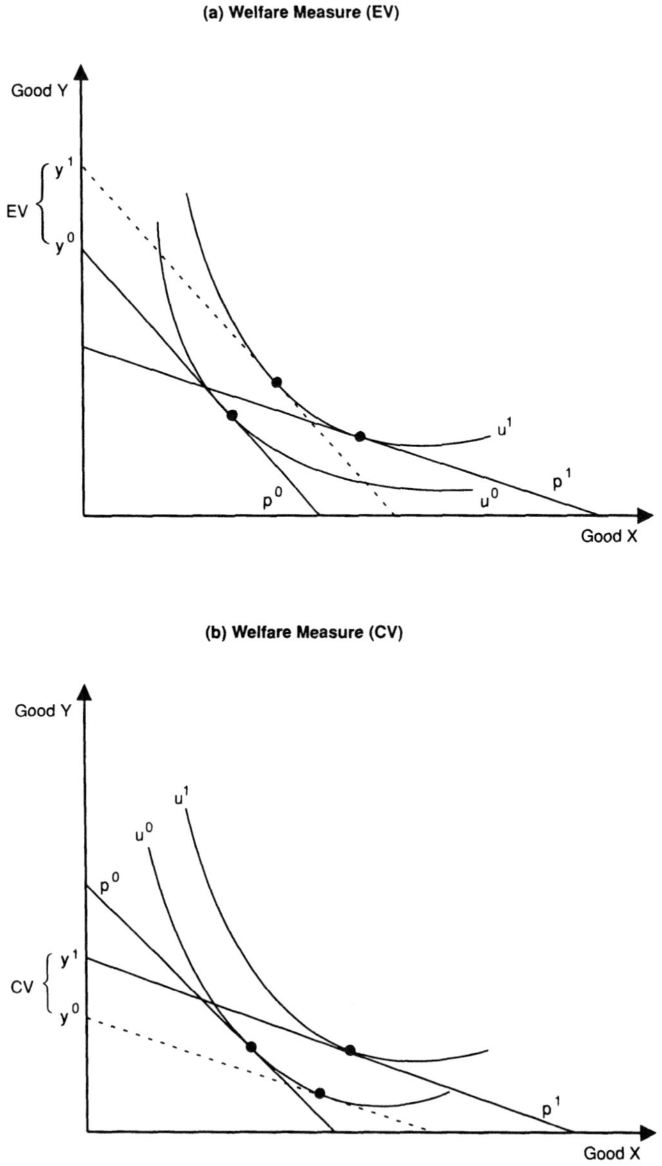

Figure 3.5
Hicksian equivalent and compensating variations: (a) welfare measure (EV); (b) welfare measure (CV)

tion is represented by

$$U = \prod_{i=1}^{n} (C_i - \lambda_i)^{\beta_i}. \tag{3A.1}$$

Maximization of equation 3A.1, subject to income and composite prices P_i, yields the demand function of equation 20. The second stage of utility maximization, resulting in equation 22, guarantees that given expenditure allocation to sector i, CD_i and CM_i will be chosen to maximize subutility C_i; equivalently any level of subutility or composite consumption C_i will be obtained at minimum cost. This maximization of subutility C_i allows us to restrict our attention to equation 3A.1 in defining our welfare measure.

Given that the demand functions represent an optimization of the consumer's maximization problem, substituting the demand function of equation 20 into the utility function results in the maximum utility obtainable given prices and income, that is, the indirect utility (IU) function:

$$IU = \prod_{i=1}^{n} \left[\left(\frac{\beta_i}{P_i}\right)(Y - \mu)\right]^{\beta_i}. \tag{3A.2}$$

Denoting $\beta = \prod_{i=1}^{n} \beta_i^{\beta_i}$, then since $\sum_{j=1}^{n} \beta_j = 1$, we can rewrite equation 3A.2 as

$$IU = \frac{\beta(Y - \mu)}{\prod_{i=1}^{n} P_i^{\beta_i}}. \tag{3A.3}$$

Inverting equation 3A.3 yields the expenditure function, that is, the minimum level of income necessary to yield utility level IU, given prices

$$E(P, IU) = \left(\frac{IU}{\beta}\right)\left(\prod_{i=1}^{n} P_i^{\beta_i}\right) + \mu, \tag{3A.4}$$

where P is the vector of final goods prices. The expenditure function in this form is known as the indirect compensation function (see Varian 1984). The expenditure function may also be expressed in terms of the direct utility function as

$$E[P, U(C)] = \left\{\left[\prod_{i=1}^{n} P_i^{\beta_i}\right]\frac{[\prod_{i=1}^{n} (C_i - \lambda_i)^{\beta_i}]}{\beta}\right\} + \mu. \tag{3A.5}$$

When written in this manner, the expenditure function is sometimes called the direct compensation function or the "money metric" utility function.

We desire a measure of how much better or worse off the representative consumer is in the initial equilibrium, facing prices P^0 and income Y^0, than in the equilibrium after the policy shift, facing prices P^1 and income Y^1. The answer depends on whether we take P^0 or P^1 as the base, but we may use the expenditure function to develop a measure.

We define

$$EV = E[P^0, IU(P^1, Y^1)] - E[P^0, IU(P^0, Y^0)] \tag{3A.6}$$

and

$$CV = E[P^1, IU(P^1, Y^1)] - E[P^1, IU(P^0, Y^0)], \tag{3A.7}$$

where EV (equivalent variation) and CV (compensating variation) are the Hicksian exact measures of the change in consumer surplus. The first term in EV is the minimum income necessary to reach utility level $IU(P^1, Y^1)$ given prices P^0. The second term in EV is the minimum income level necessary to reach utility level $IU(P^0, Y^0)$ given prices P^0; this term is equal to Y^0. If EV is positive, then the consumer is better off as a result of the policy shift. This is because, when initial prices are the constraint, an income greater than the consumer's initial income is needed to reach the new utility level. It is well known that EV and CV have the same sign.

In our case EV reduces to

$$\begin{aligned} EV &= \left[\frac{IU(P^1, Y^1)}{\beta}\right]\left[\prod_{i=1}^{n} (P_i^0)^{\beta_i}\right] + \mu^0 - Y^0 \\ &= (Y^1 - \mu^1)\left[\prod_{i=1}^{n} \left(\frac{P_i^0}{P_i^1}\right)^{\beta_i}\right] - (Y^0 - \mu^0). \end{aligned} \tag{3A.8}$$

where $\mu^t = \sum_{j=1}^{n} \lambda_j P_i^t$ and $t = 0, 1$. All of the arguments of the "unobservable" EV in this form are observable, so we take EV as our measure of the welfare change resulting from a policy shift. From the definition of the compensating variation, we have

$$CV = (Y^1 - \mu^1) - (Y^0 - \mu^0)\left[\prod_{i=1}^{n} \left(\frac{P_i^1}{P_i^0}\right)^{\beta_i}\right]. \tag{3A.9}$$

Appendix 3B: The Real Exchange Rate

This appendix discusses briefly the real exchange rate for the model presented in chapter 3. Since there is no money metric in the model, all prices are relative prices. This extends to the concept of the exchange rate. If there were assets in the model, one could define a nominal exchange rate as the relative price of two assets. In the absence of assets, the real exchange rate is the relative price of tradables to nontradables. In a multisector setting the real exchange rate is defined as a ratio of an index of the value of all tradables (on world markets) to an index of the value of all nontradables. (T is the set of tradable goods sectors.)

Based on the definitions in the model, the real exchange rate (RER) is

$$RER = \frac{\sum_{i \in T}(\alpha^i PWE_i \times ER + \beta^i PWI_i \times ER + \gamma^i PWM_i \times ER)}{\sum_{i=1}^{n} \tau^i PD_i}, \qquad (3B.1)$$

where $\sum_{i \in T}(\alpha^i + \beta^i + \gamma^i) = \sum_{i=1}^{n} \tau^i = 1$, and all the index weights in the sums are nonnegative. Expression 3B.1 can be rewritten as

$$RER = \left(\frac{ER}{\sum_{i=1}^{n} \tau^i PD_i}\right) \times \sum_{i \in T} (\alpha^i PWE_i + \beta^i PWI_i + \tau^i PWM_i). \qquad (3B.2)$$

Since $\sum_{i \in T}(\alpha^i PWE_i + \beta^i PWI_i + \tau^i PWM_i)$ is fixed unless the home country can influence the world price of some tradables, the percentage change in the real exchange rate reduces to the difference between the percentage change in the variable ER and the percentage change in the index of domestic prices. That is,

$$\widehat{RER} = \widehat{ER} - \left(\sum_{i=1}^{n} \tau^i \widehat{PD_i}\right), \qquad (3B.3)$$

where a caret indicates a percentage change in a variable. If we choose as numéraire $\sum_{i=1}^{n} \tau^i\ PD_i$ (see equation 33) and fix the value at unity, the percentage change in the variable ER is the percentage change in the real exchange rate.[9]

4 Quota Premium Rates and Rent Capture

As the description of the model in chapter 3 makes evident, estimates of the welfare costs of quantitative restrictions (QRs) in textiles and apparel and in autos depend crucially on two elements. The first is the estimate of the size of the premium resulting from QRs in the two sectors. Since there were no QRs on steel in 1984, our base year, we also need to determine the level of restraint achieved through the voluntary export restraints (VERs) negotiated on steel during 1985. The second crucial element for our welfare estimates concerns who captures the quota rents, the United States or the exporting country. This chapter looks at these two issues: How big are the quota rents, and who gets them?

In 1984, the base year for our simulations, both the auto and the textile and apparel sectors were subject to QRs. By then the VER negotiated with Japan on auto exports to the United States had been in effect for four years (since April 1, 1981).[1] QRs on textiles and apparel were much older, going back thirty years, and by 1984 the United States had negotiated export restraint agreements of various types with thirty-one countries (USITC 1985, 101). In the case of steel, the United States began in late 1984 to negotiate VERs with all significant suppliers to the US market except Canada. Since these agreements were not binding in 1984, 1984 is considered as a year with no QRs on steel.[2]

In this chapter we first discuss the theory underlying the influence of market structure on the distribution of quota rents. The remaining sections then deal with the problems associated with estimating premium rates and our solutions. We also briefly describe the US VER with Japan on autos and the US system of QRs on textiles and apparel and on steel.

4.1 Who Captures the Quota Rents?

Before getting into measurement issues, we need to look at the theory behind the capture of quota rents. To show this graphically, we character-

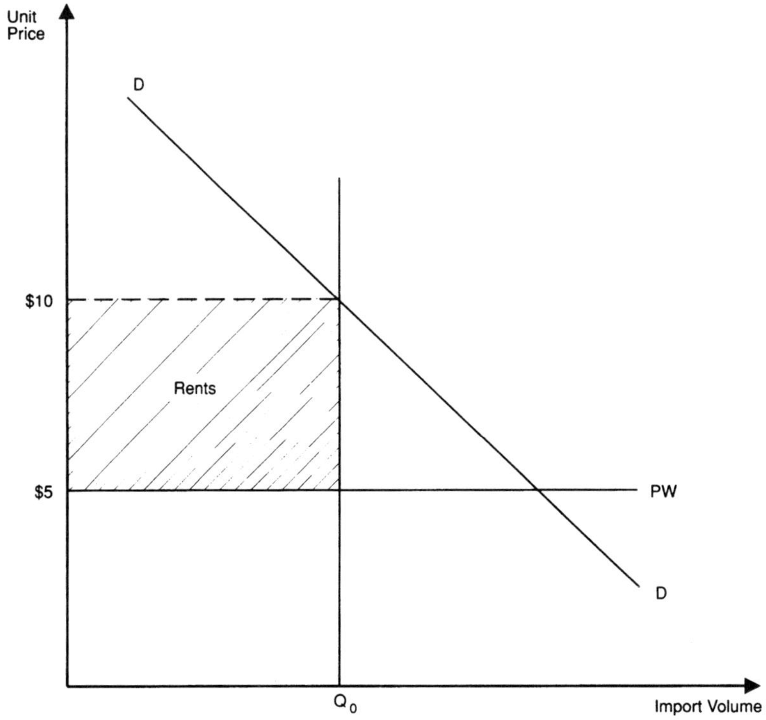

Figure 4.1
Quota rents

ize the market for imported textiles and apparel products in figure 4.1, where *DD* represents the US demand curve for imported textiles and apparel products, and Q_0 is the quantity of imported textiles and apparel allowed into the United States under the Multifiber Arrangement (MFA). We assume that imports are differentiated from domestic textiles and apparel but that imports from different countries are considered homogeneous by US consumers. (The reason for this assumption is discussed in section 4.2.2.) Given the quota, the price of imported textiles and apparel is determined by the intersection of *DD* and Q_0, which is $10 in our example. For the purposes of this illustration, we ignore tariffs and assume that the supply of imports is competitive and perfectly elastic at the price $5.

Under the MFA the United States negotiates and defines the amount of textiles and apparel products that can be imported from each country. Crucially, however, the United States allows the exporting country to allocate among domestic companies the rights to export to the United States. For example, a Hong Kong textile and apparel exporter wishing to sell to the United States has to obtain an export license from the government of Hong Kong, to which the United States has granted the right to select exporters under the quota. This system, which is the typical import quota allocation mechanism adopted by the United States, differs substantially from the US oil import quota system of the 1960s. Under that system quota rights went to US refineries, which were given the right to import oil under the quota, rather than to foreign exporters. For all the cases considered in this study, the United States, in negotiating its QRs, has allowed foreign governments to allocate quota rights among its exporters, subject only to the overall restraint of the quota.[3]

4.1.1 Monopsony, Oligopsony, and Contestable Markets in Importing

Returning to our example in figure 4.1, we see that there are potential quota rents to exporters of $5 per unit since the cost of production is $5 while the product sells for $10 in the United States. If there is monopsony power in US importing, however, some of these rents could be captured by US importers. For example, suppose there is only one US importer of textile and apparel products. This monopsonist might offer $6 per unit to exporters, who have no alternative buyer. Since suppliers earn quota rents of $1 per unit at $6, they may be willing to sell to the monopsonist at $6 rather than earn no rents at all. If they do so, four-fifths of the rents would be captured by the US monopsonist.

As we move from monopsony importing to oligopsony importing, the exporters are likely to capture a larger share of the quota rents. How the rent shares are distributed is determined, in part, by how well the oligopsonists avoid competing with each other. Through collusion they might attempt to enforce a price of $6. But because foreigners holding the quota rights possess something that is worth $10 to the oligopsonist, there is an incentive to cheat (i.e., to pay more than $6 to get a higher share of the imports) since the rent will be lost if competitors import the product.[4] Such pressures enable exporters to capture a significantly larger share of the quota rents.

If, however, the market is contestable and potential competitors can enter and exit rapidly into importing without suffering any cost disadvantage relative to incumbents, then the incumbent oligopsonists (or even monopsonist) will not be able to capture any of the rents.[5] Under the assumption of free entry, even if a monopsonist attempts to offer a price of say $9, new firms will appear that will offer a price closer to $10. The threat of entry drives the price of the imported article up to the point at which no rents remain to the importer and foreigners capture all the quota rents.

4.1.2 Competition in Importing

If there is competition in both exporting and importing, then whoever holds the quota rights gets the quota rents. In our example, though there is competitive supply in the world at $5 per unit, a company also needs to hold a license to export the product to the United States. If it holds the quota rights, a firm can obtain $10 per unit for the product. Competition among importers, to whom the product is worth $10, will ensure that no rational exporter with quota rights need accept less than $10 per unit. If an importer offers less than $10, the exporter can go to any of many other importers and obtain $10.

This simple and fundamental point about the implications of competition among importers has been the source of much confusion. It demonstrates that the exporter does not need monopoly power to capture quota rents and that even a large importing country will not capture any quota rents when there is competition among its importers for a product whose quota rights have been granted to foreigners. The same is also true for a large importing country with few importers if the market for purchasing and reselling the import is contestable and the quota rights have been granted to foreigners. To sum up, when quota rights are given to foreigners, what is crucial in determining who gets the quota rents is not the size of the importing country but the structure of the market for purchasing and reselling imports.

4.1.3 Monopoly in Exporting

The case of monopoly power in exporting, though clearly irrelevant to textiles and apparel and steel, may be relevant to autos. Suppose that there is a single foreign monopolist supplier. In this case there will be no supply curve. In terms of figure 4.1, suppose that the monopolist's marginal cost of supplying the product to the United States is $5 per unit and that the marginal revenue curve (not drawn) intersects the marginal cost curve at quantity Q_0. The monopolist will find it optimal to charge the price of $10, which is the same outcome as that discussed above for the case of competition in exporting with a quota of Q_0 allocated to foreigners. If a quota is imposed at the quantity Q_0, and the quota rights are allocated to the foreign monopolist, the outcome will be unchanged; that is, the quota is not binding.

What would be the consequences under these conditions of allocating quota rights among US firms? All those with import rights must deal with the monopolist exporter; they cannot play off competing suppliers at the marginal cost of import supply. In this case the allocation of rents from the quota depends on the price the monopolist sets. If the market in which the quota is imposed and any other of the monopolist's markets are segmented, then regardless of the quota level, it is clearly in the monopolist's interest to raise the price so that license holders get none of the rents. The same result holds even if these markets are not segmented if the quota is not too restrictive, as Krishna (1990) points out. Krishna (1989a) has shown conditions under which the result also holds with oligopoly. The basic point is that the allocation of licenses determines the pricing behavior of the oligopolistic suppliers, and this in turn determines the value of the license. If licenses are not allocated to producers, producers have an incentive to raise their price in order to capture the license rents. Thus there is little reason to expect the license price to reflect the tariff equivalent. Consequently, if the objective is to capture a share of the rents when there is significant foreign monopoly power, a tariff is superior to a quota auction.[6]

The removal of the quota altogether, however, will reduce the price to US consumers (by the amount of the estimated quota premium) because, by definition, the price under a binding quota with a monopolist supplier is above the monopolist's profit-maximizing level. Consequently our estimates of the benefits of removing the quota in autos are not affected by the possibility of monopoly power in exporting.

4.2 Quota Rent Estimates in Textiles and Apparel

4.2.1 The Multifiber Arrangement

US postwar restraints on imports of textiles and apparel go back to 1957, when a five-year VER on Japanese cotton textiles and apparel exports to the United States was negotiated. This was followed by the Long-Term Agreement on Cotton Textiles signed by nineteen countries. While this agreement was in effect from October 1962 to December 1973, the United States imposed restrictions against thirty-seven suppliers.[7] This agreement was superceded by the first Multifiber Arrangement (MFA), which was in effect from January 1974 to December 1977. Under the MFA restraints were added for wool and synthetic fibers, as well as cotton. The MFA has been extended three times, with the latest extension taking it up to July 31, 1991.[8] The newest MFA expands quota coverage to previously uncontrolled silk blends and vegetable fibers, principally linen and ramie, while dropping coverage on some textile items.[9]

As of June 1984 the United States had imposed quotas on the exports of textiles and apparel from thirty-one nations; of these, agreements with twenty-four countries were negotiated under the MFA (see USITC 1985, 101, for details). All important suppliers other than Europe and Canada are covered.[10] A characteristic of the trade restraints on textiles and apparel is that the developed countries tend to restrain the exports of developing countries but not those of each other. Because most agreements cover different types of textile and apparel products separately and because restraint levels are not immediately binding in all cases, researchers have had difficulty estimating the level of restraint created by the quotas on textiles and apparel.

Before we address this measurement problem, we look briefly at the concern sometimes expressed that US consumers will not benefit from quota removal because US retailers will simply increase their markups in response to the lower import prices. Two observations about this argument are relevant to our analysis. First, the evidence indicates that retailing is a competitive industry. This means that competition will force retailers to pass along to consumers the price decreases on imports. A survey by Cline (1979) found that imports of comparable quality sold at a lower price than domestically produced goods. Both theory and evidence suggest that retailers pass along lower prices.[11] Second, it is in any case irrelevant to our estimates of net social welfare whether retailers or import consumers capture the gains from lower prices since retailers are also US residents and consumers. If retailers capture some of the gains from lower prices as a result of quota removal, in the form of higher profits (or returns on capital), then the income and welfare of the owners of capital in that industry will increase to that extent. Since we deal with a single representative consumer, the welfare estimates are not affected. To sum up, "They may be Sons of Bitches, but they are our Sons of Bitches."

4.2.2 Measuring the Effects of the Quotas

In Hong Kong firms that hold the rights to export textile and apparel products to the United States under the MFA can sell these rights. Because this market is competitive, the price paid for the right to export the product should equal the premium earned on sales to the United States.[12] For example, suppose a producer can make a cotton shirt for \$4 and sell it in the United States for \$6. The \$4 includes all costs, (normal profit as well as delivery charges) to the United States, while the \$6 is the price from the tariff-ridden demand curve as discussed in section 3.3 of chapter 3. A producer who does not own the right to export the shirt to the United States will be willing to pay up to \$2 to obtain that right. Competition among similar producers in Hong Kong should force the price of the quota rights up to about \$2.[13] Without the quotas the price of Hong Kong shirts in the United States would be \$4 because of competition among suppliers. So, in this example, \$2, or the value of the quota rights, is the premium paid by US consumers on Hong Kong shirts because of the quota—a premium over and above any that results from tariffs on these shirts.

Morkre (1984) measured the effects of the MFA restraints on nine important categories of apparel products exported from Hong Kong to the United States, using data on the sale of quota rights in Hong Kong in 1980. Hamilton (1986, 1988) did the same, but his monthly data from January 1982 to May 1984 covered a larger group of items than did Morkre's.[14] Hamilton found that the average premium paid by US consumers of imports of Hong Kong apparel products in 1984 was 47 percent.[15]

The price paid for imported apparel products in the United States, p^{US}, is determined by the following relationship:

$$p^{US} = p^{HK}(1 + t^{HK})(1 + prc^{HK}), \tag{4.1}$$

where t^{HK} is the US tariff rate on apparel products from Hong Kong, p^{HK} is the price at which Hong Kong producers are willing to supply apparel products to the United States, and prc^{HK} is the premium rate paid by US consumers of apparel products shipped from Hong Kong. We take Hamilton's estimate of 47 percent to be representative of the quota-induced premium rate paid by US consumers of apparel products (Hamilton's data did not include textile products) from Hong Kong in 1984.[16]

An important contribution of Hamilton's work is that it allows us to infer from the Hong Kong data the quota premium in third countries. This inference is possible because of a simple but clever observation: If another country is subject to quotas on its apparel exports to the United States but is a lower-cost producer than Hong Kong, that country's premium rate is greater than Hong Kong's. Let p^x be the price at which a third country is willing to supply apparel products to the United States, t^x be the US tariff on apparel imports from this country, and prc^x be the premium rate on imports from this country. Then, as before, we have

$$p^{US} = p^x(1 + t^x)(1 + prc^x). \tag{4.2}$$

Dividing equation 4.1 by equation 4.2 and rearranging it, we get

$$\frac{p^x(1 + t^x)}{p^{HK}(1 + t^{HK})} = \frac{1 + prc^{HK}}{1 + prc^x}. \tag{4.3}$$

If country x is a lower-cost supplier than Hong Kong, p^x is less than p^{HK}, and the left side of equation 4.3 will be less than unity unless the United States applies a higher tariff rate to imports from country x than to imports from Hong Kong. If the left side is less than unity, then the premium rate paid on Hong Kong apparel products, prc^{HK}, is less than the premium paid on apparel products from country x, prc^x.

The United States does not apply preferential tariff rates for exports of textile and apparel products from developing countries. So since Hong Kong receives most-favored-nation tariff treatment, then for any other country that also receives most-favored-nation tariff treatment, equation 4.3 reduces to the following:

$$\frac{p^x}{p^{HK}} = \frac{1 + prc^{HK}}{1 + prc^x}. \tag{4.4}$$

Equation 4.4 applies to all countries discussed below under our hypothesis of no product differentiation across suppliers of apparel products.

Since the supply price is determined by relative costs, we need estimates of the costs of producing apparel products for major producers around the world. There are two sources for these estimates. One is Hamilton (1986, 1988), who argues, first, that the costs that vary most across nations are labor costs, and second, that relative to textile products, apparel products are not very capital intensive.[17] So for apparel products the relevant cost for establishing cost variations across countries is the labor cost. If we index the hourly compensation of production workers and take compensation in the US apparel industry to be 100, then Hong Kong is at 21, Brazil at 20, Taiwan at 18, South Korea at 13, India and Thailand at 6, and China at 2.[18] Thus there are a number of countries that can produce at least as efficiently as Hong Kong. A second source of estimated costs is Trella and Whalley (1990, table 2.9), who strongly support the conclusions based on Hamilton. After adjusting labor cost estimates by an index reflecting differences in labor productivity, they find that the twenty-nine other developing countries in their sample all had supply prices lower than those of Hong Kong suppliers in 1984.

Hong Kong, Taiwan, and South Korea are together known as the "Big Three" suppliers of textiles and apparel. In recent years, however, China has emerged as a major supplier. By 1986 it had passed South Korea and Hong Kong in square yards of exports to the United States. Without restraints on its exports, it could well become the dominant supplier. The share of US imports captured by the Big Three plus China was 53 percent (in value terms) in 1984 and 50 percent in 1986.[19]

It is easy to show that the extensive system of bilateral quotas greatly distorts the pattern of trade in apparel (and textile) products. For one thing, firms in some countries that are not as efficient suppliers as those in the Big Three and China nonetheless export to the United States. In a free US market they would be unable to compete. Using our example of the shirt exports, suppose that suppliers from Hong Kong can deliver a cotton shirt to the United States for $4. Because of the quotas it sells for $6. Now suppose that a supplier from Japan (which, according to US Bureau of Labor Statistics data, has labor costs almost three times those of Hong Kong) can supply the shirt for $5. Under the quotas the Japanese supplier would earn a profit of $1 on every shirt it is entitled to export, whereas in a free market, the price might fall to $4, making the Japanese supplier unable to compete.

The Japanese supplier in this example is marginally efficient and is protected in the US market, just as are domestic US firms. Indeed, the Japanese supplier is even more protected than domestic US firms because we assume there is greater product differentiation between domestic and foreign apparel products than exists between imports from different countries. It is clearly in the interest of all marginally efficient foreign suppliers (including developing country suppliers not restrained by the MFA) to support the MFA because of the price umbrella it affords in the United States and other developed countries. In a free market these marginally efficient producers would be unable to compete with countries as efficient as the Big Three and China.

To determine the quota premium rate, we need first to determine which country would be the marginally efficient supplier in a free market. The labor cost data presented above suggest that several countries can produce at least as efficiently as Hong Kong. Let us assume therefore that if a country cannot sell in the United States at prices at least as low as those of Hong Kong, it would not be able to compete in a quotaless US market for apparel. (The situation would be different for US firms, which would probably continue to operate because they benefit from product differentiation.) If Hong Kong is just able to compete in a US market without quotas, then it is the marginal free market supplier. In that case the prices of the quota premia observed in Hong Kong in 1984 would determine the quota premium rate paid by US consumers. If, however, Hong Kong could not compete in a US market without quotas, then, as explained above, the quota premium rate is higher than the quota premium rate determined from Hong Kong data.

Using the cost estimates presented above, we assume (conservatively) that Hong Kong is the marginal supplier of apparel imports in a free US market. Thus we take 47 percent as the quota premium rate on apparel products. (This 47 percent rate applies to all sales, including those of marginally inefficient suppliers and suppliers such as West Europeans who are unconstrained by the MFA because their prices would have to fall if they were to compete in a quotaless market.) The costs of the quotas will be higher than we have estimated if Hong Kong is not the marginal supplier and would be unable to compete in a quotaless market.

We illustrate the determination of the marginally efficient supplier in figure 4.2, where *DD* and Q_0 are defined as in figure 4.1. Under the quota the price of imported textiles and apparel is determined by the intersection of *DD* and Q_0 and is denoted P_0.

The supply of imported textiles and apparel *SS* is depicted as a step function. (This is not a necessary assumption for our argument, and we relax it below.) China is pictured as the low-cost world supplier, able to supply its textile and apparel products to the United States at supply price P_{China}; capacity constraints in China determine the maximum possible amount supplied by China. The next lowest supply prices are those of Korea, followed by Taiwan, Hong Kong, and Japan.

Under the quota each exporting country is allowed to export only a restrained amount to the United States. (That amount is not labeled in figure 4.2, but with binding quotas it is lower than their capacity-constrained exports would be.) Thus any country that can produce at a price less than P_0 and has quota rights can obtain rents by exporting to the United States. Since rents per unit are the difference between price $P_0/(1 + tm)$ and a country's supply price, the lower the costs the higher the per unit rent.

If the quotas were removed, the equilibrium price would be reduced to the intersection of demand curve *DD* and supply curve *SS*, or to price $P_{\text{Hong Kong}}$ in figure 4.2. Low-cost suppliers such as China and Korea would not be restrained by the quota and would be able to ship up to their capacity constraints. As shown in the figure, China would supply $\bar{Q}_{\text{China}}$, and Korea would supply $\bar{Q}_{\text{Korea}}$, with $\bar{Q}_{\text{China}} + \bar{Q}_{\text{Korea}}$ being the sum of their supply.

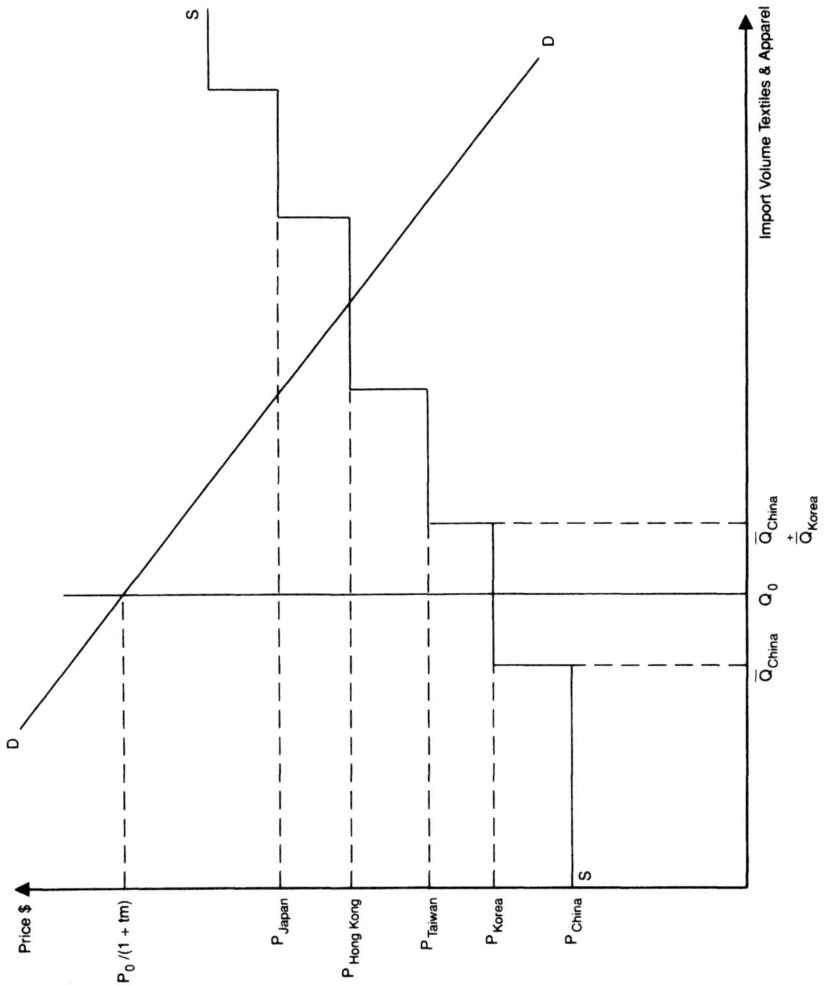

Figure 4.2
Determination of marginal textile supplier

China would continue to earn rents, but these entirely inframarginal rents (rather than quota rents) would be reduced to $P_{\text{Hong Kong}} - P_{\text{China}}$. Suppliers with costs higher than those of Hong Kong would not be able to compete and would be excluded from an open US textile and apparel market even though they had been earning rents under the quota regime.

While we illustrated our argument by assuming that all countries have perfectly elastic supply curves and capacity constraints, this is not necessary for our conclusion. If supply curves for each country slope upward, indicating the inclusion of progressively less efficient firms, removal of US quotas would be expected to force some of a country's firms out of the US market. The important point is that there were enough producers in the world adequately efficient to earn a quota premium rate of at least 47 percent in 1984.

Generally under the MFA the major industrial countries do not apply restrictions against each other's textile or apparel products. Since most of the European Community countries are high-cost producers, they would also be squeezed out of an open US market. But because their costs are not below those of the marginally efficient supplier, they are not relevant to the estimate of quota premia. They earn a rent on their sales that is not a quota rent and that is lower than the quota rent earned on sales from Hong Kong.

The assumption of no product differentiation across import suppliers is a simplification that eases the difficult task of estimating premium rates. Relaxing this assumption would require estimates of the elasticities of substitution across suppliers for apparel products, and these estimates are not available. With product differentiation across supplying countries, it is possible that all countries would continue to sell in the United States if quotas were removed. In that case, under the quota system the United States would capture less of the quota rents from marginally inefficient suppliers and more of the quota rents from marginally efficient suppliers.

To obtain the overall textile and apparel quota premium rate, we also need the quota premium rate on textile products. A recent report by the US International Trade Commission (USITC 1987b, 3.4–3.15) found that a significant percentage of the textile product categories are subject to binding quotas. In particular, 81 percent of imported cotton fabric, 31 percent of wool, and 67 percent of synthetic fiber fabrics are subject to binding quotas.[20] Cline (1987, 117) estimates that the quota premium rate on textiles was 5 percent during the Long-Term Agreement, 10 percent from 1974 to 1981, and 15 percent thereafter, reflecting successive tightening of the agreements. In the absence of hard data, such as Morkre or Hamilton present for apparel, and with the knowledge that the US textile industry is more competitive internationally than the US apparel industry (Morkre and Tarr 1980), we take 5 percent as our estimate of the quota premium rate on textiles. Considering the vehemence with which the textile industry lobbies to maintain the quotas and the evidence cited in USITC (1987b), this estimate is likely to be conservative.

The overall quota premium rate on textiles and apparel products is a weighted average of the quota premium rates of the two segments of the industry. Since the value of textile imports was 15.4 percent of the total value of textile and apparel imports into the United States in 1984,[21] the overall quota premium rate was 40.5 percent:

$$prc = 0.154(5) + 0.846(47). \qquad (4.5)$$

So for textiles and apparel we use 0.405 as the value for prc_i and pri_i in equations 16 and 17 of table 3.1.

4.2.3 Lower-Bound Estimate of Quota Rents Captured by Exporters

Because quota rights to sell apparel products in the United States command a price in Hong Kong, there are quota rents associated with exporting to the United States that are captured in Hong Kong. The cost of production for a rational Hong Kong supplier must be less than the price for which they are sold to the US importer by an amount at least as great as the price paid for the quota rights. Otherwise, the producer would not have paid such a high price for the quota rights. This means that the quota rents captured in Hong Kong must be at least as great as the amount paid for the quota rights to export to the United States.[22]

As was discussed in subsection 4.1.1, if there is monopsony power in US importing of textile and apparel products and the market is not contestable, US importers may capture quota rents in addition to the quota rents captured in Hong Kong. In that case the total quota rents are greater than the quota rents captured by Hong Kong exporters alone. However, the quota sales data do establish a lower bound estimate of the rents received by Hong Kong exporters.

Any quota rents captured by Hong Kong exporters are a loss to the United States because US citizens are paying a price that includes the quota rents for goods that could be obtained without the quota rent cost. Since our methodology is based on the quota sales data, it overestimates neither the quota rents captured in Hong Kong nor, by implication, the losses suffered by US consumers because of quota rents.

Finally, although it is irrelevent to our estimates of quota rents, it is our assessment that textile and apparel retailing and importing in the United States is better described as a competitive industry than as any of the alternatives we discussed, which attribute monopoly rents to importing. This seems to be particularly the case for apparel, for which there are over 40,000 US importers (Bergsten et al. 1987, 165; see also Morkre 1984 and Cline 1979). So despite the theoretical possibility to the contrary, we believe that US retailers capture very little rent from the textile and apparel quotas. For this reason, when we use the term "quota rents," we usually mean the quota rents captured by foreigners.

Nonetheless, for the benefit of readers who believe that US importers capture monopsony rents on textiles and apparel imports, we perform some experiments in chapter 5 in which US importers of textiles and apparel capture some of the rents. In these experiments we increase the premium rate paid by US consumers on imported textiles and apparel so that US importers capture 25 percent of the total rents without changing the amount of rents captured by foreigners.

4.3 Quota Rent Estimates for Automobiles from Japan and Europe

In the spring of 1981, after negotiations with US government officials, the Japanese government announced that it would voluntarily restrain its exports of autos to the United States to 1.68 million vehicles a year between April 1, 1981, and March 31, 1984.[23] This action was taken at a time of falling US production and employment in the automobile sector, when a number of legislative attempts were underway to curb Japanese imports.[24] Between April 1, 1984, and March 31, 1985, Japan agreed to limit its auto exports to the United States to 1.85 million vehicles.

4.3.1 How a Voluntary Export Restraint Can Induce Quality Upgrading

It is well documented that the price of Japanese autos in the United States rose considerably during the period in which the VER with Japan was in effect (Crandall 1984, 1985; Feenstra 1984, 1985, 1988; Tarr and Morkre 1984). Not all of the price increase was due to the VER, however. Some of it came about because Japan began to ship higher-quality autos during the VER period.

To show how a VER may lead to quality upgrading, we examine a case that corresponds closely to the VER on autos negotiated between the United States and Japan (figure 4.3). Firms in the exporting country pro-

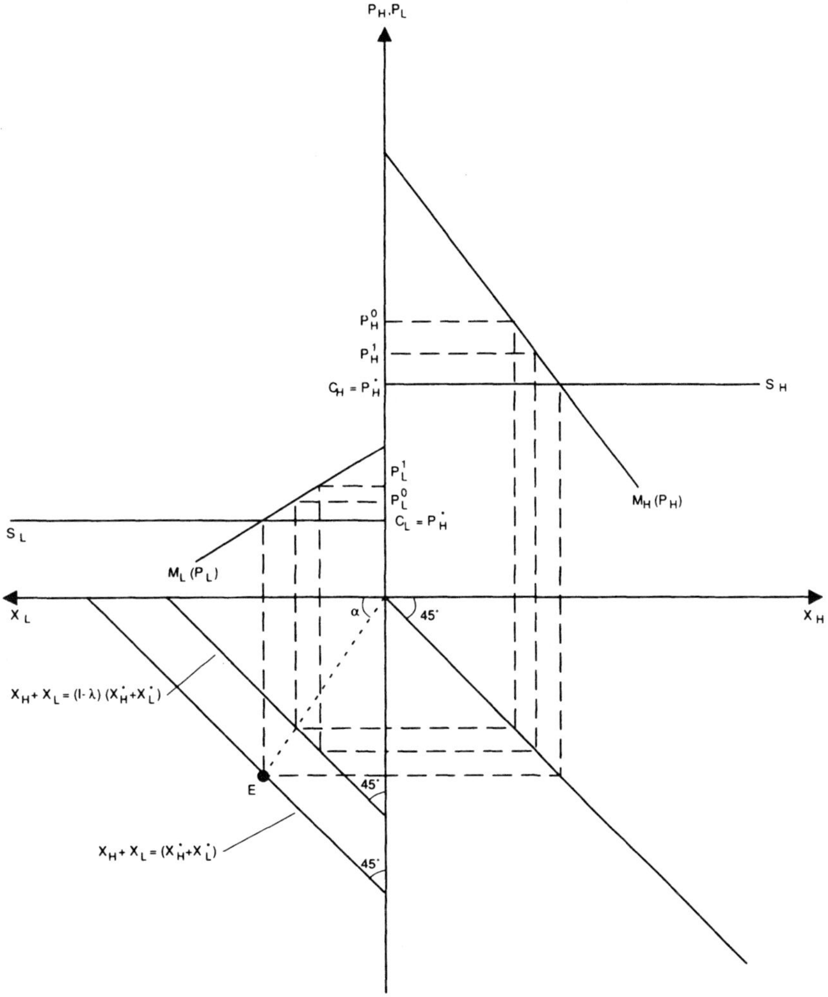

Figure 4.3
Quality upgrading under a VER

duce for the export market two different products that are not cross-substitutable in demand, an expensive product X_H and an inexpensive product X_L.[25] Production occurs under constant costs for the relevant range, with C_H and C_L representing the marginal and average cost curves for the two products. Firms face downward- sloping demand functions $M_H(P_H)$ and $M_L(P_L)$ in the country with which the VER has been negotiated. Finally, the free trade equilibrium prices are P_H^* and P_L^*, with a higher price for the expensive product ($P_H^* > P_L^*$).

The free trade equilibrium is described in figure 4.3, where the demand and supply schedules for the expensive product (X_H) are depicted in the northeast quadrant and those for the inexpensive product (X_L) in the northwest quadrant.[26] The 45-degree line in the southeast quadrant maps X_H, which is measured horizontally, to an equal value on the lower vertical axis. The 45-degree line in the southwest quadrant performs the same mapping for X_L but at the same time is a family of constant total output curves ($X_H + X_L$). Under free trade exports total $X_H^* + X_L^*$, and the quality mix (α) is described by the ray *OE*. An agreed-on reduction in total exports of cars of λ percent will shift the 45-degree schedule in the southwest quadrant inward by λ percent. With no change in the product mix, prices rise to P_H^0 and P_L^0.

If export licenses are based on past export performance and cannot be traded and if firms are unable to substitute products in production, there will be no change in product mix. However, if licenses can be traded, profit maximization will lead firms to trade licenses in order to achieve equal quota premia per unit. Provided that $P_H^0 - C_H > P_L^0 - C_L$, the product mix will shift toward the expensive product, as depicted in figure 4.3, where the output mix shifts until $P_H^1 - C_H = P_L^1 - C_L$.[27] As one can see from the figure, the more inelastic the demand for the high-priced product and the more elastic the demand for the low-priced product, the more likely that this condition for product upgrading will hold.[28] The same reasoning would apply to a multiproduct firm, which would shift its product mix until it achieved equal premium rates in the restricted market. What this analysis establishes is that quality upgrading in response to a VER is not guaranteed. It depends on elasticities. Although quality upgrading under VERs is a widely observed phenomenon, it nonetheless suggests that firms generally perceive the more expensive product to have a less elastic demand.[29]

4.3.2 The Effect on the Price of Japanese Automobiles

For the case of autos, the technique of hedonic regression is helpful in detecting whether a VER leads to quality upgrading. Feenstra (1988) used this technique to estimate how much quality upgrading occurred during the VER period. The technique involves estimating how much consumers are willing to pay for various characteristics of a product. Suppose, for example, that we can estimate that consumers are willing to pay $500 for air conditioning on Japanese autos. Suppose also that in the period before the VER, a specific model came without air-conditioning but during the VER period air-conditioning was a standard feature. If the price of the vehicle went up by $700, and all other things remained the same, we should not attribute all of the price increase to the VER. Part of the increase is due to the addition of air-conditioning. The technique of hedonic regression would predict a price increase for the air-conditioned vehicle of $500 and would attribute only the excess price increase to the VER. Since some consumers would choose not to purchase air-conditioning if provided with the option (i.e., air-conditioning is worth less than $500 to them), the technique of hedonic regression overestimates the value to consumers of the quality increase. So to the extent that consumers value higher quality at less than the value estimated from Feenstra's hedonic regressions, our estimates of the costs to the economy of the VERs are conservative.[30]

Feenstra (1988) also adjusted for the appreciating value of the US dollar during 1981–84. Furthermore, since Japanese trucks were subject to a higher tariff rather than to a VER, Feenstra assumed that without the VER Japanese auto and truck prices, adjusted for quality and tariff changes, would have moved together. Feenstra estimated that by 1984 the VER had caused Japanese auto prices in the United States to rise by $1,096 per vehicle. Although Japanese prices went up by more than $2,300 between 1980 and 1984, much of this increase was accounted for by quality improvements. Since the average unit value of an imported Japanese car was $7,518 in 1984 (Feenstra 1988, table 2), the $1,096 per vehicle attributable to the VER represents a 17.1 percent premium.

4.3.3 The Effect on the Price of European Automobiles

Dinopoulos and Kreinin (1988) provide evidence that the price of European autos in the United States also increased considerably during the period of the Japanese VER. There are several possible reasons for this increase. The European export supply curve to the United States may be inelastic in the short run, the Europeans may have been acting to extract higher prices in monopolylike fashion, or the Europeans may have feared that the United States would try to restrain their exports if they increased their quantity. Dinopoulos and Kreinin observe that a failure to account for the increase in the price of the European vehicles induced by the Japanese VER leads to a significant underestimation of the welfare costs of the VER.

Like Feenstra, Dinopoulos and Kreinin recognize that it is important to adjust the price increase for the effects of quality upgrading. To estimate the amount of the price increase in European cars attributable to the Japanese VER, they used both hedonic regressions and supply function estimation. Using hedonic regressions, Dinopoulos and Kreinin find that after adjusting for quality increases, the average price of an imported European auto increased by $6,212. Using a supply function estimation technique, which adjusts for the higher costs of supplying higher-quality products, they find that the VER induced a price increase in European cars of $6,912. Averaging the two results yields an estimate of $6,562 per auto attributable to the Japanese VER.[31] Since the average unit value of a European import was $18,933 in 1984, $6,562 represents a premium rate of 53.0 percent of the total value. Dinopoulos and Kreinin attribute the relatively higher premium rate on European imports than on Japanese imports to relatively less quality upgrading.

4.3.4 The Overall Premium Rate

The value of US imports of Japanese autos was 59 percent of the total value of Japanese and European auto imports in 1984. So the overall Japanese–European weighted average premium rate is 31.8 percent:

$$prc = 0.59(17.1) + 0.41(53.0). \tag{4.6}$$

We take that premium rate to be representative of the premium rate for all auto imports.

4.3.5 Quota Rent Capture in Automobiles

To estimate the premium rate on autos, we used prices actually paid to the large foreign auto manufacturers by their networks of US dealers. We adjusted that price for cost and quality increases, so our estimate of a 31.8 percent premium rate is for rents actually received by foreign firms.

There is some evidence, however, that during the VER period, Japanese manufacturers allowed their US dealers to capture some of the rents.[32] Their motivation may have been to foster goodwill among their US dealers and so create a strong, loyal network of dealers in the United States. If this indeed occurred, this implies that the total premium rate in autos was higher than 31.8 percent, with the quota rents above 31.8 percent going to

US dealers. Therefore, based on our reading of the trade press, in our estimates of the welfare cost of VERs, we also estimate the effects of assuming that the US dealers of Japanese autos captured rents of $500 per vehicle while US dealers of European autos captured no VER-induced rents. This implies that the premium rate on Japanese autos is 24.8 percent and that the weighted average premium is 36.4 percent. We show in appendix A that this implies that the share of rents captured by foreigners is 90 percent.

4.4 Voluntary Export Restraints on Steel

In early 1984 the United Steelworkers Union and Bethlehem Steel Corporation petitioned the US International Trade Commission for protection from imports under section 201 of the Trade Act of 1974. They requested that quotas be imposed on carbon and alloy steel at a level that would restrain imports to no more than 15 percent of domestic apparent consumption. The president, in response to an affirmative USITC decision for part of the industry, rejected quotas through the 201 process, instead directing the US trade representative to negotiate VERs with foreign governments that would limit the imports of carbon and alloy steel products to 18.5 percent of domestic apparent consumption. In 1984 imports were 26.4 percent of domestic apparent consumption.[33] By mid-1985 the United States had negotiated bilateral VERs with virtually all significant suppliers of steel to the United States except Canada.

While the stated goal of the VERs for steel was to reduce imports to 70 percent of their level in 1984, we will assume that the restraints were not severe enough to achieve that great a reduction. Since imports averaged 22.3 percent of US apparent consumption during 1986 and 1987, we assume that the VERs reduced imports only to 85 percent of domestic apparent consumption.[34]

The US agreements with Korea and Japan are typical of the US agreements with non-EC countries. In the case of Korea, the VER is an "arrangement" between the two governments stipulating that Korea will issue export licenses and certificates and that the United States will require their presentation as a condition of import into the United States. Korea is given specific quantity allowances for particular products on roughly an annual basis, with quarterly adjustments based on demand forecasts for the US market provided by the US Department of Commerce. The Korean Ministry of Trade and Industry (MTI) administers the export certificate scheme, allocating shares of the total allowed exports among Korean steel companies, reportedly on the basis of 1983–84 benchmark export performance. MTI has delegated the administrative responsibility for issuing certificates and monitoring adherence to the arrangement to steel industry associations in Korea.[35]

The arrangement between the governments of the United States and Japan is very similar. Using US Department of Commerce quarterly ceiling data, the Japanese Ministry of International Trade and Industry determines shares for each company based on its export performance during 1981–84. The administrative functions are also handled by an industry organization, the Japan Iron and Steel Exporters Association–USA, formed explicitly for this purpose.

Since foreigners are granted the quota rights and we assess steel import markets to be such that importers are incapable of significantly affecting the supply price, foreigners are assumed to capture the quota rents.

5 Welfare Costs of US Quotas in Textiles and Apparel, Automobiles, and Steel in the Basic Model

This chapter presents the results of simulating the effects on welfare and resource allocation of eliminating quantitative restrictions (QRs) on textiles and apparel, autos, and steel.[1] The chapter also estimates the welfare gains from eliminating tariff protection. Simulations are done for a high elasticity scenario, a central (or best-estimate) scenario, and a low elasticity scenario. The effects of removing QRs in each sector individually are simulated first, followed by a simulation of the effects of a joint removal of QRs in the three sectors. Before discussing our results, we present a brief intuitive description of our welfare measure, which takes into account the two components of the welfare costs of QRs: quota rents, which because of the way quotas are administered by the United States, go primarily to the exporting country (see chapter 4), and distortionary costs.[2]

As an example, let us first consider the welfare gain from retaining QRs in textiles and apparel, adding the assumption that the United States introduces a mechanism enabling US residents to capture quota rents (e.g., a quota auction). Using the graphical example of figure 4.1 in chapter 4, this would mean that the rectangular area marked "rents" is no longer transferred to the exporting countries. (We simulate this effect by changing the value of θ_k [*k* for textiles and apparel] from 1 to 0 in model equations 30 and 31; see table 3.1 in chapter 3.) However, significant political economy issues are involved in transferring quota rents from abroad that could make such a policy change unlikely (these are touched on briefly in section 5.5.2).

The distortionary cost component of QRs (the triangular area under the *DD* curve in figure 4.1) includes both consumption and production effects. On the consumption side consumer choices are distorted by the set of prices under the quota. With QR removal, prices for textile and apparel products fall, inducing consumers to switch from other products into textile and apparel products, which they now value more highly than some of their previous purchases of other goods. On the production side relative price changes also occur after removal of the quota, inducing firms to shift production across sectors. Factors of production move to sectors where they are valued more highly at the new undistorted prices. Similarly firms substitute imported textiles for domestic textiles as inputs into production.

At the new equilibrium, with the new level of income, the economy produces a new bundle of commodities. How the representative consumer of our model values the new bundle of commodities relative to the initial bundle is assessed using the Hicksian equivalent variation (*EV*) measure presented in chapter 3. This measure covers the combined impact of both the rent capture and the distortion effects. It also takes into account any other distortions in the economy that lead to second-best effects (as assumed in chapter 6). The Hicksian compensating variation (*CV*) measure also takes these into account. For our static one-period model with a single representative consumer and no government sector, the *EV* and *CV* measures provide the boundaries for the welfare change between equilibria. We do not report results for the *CV* measure here, however, since the difference between the two measures is always extremely small, with the *EV* never exceeding the *CV* by more than 0.5 percent.

In general, QRs impose costs on the economy, so their removal benefits the economy. Normally we use this terminology interchangeably, speaking sometimes of "the costs of QRs" or the "costs of imposing QRs," and sometimes of the "gains from removing QRs." As we discuss in some detail in this chapter, however, there is an asymmetry with respect to the impact of differing elasticities on the estimates of the effects of imposing or removing QRs. For two of the three sectors on which we focus, QRs existed in the base year of the model, and we estimate the costs of these QRs by counterfactually simulating their removal. For the third sector, steel, QRs did not exist in the base year, and we estimate their effects by counterfactually simulating the imposition of QRs. It is therefore necessary to distinguish between the imposition and the removal of QRs in our counterfactual experiment when we consider the sensitivity of the estimates to elasticities. In other cases the distinction is less important, and we speak interchangeably of the costs of QRs and the benefits of their removal.

In the following sections we first briefly describe the elasticity specifications in section 5.1. In sections 5.2, 5.3, and 5.4 we look at the benefits of removing QRs individually in the three sectors, treating separately the distortionary and rent transfer elements. In section 5.5 we consider the benefits of the simultaneous removal of QRs in all three sectors. Section 5.6 introduces the large-country assumption into the welfare estimates. The chapter closes with a comparison of our results with those of earlier studies. The appendix examines the sensitivity of the results to two assumptions: that quota premia remain unchanged in other sectors when quotas are removed in the sector and that steel imports are rationed in the aggregate rather than by sector.

5.1 Elasticity Specification

The estimates in this chapter are computed for the three sets of elasticities: low, central, and high. Sources for each set of elasticities and their interpretation are discussed in appendix B at the end of this book. The three sets of price elasticities are reported in table 5.1. In general, the low and high sets of elasticities are derived from the central elasticity estimate by subtracting or adding one standard deviation. The central elasticity estimates are our preferred estimates.

Table 5.2 describes the structure of production and demand in the three sectors in 1984, when QRs were in effect for textiles and apparel and autos. For all three sectors exports constitute a very small share of total sales (5.5 percent or less). Otherwise, the three sectors are very different. Steel is virtually a pure intermediate-producing sector, and all its sales are intermediate sales. At the opposite extreme is the auto sector, with more than 90 percent of its output as final goods. The textile and apparel sector splits its sales between intermediate and final demand sales. This structure of sales is also reflected by construction in the structure of import demand (see appendix A): All steel imports are intermediate imports, and over 90 percent of auto imports are final consumption imports.[3]

In the following sections we present economywide estimates of the welfare gain and employment dislocation from quota removal for the low, central, and high elasticity sets for each of the three sectors. We summarize the total welfare gain of the QRs and that component of the gain due to the capture of quota rents from foreigners. In our discussion of the welfare gains from removing QRs one sector at a time, we concentrate on the central (our preferred) elasticity estimates. While we also report the results for the high and low elasticity estimates, their analysis is generally left up to the reader.

We also estimate the economywide employment relocation effects from removal of the quotas. We define economywide relocation as half the sum of the absolute value of the employment changes in the ten sectors of our model. It is a measure of the total employment shift among the aggregated sectors of our model. Our aggregate estimate probably underestimates

Table 5.1
Elasticity specifications

Sector	Elasticity of substitution: intermediates			Elasticity of substitution: capital/labor			Elasticity of transformation: domestic/export sales			Elasticities of final demand: Price elasticities of composite final goods[a]			Elasticities of final demand: Elasticity of substitution domestic/import		
	Low	Central	High	Low	Central	High	Low	Central	High	Low	Central	High	Low	Central	High
Agriculture	0.85	1.42	1.99	0.48	0.61	0.74	2.6	3.9	5.2	0.15	0.28	0.59	0.85	1.42	1.99
Food	0.15	0.31	3.57	0.62	0.79	0.96	1.6	2.9	4.2	0.16	0.29	0.59	0.15	0.31	3.57
Mining	0.25	0.50	1.10	0.60	0.80	1.00	1.6	2.9	4.2	0.42	0.81	1.65	0.25	0.50	1.10
Steel	1.10	3.05	5.00	0.84	1.00	1.16	1.6	2.9	4.2	0.42	0.81	1.64	1.10	3.05	5.00
Automobiles	0.50	2.01	8.39	0.50	0.81	1.12	1.6	2.9	4.2	0.41	0.82	1.65	1.08	1.88	2.56
Textiles and apparel	0.60	2.58	4.56	0.83	1.00	1.17	1.6	2.9	4.2	0.50	1.06	2.08	0.60	2.58	4.56
Other manufactures	0.13	3.55	6.97	0.60	0.80	1.00	1.6	2.9	4.2	0.54	0.98	1.96	0.13	3.55	6.97
Other consumer goods	1.58	3.15	6.30	0.60	0.80	1.00	1.6	2.9	4.2	0.61	1.17	2.37	1.58	3.15	6.30
Traded services	0.90	2.00	4.00	0.60	0.80	1.00	0.3	0.7	1.1	0.50	0.97	1.97	0.90	2.00	4.00
Nontraded services				0.60	0.80	1.00				0.49	0.98	1.95			

Note: CES and CET functions imply that the corresponding elasticities of substitution or transformation correspond to compensated import demand or export supply elasticities. See chapter 2 and appendix B at the end of this book.
a. Absolute values are listed.

Table 5.2
Production and demand structure in textiles and apparel, automobiles, and steel (base year data: 1984)

Item	Textiles	Autos	Steel
Gross output (*X*) ($ billion)	122.8	124.2	57.5
Employment (*L*) (1,000 person-years)	1,969.0	536.5	531.0
Imports[a] ($ billion)			
Intermediates (*VTM*)	11.8	2.3	12.7
Final (*CM*)	11.8	30.3	0.0
Sales ($ billion)			
Exports (*E*)	6.8	4.9	1.4
Domestic final (*CD*)	57.9	111.0	0.0
Domestic intermediates (*VTD*)	58.1	8.3	56.1
Tariff rate (*tm*) (%)	17.7	2.7	5.3
Premium (*prc, pri*) (%)	40.5	31.8	0.0[b]

Note: Variables are defined in tables 3.2 and 3.3 in chapter 3. Tariff and premium rates are ad valorem rates.
a. Imports are valued at border prices exclusive of tariffs and premia.
b. Steel has a zero premium rate because QRs on steel were not in effect until 1985.

total employment changes in the economy, however, because it masks any employment shifts within subsectors. The more disaggregated the model, the greater would be the economywide dislocation estimate.

In analyzing the welfare and employment effects for individual sectors (sections 5.2, 5.3, and 5.4), we remove QRs only in the sector being examined in order to simplify the interpretation of results. Premium rates on the quotas in the other sectors are held constant. As we show in appendix 5A, treating QRs this way in terms of their tariff equivalent does not significantly affect our results. The alternative case in which premium rates are endogenous in the other two sectors when individual QRs are removed is treated in appendix 5A.

5.2 Removing Quotas on Textiles and Apparel

The welfare gains from eliminating quotas on textiles and apparel alone (table 5.3) range from $6.9 billion (low elasticity case) to $15.0 billion (high elasticity case). In the low elasticity case there is relatively little resource reallocation because of the combined effect of low elasticities of supply and demand. For the best-estimate case (central elasticity), employment in textiles and apparel declines by 247,000 jobs as a result of removing the quotas, but employment in all other sectors increases. For example, the

Table 5.3
Welfare gains and employment effects of removing quotas in textiles and apparel

Policy change/ elasticity estimate	Welfare gain[a]	Employment change in textiles	Economywide relocation[b]
Remove quotas			
Low elasticity case	6.89	−18.0	35.8 (0.03)
Central elasticity case	10.40[c]	−246.9	246.9 (0.24)
High elasticity case	14.95	−449.8	449.8 (0.43)
Capture quota rents			
Low elasticity case	5.87	−0.68	41.68 (0.04)
Central elasticity case	5.94[c]	−2.81	53.11 (0.05)
High elasticity case	5.96	−3.20	55.82 (0.05)

Note: The results reported under "remove quotas" include recovery of both distortionary costs and quota rents; "capture quota rents" is also reported separately to highlight the magnitude of this effect. The difference between the two is the distortionary cost component.

a. Welfare is the equivalent variation measure defined in appendix 3A in chapter 3 and expressed in billions of 1984 US dollars.

b. Computed as half the sum of the absolute value of the employment changes expressed in thousands of work-years. The numbers in parenthesis are the percentage of workers in the economy that must relocate.

c. The welfare gain from removing textile quotas is $13.70 billion if we assume that under the quotas US firms are capturing rents in addition to those captured by foreigners. The gain from capturing quota rents from foreigners in this case is $5.96 billion.

combined increase in employment in other manufactures and traded and nontraded services is 202,700 new jobs (see table 5.7 in section 5.5); 0.24 percent of the labor force would have to relocate.

The gains from capturing quota rents on textiles and apparel are almost $6.0 billion. (This estimate changes very little with the elasticity specification.) Thus in the central elasticity case over half of the costs to the United States of the quotas on textiles and apparel are due to the capture of quota rents by foreigners. The United States could thus achieve roughly the same level of protection of textiles and apparel (in terms of employment and output effects) at less than half the cost by substituting tariff protection for QRs or by auctioning the quota rights. Note, however, that because of

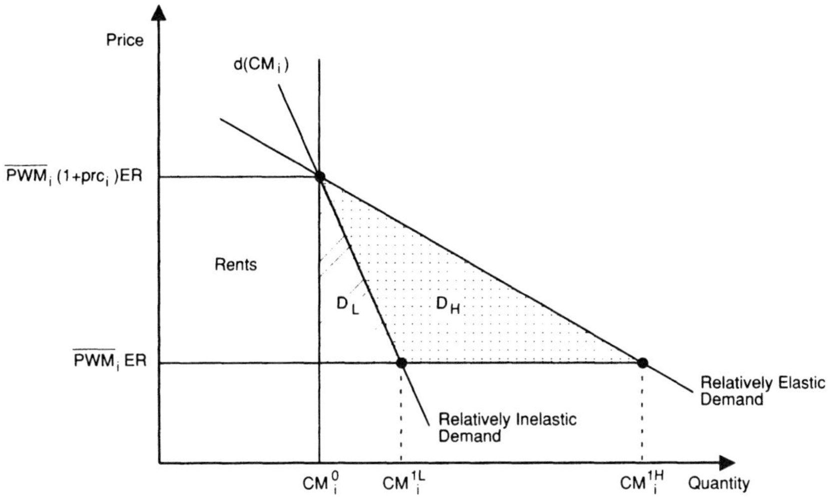

Figure 5.1
Distortionary cost of QRs under different elasticities of import demand for final goods with and without quota

income effects and differing income elasticities of demand across sectors, an auction quota or tariff would not yield exactly the same level of protection as the quota. For example, in the central elasticity case, because of the low income elasticity of demand for domestic textiles and apparel, an auction quota would reduce employment in the textile and apparel sector by 2,810 jobs. This employment effect is not captured in a partial equilibrium approach.

The distortionary costs of QRs are considerably higher in textiles and apparel (43 percent or $4.46 billion) than in autos (20 percent or $1.94 billion) for the central elasticity case, even though the two sectors are about the same size and the initial value of textile imports is less than three-fourths of the value of auto imports. This is so for two reasons. First, the estimates of the elasticity of demand for imports and of the elasticities of substitution in demand are high in textiles and apparel relative to autos. This means that the higher prices caused by the quotas induce a relatively larger switch by consumers out of imported textile and apparel products than out of autos. This in turn implies that the distortion costs in textiles and apparel are higher since consumer purchases diverge more from the desired optimum choice (with no quotas) than in the case of automobiles.

Figure 5.1 illustrates the partial equilibrium effect on the estimated value of the distortionary cost component of a QR as a result of varying the elasticity of demand for imports of a final good with infinite elasticity of import supply. Initially a quota exists for the final good such that (using the notation of chapter 3) the initial distorted price is $\overline{PWM}_i(1 + prc_i)ER$ and the initial quantity demanded is CM_i^0. Removing the quota reduces the price to $\overline{PWM}_iER$. The quantity demanded increases to CM_i^{1L} or CM_i^{1H}, depending on the elasticity of demand. The distortionary costs recovered by consumers through lower prices are measured by the deadweight loss indicated by triangle D_L or D_H, which increases as demand elasticity increases.[4] (Note that the value of rents is insensitive to the elasticity specification.)

The second reason for the higher distortionary costs in textiles and apparel than in autos is that textiles and apparel have a much higher tariff rate and a higher quota premium rate (see table 5.2). With this combination of tariffs and quotas, US consumers of textiles and apparel paid, on average, about 58 percent more than they would have in 1984 had these restraints not been in effect. As mentioned in chapter 2, the distortion costs increase more than proportionately with the price distortion wedge. As the price distortion wedge increases, with no change in the elasticity, the quantity change also increases, which acts multiplicatively on the price distortion wedge in contributing to welfare change.

As mentioned in chapter 4, it is conceivable, although unlikely, that the Multifiber Arrangement (MFA) on textiles and apparel allows US importers to capture some of the quota rents because of monopoly power in importing. To get some idea of the size of this potential effect, we recalibrate the model with the assumption that US importers capture 25 percent of total rents while exporters continue to capture the same *dollar value* of rents. As explained in appendix A, this implies that the new initial premium rate is 62.5 percent instead of 40.5 percent and that θ_k for textiles and apparel in equations 30 and 31 is set to 0.75 instead of 1. Under these assumptions the total gain in the central elasticity case from removing quotas would be $13.7 billion, of which $7.74 billion is the recovery of the distortionary cost. The benefits of quota rent capture remain approximately unchanged. Thus a 54 percent increase in the premium rate results in a 74 percent increase in the distortionary cost of QRs in textiles and apparel. This result emphasizes again that distortionary costs increase more than proportionately with increases in protection.[5]

The estimated employment changes in each of the ten sectors as a result of quota removal (see table 5.7 in section 5.5) are summarized in table 5.3 by the "economywide relocation" measure, which is the absolute value of the sum of the employment losses in all industries that lose jobs when quotas are removed. As mentioned, this is an underestimate of economy-wide relocation since our level of aggregation masks subsectoral job losses.

5.3 Removing Voluntary Export Restraints on Japanese Automobiles

For the estimated gains of eliminating the VER on Japanese auto imports shown in table 5.4, the low, central, and high elasticity cases assume that the United States does *not* possess monopsony power in auto imports. For the central elasticity case with terms-of-trade effects, however, the United States is assumed to possess monopsony power in the purchase of autos from the rest of the world but not to have monopoly or monopsony power in any other sector. The value assumed for the foreign elasticity of supply of autos is 5.

The gains from removing the VER on Japanese auto imports range from \$8.9 billion to \$10.8 billion without terms-of-trade effects. As in the case of textiles, the gains are greater the greater the elasticities. When terms-of-trade effects are incorporated, the United States gains less from removing the VER (\$7.3 billion). This reflects the assumption that when the United States possesses monopsony power in importing, it is able to induce foreign suppliers to supply autos at a lower price by purchasing fewer automobiles.

Since there is evidence to indicate that US dealers of Japanese autos captured some rents during the VER period (see chapter 4), we simulated the effect of US dealers capturing about \$500 per unit on Japanese vehicles and no rents on non-Japanese imports, while keeping the dollar value of rents captured by foreigners unchanged. This implies (see appendix A) that the premium rate on autos increases from 31.8 to 36.4 percent and that foreigners capture 90 percent of the quota rents. Under this scenario the welfare gain from removal of the VER is \$10.3 billion. The rent capture estimate does not change significantly as a result of the additional rents assigned to US residents, implying that about \$0.4 billion is added to distortion costs when the likely additional quota rents of US dealers are included.

The labor relocation caused by removing QRs is much less in autos than in textiles and apparel because the automobile sector employs fewer people, is less labor intensive, and has lower elasticities than the textile and apparel sector, implying less resource reallocation. In the central elasticity case removal of the VER on Japanese autos results in a loss of 36,200 jobs in the auto sector.

Table 5.4
Welfare gains and employment effects of removing voluntary export restraints in automobiles

Policy change/ elasticity estimate	Welfare gain[a]	Employment change in automobiles	Economywide relocation[b]
Remove voluntary export restraint			
Low elasticity case	8.92	−22.8	49.39 (0.05)
Central elasticity case	9.82	−36.2	43.23 (0.04)
With United States capturing some quota rents	10.28	−40.9	43.5 (0.05)
With terms-of-trade effects	7.31	−27.2	32.44 (0.03)
High elasticity case	10.84	−34.1	88.91 (0.08)
Capture quota rents			
Low elasticity case	7.83	−0.25	55.48 (0.053)
Central elasticity case	7.88[c]	0.02	70.35 (0.067)
With terms-of-trade effects	7.83	0.19	70.34 (0.067)
High elasticity case	7.88	0.14	73.85 (0.070)

Note: The results reported under "remove voluntary export restraints" include recovery of both distortionary costs and quota rents; "capture quota rents" is also reported separately to highlight the magnitude of this effect. The difference between the two is the distortionary cost component.

a. Welfare is the equivalent variation measure defined in appendix 3A in chapter 3 and expressed in billions of 1984 US dollars.

b. Computed as half the sum of the absolute value of the employment changes expressed in thousands of work-years. Numbers in parenthesis are the percentage of workers in the economy that must relocate.

c. If rents are captured only on Japanese auto imports and not on European imports, the welfare gain is $4.63 billion.

Unlike most of our results for other sectors, the employment loss in the auto sector is less in the high elasticity case (34,100 jobs) than in the central elasticity case. This occurs because imported and domestic autos are not as good substitutes for each other in the high elasticity case as in the central case, which can be understood through reference to equation 2.9 or 2.11 in chapter 2. The extent to which imported and domestic autos are gross substitutes for each other depends on the size of the difference between two elasticities: (1) the elasticity of substitution between imported and domestic autos in the CES nest of composite autos and (2) the elasticity of demand for composite autos. When imported autos decrease in price because VERs are removed, the demand for domestic autos decreases as the elasticity of substitution increases, but it increases as the elasticity for composite autos increases. Although both elasticities increase in moving from the central to the high elasticity case (see table 5.1), their difference decreases from 1.06 (1.88 minus 0.82) to 0.91 (2.56 minus 1.65). Consequently (from equation 2.9) imported and domestic autos are not as good substitutes for each other in the high elasticity case as in the central case, and there is less resource movement following the removal of the VER.

The gain from capturing the quota rents accruing to Japanese and European suppliers as a result of the VER with Japan is estimated at $7.9 billion. As in the case of textiles and apparel, the elasticities do not significantly affect the estimates of the gains to the United States in this policy experiment. The gains are approximately $7.8–$7.9 billion in all cases. Note that in this case we have assumed implicitly that the premium above the world supply price received by European suppliers would fall to zero after the VER with Japan is eliminated, since it was the VER with Japan that induced the price increase on European autos sold in the United States.

If, however, the United States decides to capture the quota rents on Japanese car imports through an auction quota, a tariff, or some other domestic quota allocation scheme, then a separate mechanism is also required to capture the quota rents on European car imports (rents that exist only while the VER on Japanese imports is in place), even though European imports were not restrained by the United States. Whether the Europeans restrained their car exports to exploit monopoly power gained as a result of the US restraint on Japanese imports or whether they simply have a very inelastic supply curve to the United States, the United States would need to impose a tariff on European imports (equal to the premium rate) to capture these rents while the VER with Japan remains in effect. (However, in the quota-rent capture estimates, we do not measure the welfare costs of imposing a tariff on European exports alone.) If the United States establishes an auction quota on Japanese auto imports without establishing a tariff to capture the rents on European auto imports, the United States would, in the central elasticity case, capture only $4.6 billion instead of $7.9 billion.

In the cases without terms-of-trade effects, the gains from capturing the quota rents on imported Japanese and European autos are between 72 and 88 percent of the total gains from removing the quotas. This means that the United States could obtain roughly the same level of protection for the car industry as that achieved through the VER at only 12 to 28 percent of the costs if it employed a policy that captured the quota rents.

When terms-of-trade effects are taken into account, the United States actually gains more from a policy of capturing quota rents than it does from removing the quotas. This occurs because the United States has monopsony import power in the terms-of-trade case, which goes unexploited when the VER is removed. Monopsony power implies that there is an optimal degree of import restriction. Indeed, as the simulation results suggest, removing the VER puts the United States further away from the level of imports that would maximize its welfare than when the VER is in place.

5.4 Imposing Voluntary Export Restraints on Steel

Because the bilaterally negotiated VERs on steel exports to the United States did not go into effect until 1985, our estimate of the welfare costs of VERs in steel is obtained by simulating the restraint of steel imports to 85 percent of their actual volume in 1984 (see section 4.4 of chapter 4).[6] When we estimate the welfare costs of the joint removal of QRs in the three sectors (see section 5.5 below), we also calculate the welfare costs from a solution in which steel imports are restrained.[7]

The welfare costs of the bilateral VERs with all major suppliers of steel to the United States (table 5.5) range from $2.43 billion (low elasticity case) to $0.54 billion (high elasticity case). The lower the value of the elasticity of demand, the higher is the welfare costs of imposing a quota. Why this is so is shown in a partial equilibrium analysis in figure 5.2.

Imposing a quota at $\overline{VTM_i^1} < VTM_i^0$ leads to a price increase. The less elastic the demand curve, the greater is the price increase required to reduce the quantity demanded and so the greater are the distortion costs (triangle D_L) and the rent costs (rectangular area in figure 5.2).

Note that the effect of elasticities on the distortion costs is asymmetrical between imposing QRs (as in figure 5.2) and removing QRs (as in figure 5.1). Also note that the value of rents is sensitive to the assumed value of the elasticity of demand in the case of imposing a QR but not in the case

Table 5.5
Welfare costs and employment effects of imposing voluntary export restraints in steel

Policy change/ elasticity estimate	Welfare cost[a]	Employment change in steel	Economywide relocation[b]
Impose voluntary export restraint			
Low elasticity case	2.43	22.3	24.44 (0.02)
Central elasticity case	0.86	20.8	21.2 (0.02)
High elasticity case	0.54	20.4	20.83 (0.02)
Quota rent capture by foreigners			
Low elasticity case	2.16	0.35	15.5 (0.015)
Central elasticity case	0.74	0.18	6.6 (0.006)
High elasticity case	0.44	0.11	4.17 (0.004)

Note: The results reported under "impose voluntary export restraints" include both distortionary costs and the capture of quota rents by foreigners; "quota rent capture by foreigners" is also reported separately to highlight the magnitude of this effect. The difference between the two is the distortionary cost component.
a. Welfare is the equivalent variation measure defined in appendix 3A in chapter 3 and expressed in billions of 1984 US dollars.
b. Computed as half the sum of the absolute value of the employment changes expressed in thousands of work-years. Numbers in parenthesis are the percentage of workers in the economy that must relocate.

of removing a QR. This result follows from the fact that imposition of a QR is naturally modeled as a quantity reduction constraint, whereas removal of a QR must be modeled as a reduction in the import price since a preexisting QR is assessed in terms of its price impact.[8]

The distortionary cost component of VERs on steel ranges from $0.27 billion (low elasticity case) to $0.10 billion (high elasticity case). The distortionary cost is relatively small because of the high value of the elasticity of substitution (from 1.10 to 5.0), reflecting steel's relative homogeneity.

US capture of the quota rents from the VERs on steel would result in a gain of between $0.4 billion (high elasticity case) and $2.2 billion (low elasticity case). Since these gains are between 81 and 89 percent of the total welfare losses due to the VERs on steel, the United States could achieve roughly the same level of protection for steel at 15 percent of the cost by introducing a protection mechanism that captures the quota rents.

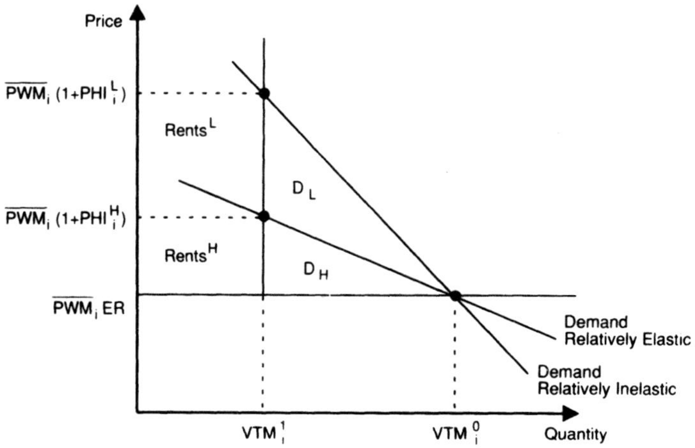

Figure 5.2
Distortionary cost of imposing QRs under different elasticities of import demand for intermediate goods

The steel industry is estimated to gain between 20,400 and 22,300 jobs from the imposition of the VERs. Mining is the only other sector that gains jobs under all elasticity scenarios for the imposition of VERs on steel (see table 5.7 in section 5.5), which is not surprising since mining products are important inputs into steel. Most other sectors lose employment under most of the elasticity scenarios, especially other manufactures (12,400 jobs in the central elasticity case).

5.5 Joint Removal of Quotas in the Three Sectors

5.5.1 Benefits from Removing Quotas

The welfare gains to the United States from the joint removal of QRs in all three sectors would be between \$18.3 billion and \$26.2 billion annually (table 5.6). For the central elasticity case the estimated gain is \$21.05 billion, or almost the same as that derived by adding the individual estimates in tables 5.3, 5.4, and 5.5 (\$21.08 billion). The estimates are not strictly comparable, however, because the joint estimates (table 5.6) are measured from a counterfactually created base that includes VERs on steel, whereas the results for steel alone (table 5.5) are measured from a base without VERs on steel. Nevertheless, since the individual sector estimates are general equilibrium estimates, they properly account for general equilibrium linkages including the balance of trade constraint. (As we discuss in

Table 5.6
Changes in welfare, real wages, and the real exchange rate from the joint removal of quotas and elimination of all tariffs

Policy change/ elasticity estimate	Welfare gain[a]	Real wage (% change)	Real exchange rate (% change)[b]
Remove quotas			
Low elasticity case	18.27	0.11	−0.6
Central elasticity case	21.05	0.03	0.8
High elasticity case	26.19	−0.01	1.3
Capture quota rents			
Low elasticity case	15.92	−0.15	−2.77
Central elasticity case	14.65	−0.03	−1.8
High elasticity case	14.38	−0.03	−0.5
Remove all tariffs[c]			
Low elasticity case	0.22	0.190	1.01
Central elasticity case	0.85	0.197	2.04
High elasticity case	1.78	0.204	2.37

Note: Quotas are removed jointly in textiles and apparel, automobiles, and steel after counterfactually creating an equilibrium with VERs in steel.
a. Welfare is the equivalent variation measure defined in appendix 3A in chapter 3 and expressed in billions of 1984 US dollars.
b. A negative value indicates an appreciation of the real exchange rate.
c. Changes are calculated from the quota-free solution.

section 5.7, partial equilibrium estimates, which do not recognize the pressure of a balance of trade constraint expressed in appropriate foreign units, are seriously biased upward.)

As discussed in section 2.3.2, the capturing of quota rents leads to an appreciation of the real exchange rate; the appreciation is between 2.8 percent (low elasticity case) and 0.5 percent (high elasticity case). The degree of appreciation changes with the elasticities because of the need to maintain external equilibrium. The domestic capture of quota rents raises income and hence raises demand for both domestically produced (i.e., nontraded) goods as well as imports. With exogenous terms-of-trade the price of imports is fixed, so the increased demand for domestic goods requires an increase in the relative price of domestically produced goods; that is, the real exchange rate must appreciate to restore equilibrium in the balance of trade. How much it must appreciate depends on the elasticity of excess demand for domestically produced goods. The greater that elasticity, the less the real exchange rate must appreciate to induce the required decrease in exports and increase in imports to restore external equilibrium.

In interpreting the change in the real exchange rate when QRs are removed, we need to consider two opposite effects on the demand for imports: rent capture, which leads to a real exchange rate appreciation, and distortion removal, which leads to a real exchange rate depreciation because of the substitution toward imports. For low elasticities the rent-capture effect dominates, so there is a real exchange rate appreciation. In the central and high elasticity cases removal of QRs leads to depreciation of the real exchange rate. Thus, if quotas are of the type that do not allow domestic rent capture, their removal results in an increased demand for imports and depreciation of the real exchange rate. Similarly, since tariff removal does not involve rent capture, it results in an increased demand for imports independent of elasticities. Thus with tariff removal a real exchange rate depreciation is required in all elasticity cases to restore equilibrium in the balance of trade.

Removing QRs jointly in the three sectors would also lead to a very small increase in the real wage because relative factor intensities are not very different across sectors at our level of aggregation.[9] It is also conceivable, however, that a model that incorporates several skill classes would reveal a fall in the real wage of lower-skill classes with the removal of QR protection in sectors that use these classes intensively.

The employment implications of eliminating QRs in the three sectors are shown in table 5.7, which also shows the employment changes in in-

Table 5.7
Sectoral changes in employment from removing quotas in textiles and apparel, automobiles, and steel separately and together and from removing all tariffs: central elasticity case (thousands of work-years)

	Remove quotas				Remove
Sector	Textiles and apparel	Automobiles	Steel	All three industries	all tariffs[a]
Agriculture	7.8	9.9	1.3	19.2	54.0
Food	3.6	0.8	0.1	4.5	4.4
Mining	4.5	0.2	−0.4	4.3	4.5
Textiles and apparel	−246.9	−0.4	1.0	−245.0	−98.9
Automobiles	4.1	−36.2	0.4	−31.8	2.9
Steel	3.9	0.3	−20.8	−16.7	−8.2
Other consumer goods	20.2	6.7	2.7	29.6	−33.7
Other manufactures	63.4	−6.6	12.4	68.7	56.9
Traded services	70.5	13.5	1.7	85.3	49.7
Nontraded services	68.8	11.8	1.6	81.9	−31.6

a. Employment changes are calculated from the quota-free solution.

dividual sectors. When QRs are removed jointly in all three sectors, only the sectors that had been protected by QRs lose employment. Although the auto industry gains from cheaper steel input prices, the substitution effect toward cheaper auto imports dominates. All three sectors lose jobs, but job losses are especially concentrated in the textile and apparel sector.

Our simulations assume a balance of trade constraint, which implies that the value of imports must always equal the value of exports (both expressed in foreign units). This assumption makes the interpretation of the welfare costs of protection more transparent.

The sectoral changes in the volume of imports and exports that result when all QRs are jointly removed are reported in table 5.8. Not surprisingly, since the QRs are all in manufacturing sectors, removing them benefits agriculture, which expands its exports. The "other manufactures" sector benefits from lower input costs, and its exports expand significantly. The small increase in export volume for other sectors is attributable to the small depreciation of the real exchange rate. As expected, imports increase for the three sectors for which QRs are removed and decrease for most other sectors.

5.5.2 Benefits from Capturing Quota Rents

The quota rent component of the welfare gains from removal of QRs in all three sectors is between $14.4 billion (high elasticity case) and $15.9 billion (low elasticity case). This means that in the aggregate the capture of rents by foreigners accounts for about two-thirds of the costs of the quotas. If tariffs were used instead of QRs, roughly the same level of protection could

Table 5.8
Sectoral changes in exports and imports as a result of simultaneously eliminating quotas in textiles and apparel, automobiles, and steel: central elasticity case (billions of US dollars)

Sector	Exports	Imports
Agriculture	1.33	−0.04
Food	0.15	0.07
Mining	0.09	0.41
Textiles and apparel	0.04	7.66
Automobiles	−0.04	5.63
Steel	0.00	1.07
Other consumer goods	0.51	−0.46
Other manufactures	4.87	−3.60
Traded services	1.34	−0.30

be achieved at one-third the cost. However, such a shift in trade policy would present the United States with a problem in trade relations. Since the United States is a member of the General Agreement on Tariffs and Trade (GATT), it cannot unilaterally raise tariffs without offering compensation in the form of tariff reductions on other commodities. Of the other alternatives, shifting to auction quotas, as suggested by Bergsten et al. (1987), would probably be less costly than granting import licenses directly because a system of free import licenses provides incentives for rent seeking, inducing importers to use resources unproductively in trying to obtain the licenses.[10]

It is also important to consider, however, that quota rents are a means of compensating foreigners for US protection. If the United States changed its policy to capture these rents, foreign governments might retaliate. So in political economy terms, auctioning quota rents is not a straightforward story. Furthermore, if the United States captured the quota rents, the income effect associated with the transfer would induce a number of changes. The real exchange rate would appreciate, and because consumers have different income elasticities of demand for final goods, resource reallocation would also take place. So the capture of quota rents cannot be viewed as a pure transfer; from the rent transfer gain, one would have to subtract the relocation costs incurred by workers who must find new jobs.

5.5.3 Benefits of Free Trade

In a final exercise we measure the additional benefits of removing all import tariffs in all ten sectors once the new equilibrium has been achieved after the removal of QRs on textiles and apparel, autos, and steel. The welfare benefits (table 5.6), which range from $0.2 to $1.8 billion, are significantly lower than those from removing QRs. Once again this result emphasizes the high costs of QRs, especially when the quota rents are captured abroad. (Appendix 5A shows that removing tariffs while QRs remain would result in a welfare loss because tariff removal results in a rent transfer to foreigners.)

The largest employment effect from the removal of tariffs occurs in the textile and apparel sector (table 5.7) which has the highest tariff rate and loses the most jobs. Agriculture gains a larger number of jobs from tariff removal than from quota removal. The gain in agricultural employment is greater because tariff removal induces greater depreciation of the real exchange rate than does quota removal and consequently greater expansion of exports, which especially helps agriculture.

5.6 Introducing Terms-of-Trade Effects

We have argued that, as a first approximation, the United States can be considered as a price taker in world markets despite its large size, at least for policy changes of the size considered here. It may be argued, however, that the United States has monopsony power in the market for autos because it absorbs a significant share of Japanese production and because US environmental and safety standards lead to a differentiated product. For that reason we considered an import supply elasticity of 5 for auto imports (see section 5.3). We would also argue that the United States is likely to have some monopoly power in its foreign sales of agricultural products as agricultural exports expand significantly with the joint removal of QRs in all three sectors. Because of this large US share in the world market for agricultural products, our preferred foreign elasticity of demand for US exports of agricultural products is 4.

The effect of making terms of trade endogenous for the foreign supply of auto imports and the foreign demand for agricultural exports appears in column 1 of table 5.9. We consider this estimate the most plausible for the welfare costs of QRs in textiles and apparel, autos, and steel. Because of terms-of-trade losses, the aggregate gain from removing QRs in the central elasticity case is reduced by \$2.58 billion (from \$21.05 to \$18.47). The distortionary cost is reduced by \$2.65 billion because auto imports expand and because agriculture is one of the sectors whose exports expand the

Table 5.9
Welfare effects of quotas with large-country assumption: central elasticity case

Policy change	$\varepsilon^s_{autos} = 5$ $\varepsilon^d_{agr} = 4$[a] (1)	$\varepsilon^d_k = 3$[b] (2)	$\varepsilon^s_k = 4$[c] (3)	$\varepsilon^s_k = 4$ $\varepsilon^d_k = 3$[d] (4)
Remove quota	18.47	19.51	15.49	14.64
Capture rents from foreigners while retaining quotas	14.72	16.42	13.54	14.94

Note: ε^d_k = elasticity of demand for exports of sector k, and ε^s_k = elasticity of supply of imports in sector k.
a. Let $\varepsilon^d_k = 4$ for k = agriculture; $\varepsilon^s_k = 5$ for k = autos; small-country assumption for all other sectors.
b. Let $\varepsilon^d_k = 3$ for all traded sectors; small-country assumption for ε^s_k.
c. Let $\varepsilon^s_k = 4$ for all traded sectors; small-country assumption for ε^d_k.
d. Let $\varepsilon^s_k = 4$ and $\varepsilon^d_k = 3$ for all traded sectors.

most when QRs are removed. The QRs impose about 25 percent less distortionary cost in this case because they partially exploit the assumed monopoly power in agricultural exports and monopsony power in auto imports.

Previous global modeling exercises (discussed in section 5.7) have shown very strong terms-of-trade effects when protection is reduced unilaterally. For this reason we conducted a systematic sensitivity analysis with respect to the degree of US monopoly and monopsony power in world markets, even though we do not think that such an assumption is a good approximation for the long- run comparisons made in this chapter.

We report the results of three sensitivity experiments in columns 2 through 4 of table 5.9: (1) under generalized monopoly power with a foreign elasticity of demand of 3 for US exports (column 2), (2) under conditions of generalized monopsony power with a foreign import supply elasticity of 4 for all sectors (column 3), and (3) under a combination of these two. Before discussing these results, we remind the reader that along the offer curve, the import supply and export demand elasticities are not independent. This means that in the aggregate the elasticity of demand for exports is less than 3 and the elasticity of supply of imports is less than 4.[11]

The results show that the welfare gain from removing QRs decreases as the degree of monopoly or monopsony power increases. By restraining trade, the QRs are partially exploiting that market power, although not optimally.

The results reported in column 2 are an application of the Lerner symmetry theorem, namely, that a tax on imports is equivalent to a tax on exports. Because of the balance of trade constraint, the QRs on imports indirectly reduce exports, so removing the QRs increases exports and results in a terms-of-trade loss. Thus the welfare gains reported in column 2 of table 5.9 are lower than those for the central elasticity case reported in table 5.6. The welfare gains from removing QRs are lower still under column 3 because the QRs in textiles, autos, and steel act directly to exploit the assumed monopoly power in those sectors.

With both monopsony and monopoly power the induced terms-of-trade loss is slightly greater than the distortionary cost. Thus one can conclude that with a foreign elasticity of demand for US exports of 3 and a foreign elasticity of import supply of 4, the distortionary cost of QRs would be more than offset by the induced terms-of-trade loss. However, because of rent transfer there would still be a welfare gain of $14.6 billion with QR removal under conditions of generalized monopoly and monopsony power.

5.7 Comparisons with Earlier Estimates

We conclude this chapter by comparing our results with earlier estimates. First, we explain why our results are so different from the partial equilibrium estimates reported in chapter 1 (table 1.1). Then, we discuss briefly why our results are also different from other general equilibrium estimates.

5.7.1 Partial Equilibrium Estimates

In chapter 1 we argued that partial equilibrium estimates are upwardly biased because they fail to account for the effect of a balance of trade constraint and so for changes in the real exchange rate. Trade liberalization in autos, for example, will increase auto imports, resulting in a trade balance deficit and depreciation of the real exchange rate. At the same time imports in other sectors will decrease, and exports will increase to restore equilibrium in the balance of trade. But the reduction of imports in other sectors and the increase in exports represent a reduction of welfare that partial equilibrium estimates fail to capture.

We estimate the magnitude of this bias by doing what is typically done implicitly in partial equilibrium studies: fixing the real exchange rate and allowing the balance of trade to vary. For the central elasticity specification, removing quotas in all three sectors leads to a current account deterioration of $14.3 billion and a welfare gain to the US economy of $35.8 billion. This estimate is about 1.5 times that obtained when the balance of trade is properly taken into account. Welfare analysis based on this scenario assumes that the rest of the world will provide the United States with a free lunch of $14.3 billion annually. Obviously this is not realistic. Thus economywide welfare estimates obtained by adding up partial equilibrium estimates for individual sectors are likely to be significantly biased upward.[12]

Despite this inherent upward bias, our summary of the partial equilibrium estimates of the costs of protection in the textile and apparel, auto, and steel sectors reveals estimates of the welfare costs of protection that are smaller than those we obtained. The main explanation for this difference is that our study benefited from the detailed work on quota-induced premium estimates of Hamilton (1988), Feenstra (1988), and Dinopolous and Kreinin (1988).[13] Our premium estimates are higher or cover a wider portion of the industry than those of most studies surveyed.

There are, however, other reasons as well for the differences in results, one of which we mention here. That is the distinction made in partial equilibrium analysis between welfare costs and consumer costs, a distinction that is inappropriate in our welfare estimates. Partial equilibrium estimates do not model the flow from labor and capital income to consumers, so they need to separate individuals in their roles as consumers and as workers and capital owners. Partial equilibrium studies often estimate that the cost to consumers is larger than the cost to the economy because consumers are presumed to lose what firms earn as profits (or what the government takes as tariff revenue). Since neither assumption is appropriate under an economywide perspective, the distinction between welfare cost and consumer cost is also inappropriate.[14]

5.7.2 General Equilibrium Estimates

Our estimates of the welfare benefits of quota removal are also significantly higher than most previous general equilibrium estimates. Deardorff and Stern (1986, table 4.6) estimate small welfare gains from quota removal. Whalley (1985, table 10.2) finds that the United States, as well as the other countries or regions in his model, suffers welfare losses if it unilaterally removes tariffs or nontariff barriers.

These studies use tariff equivalents to capture the effects of quotas. While this procedure may be satisfactory for importing countries that capture the rents from their quotas, that is not the case for countries like the United States, whose quota allocation systems allow the exporting country to capture all or most of the quota rents. For example, in the central elasticity case we estimated that the US economy would gain $21.1 billion from removing quotas in the three sectors. Of this gain $14.7 billion is recaptured quota rents. Had we treated the quotas by using their tariff equivalent, the estimated gain to the United States of removing the quotas in the three sectors would have been only $6.4 billion. Thus one source of discrepancy between our estimates and previous general equilibrium estimates derives from the fact that we have properly accounted for the $14.7 billion in rent transfer associated with the US system of quotas.

Our estimates of the distortion costs of the quotas are also higher than previous general equilibrium estimates because our estimates are not dominated by terms-of-trade effects, a problem that we believe has plagued previous general equilibrium models. If a country has monopoly power in a particular export market or monopsony power in an import market, it will influence the price it receives or pays for the product in foreign units. In that case a departure from free trade is optimal. In our view any terms-of-trade effects are likely to be quite small for most countries. It seems highly unlikely, for example, that countries such as Israel or Luxembourg are large enough in world markets to significantly affect world prices over the broad range of products in which they trade. Yet in the general equilibrium estimates mentioned above, the terms-of-trade effects are so strong that Israel and Luxembourg have been found to lose welfare from unilateral trade liberalization.[15]

We conclude that even in the unlikely event that the United States has generalized monopoly and monopsony power in each traded sector, the removal of quotas in the three sectors would yield a welfare gain of $14.6 billion (table 5.9, column 4). Taking into consideration that quotas may induce monopoly rents for US auto dealers would add an extra $1.3 billion in distortionary costs. So, under any plausible set of assumptions, there is a substantial welfare cost from quotas in textiles and apparel, autos, and steel.

Appendix 5A: Liberalization with Endogenous Quota Premia and Sectoral Rationing of Steel

This appendix examines the sensitivity of the results presented in chapter 5 to two assumptions about the treatment of QRs. In section 5A.1 we estimate the effects of QR removal when QRs remain binding in other sectors. In section 5A.2 we estimate the extra welfare loss from rationing steel imports to individual sectors instead of aggregate steel imports.

5A.1. Liberalization with Endogenous Quota Premia

In our welfare cost calculations of the VER on Japanese auto imports (section 5.3), we assumed that when the VER was removed, imported textile products would still be purchased at the same exogenously given premium rate. Likewise, when calculating the welfare effects of removing QRs on textiles and apparel (section 5.2) or applying them on steel (section 5.4), we kept the premium rate on autos at its initial estimated value and allowed import volumes to adjust. In effect this amounts to treating QRs as tariff equivalents (except for rent transfer) since the premium rates were kept at the exogenously given levels estimated in chapter 4. As we explained, we introduced this assumption to ease the interpretation of results. Now we relax this assumption.

Through general equilibrium effects the removal of a QR in one sector will affect the demand for imports in all other sectors. In turn the quota premium rate is determined endogenously from the tariff-ridden demand curve. Therefore one should allow premium rates in sectors subject to QRs to adjust endogenously when QRs in other sectors are removed (or im-

Table 5A.1
Welfare changes from removing quotas and tariffs with endogenous premia in other sectors: central elasticity case

Policy change	Textiles and apparel	Automobiles	Steel	All sectors
Remove quotas (welfare change)				
With endogenous premia	10.57	9.8	0.89	
With exogenous premia[a]	10.40	9.8	0.86	
Remove all tariffs but leave quotas				
Welfare change[b]				−3.55
Quota premium rates (%)				
After removal	62.4	32.8	11.3	
Before removal	40.5	30.8	7.0	
Markup above world prices (%)[c]				
After removal	62.4	32.8	11.3	
Before removal	65.4	34.3	12.7	

Note: Welfare is the equivalent variation measure defined in appendix 3A in chapter 3 and expressed in billions of 1984 dollars.
a. These figures are the estimates presented in tables 5.3, 5.4, and 5.5.
b. Welfare change is measured from the solution with binding quotas in textiles, autos, and steel.
c. From equation 17 or 26 of table 3.1, the percentage markup in final goods over world prices is p_i, solved from $(1 + p_i) = (1 + tm_i)(1 + PRC_i)$. After tariff removal this markup is the quota premium rate; before tariff removal the markup is calculated from the solution with binding quotas in textiles, autos, and steel.

posed, as in the case of steel). We do that here, and we also estimate the welfare effect of removing all tariffs, starting from a solution with binding QRs in all three sectors. In this experiment the premium rates in textiles and apparel, autos, and steel are determined endogenously. When QRs are binding and rents accrue to foreigners, tariff removal will increase the rent transfer to foreigners, especially if the highest tariffs are in the sectors with QRs (as is the case in textiles).

The results of these experiments are reported in table 5A.1. All experiments are for the central elasticity specification under the small-country assumption.

Two conclusions are particularly notable. First, these welfare estimates are virtually identical to those obtained by treating QRs as tariff equivalents (except for the rent transfer component). This means that the results presented in the main body of the text are not affected by our assumption about the treatment of QRs. Second, removing tariffs while QRs remain in effect would result in a substantial welfare loss of $3.55 billion because of increased rent transfer abroad. When tariffs are removed, the endogenously determined quota premium rates increase in all sectors. This outcome is a direct application of the discussion in section 3.3, summarized in figure 3.4. It is also interesting to note that the markup over world prices (including both tariffs and quota premia) declines after tariff removal because tariff removal transfers rents to foreigners and reduces domestic income. The reduction in income reduces demand for all products, implying a lower endogenously determined premium rate.

5A.2 Quotas on Steel by Sector

In the results in the main text of this chapter, we assumed that the constraint on imported steel was on aggregate imports of steel rather than on imports demanded by individual sectors. This means that the quota-constrained steel went to the highest bidder and that an equal premium rate was established across all users. An alternative assumption is that licenses to import steel are not transferable across sectors, so each sector is individually constrained. Although this is not the case in US steel markets, such rationing schemes are frequent, especially among developing countries facing balance of payments crises.

Our model can be easily modified to accommodate individual rationing by sectors. In this case equation 25 (from table 3.1) is replaced by

$$\overline{VM}_{ki}^{1} < VM_{ki}^{0} \Rightarrow PMI_{ki}^{v} = PWI_k(1 + tm_k)(1 + PRI_{ki})ER, \quad i \in T, \qquad (25')$$

where k represents steel, and $\overline{VM}_{ki}^{1}$ is the amount of rationed imported steel allotted to sector i. With this end-user rationing scheme, generally $PMI_{ki}^{v} \neq PMI_{kj}^{v}$ because the endogenously determined rates will differ by end user. Because US input-output tables do not distinguish between domestic and imported intermediate transaction flows (see appendix A), we had to assume that all purchasers of steel use domestic and foreign steel in the same proportion, thereby limiting the scope for variations in premium rates. However, because all sectors do not use steel inputs with the same intensity, premium rates can still differ across sectors.

Table 5A.2 compares the costs of rationing each end user of steel by 15 percent (the same percentage decrease as that used in the main body of the text) with the costs when the constraint is on aggregate steel imports. The results show a very small increase in welfare costs with sectoral rather than aggregate rationing. When steel is rationed in the aggregate, the marginal rate of substitution between imported and domestic steel will be equal

Table 5A.2
Welfare costs of rationing steel by sector

Elasticity case	Total welfare cost[a]	Distortionary cost[b]
Low elasticity case		
Constraint by sectors	2.448	0.272
Constraint on aggregate imports[c]	2.433	0.271
Central elasticity case		
Constraint by sectors	0.868	0.129
Constraint on aggregate imports[c]	0.864	0.128
High elasticity case		
Constraint by sectors	0.544	0.099
Constraint on aggregate imports[c]	0.541	0.098

a. Welfare is the equivalent variation measure defined in appendix 3A of chapter 3 and expressed in billions of 1984 US dollars.
b. The distortionary cost component is the total welfare cost less the rent transfer component.
c. These results are from table 5.5 in section 5.4.

across sectors, ensuring a uniform premium rate. When individual users are rationed by sector, they cannot equate their marginal rates of substitution between domestic and imported steel across sectors (i.e., Pareto-optimal trades are foreclosed).

6 Welfare Costs of Quantitative Restrictions under Different Factor Market Assumptions

This is the first of two chapters that introduce behavioral modifications to the basic model presented in chapter 3. This chapter concentrates on the implications of different behavioral assumptions in factor markets; chapter 7 extends the model to account for modifications in commodity markets due to economies of scale in autos and steel. In this chapter we deal with four extensions of the model: (1) endogenous labor supply, through the introduction of labor-leisure choice in the utility function; (2) the implications of removing quantitative restrictions (QRs) in autos and steel if workers in these sectors receive a high distorted wage so that the value of their marginal product is greater than the value of the marginal product of workers in other sectors; (3) short-run costs of QRs under the assumption of sectoral specificity of capital; and (4) welfare costs of QRs with international capital mobility.

Each extension of the model in this and the following chapter is introduced as a separate departure from the basic model. So, when we analyze the implications of wage distortions, for example, we assume that labor supply is fixed, as we did in the simulations reported in chapter 5, rather than endogenous, as in our first extension with labor-leisure choice. This approach makes the interpretation of results more transparent than would be the case were we to introduce extensions cumulatively. In section 6.1 we treat labor- leisure choice; in section 6.2, the implications of wage distortions; in section 6.3, labor union behavior. In section 6.4 we report results for capital specific to its sector, and in section 6.5 we examine the effect of international mobility of capital.

6.1 Labor-Leisure Choice

6.1.1 Modifying the Basic Model

We introduce labor-leisure choice by modifying the Stone-Geary utility indicator of appendix 3A (equation 3A.1):

$$U = \prod_{i=0}^{n} (C_i - \lambda_i)^{\beta_i}, \tag{6.1}$$

where $\sum_{i=0}^{n} \beta_i = 1$ and C_0 is leisure. The C_i terms for $i = 1, \ldots, n$ are composite commodities, as in chapter 3. With this extended Stone-Geary utility function, labor supply becomes endogenous. The implications of equation 6.1 are discussed in appendix 6A, where we show that the following equation for labor supply must be added to our basic model:

$$LS = \overline{\text{MAXHOURS}} - \left(\frac{\beta_0}{W}\right)\left[\frac{Y - \sum_{i=1}^{n} PC_j\lambda_j}{1 - \beta_0}\right]. \tag{6.2}$$

We also show in appendix 6A that the consumer demand functions for composite commodities (equation 20 of table 3.1) must be modified as follows:

$$C_i = \lambda_i + \left[\frac{\beta_i}{(1 - \beta_0)PC_i}\right](Y - \text{COMIT}), \qquad i \in N, \tag{20$'$}$$

where

$$\text{COMIT} = \sum_{j \in N} PC_j\lambda_j, \qquad 1 > \beta_i > 0, \qquad i \in N.$$

When there is no labor-leisure choice, $\beta_0 = 0$, and equation 20′ reduces to equation 20. The other equations of the basic model remain unchanged.

Figure 6.1 shows the nesting implied by extending the utility function to include labor-leisure choice. We have simply added another branch at the top level to reflect the simultaneous labor-leisure and commodity choice. At the lower level, a constant elasticity of substitution (CES) functional form describes the choice between domestic and imported commodities for each composite commodity group. Note, however, that because of the weak separability of equation 6.1, we could alternatively have relied on three-stage budgeting, where in the first stage the labor-leisure choice depends on the price of leisure relative to the price of an aggregate index of commodities (see Tarr 1989).

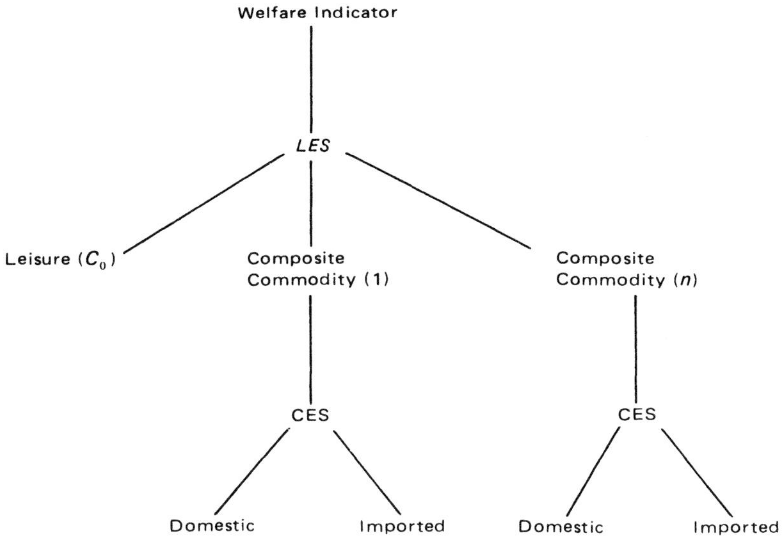

Figure 6.1
Extended utility choice

The central form of the Stone-Geary utility function ($\lambda_i = 0$ for $i = 1, \ldots, n$) implies that the own-elasticity of demand is unity for all commodity groups and that they are all on the border between gross substitutes and complements with each other in the resulting linear expenditure system (*LES*). Because this is a very limiting and unsatisfactory property, we have chosen the empirically more relevant noncentral LES form estimated in most demand studies.[1]

In appendix B to this book we present a summary of the recent estimates of the elasticity of US labor supply with respect to income and the real wage. We select an elasticity of US labor supply to income of -0.12. The elasticity with respect to the real wage is positive but quite small. Consequently in the central elasticity case we choose a parameter value for β_0 in equation 6.2 such that the elasticity of US labor supply is -0.12 with respect to income and 0.055 with respect to the real wage. In the high labor supply elasticity case the respective elasticities are -0.24 and 0.093.

6.1.2 Costs of Quotas with Labor-Leisure Choice

Table 6.1 presents the results of the welfare experiments with labor-leisure choice and compares them with the fixed labor supply case of chapter 5. In all the experiments we use the central elasticity estimates for all elasticities

Table 6.1
Welfare costs of quotas with labor-leisure choice: central elasticity case (billions of 1984 dollars)

Cost component elasticity case	Textiles and apparel	Automobiles	Steel	Costs of quotas in the three sectors
Welfare cost				
Fixed labor supply[a]	10.396	9.816	0.864	21.048
Central labor supply elasticity	10.395	9.815	0.864	21.044
High labor supply elasticity	10.394	9.815	0.864	21.041
Quota rent capture				
Fixed labor supply[a]	5.943	7.877	0.736	14.653
Central labor supply elasticity	5.942	7.876	0.736	14.650
High labor supply elasticity	5.942	7.874	0.736	14.646

Note: Welfare is the equivalent variation measure defined in appendix 6A.
a. These results are from chapter 5, tables 5.3–5.6.

except labor supply elasticities. The fixed labor supply case of chapter 5 corresponds to the low labor elasticity case presented here.

Introducing labor-leisure choice affects estimates in the following way. Removing protection raises income. In this model leisure is a substitute for all goods, so part of the increased income is spent on leisure. This means that the worker-consumer supplies fewer work hours. In terms of the diagrammatic presentation in figure 5.1 in chapter 5, the worker-consumer consumes less textiles so that relative to a fixed labor supply, the demand curve for textiles shifts in and the resulting welfare gain is less because the triangle is smaller. In other words, abolishing protection removes the price wedge between domestic and world prices. The size of the triangle representing the benefits of removing protection is greater the more the worker-consumer increases purchases of the formerly protected product. Substituting leisure for commodity consumption and consuming less of the formerly protected product reduces the gains from quota removal. The greater the elasticity of labor supply with respect to income (in absolute value), the less the increase in commodity consumption after removal of protection and so the lower the benefits accompanying the removal. In a more general specification in which leisure is a complement with some protected commodities (e.g., autos), removing the quota on those commodities would result in a greater welfare gain with labor-leisure choice because more of those commodities would be consumed than in the absence of labor-leisure choice.

Table 6.2
Employment effects of removing quotas on textiles and apparel, automobiles, and steel with labor-leisure choice: central elasticity case (change in employment by industry in thousands of jobs)

Sector	Fixed labor supply	Central labor elasticity	High labor elasticity
Agriculture	19.2	18.7	18.4
Food	4.5	4.2	4.0
Mining	4.3	4.0	3.8
Textiles and apparel	−245.0	−245.5	−245.8
Automobiles	−31.8	−31.9	−32.0
Steel	−16.7	−16.8	−16.9
Other consumer goods	29.6	29.0	28.5
Other manufactures	68.7	65.8	63.6
Traded services	85.3	76.8	70.1
Nontraded services	81.9	73.9	67.6
Total employment change	0.0	−21.6	−38.8

Note: A positive number means that employment is estimated to increase.

Incorporating labor-leisure choice results in almost identical, but slightly lower, estimates of the costs of QRs. The welfare estimates are reduced only slightly because the reduction in labor supply is small (see table 6.2) and the reduction in consumption is dispersed across all sectors. Since incorporating labor-leisure choice is shown to have little effect on the costs of trade protection, we revert to the fixed labor supply assumption for all remaining simulations.[2]

The employment effects of removing quotas in all three sectors are shown in table 6.2. In the central labor elasticity case, aggregate employment declines by 22,000 jobs, or 0.02 percent of the labor force. The decline occurs because the worker-consumer is wealthier after the QR is removed and so works fewer hours. While the real wage increases slightly (0.06 percent), which has the opposite effect, the income effect dominates because the change in income is larger than the change in the real wage and because the elasticity of the labor supply to the real wage is low. Thus the removal of QR protection leads to a small decline in hours worked.

6.2 Welfare Costs of Quotas in Steel and Automobiles in the Presence of Wage Distortions

We now consider how wage distortions (for which we give supporting evidence in section 6.2.1) affect our estimates of the costs of QRs in steel and autos. Wage distortions introduce a second-best effect in the initial situation with quotas, which affects our welfare cost estimates. We also consider whether trade policy affects the distortion level itself. This may happen if unions have a utility function with wages and employment as arguments. We treat wage distortions first as exogenous and then as endogenous by modeling labor union activity in the auto and steel sectors (section 6.3). In both cases we introduce modifications to the basic model with fixed labor supply.

6.2.1 Evidence of Wage Distortions in Automobiles and Steel

Most wage rates in the auto and steel sectors are negotiated by the United Autoworkers and the United Steelworkers unions.[3] Once the wage and compensation package is negotiated, firms are free to hire as many workers as they choose, but they must do so at the negotiated wage rate.

Several authors (Kreinin 1984; Tarr 1985; Crandall 1987) have argued that worker compensation in the auto and steel industries makes it difficult for these industries to be internationally competitive. Here we assess a related question: Are the wage rates in these sectors above the opportunity costs of workers of comparable skill for work of comparable attractiveness? We will call the latter wage the "competitive wage." In principle, it is possible that wage rates in these sectors are not above the competitive wage, in which case the United States has no comparative advantage in these sectors. In that case wage rates will be too high to maintain international competitiveness but cannot go any lower without inducing workers to leave for other sectors of the economy that pay a competitive wage. If, however, wage rates are above the competitive wage, then there is a distortion, and the United States has a comparative disadvantage because of the wage distortion. Incorporating that distortion in the model may significantly affect the results presented in chapter 5.

We provide estimates of wage distortions in autos and steel from two methods. One method compares hourly compensation of steel and auto workers in 1984 in the important producing countries around the world. As the data in table 6.3 reveal, steel and auto workers in almost all countries receive a premium above the wage earned by the average manufacturing worker. However, that premium was significantly higher in both industries in the United States than in other countries, with the exception of the case of the steel industry in Japan and Korea.

US steelworkers earned 63 percent above the average of all US manufacturing workers in 1984. By comparison the premium earned by steel-

Table 6.3
International comparisons of hourly compensation costs for production workers in iron and steel and motor vehicles and equipment, 1984

	Hourly compensation (US dollars)		Compensation relative to that of average production worker the same country	
Country	Motor vehicles and equipment	Iron and steel	Motor vehicles and equipment	Iron and steel
United States	18.92	20.26	1.53	1.63
Canada	13.18	15.38	1.19	1.39
Brazil	1.68	1.68	1.45	1.45
Mexico	2.55	2.58	1.25	1.26
Australia	9.56	na	1.02	na
Japan	7.92	11.14	1.25	1.75
Korea	1.94	2.23	1.38	1.58
Taiwan	2.05	na	1.39	na
Austria	na	8.96	na	1.27
Belgium	9.64	10.72	1.12	1.24
Denmark	7.53	na	0.93	na
France	8.42	9.15	1.13	1.22
Germany	11.92	10.63	1.26	1.13
Ireland	4.05	na	1.10	na
Italy	7.72	8.87	1.05	1.20
Netherlands	8.14	10.74	0.93	1.23
Spain	5.35	na	1.17	na
Sweden	9.64	na	1.05	na
United Kingdom	4.67	7.19	1.13	1.22
Average (excluding the United States)	7.06	8.27	1.16	1.33
US premium/average premium	11.86	11.99	1.31	1.23

Source: Based on data from the US Department of Labor, Bureau of Labor Statistics, Office of Productivity and Technology, November 1986.
Note: na means not available.

workers in European countries over their respective manufacturing workers ranged from a low of 13 percent in Germany to a high of 27 percent in Austria. US workers in motor vehicle and equipment manufacturing earned 53 percent more than the average US manufacturing worker in 1984. The premium in the United States was higher than the premium in any other country, and in seven of the countries listed in table 6.3, the premium earned was 13 percent or less.

To get an estimate of the relative wage distortion in the two industries in the United States, we divide the premium for the United States in each industry by the average of the premia for the respective industry in the other countries, which yields a distortion value of 1.23 in steel and 1.31 in autos. We use these estimates of the wage distortions in iron and steel and motor vehicles in our simulations.

A second method of estimating wage distortions is that of Krueger and Summers (1988), who base their estimates on studies of wages that control for gender, age, full-time work, fringe benefits, and other worker characteristics. They estimate that US workers in the transport equipment sector earn a compensation premium of 27 percent above the industrywide average wage and that workers in primary metals (the closest industry in their sample to steel) earn a 26 percent premium (Krueger and Summers 1988, table 2). These estimates are very close to ours and to those of Katz and Summers (1989b, table 1), who also argue that it is difficult to account convincingly for persistent interindustry wage differentials on the basis of unobserved ability differences or equalizing differences. Rather, they argue, workers in a number of industries appear to earn rents which would justify our focus on trade policy changes in the presence of wage differentials.[4]

6.2.2 Eliminating Exogenous Wage Distortions

The only modification we introduce to our basic model is to substitute $W\phi_i$ for the wage rate entering the labor demand equation (equation 3 in table 3.1), where $\phi_i > 1$ is the distortionary component of the wage for steel (1.23) and autos (1.31) estimated in section 6.2.1. We also also need to modify income equation 31, changing $\overline{WLS}$ to $W\sum_{i=1}^{n} L_i\phi_i$ to reflect the assumption that workers in steel and autos receive wage income higher than the competitive wage W.

Since the wage rate (adjusted for skill mix and attractiveness of the work) in steel and autos is higher than in the rest of the economy, the value of the marginal product of workers is higher in these two industries than elsewhere. This means that US welfare would improve if a worker shifted

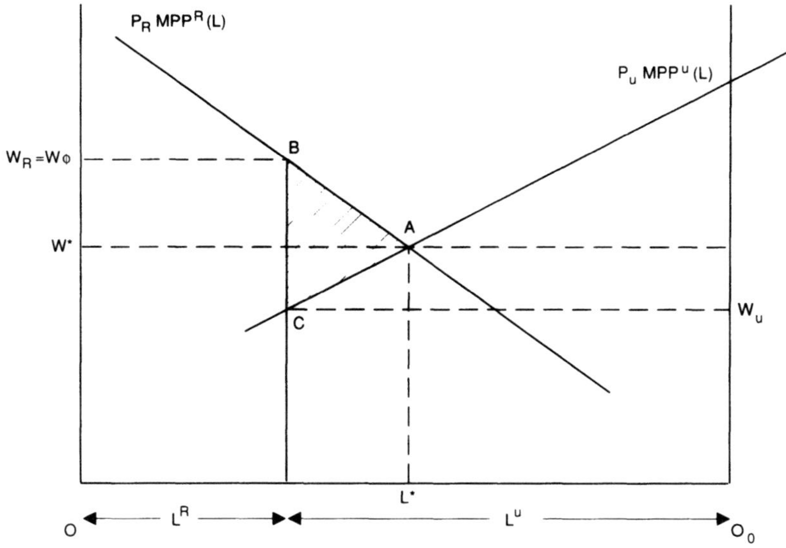

Figure 6.2
Distortions from interindustry wage differentials

into the steel or auto industry from elsewhere in the economy where the value of marginal product is lower.

Figure 6.2 illustrates in partial equilibrium the welfare gain from removing a distortionary wage differential in a two-sector (*R* and *U*) price-taking open economy. A wage differential in favor of sector *R* leads to too little employment in that sector and to too much employment in sector *U*. If there are no other market imperfections, the social costs of the rents accruing to labor in sector *R* are equal to the private costs, or area *ABC*. If there are other market imperfections, however, such as protection in sector *R*, the private benefits from removing the wage differential will exceed the social benefits because protection in effect shifts out the social demand curve for labor in sector *R* and shifts in the social demand curve for labor in sector *U*.[5]

Given different wage premia across industries and the desirability of increasing employment in sectors with high-labor rents, Katz and Summers (1989a, 1989b) suggest that a case can be made for industrial policies aimed at increasing employment in sectors with high-wage premia. They contend that interindustry wage differentials are more important for industrial policy than are product market imperfections. That is, there is relatively little opportunity for international profit shifting along the lines first suggested

Table 6.4
Welfare effects of removing wage distortions in automobiles and steel, separately and together: central elasticity case (billions of 1984 US dollars)

Sector	Welfare gain
Automobiles	0.23
Steel	0.64
Automobiles and steel	0.87

Note: Wage distortions are removed while protection remains in all three sectors. Welfare is the equivalent variation measure defined in appendix 3A in chapter 3.

by Brander and Spencer (1983, 1984) compared with increasing labor rents. Observing that sectors with high-wage premia are generally export industries, Katz and Summers (1989a) argue for export incentive policies instead of import substitution policies. They note, however, that the steel and auto sectors are exceptions from most other high-wage premia sectors in two important ways: (1) they do little exporting and are faced with significant import competition, and (2) their high wages are better explained by strong union behavior than by efficiency wage theories.

While Katz and Summers carefully point out that the case for an activist industrial policy is substantially weakened by the strong likelihood that theoretically optimal policies will not be implemented in practice, it is nonetheless informative to assess the benefits of industrial policy in the presence of wage distortions. To do this, we first consider the effects of eliminating the wage premia. One way to do this is to provide wage subsidies. As the work of Bhagwati and Srinivasan (1969) suggests, the optimal instrument for attacking exogenous wage distortions is not protection but an instrument that operates most directly on the relevant margin. An alternative to wage subsidies is a policy to reduce or eliminate union power in autos and steel. This is probably a better approach since unions are likely to raise wage demands in response to government subsidies to eliminate labor misallocation due to wage distortions, resulting in spiraling government subsidies.[6] (In section 6.2.3 we evaluate whether there are welfare gains from removing QRs in autos and steel in the presence of wage distortions in both sectors. In section 6.3 we generalize the analysis to the more realistic case of endogenous wage distortions.)

Table 6.4 shows the welfare gains from the removal of wage distortions. The economy gains more from the removal of wage distortions in steel than in autos because steel is the more labor intensive of the two sectors.

Table 6.5 shows the employment effects by industry of the removal of wage distortions. When distortions are removed in both sectors, employment increases by 63,000 jobs in steel and by 86,000 jobs in autos.

Table 6.5
Employment effects of removing wage distortions in automobiles and steel, separately and together: central elasticity case (employment change by sector in thousands of jobs)

Sector	Automobiles	Steel	Automobiles and steel
Agriculture	−4.15	−5.77	−9.92
Food	−1.94	−1.51	−3.45
Mining	−0.61	−0.36	−0.97
Textiles and apparel	−0.42	−3.15	−3.57
Automobiles	85.82	0.33	86.24
Steel	0.51	62.24	62.80
Other consumer goods	−3.99	0.28	−3.72
Other manufactures	4.16	6.16	10.34
Traded services	−36.37	−34.80	−71.22
Nontraded services	−43.04	−23.41	−66.54

Note: A positive number means that employment is estimated to increase.

Employment decreases in all other sectors (especially in the two service sectors) except other manufactures, where it increases slightly because steel is used as an intermediate product. The lower wage in autos and steel reduces prices in these sectors, enabling other manufacturing industries to produce their products more cheaply. Consequently quantity demanded for other manufactures increases, which explains the sector's increased use of labor. Other sectors lose employment to the steel and auto sectors because steel and autos are not as important as intermediate inputs to other sectors as they are to other manufactures. When wage distortions are removed on steel and autos separately, the pattern is similar, with other manufactures gaining employment in both cases.

It is interesting to compare the distortion costs of interindustry wage differences with the distortion costs of the QRs in autos and steel. In chapter 5 we estimated that the distortionary cost component of QRs in autos and steel in the central elasticity case was about $2.06 billion. The distortion costs of the interindustry wage differences in autos and steel are about $0.87 billion (table 6.4), or about four-tenths of the distortion costs of QRs in those sectors. So at least for sectors with significant restrictions to free trade, such as autos and steel, our results indicate that the distortion costs of QRs are larger than the costs of wage distortions.

6.2.3 Costs of Quotas in the Presence of Wage Distortions

In theory it can be argued that removing QRs in the presence of wage distortions would yield little, if any, welfare gain. The rationale is that

Table 6.6
Welfare costs of quotas in the presence of wage distortions in automobiles and steel: central elasticity case (billions of 1984 US dollars)

Sector	Welfare change
Automobiles	
With wage distortions	9.615
Without wage distortions[a]	9.816
Steel	
With wage distortions	0.780
Without wage distortions[a]	0.864
Textiles and apparel, automobiles, and steel[b]	
With wage distortion	20.799
Without wage distortions[a]	21.048

Note: Welfare is the equivalent variation measure defined in appendix 3A of chapter 3.
a. Estimates of the welfare gains of removing quotas in the absence of wage distortions are from chapter 5, tables 5.4, 5.5, and 5.6.
b. Joint costs are estimated by removing quotas in all three sectors from a counterfactually created equilibrium with quotas on steel.

removing quotas in autos and steel will induce labor to move out of these sectors, where the value of the marginal product is higher than in the rest of the economy (figure 6.2). Society would then bear a cost approximately equal to the difference between the value of the marginal product in steel and autos and the value of the marginal product elsewhere in the economy. So because of the wage distortion, there is a trade-off between the welfare gain of removing the quota and the costs of moving employees out of the sectors where the value of their marginal product is highest. Under this second-best situation the policy of removing the quota is not necessarily optimal, given the presence of another distortion in the economy. It is therefore of interest to estimate the effects of removing the quota in the presence of wage distortions and observe which of the two effects dominates.

The welfare gains from removing the quotas, either separately or together, are less (in absolute value) in all cases when wage distortions are present (table 6.6), but the attenuating effect of the wage distortions is extremely small. Similarly the changes in employment (table 6.7) are very close to those obtained in the absence of wage distortions. Removing quotas in autos and steel yields strong welfare gains even in the presence of wage distortions in both industries. Clearly wage distortions are not a justification for maintaining QR protection.

Table 6.7
Employment effects of removing quotas separately and together in the presence of wage distortions in automobiles and steel: central elasticity case (change in employment by industry in thousands of jobs)

Sector	Automobiles	Steel[a]	Textiles, automobiles, and steel[b]
Agriculture	9.97	−1.30	19.18
Food	0.88	−0.13	4.60
Mining	0.24	0.39	4.33
Textiles and apparel	−0.43	−0.99	−245.05
Automobiles	−36.20	−0.39	−31.86
Steel	0.32	20.80	−16.73
Other consumer goods	6.64	−2.69	29.55
Other manufactures	−6.63	−12.41	68.77
Traded services	13.35	−1.63	85.14
Nontraded services	11.87	−1.64	82.08

Note: A positive number means that employment is estimated to increase.
a. For steel alone, the estimates are for the imposition of quotas.
b. Joint effects are estimated by removing quotas in all three sectors from a counterfactually created equilibrium with quotas on steel.

6.3 Modeling Labor Unions in the Automobile and Steel Sectors

Unions in the auto and steel industries can be viewed as instruments used by employees to generate (or extract) the monopoly rents deriving from regulations or imperfections in the product market. If the union can organize enough workers in the industry, it can restrict the labor supply and collect these rents in classic monopoly fashion. When the conditions that led to the generation of the rents change, however, the premium earned by workers will change as well.[7] This implies that the premium should be considered endogenous with respect to a change in protection. For example, with intensification of international competition in the steel and auto industries because of a US reduction in protection, the United Steelworkers and the United Autoworkers unions would control a smaller share of the internationally relevant supply of labor and so would be able to extract a smaller wage premium.

In the following section we discuss alternative ways to model labor union behavior. The reader who is interested only in the impact of endogenous wage distortions on the costs of QRs may skip to section 6.3.2.

6.3.1 Labor Unions and Wage and Employment Determination

As do most analyses of union behavior, we begin with the assumption that the union has a quasi-concave utility function of wages and employment. Empirical applications require a specific functional form, and once again, we choose the generalized Stone-Geary:

$$U = \bar{A}(W\phi - \overline{W}_0)^{\gamma}(L - \bar{L}_0)^{\delta}, \qquad \bar{A}, \gamma, \delta > 0, \tag{6.3}$$

where W is the wage rate in the competitive labor market (the opportunity cost of labor) and $\phi > 1$ implies the existence of a wage premium in the sector. (For expositional purposes we suppress industry subscripts and use a bar over a variable to indicate that it is exogenous.) Note that ϕ is now an endogenous variable. In this specification the parameters $\overline{W}_0$ and $\bar{L}_0$ are the minimum acceptable wage and employment levels. It is natural to take $\overline{W}_0$ to be W, which we do below. $\bar{L}_0$ has no such obvious interpretation, and we discuss below how we determine its value.

This functional form has the advantage that many of the hypotheses traditionally offered as an explanation of union behavior are special cases of this general formulation. In particular, we have the following special cases:

$$U = \bar{A}(W\phi - \overline{W}_0)L, \tag{6.4}$$

which corresponds to the assumption that the union maximizes rents, and

$$U = \bar{A}W\phi L, \tag{6.5}$$

which corresponds to the assumption that the union maximizes the wage bill.

We assume that the union either sets the wage rate unilaterally or negotiates it with the firm, but that the firm unilaterally determines the level of employment. However, as discussed below, there are advantages and disadvantages to this assumption, and our choice will be determined by the relevant empirical evidence.

Suppose for now that the firm takes the wage rate as given and chooses the employment level that maximizes profits at this wage rate. This yields a negatively sloping labor demand schedule for the firm, which we denote by

$$L = L(W\phi), \tag{6.6}$$

which is the type of labor demand schedule discussed in section 6.2. Given

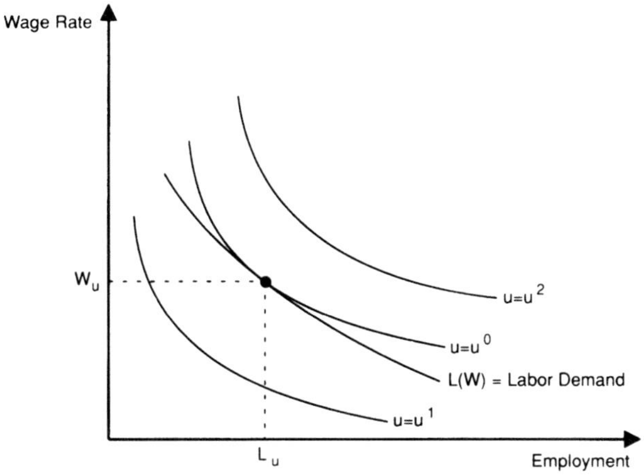

Figure 6.3
Employment determination with passive firm

this behavior by the firm, the union will seek to maximize its utility function (equation 6.3) subject to the labor demand schedule (equation 6.6) of the firm. The outcome is depicted in figure 6.3, where the optimal combination is W_u, L_u.

The profits of the firm, however, are a monotonically decreasing function of the wage rate. Thus the firm would prefer to pay as low a wage as possible. Since workers can always earn their opportunity wage W in other industries, the firm cannot offer anything lower than W and so wants to pay W. Wage negotiations between the firm and the union, which subsequently leave the firm free to choose the employment level, will result in a wage rate somewhere between W_u and W, but on the firm's labor demand curve (equation 6.6). A possible outcome of the negotiated agreement between the firm and the union is depicted in figure 6.4 as W_n, L_n.

Extensive empirical research has been conducted using equation 6.3 to test union behavior and the assumption that the firm reacts passively to the union's wage offer (see Farber 1986 for a survey of the research). The results indicate that the special cases of equations 6.4 and 6.5 must be rejected. That is, unions appear to value employment maximization more highly than pure rent maximization or wage bill maximization. Moreover, if one accepts a model of wage determination in which *firms react passively* to the wage demand and set employment according to their labor demand schedule, then the weight assigned to employment in the utility function (equation 6.3) is probably relatively high. A potential problem of these

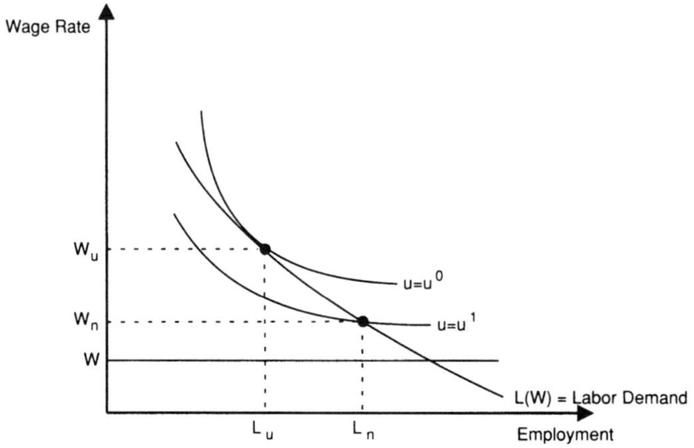

Figure 6.4
Employment determination through negotiation

studies is that they may be misattributing the impact of an active firm (whose actions would lower the wage and increase employment) to union preferences for more employment.

Consider the alternative in which the union and the firm jointly negotiate both wages and employment. We can define a contract curve in wage-employment space between the firm and the union. (The contract curve is the set of efficient bargaining outcomes.) It is well established (see McDonald and Solow 1981) that the contract curve lies to the right of the labor demand curve.[8] The relationship between the labor demand and contract curves is depicted in figure 6.5, where *CC* is the contract curve and the Π_t curves are isoprofit curves with $\Pi_t > \Pi_{t+1}$. Thus the firm cannot be simultaneously on the contract curve and on its own labor demand function. It follows that bargaining over *L* in addition to *W* (as we assumed above) is a necessary but not sufficient condition for being on the contract curve. Otherwise, merely setting *W* allows the firm to go to *L*(*W*), which is off the contract curve. Given any agreement on the contract curve, the firm will have an incentive to lower the level of employment if the wage rate does not change. That is, the firm will have an incentive to cheat.

Our reading of the evidence is that it is more reasonable to assume that the firm is on its labor demand schedule than to assume that wage and employment levels are on the contract curve. The empirical evidence suggests that labor contracts do not stipulate employment levels (see Oswald 1982). The reason appears to be that it is too difficult to design contracts with employment guarantees.[9] Thus we believe that we are justified in

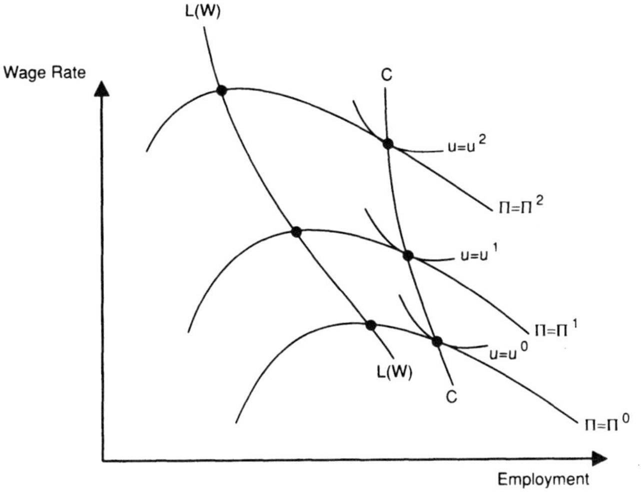

Figure 6.5
The union-firm contract curve

assuming that the union and the firm do not determine the employment level through negotiation.

For labor economists interested in explaining union behavior, the distinction between an active and a passive firm is crucial. We are interested in approximating wage and employment levels in the steel and auto industries in response to a change in policy, so we need to know only where we are along the firm's labor demand schedule, not whether the firm actively influenced the wage offer. As we illustrate below, increasing the weight on employment in equation 6.3 has the same effect on the wage-employment outcome as does using a lower employment weight and assuming active firm influence on the wage decision. We assume that the firm sets the employment level after reacting passively to wage setting by the union. We experiment with different values for the weights given by the union to wages and employment in equation 6.3, but we read the evidence as suggesting that the weight assigned to employment is relatively high—which, for our purpose, may be due to active firm behavior.

The cost function (equation 1 of table 3.1) for sectors with a wage distortion ϕ_i is modified by replacing W with $W\phi_i$. Applying Shephard's lemma to the modified cost function implies that labor demand in equation 6.3 is given by (sector subscripts omitted)

$$L^d = \left(\frac{\alpha PVC}{W\phi}\right)^{\sigma}\left(\frac{X}{\overline{AX}}\right)^{1-\sigma}. \qquad (6.7)$$

We use equation 6.7 to substitute for L in equation 6.3. Then maximizing U gives, after manipulation (see appendix 6B), the following equation for determining the endogenous wage differential ϕ:

$$\frac{\phi - 1}{\phi} = \left(\frac{L^d - \bar{L}_0}{L^d}\right)\frac{\gamma}{\delta\sigma}. \tag{6.8}$$

We take $\gamma + \delta = 1$, and experiment with $\gamma = 0.2$, 0.5, and 0.8. Since we have values for employment and for the wage differential in steel and autos for the base-year equilibrium, we determine $\bar{L}_0$ by solving equation 6.8 for $\bar{L}_0$. Thus, for the following experiments, the basic model of chapter 3 is modified to include wage differentials for steel and autos, ϕ_i (as described in section 6.2.2), which are determined endogenously by equation 6.8.

6.3.2 Welfare Costs of Quotas in the Presence of Endogenous Wage Distortions

The results of removing quotas in autos and imposing quotas in steel in the presence of endogenous wage distortions are given in table 6.8 for the central elasticity case. For comparison, results for exogenous wage distortions (from tables 6.6 and 6.7) are presented as well as case 0. Three other sets of results are reported: case 1 in which the union gives more weight to maximizing employment than to maximizing the wage premium, case 2 in which the union gives equal weights to wages and employment, and case 3 in which the union gives more weight to maximizing the wage premium than to maximizing employment. Since similar effects operate in both cases, we discuss only results for the steel case.

In the case of steel, imposing QRs (note that we now measure changes from the solution with steel unrestricted) raises the demand for labor in the steel industry. The steelworkers union now chooses a higher wage in order to maximize its utility. The higher wage results in greater distortion costs to the economy. So the greater the relative weight the union places on wages, the higher will be the wage premium for steelworkers for the given increase in labor demand and, as expected, the greater will be the costs of imposing the QR. The welfare cost increases monotonically in cases 1, 2, and 3 because the union sets a higher wage premium when the demand for labor increases with the imposition of the QR.

The distortionary costs of imposing QRs in steel (the total welfare cost minus the quota rent capture component) rise from \$45 million in case 0 to \$119 million in case 3, indicating that union behavior increases the distortionary costs by 164 percent.[10] Note also that with a high weight on

Table 6.8
Welfare costs of quotas in the presence of endogenous wage distortions in automobiles and steel: central elasticity case

Sector	Welfare change (billions of 1984 dollars)[a]					Employment change (thousands of jobs)				Wage differential (% distortion relative to unity)			
	Case 0	Case 1	Case 2	Case 3		Case 0	Case 1	Case 2	Case 3	Case 0	Case 1	Case 2	Case 3
Automobiles (A)	9.62	9.63	9.69	9.74	(A)	−36.20	−34.40	−21.29	−8.65	1.31	1.30	1.24	1.19
					(S)	0.32	0.30	0.21	0.09	1.23	1.23	1.23	1.23
					(A)	−0.39	−0.37	−0.25	−0.11	1.31	1.31	1.31	1.31
Steel (S)[b]	−0.78	−0.79	−0.88	−0.99	(S)	20.80	20.00	13.64	5.92	1.23	1.233	1.26	1.30
Textiles, auto-					(A)	−31.86	−30.27	−18.66	−7.53	1.31	1.30	1.25	1.20
mobiles, and steel[c]	20.80	20.82	20.96	21.11	(S)	−16.73	−16.12	−11.16	−4.91	1.23	1.231	1.24	1.24

Note: Case 0 is the exogenous wage differential case from table 6.6. Case 1 gives more weight to employment ($\delta = 0.8$) and less to wages ($\gamma = 0.2$). Case 2 gives equal weights to wages ($\gamma = 0.5$) and employment ($\delta = 0.5$). Case 3 gives more weight to wages ($\gamma = 0.8$) and less to employment ($\delta = 0.2$).

a. Welfare is the equivalent variation measure defined in appendix 3A of chapter 3.

b. For steel the changes are the result of imposing rather than removing quotas as in autos.

c. Estimates are for the effects of joint removal of quotas from a counterfactually created equilibrium with quotas on steel.

wages, employment gains fall to less than 30 percent of the gains achieved when there is no endogenous union wage determination. Introducing union behavior in the auto sector yields similar results. Labor union activity cuts the estimated loss in employment from removing QRs to 34,000 jobs when the union puts more weight on employment and to 9,000 jobs when wages predominate.

For steel note also that the estimated welfare costs of QRs with endogenous wage distortions are higher than the estimated costs with no wage distortions (from chapter 5) when the union weight on wages is higher than 0.5 (case 3) and lower when the weight is lower than 0.5 (case 1). With a weight for wages of 0.5 (case 2), the costs are about equal with and without endogenous wage distortions.

Our results cast serious doubts on the arguments for an industrial policy based on wage distortions. The arguments are based on the observation that more labor should be employed in sectors with high wage distortions and on the presumption that the costs of protection are lower if significant wage distortions exist. *When wage distortions are endogenous, however, protection increases the distortion, and those added costs of protection can outweigh the benefits of increased employment in the sector.* This means that QRs have a higher cost in sectors with endogenous wage distortions than in sectors without them and that the presumption that wage distortions justify support for protection or for a more general industrial policy does not hold in sectors with endogenous wage distortions.[11]

6.4 Short-Run Welfare Costs of Quotas in Textiles and Apparel, Automobiles, and Steel

In the basic model we assumed a time period long enough for capital to move across sectors until rental rates were equalized. We now give Marshallian short-run welfare calculations in which capital is fixed in each sector.

With fixed capital in each sector, $\bar{K}_i$, we have an endogenously determined rental rate for each sector, R_i. So in the short-run model the rental rate rather than capital varies across sectors, rising in expanding sectors and falling in contracting sectors. To model this change, we drop the economy-wide capital stock constraint (equation 4 in table 3.1) from the model. Total capital stock remains fixed implicitly because capital stock is fixed for each sector.

The welfare effects of removing QRs in textiles and apparel, autos, and steel are reported in table 6.9 for the central elasticity case; employment

Table 6.9
Welfare effects of removing quotas and tariffs with fixed capital stocks in each sector: central elasticity case

Policy change/sector	Welfare effect[a]	Sectoral rental rate (R_i)[b]
Remove quotas		
Textiles and apparel		
With fixed capital stock	10.34	0.051
With intersectoral capital mobility[c]	10.40	0.058
Automobiles		
With fixed capital stock	9.74	0.050
With intersectoral capital mobility[c]	9.82	0.058
Steel[d]		
With fixed capital stock	−1.17	0.063
With intersectoral capital mobility[c]	−0.86	0.058
Textiles and apparel, automobiles, and steel		
With fixed capital stock	21.23	
With intersectoral capital mobility[c]	21.05	[e]0.058
Remove all tariffs		
With fixed capital stock	0.82	na
With intersectoral capital mobility[c]	0.85	

a. Welfare is the equivalent variation measure defined in appendix 3A of chapter 3 and expressed in billions of 1984 US dollars.
b. Rental rate for the sector affected by QR removal.
c. These values are from the corresponding experiment with intersectoral capital mobility in chapter 5 (tables 5.3–5.6).
d. For steel, estimates are for the imposition of QRs.
e. Rental rates have the same values as in individual cases, except for steel, because estimation is for the removal of QRs.

changes are presented in table 6.10. Fixing the capital stock in each sector has a welfare effect analogous to that of moving to a lower elasticity regime because a firm's elasticity of supply is lower with fixed capital stock than when all factors are variable. This intuitive proposition is an application of the Le Chatelier principle that the more variable a firm's factors, the higher will be its price elasticity of supply (see Varian 1984, 56–57).[12] The smaller the elasticity of supply, the larger will be the expected costs of imposing a quota, as in the steel industry. Conversely, for the removal of quotas as in the textile and apparel and auto experiments, the smaller the elasticity of supply, the less able is the economy to adjust and benefit from quota removal. Although this result has intuitive appeal, the opposite is true for tariff removal: The larger the elasticity of supply, the larger will be the gains from tariff removal.

Table 6.10
Employment effects of quotas with fixed capital stocks in each sector: central elasticity case (change in employment by industry in thousands of jobs)

Sector	Remove quotas on: Textiles and apparel	Remove quotas on: Automobiles	Impose quota on steel
Agriculture	21.08	10.07	−0.11
Food	4.87	13.30	−0.34
Mining	10.20	2.44	1.00
Textiles	−246.22	1.14	−5.90
Automobiles	−53.84	−60.52	−1.15
Steel	−43.16	1.29	49.22
Other consumer goods	31.46	6.06	−4.41
Other manufactures	107.71	7.33	−31.88
Traded services	91.52	20.79	−2.35
Nontraded services	76.40	10.08	−9.39

Note: A positive number means that employment is estimated to increase.

In this section we provide a straightforward partial equilibrium interpretation of these results. Neary (1988) has established analogous results in general equilibrium, and we discuss those in section 6.5.

First consider the case, depicted in figure 6.6, of removing a tariff on a homogeneous product. Let D be the demand curve, S_I be the relatively inelastic domestic supply curve and S_e the relatively elastic supply curve, $\overline{PW} \times \overline{ER}$ be the border price of imports, and tm be the tariff rate. Initial imports are BM, increasing to either CN or DN after tariff removal depending on elasticities. With tariff removal the production deadweight loss ABD is regained in the high elasticity case, and loss ABC is regained in the low elasticity case. Thus the benefits of removing tariffs are greater in the high elasticity case, which explains the result in the last row of table 6.9.[13]

Now consider the case of quota removal with product differentiation, as depicted in figure 6.7. Although the explanation is simpler with product homogeneity, we illustrate the result with product differentiation because our model incorporates differentiation between the home and imported product. In panel A, Q_0, P_0 is the quantity-price equilibrium at the intersection of the initial domestic demand D^0 and domestic supply S_I or S_e. In panel B, q_0 is the initial quota-restrained import quantity and d^0 is the initial demand for imports. The import and the domestic product are gross substitutes; thus when the quota is removed, the import price falls to $\overline{PW} \times ER$, inducing a reduction in domestic demand to D^1. The domestic price

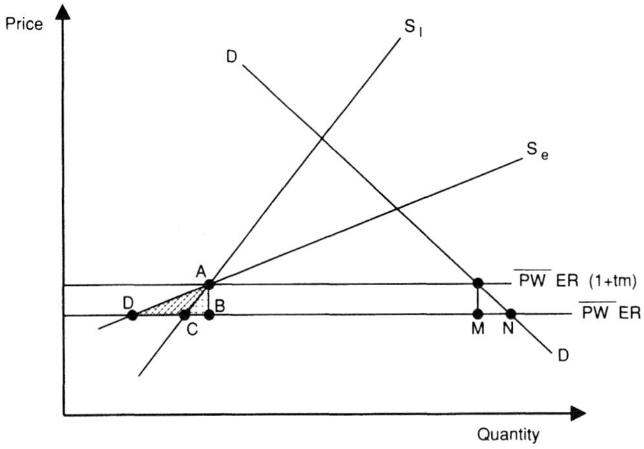

Figure 6.6
Benefits of tariff removal depending on supply elasticity homogeneous product

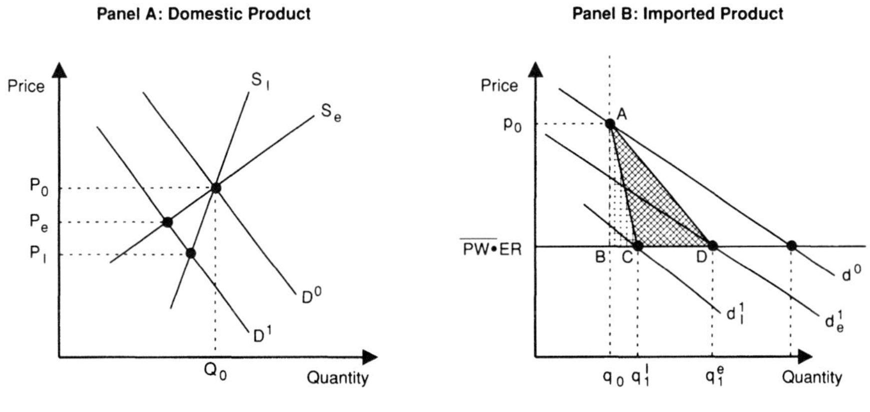

Figure 6.7
Benefits of quota removal depending on supply elasticity for differentiated product

will fall to P_e in the high elasticity case, inducing a relatively small downward shift in import demand, or to P_I in the low elasticity case, inducing a relatively large downward shift in import demand. The welfare gains from quota removal are larger the greater the elasticity of supply.[14] Since supply elasticities are lower with fixed capital stocks, this explains the estimates for textiles and apparel and autos in table 6.9.

Unlike the case for tariffs, however, there is asymmetry in the effects of removing or imposing QRs. The costs of imposing QRs are greater the lower the elasticity of supply. (This is easily verified using a diagram such as that in figure 6.6 or 6.7.) Thus, as shown in table 6.9, the imposition of QRs on steel costs the economy more with fixed capital stocks. Consequently the outcome for the combined case of textiles and apparel, autos, and steel is ambiguous because of the mixture of imposing and removing QRs. Note that these observations on the asymmetry of the effects of supply elasticities on the costs of QRs are the same as those we discussed in chapter 5 on the effects of demand elastiticies on the costs of QRs.

6.5 Welfare Costs of Quotas with International Capital Mobility

The share of US capital stock owned by foreigners increased from 1 percent in 1984 to 4 percent in 1988. With the increasing integration of international capital markets in recent years, trade policy changes can be expected to affect direct foreign investment. This means that an evaluation of the costs of protection needs to consider the effects of international capital mobility.

In this section we assume that the United States faces an infinitely elastic supply of capital at a fixed interest rate and that the proceeds from foreign direct investment accrue to the owners of the capital stock. As an example, take the labor-intensive textile and apparel sector. Removal of protection puts upward pressure on the rental–wage ratio, inducing an inflow of foreign capital and an outflow of service payments to the foreign owners of capital. To simplify calibration of the model and maintain the same initial solution as in chapter 5, we assume no foreign ownership of capital in the base solution.[15]

In terms of the basic model presented in chapter 3 (table 3.1), we drop equation 4, which fixes the economywide capital stock, and fix the value of the rental rate R in terms of the numéraire so that $R = \overline{R}_0$, where R_0 is the rental rate before protection is removed. We replace equations 30 and 31 in the basic model by the following:

$$\bar{B} = \sum_{k \in T} \left(PWE_k E_k - PWM_k CM_k - PWI_k VTM_k \right)$$

$$- \frac{\sum_{k \in T} \theta_k (\text{RENTC}_k + \text{RENTI}_k)}{ER} - \frac{RKF}{ER} \qquad (30')$$

and

$$Y = W\overline{LS} + RKD + GR + \sum_{k \in T} (1 - \theta_k)(\text{RENTC}_k + \text{RENTI}_k) - \bar{B}ER, \qquad (31')$$

where KF is the amount of foreign-owned capital stock and $KD = KS - KF$ is the amount of domestic-owned capital stock.

Table 6.11 compares the results of five simulations with and without international capital mobility. The table also reports the amount of international capital inflow or outflow. The results point to a combination of two effects: (1) an elasticity effect, described in the previous section, which can be interpreted in partial equilibrium, and (2) a general equilibrium valuation of the imported capital services.

The impact of international capital mobility on welfare is another application of the impact of differing elasticities on the welfare effects of QRs. When capital is allowed to move freely across countries, the elasticity of supply increases. The elasticity effects of international capital mobility can be derived from figures 6.6 and 6.7 and the analysis presented in section 6.4. In particular, international capital mobility in response to a tariff increase or decrease would be expected to increase symmetrically the absolute value of the change in welfare. A change in QRs, however, has an asymmetric effect on welfare: Removing a QR results in a greater absolute value of the welfare change, and imposing a QR results in a smaller absolute value of the welfare change.

In recent general equilibrium theoretical work, Neary (1988) and Neary and Ruane (1988) derive the result that international capital mobility increases the costs of imposing a tariff. They also show that a quota will impose less costs on the economy with international capital mobility than without it. These results are all consistent with our discussion. But because their work does not show asymmetry between imposing and removing quotas as ours does, they find that quota removal with international capital mobility results in lower benefits to the economy than quota removal without international capital mobility.

Neary and Ruane treat quota removal and quota imposition symmetrically, considering both as a change in quantity. We treat quota removal as

Table 6.11
Welfare and employment effects of removing quotas in the presence of internationally mobile capital

Policy change/sector	Total welfare effect[a]	Rent capture[a]	Change in employment[b]	Change in aggregate value of capital stock[c]
Remove quotas				
Textiles and apparel				
With international capital mobility	10.28	5.95	−242.18	145.984
Without international mobility[d]	10.40	5.94	−246.9	−4.43*
Automobiles				
With international capital mobility	9.819	7.89	−36.22	−2.452
Without international mobility[d]	9.816	7.88	−36.2	−5.813*
Steel[e]				
With international capital mobility	−0.855	0.74	20.64	−11.720
Without international mobility[d]	−0.864	0.74	20.80	−12.346*
All three[f]				
With international capital mobility	20.93	14.69	na	155.256
Without international mobility[d]	21.05	14.65	na	−11.609*
Remove all tariffs				
With international capital mobility	1.12	na	na	184.342
Without international mobility[d]	0.85	na	na	na

Note: na means not applicable.
a. Welfare (and rent capture) is the equivalent variation measure defined in appendix 3A of chapter 3 and expressed in billions of 1984 US dollars.
b. Change in employment in the sector affected by the policy change in thousands of work-years.
c. The change in billions of 1984 dollars. A positive value indicates that capital is imported.
d. Results are from corresponding experiments with no international capital mobility reported in chapter 5 (tables 5.3–5.6). Asterisks refer to capital movements from rent capture.
e. For steel, estimates are for the imposition of quotas for aggregate steel imports.
f. Estimates are for the effects of removing quotas in all three sectors from a counterfactually created equilibrium with quotas on steel.

a change in the tariff equivalent of the quota and therefore as a change in price. Both approaches are correct on theoretical grounds; in applied work, however, our approach is the only practical choice. As an example, consider the removal of US quotas on textiles and apparel. Because the quota system has been in effect for so long, it would be very difficult to estimate the quantity effect of removing the quotas. By contrast, as we discussed in chapter 4, the price reduction that results with removal of the quotas can be reasonably estimated.

Now consider the second effect described above: the general equilibrium valuation of imported capital services. First, we consider the case of textiles and apparel. The welfare benefits of removing quotas are less with international capital mobility than without (table 6.11). This outcome is contrary to the expected impact of international capital mobility on welfare through an elasticity effect (figure 6.7). With removal of the quota, the economy imports $146 billion in capital.[16] Why does the import of capital lead to a welfare loss? Recall that the United States is assumed to pay the international rental rate on capital and that the earnings from foreign investment are repatriated. Brecher and Díaz-Alejandro (1977) have shown that capital import will reduce welfare if the marginal product of imported capital (valued at world prices, to reflect the value of the social marginal product) is less than the rental rate on the capital. Given that there are distortions in the economy, most notably in steel and autos, some capital is going to sectors that use too many resources based on world prices. Capital will be imported into these distorted sectors until, at the margin, the value of the private marginal product (based on distorted prices, which are too high) equals the rental rate on capital. Thus the social marginal product of the capital imported into autos and steel is less than the private marginal product. Since private marginal product equals the rental rate on capital, the economy's welfare is reduced because of this imported capital.[17]

So the benefits of removing quotas on textile and apparel are less with international capital mobility than without because the economy is paying more than the value of the social marginal product for the imported capital. This effect dominates the elasticity effect, which alone would lead to larger benefits with international capital mobility.

Next we consider autos and steel. In these cases the elasticity and capital flow effects reinforce each other. The capital flows are small, however, so the results of removing QRs are very close to the results without international capital mobility (table 6.11). For autos the benefits are slightly larger with international capital mobility because of the greater elasticity. Moreover, by inverse reasoning to the textile and apparel case, the export of capital is a slight benefit to the economy because some of the capital that leaves the previously protected auto sector goes abroad instead of into the still protected sectors of textiles and apparel or steel. The difference is very small, however, because the impact of international capital mobility on the supply elasticity is small. With steel we find the asymmetric effect that the cost of imposing QRs is less with international capital mobility than without, as suggested by the elasticity argument and because of the capital outflow which is a source of benefit.

Finally, we consider the effects of removing all tariffs after QRs have already been removed. Now capital imports are considerable, largely because the labor-intensive textile and apparel sector (which had the highest tariff rate) contracts more than the other sectors. Since this scenario involves moving to free trade, there are no second-best considerations regarding valuation of the imported capital. This means that the benefits are greater with international capital mobility, as predicted from elasticity considerations.

6.6 Conclusion

This chapter examined the sensitivity of the welfare and employment estimates presented in chapter 5 to factor market assumptions. In chapter 5 the economy was assumed to be in the simplest neoclassical equilibrium, except for distortions in foreign trade due to tariffs and QRs. In this chapter we considered alternative factor market assumptions to allow for an endogenous labor supply, wage distortions (exogenous and endogenous) in autos and steel, sectoral specificity of capital, and international capital mobility. The general conclusions of chapter 5 about the welfare effects of QRs in textiles and apparel, autos, and steel are maintained, although their magnitudes are different.

Introducing labor-leisure choice reduces only very slightly the welfare estimates of chapter 5. The results suggest that removing QRs in the three sectors would reduce employment by 20,000 to 40,000 jobs, mainly because of higher incomes following removal of QRs.

In examining the impact of wage distortions in autos and steel, we found that if wage distortions are exogenous, the welfare gains of eliminating QRs in these sectors are attenuated slightly by increased labor misallocation. However, this effect is extremely small, so QR removal results in strong welfare gains even in the presence of exogenous wage distortions.

When we considered the more realistic case of endogenous wage distortions in autos and steel by incorporating union behavior, we found that the removal of QRs on autos lowered the wage distortion and that the imposition of QRs on steel increased the wage distortion. Because wage distortions increase with the imposition of QRs, the welfare cost of imposing QRs on steel could rise by as much as 15 percent and the jobs saved in the sector could drop by as much as one-quarter when there is union activity and when unions value wages more than employment. Thus, once we incorporate endogenous wage distortions, there is no presumption that wage distortions reduce the costs of protection.

When we assumed sectoral specificity of capital—a short-run assumption—our estimates of the welfare benefits of removing quotas increased, but not by much. Introducing international capital mobility significantly raised the welfare benefits of removing the remaining *tariff* protection after QRs had been removed. International capital mobility was found to reduce the benefit of removing QRs in textiles and apparel by increasing capital inflows whose marginal social product is lower than the rental rate on capital.

Appendix 6A: The Welfare Measure and Labor-Leisure Trade-off

6A.1 The Extended Stone-Geary Utility Function

Equation 6.2 was derived from an extended Stone-Geary utility function (equation 6.1). Let P_i denote the price of the respective final consumption products, $i = 1$ through n, and let

$$COMIT = \sum_{j=1}^{n} \lambda_j P_j = \mu.$$

We define the extended top-level Stone-Geary utility function of the worker-consumer as

$$U(C_0, C_1, \ldots, C_m) = \prod_{i=0}^{n} (C_i - \lambda_i)^{\beta_i} \qquad (6A.1)$$

subject to $1 > \beta_i > 0$ and $(C_i - \lambda_i) > 0$ for $i = 0, 1, \ldots, n$, where C_0 is leisure and $\sum_{i=0}^{n} \beta_i = 1$. The worker-consumer earns the wage rate WG for every hour worked, allocating total time between labor supply and leisure. The commodities C_i, $i = 1, \ldots, n$, remain CES aggregates of the imported and domestic variety of the products in the sector.

6A.2 Labor Supply and Leisure Demand

The worker-consumer maximizes the utility function of equation 6A.1 subject to $\sum_{i=0}^{n} P_i C_i = X$, where X is full income and is defined as nonlabor income Y_{NL}, plus the inputed value of time $X = Y_{NL} + WG \times T$, where T is total time available (see Deaton and Muellbauer 1980; Abbott and Ashenfelter 1976). Abbot and Ashenfelter (1976) have shown that the demand functions for all goods (including leisure) in the extended LES satisfy the standard LES form:

$$C_i = \lambda_i + \left(\frac{\beta_i}{P_i}\right)\left(X - \sum_{j=0}^{n} P_j \lambda_j\right), \qquad j = 0, \ldots, n, \tag{6A.2}$$

where we have written the wage rate WG as P_0 to simplify notation.

Since labor supply LS satisfies $LS + C_0 = T$, we substitute for C_0 in equation 6A.2 and rearrange to obtain the following:

$$LS = \overline{\text{MAXHOURS}} - \left(\frac{\beta_0}{WG}\right)\left(X - \sum_{j=0}^{n} P_j \lambda_j\right), \tag{6A.3}$$

where $\overline{\text{MAXHOURS}} = T - \lambda_0$. Since time is spent either working or in leisure, we have

$$X = Y + WG \times C_0. \tag{6A.4}$$

Substituting for X from equation 6A.4 into equation 6A.2 with $i = 0$ and rearranging the equation, we get

$$C_0 - \lambda_0 = \left(\frac{\beta_0}{WG}\right)\left(\frac{(Y - \sum_{j=1}^{n} P_j \lambda_j)}{1 - \beta_0}\right). \tag{6A.5}$$

Subtracting $WG \times \lambda_0 + \sum_{j=1}^{n} P_j \lambda_j$ from both sides of equation 6A.4 and substituting the right side of equation 6A.5 for $C_0 - \lambda_0$, we obtain, after rearranging the equation,

$$X - \sum_{j=1}^{n} P_j \lambda_j - WG \times \lambda_0 = \frac{Y - \sum_{j=1}^{n} P_j \lambda_j}{1 - \beta_0}. \tag{6A.6}$$

Substituting the right side of equation 6A.6 for the left side of equation 6A.6 in equation 6A.3, gives equation 6.2, the labor supply function. A similar substitution into equation 6A.2 yields the commodity demand functions (20′) of section 6.1. Equation 6A.6 shows that when the worker-consumer optimally allocates full income between leisure and commodities, there is a relationship between full income and money income. We make repeated use of equations 6A.5 and 6A.6. Then the labor supply function derived from an extended Stone-Geary utility function, the commodity demand functions, and the Hicksian equivalent and compensating variations discussed below may be written without having to make an arbitrary assumption regarding the time available to the worker-consumer.[18]

Had we assumed that the total work force (or time) available is some scalar multiple of the initial work force (or time), we would have stopped at equation 6A.3, which is dependent on λ_0 and hence total time available. Ballard et al. (1985) have chosen this approach. The problem, however, as they note (p. 135), is that their results depend heavily on the assumed value of the scalar multiple, a parameter about which little is known. Thus our approach eliminates an element of arbitrariness.

6A.3 Welfare Analysis with a Labor-Leisure Trade-off

In this section we proceed analogously to our approach in appendix 3A. We seek expressions for the Hicksian equivalent and compensating variations in terms of "full income." Consequently we first derive the indirect utility function and the expenditure function.

To obtain the indirect utility function, we must substitute the optimum values of C_i, $i = 0, 1, \ldots, n$, into equation 6A.1. As we discussed in appendix 3A, our measure of welfare can ignore explicit inclusion of CD_i and CM_i of the components of C_i, $i = 1, \ldots, n$ due to two-stage maximization.

Substitute equation 6A.2 into equation 6A.1 and simplify to obtain the indirect utility function IU:

$$IU = \prod_{i=0}^{n} \left(\frac{\beta_i}{P_i}\right)^{\beta_i} \left(X - \sum_{j=0}^{n} P_j\lambda_j\right). \tag{6A.7}$$

Use equation 6A.6 to obtain

$$IU = \prod_{i=0}^{n} \left(\frac{\beta_i}{P_i}\right)^{\beta_i} \left(\frac{[Y - \sum_{j=1}^{n} P_j\lambda_j]}{1 - \beta_0}\right). \tag{6A.8}$$

Solve equation 6A.7 for X to obtain the expenditure function:

$$E[P, IU] = \prod_{i=0}^{n} \left(\frac{P_i}{\beta_i}\right)^{\beta_i} \times IU + \sum_{j=0}^{n} P_j\lambda_j. \tag{6A.9}$$

Define

$$EV = E[P^0, IU(P^1, X^1)] - X^0 \tag{6A.10}$$

and

$$CV = X^1 - E[P^1, IU(P^0, X^0)] \tag{6A.11}$$

as the Hicksian equivalent and compensating variation measures, respectively.

Use equations 6A.8 and 6A.6 to obtain

$$EV = \left(\frac{1}{1-\beta_0}\right)\left[\left(Y^1 - \sum_{j=1}^{n} P_j^1\lambda_j\right)\prod_{i=0}^{n}\left(\frac{P_i^0}{P_i^1}\right)^{\beta_i} - \left(Y^0 - \sum_{j=1}^{n} P_j^0\lambda_j\right)\right] \tag{6A.12}$$

and

$$CV = \left(\frac{1}{1-\beta_0}\right)\left[\left(Y^1 - \sum_{j=1}^{n} P_j^1\lambda_j\right) - \left(Y^0 - \sum_{j=1}^{n} P_j^0\lambda_j\right)\prod_{i=0}^{n}\left(\frac{P_i^1}{P_i^0}\right)^{\beta_i}\right]. \tag{6A.13}$$

Note that we have obtained expressions for EV and CV in equations 6A.12 and 6A.13 that do not involve λ_0 or T.

Appendix 6B: Derivation of Labor Union Wage Differential

We omit sector subscripts. As explained in the text, the union maximizes

$$U = \bar{A}(W\phi - \overline{W}_0)^{\gamma}(L - \bar{L}_0)^{\delta}, \qquad \bar{A},\ \gamma,\ \delta > 0, \tag{6B.1}$$

taking labor demand as given. From Shephard's lemma the firm's labor demand is given by

$$L^d = \left(\frac{X}{\overline{\overline{AX}}}\right)^{1-\sigma}\left(\alpha \times \frac{PVC}{W\phi}\right)^{\sigma}. \tag{6B.2}$$

Substitute for L from equation 6B.2 into equation 6B.1. Then maximizing U by setting $dU/d\phi = 0$ gives, after some manipulation,

$$\gamma W(L^d - \bar{L}_0) = \delta\sigma(W\phi - \overline{W}_0)L^d\left(\frac{1}{\phi}\right). \tag{6B.3}$$

Since the union need not accept a wage lower than the competitive wage W, we set the minimum acceptable wage $\overline{W}_0$:

$$\overline{W}_0 = W. \tag{6B.4}$$

Then equation 6B.3 reduces to equation 6.8 of the text.

We calibrate $\overline{L}_0$ to be consistent with the initial data, ensuring an equilibrium (see appendix A for further details on calibration) so that

$$\overline{L}_0 = L_0^d \left(1 - \left(\frac{\delta}{\gamma} \right) \sigma \frac{\phi - 1}{\phi} \right), \tag{6B.5}$$

where L_0^d is initial employment.

7 Welfare Costs of Quantitative Restrictions with Imperfect Competition in Automobiles and Steel

In this chapter we introduce economies of scale into our estimates of the welfare costs of quantitative restrictions (QRs). This complicates our assessment of the welfare costs of QRs in several ways. To begin with, the measurement of economies of scale is itself difficult. For example, is it correct to consider low average plant output levels in a year of weak demand as a departure from minimum efficient scale when it could be due to excess capacity caused by cyclical fluctuations? Another problem is which pricing rule to apply with increasing returns to scale. We incorporate several alternatives into the model, each representative of a different interpretation of industry structure. We report the available evidence on how representative each pricing rule is of industry behavior in autos and steel, but the evidence cannot be considered conclusive.

Faced with these difficulties, we proceed cautiously. For an economy like the United States, with a large internal domestic market, the scope for unexploited economies of scale is relatively limited. In section 7.1 we provide evidence, however, suggesting that economies of scale may not be fully exploited in autos and steel and that the US auto industry made abnormally high profits in 1984. Since QRs were in effect that year, we explore numerically the implications of an endogenous market structure in the US auto industry and consider the possibility that the abnormally high profits were the result of the voluntary export restraint (VER) on Japanese autos. However, since the evidence on economies of scale and market structure is not as firmly grounded as the evidence on which the rest of our modeling assumptions rest—including those in chapter 6—we view the results in this chapter as more tentative than the others.

The chapter is organized as follows: Section 7.1 presents evidence on economies of scale and pricing rules in the steel and auto industries. Section 7.2 introduces the modifications to the basic model needed to accommodate imperfect competition. Welfare cost estimates with the modified model are presented in section 7.3.

7.1 Evidence on Economies of Scale and Pricing Rules in Steel and Automobiles

Our modeling of economies of scale (section 7.2) requires an estimate of the cost disadvantage ratio (*CDR*). Under constant marginal costs the *CDR* is related to the scale efficiency parameter (*S*), where $S = AC/MC$ (*AC* is average cost and *MC* is marginal cost) by $CDR = 1 - (1/S)$. Thus for a single product case, there are locally increasing returns to scale if *S* is greater than unity (i.e., if the value of *CDR* is positive) and decreasing returns to scale if *S* is less than unity and *CDR* is negative.

7.1.1 Steel Industry

Economies of Scale

Estimates of economies of scale for steel have been based on detailed engineering studies and on the costs of operating many plants throughout the world. These estimates have revealed that virtually all the advantages of large-scale operation can be achieved at a substantially lower level of operation—the minimum efficient scale (*MES*)—than that at which the larger Japanese plants can operate (about 15 million tons a year). For an integrated facility Barnett and Schorsch (1982) estimate that *MES* operation can be achieved at 4 million tons a year, and Tarr (1984) estimates a level of 6 million tons a year. For the range of products that can be produced by a "minimill" (approximately 25 percent of US output), *MES* operation can be achieved at about 0.5 to 0.75 million tons a year. In 1980 the average integrated plant in the United States had a capacity of 4 million tons a year (Barnett and Schorsch, p. 197), and minimills generally operated in the MES range. Based on the Barnett and Schorsch estimates, the *CDR* for US steel plants would be zero, implying that there were no economies of scale and that the results of chapter 5 hold. Applying the methodology discussed in appendix A to Tarr's estimates, however, suggests a *CDR* of 0.04, which we use in this chapter as the estimate for unexploited economies of scale in the steel industry.[1]

Pricing

Evidence suggests that pricing practices in the US steel industry changed after 1960, with higher than competitive pricing before 1960 and more closely competitive pricing after 1960. Stigler (1968) has argued that US steel pricing before 1960 was characterized by dominant firm pricing, and Parsons and Ray (1975) found dominant cartel pricing.[2] That steel pricing in the United States became much more competitive after 1960 has been documented by the Federal Trade Commission (FTC Staff Report 1977, ch. 4). Econometric estimates of Rippe (1970) and Mancke (1968) also indicate a change in the steel price-setting mechanism after 1960.[3] Further recent econometric evidence from Harrison (1988), based on estimates of the pass-through effect of exchange rate changes on the US steel industry, also points toward competitive pricing in the US steel industry.

Three factors, in particular, contributed to more competitive steel pricing after 1960. First, the United States became a net importer of steel in 1959 (imports rose from 1.2 percent of apparent steel consumption in 1955 to 17.1 percent in 1971 and to over 25 percent in 1984). Second, US Steel Corporation's market share fell from 65.4 percent in 1902 to 25.7 percent in 1961 and to 22.1 percent in 1976. After 1960 US Steel could no longer price like a dominant firm and instead joined the "chiselers" in offering discounts. And third, minimills emerged as a significant competitive force in the steel industry, increasing their share of US production from about 3 percent in 1960 to about 20 percent in 1984 (Congressional Budget Office 1984, 3). These relatively small and efficient producers generally regard their output and pricing decisions as too small to affect industrywide prices, but collectively they are important. In addition the steel industry has been in a precarious position since 1974. Earnings fell from profits of $2.5 billion in 1974 to losses of $3.4 billion in 1982 and $0.2 billion in 1984 (*Annual Statistical Report* of the American Iron and Steel Institute 1984). These losses have been associated with significant capacity reductions (*Steel Industry Quarterly*, April 1988), suggesting that these recorded losses are indeed economic losses.

Based on the evidence presented here, we conclude that pricing practices in the US steel industry are best characterized as competitive or contestable. However, for the sake of illustration, we also calculate welfare effects based on the assumption of Chamberlinian monopolistic competition, since in the long run, the Chamberlinian model does not allow profits.

7.1.2 Automobile Industry

Economies of Scale

Unlike the case for steel, the evidence for economies of scale in autos is based on econometric rather than engineering estimates. Thus the estimates of economies of scale for steel and autos are not strictly comparable.

Friedlaender, Winston, and Wang (1984) note that the auto industry is characterized by long planning horizons and extremely large fixed costs associated with the introduction of new car designs. In addition they note that the same dies are used to produce parts for a wide range of models and that some parts and even major components are similarly interchangeable. This means that there are economies related to the scale of operation or to the composition of output at the *firm* level, and it is appropriate therefore to estimate the cost function at the firm rather than the plant level.

Using the measure developed by Panzar and Willig (1977), Winston and Associates (1987) estimate the degree of multiproduct scale economies at the output level achieved by General Motors, Ford, and Chrysler for each year from 1958 to 1983. In the single product case this measure, $SM = C(Y)/[\sum Y_i \times (dC/dY_i)]$ (where C is the cost function, Y_i is the output of the ith product, and Y is the vector of the Y_i), reduces to the measure introduced above, namely, $S = AC/MC$.

For the sample period as a whole, Winston and Associates estimate that $S = 1.03$. For 1982 or 1983 alone, they estimate that $S = 1.12$. That is, firmwide economies of scale, averaged over the industry and the entire sample period, were increasing, but they were increasing more strongly in 1982 and 1983, the last years for which they estimate. Expressed in terms of the cost disadvantage ratio, the estimate is 0.029 for the whole sample period and 0.107 in 1982 and 1983. Since 1984 is our benchmark year, we take as our estimate of economies of scale in autos the *CDR* estimates of 0.107 for 1982 and 1983 rather than an average taken over the period going back to 1958.

Pricing

The most striking aspect of the US auto industry in our benchmark year of 1984 is that it earned record profits of $10.4 billion. This was almost double the profits of the previous year and followed four years of losses (see table 7.1). We assume that approximately $1 billion of these profits were normal profits, so that $9.4 billion were pure profits, which is close to the econometric estimates of Winston and Associates.[4]

The natural question to ask is whether these profits were linked to the VER on Japanese auto exports to the United States. In the absence of further information, we consider a range of pricing rules and profit assumptions. In our preferred simulations, however, we assume that the auto industry was pricing above average costs in 1984 by a margin sufficient to capture $9.4 billion in pure profits. Since revenue was $124.2 billion in 1984, this implies a profit rate of 8.0 percent.

Theory tells us that a quota can act as a facilitating practice in the pricing practices of the US auto industry (Krishna 1985). Without a quota, firms

Table 7.1
Profits in the US automobile industry, 1979–84 (billions of dollars)

Year	Profits
1979	−0.4
1980	−4.7
1981	−2.3
1982	−0.6
1983	5.3
1984	10.4

Source: US International Trade Commission (1985, 13).

may not be able to collude or may regard their market power as inconsequential and so price close to marginal costs. In the presence of a quota, however, especially when firms are few, they need only concern themselves with their domestic competitors because foreign competitors will not be able to increase their shipments in response to higher prices. With import competition choked off, domestic firms may perceive that their pricing and output decisions have a greater influence on domestic competitors. As a result their pricing and output decisions may become less competitive. In this way a quota may increase the degree of collusion or monopolylike pricing practices.

Support for this view is found in the empirical literature that tests the import discipline hypothesis. Studies by Marvel (1980), De Rosa and Goldstein (1981), Pugel (1978), and Domowitz, Hubbard, and Petersen (1986) have found that import competition has restrained price-cost margins in the United States.[5] Thus the VER on Japanese autos may have allowed US firms to earn above normal profits.

We model endogenous market structure with two pricing rules. In one alternative we assume that removing the VER forces contestable markets. That is, because of the greater threat of entry without VERs, pricing reverts to contestable market pricing, eliminating profits. Under this scenario there is no firm entry. The other alternative is to consider a monopolistic competition model. The quota generates profits in the short run. However, market entry (which is possible only by building domestic plants in response to the profits generated by the VER) continues until the profits are eliminated in the long run. Thus the profits generated by the VER are not sustainable in the long run.

In the monopolistic competition model one must assess the competitiveness of firms. Dixit (1988), who estimated the extent of collusion or noncompetitive pricing in autos for 1979, 1980, and 1983, concluded that pricing was most competitive in 1980 and least competitive in 1979. If domestic firms are counted by corporation rather than by division, Dixit's results indicate that pricing is more competitive than Cournot in all three years examined. Krishna, Hogan, and Swagel (1989) also found an increase in competition among US companies between 1979 and 1980. Unlike Dixit, however, they found less collusive pricing in both 1979 and 1980 than in 1984. For all years, however, they found domestic auto pricing more competitive than Cournot (or even than Bertrand).[6]

Both contestable markets and monopolistic competition in the long run result in prices equal to average costs because of the threat of entry or actual entry, respectively. In assessing which structure seems to be most representative of the US auto industry, we note that there was a dramatic surge in foreign direct investment in the US auto industry in the mid-1980s (see appendix B). Six Japanese firms established auto assembly facilities in the United States between 1984 and 1987, followed by investments in parts plants. (The decision to invest in the United States was probably influenced by the VER or the fear of its reintroduction.) In addition there has been substantial exit from the US auto industry over the long run (e.g., the firms producing Studebaker, Hudson, and Packard autos).

We therefore conclude that the US auto industry is better represented by a monopolistic competition model with free entry and exit than by a contestable-market model with pricing that deters entry. We also see a need for a formulation that allows international capital mobility through foreign direct investment. Since entry is reasonable only in response to pure profits, the most plausible assumption is that foreign investment occurred to eliminate the substantial pure profits that existed in the US auto industry in 1984, the last full year of the VER. For this reason we consider a closure with international capital mobility to eliminate profits in the auto industry. The formulation is the same as that presented in section 6.5.

7.2 Modifications to the Basic Model to Accommodate Imperfect Competition

We discuss first how we model decreasing costs, then how we deal with pricing. Since we no longer assume constant returns to scale in autos and steel, the number of firms in those industries now matters. We make two assumptions with respect to firm entry: (1) no entry in the short run, so that the number of firms in sector i (N_i) is fixed, and (2) free entry and exit in the long run, as firms enter when the industry makes profits and exit when it has losses. Although the number of firms in fact is an integer variable, for computational reasons we model N_i as a continuous variable. This is obviously a less damaging departure from reality for the steel industry, which has many firms, than for the auto industry, which is dominated by three car producers (Ford, General Motors, and Chrysler). But even for the auto industry, one could argue that the assumption of continuity is not damaging since there are several foreign-owned assembly plants. Alternatively, in the short run, in view of the large share of fixed costs in total costs in the auto industry and the small number of firms, the assumption of no entry/exit may be viewed as the more relevant assumption about firm mobility.

In autos and steel, sectoral output XD_i is assumed to be produced by N_i identical firms so that $XD_i = N_i xd_i$, where xd_i is firm output.

We define total costs TC_i and average costs AC_i as[7]

$$TC_i = FC_i + CV_i, \quad AC_i = \frac{TC_i}{XD_i}, \tag{7.1}$$

where CV_i, variable costs, is defined by equation 1 of table 3.1. Note that the variable cost component of equation 7.1 is subject to constant returns to scale so that marginal costs are constant and equal to average variable costs (CV_i/XD_i). Fixed costs are defined by

$$FC_i = \left(\frac{N_i}{\bar{N}_i}\right) \times (\overline{KF}_i \times R + \overline{LF}_i \times W), \tag{7.2}$$

where $\overline{KF}_i$ is the firm's fixed capital costs, $\overline{LF}_i$ is the firm's fixed labor costs, and $\bar{N}_i$ is the initial number of firms.[8] Since our results are quite insensitive to the assumed distribution of fixed costs between labor and capital, we weigh these two components of fixed costs equally.[9]

With increasing returns to scale, we are forced to abandon the hypothesis of perfectly competitive marginal cost pricing. As is evident from the cost function measure of scale economies, increasing returns implies that marginal cost is less than average cost ($CV_i/XD_i < AC_i$) so that marginal cost pricing ($PX_i = CV_i/XD_i$) leads to unprofitable firms. There are a number of ways to replace the marginal cost pricing rule. One is to specify a pricing rule-of-thumb, as do Harris (1984) and Cox and Harris (1985) who assume, among their alternatives, that domestic firms price to match imported competition (sometimes referred to as the Eastman-Stykolt [1960] hypothesis) or to achieve a "normal" markup over marginal cost. While at first glance this approach is intuitively appealing, the selection of the markup is arbitrary. We prefer a profit-maximizing approach, even though it raises further issues.

To begin with, we must decide how much product differentiation to accommodate in the model. One approach would be to assume that the number of product varieties is a function of trade policy, perhaps combined with a constant elasticity of substitution across all varieties (as in Spence 1976 and Dixit and Stiglitz 1977). Applied trade models incorporating product variety yield estimates of the benefits of trade liberalization that are somewhat larger than otherwise because of the greater variety of products available to consumers through increased trade.[10] More simply we assume that the products are differentiated by home or import variety; the products of all firms within a sector are otherwise perfect substitutes. Therefore our results are likely to underestimate the benefits of trade liberalization because we have not incorporated the benefits of additional variety that would occur with trade liberalization.

Another basic issue raised by imperfect competition concerns how other firms will price their output. We consider two pricing hypotheses that differ with respect to pricing for domestic markets but not for export markets, where firms are assumed to price competitively. In world markets US exports face close substitutes and therefore stiff competition, so this assumption is plausible; in any case it is of little consequence since auto and steel exports do not exceed 5 percent of total sales.

The first domestic pricing hypothesis we consider is the contestable market assumption. This case is the analogue to perfect competition for the case of increasing returns to scale. It is based on the assumption of low-cost entry and exit so that the threat of entry forces firms to price at average costs. In this contestable market scenario, equation 32 of our model (from table 3.1) is replaced by

$$PX_i = AC_i. \tag{7.3}$$

This pricing rule represents only a small departure from the competitive pricing rule since price also equals average cost in the long-run equilibrium of the competitive model.

The second case we consider assumes that each firm behaves in the domestic market as an oligopolist facing a downward sloping demand curve. Analogously to Cournot, we assume that firms adjust output to maximize profits, with price as the equilibrating variable.[11] In this process firms assess the reactions of their competitors to their output decision.[12] We rely on the conjectural variation approach of Frisch (1933), since the various oligopoly reaction assumptions can be subsumed as special cases.

Dropping sectoral subscripts, and omitting exports for simplicity, we denote by $Q = N_i Q_i$ the homogeneous output produced for the domestic market by the N_i identical firms. The market elasticity of demand is defined as $\varepsilon^d \equiv -(dQ/dPD)(PD/Q)$. When the ith firm changes its output, its conjecture with respect to the change in industry output is represented by $\Omega_i \equiv dQ/dQ_i$. The assumption of common conjectures allows us to write $\Omega = \Omega_i$, for all i.

Each firm maximizes profits, which are given by

$$\Pi_i = PD(Q)Q_i - TC_i. \tag{7.4}$$

The first-order condition for profit maximization for firm i yields

$$\frac{d\Pi_i}{dQ_i} = PD(Q) + Q_i \frac{dPD}{dQ}\frac{dQ}{dQ_i} - \frac{dTC_i}{dQ_i} = 0. \tag{7.5}$$

Substituting the definitions presented above and noting that marginal costs are given by $CV_i/Q_i = dTC_i/dQ_i$, expression 7.5 can be rewritten as[13]

$$PD = \frac{CV}{Q} + \frac{Q}{N}\frac{1}{\varepsilon^d}\frac{PD}{Q}\Omega, \tag{7.6}$$

which can be rewritten as

$$\frac{PD_i - C_i'}{PD_i} = \frac{\Omega_i}{N_i \varepsilon_i^d}, \tag{7.7}$$

where the i subscript again denotes the sector and $C_i' = CV_i/XD_i =$ marginal costs.

Expression 7.7 shows that the percentage markup of price over marginal costs decreases with the number of firms and the elasticity of demand. With $\Omega_i = 1$, we have Cournot conjectures, that is, the firm believes that the other firms will not change their output decisions, so a one-unit change in its output will lead to a one-unit change in industry output. With $\Omega_i = 0$, we have competitive behavior, that is, the firm believes that a change in its output decision will not change industry output, so price equals marginal costs. With $\Omega_i = N_i$ we have the monopoly, or perfectly collusive, solution where the markup equals the inverse of the market elasticity of demand.

An additional issue is how conjectures may change as a result of firm entry. Intuitively one might argue that as the number of firms increases, in the limit the industry becomes competitive and conjectures should approach competitive behavior.[14] Since price equals marginal costs in a competitive industry, Ω_i must equal zero as the number of firms increases without limit. Thus, when we conduct policy experiments, we simulate the effect on conjectures of the additional competition from firm entry by assuming that

$$\Omega_i = \frac{\Omega_i^0}{N_i/\overline{N}_i}, \tag{7.8}$$

where the Ω_i^0 terms are the conjectures of firms in the industry in the initial equilibrium. With this hypothesis conjectures become more competitive as firms enter and, in the limit, approach competitive conjectures. We refer to simulations with this hypothesis as "endogenous conjectures."

The market elasticity of demand in each sector is a share-weighted sum of elasticities of demand for final sales (ε_i^F) and for intermediate sales (ε_i^v):

$$\varepsilon_i^d = \varepsilon_i^F S_i^F + \varepsilon_i^v S_i^v, \tag{7.9}$$

where $S_i^F = CD_i/D_i$ and $S_i^v = VTD_i/D_i$ are the quantity-weighted shares of final and intermediate demand, respectively, in sector i. (The derivation of the elasticity of demand is given in appendix 7A, and the full expression in terms of underlying parameters of the model is given in equation 7A.22.)

The introduction of pure profits also requires a change in the equation defining income (equation 31 in table 3.1), which is now replaced by

$$Y = W\overline{LS} + R\overline{KS} + GR + \sum_{k \in T} (1 - \theta_k)(\text{RENT}C_k + \text{RENT}I_k) - \overline{B}ER + \sum_{i \in N} PROF_i XD_i, \tag{7.10}$$

where $PROF_i$ is profit per unit of output. The factor constraints (equation 4 in table 3.1) are also replaced by

$$\left(\sum_i L_i^d + N_i\overline{KL}_i\right) = \overline{LS}, \quad \left(\sum_i K_i^d + N_i\overline{KF}_i\right) = \overline{KS}. \tag{7.11}$$

In the scenarios that allow for firm entry and exit, long-run equilibrium is reached when firm entry drives profits to zero, satisfying the following additional equation:

$$PROF_i = 0. \tag{7.12}$$

This completes the changes brought to the basic model of chapter 3.

With imperfect competition and scale economies, model calibration must be decomposed into two parts: (1) How much do average costs depart from marginal costs (due to scale economies), and (2) what is the markup of price over average costs (due to imperfect competition)? (Model calibration is described in detail in appendix A.) Independent of initial profits in autos, fixed costs are determined from total costs and the exogenously estimated cost disadvantage ratio, discussed in section 7.1 and appendix A. To incorporate fixed costs while replicating observed prices and quantities in the constant-returns-to-scale case, the primary variable cost component of total costs (see equation 1 in table 3.1) is reduced by the amount of fixed costs (using equation 7.1).

With respect to pricing in relation to average costs, we first consider the case of no initial profits. One possibility is to assume contestable pricing (equation 7.3), in which case no further modifications are necessary and the calibration is complete. Alternatively, we can assume that oligopolists play an output game that leads to the pricing rule in equation 7.7, where marginal costs have already been determined. In this case we solve the equation for the value of Ω_i such that profits are zero in the initial equilibrium. A fully equivalent approach is to read in Cournot conjectures, $\Omega_i = 1$, and solve for N_i, the Cournot equivalent number of firms. We believe that data on the elasticity of demand and on price-cost margins are better than data on conjectures, so we prefer to calibrate conjectures rather than to adjust elasticities or marginal costs to an assumed value of conjectures.[15] We refer to simulations where the conjecture Ω_i is calibrated and fixed in this manner as "monopolistic competition." It should be clear, however, that this situation is not "Chamberlinian" monopolistic competition, which requires Cournot conjectures (i.e., $\Omega_i = 1$). Note also that the elasticity of demand ε_i^d is endogenous because the shares of domestic and foreign goods in total demand are themselves endogenous since they change in response to changes in trade policy.

Next we consider the case of initial profits in autos. Again the first step is to allocate fixed costs out of initial primary variable costs. In a second step, given the profit rate per unit of domestic sales and the quantities and foreign prices (expressed in domestic currency units), we solve for the prices that satisfy the firm's budget constraint.[16] This calibration is indicated in figure 7.1, which compares an initial equilibrium in autos without initial profits ($PD_0 = 1$) and one with initial profits of \$9.4 billion ($PD_0 = 1.08$). As figure 7.1 suggests, the calibration of Ω_i is obtained, as before, from equation 7.7, but with the newly calculated set of domestic prices.

The calibration steps described above result in the following initial values for the elasticity of demand (ε_i^d) and conjecture (Ω_i): for steel, $\varepsilon_s^d = 2.34$ and $\Omega_s = 0.63$, and for autos, $\varepsilon_a^d = 1.37$ and $\Omega_a = 0.72$.[17] These calculations are based on the assumption that there are three auto firms and seven steel firms.[18] Thus both industries are acting more competitively

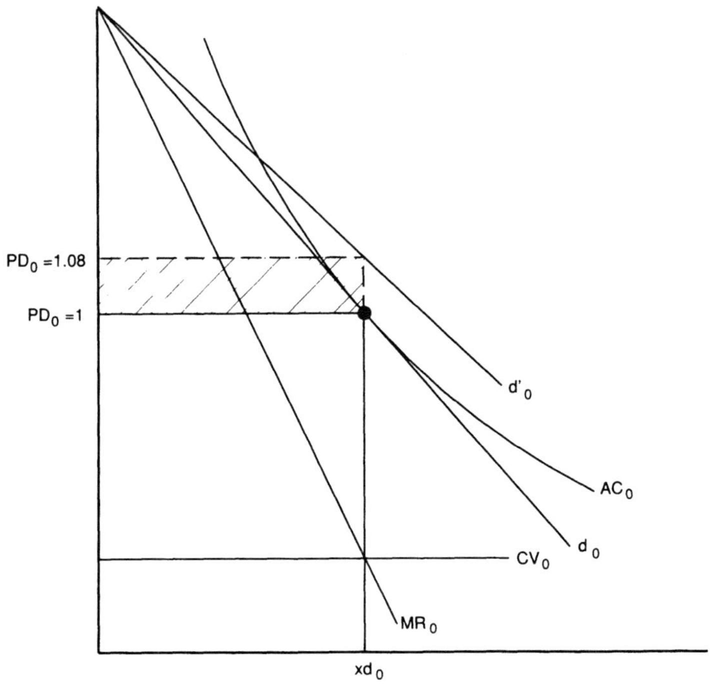

Figure 7.1
Calibration with initial profits in automobiles

than Cournot. It is perhaps more instructive to follow Dixit (1988) and calculate the Cournot equivalent number of firms: That is, if $\Omega_i = 1$, what value of N_i is required to satisfy equation 7.7? The higher the number, the more competitive is the industry. For autos the number is 4.17, and for steel it is 11.1. Since Dixit calibrated 13.85 as the Cournot equivalent number of auto firms in 1983, we find the auto industry is considerably less competitive in 1984. In view of the profit data shown in table 7.1, this should not be surprising. Steel is seen to be the more competitive of the two industries, which is consistent with the discussion presented in section 7.1.

7.3 Welfare Costs of Quantitative Restrictions with Imperfect Competition

Before comparing the results with the modifications introduced in section 7.2 with the results in chapter 5, it is instructive to recall how the departure from marginal cost pricing implied by increasing returns to scale modifies the standard costs of protection. Following Rodrik (1988), we simplify the discussion and assume that domestic and foreign goods are perfect substitutes, where P_i represents the price in the domestic market. The supply side is represented by the unit average cost function in each sector, $AC_i(w, XD_i)$, where w is the vector of factor prices; average costs are written as a function of output XD_i to allow for increasing returns to scale. The demand side is represented by a single consumer with expenditure function $E\ (P_1, \ldots P_n, W)$, where W is a welfare index. The initial equilibrium of the economy can be represented using the equality between national income and expenditure. National income is usefully decomposed into factor income, "pure" profits, and quota rents or tariff revenues. Therefore the income-expenditure equality can be represented as

$$E(\cdot) = W(\overline{LS}) + R\overline{KS} + \sum_i (P_i - AC_i)XD_i + \sum_i (P_i - P_i^*)M_i, \qquad (7.13)$$

where M_i is imports of sector i and P_i^* is the world price of good i.[19]

To consider the effects of a trade reform, we totally differentiate both sides of the income-expenditure equality and evaluate at the initial equilibrium. After some algebraic manipulation in which we invoke Shephard's lemma, we have

$$E_W dW = \sum_i (P_i - P_i^*)dM_i + \sum_i (P_i - AC_i)dXD_i$$

$$+ \sum_i N_i AC_i\left(1 - \frac{MC_i}{AC_i}\right)dXD_i, \qquad (7.14)$$

where N_i is the number of symmetric firms in an industry i with increasing returns to scale.

Expression 7.14 decomposes the welfare change into three effects. The first term states the familiar effect that imports should be expanded whenever the domestic price exceeds the world price. The second term states that domestic output should be expanded whenever domestic price exceeds average costs. This is the familiar proposition that output should be expanded when it is restricted because of monopoly pricing. Finally, since AC > MC whenever there are increasing returns to scale, the third term states that for a fixed number of firms, production should be expanded whenever there are unexploited economies of scale. Thus expression 7.14 highlights policy trade-offs from trade liberalization in the presence of imperfect competition and scale economies. Trade liberalization will result in benefits through the effect of the first term but may result in losses from the other two.

When we use the monopolistic competition pricing rule (equation 7.7), two other effects also influence the welfare effects of trade policy changes. If quotas are binding, their elimination tends to raise the elasticity of demand facing domestic firms because imports can substitute for domestic output in response to a domestic price increase. The more elastic the demand curve for sales on the domestic market, the closer to marginal cost is the pricing for domestic sales.[20] The second effect comes from the introduction of endogenous conjectures, which makes firm entry equivalent to an increase in the elasticity of demand. Firm entry would shift inward the demand curve facing the representative firm. With endogenous conjectures, $\Omega_i = \Omega_i^0 | (N_i/\bar{N}_i)$, so firms act less collusively than under exogenous conjectures if there is firm entry.

The implication of this discussion of how departures from marginal cost pricing affect the standard costs of protection is that we should expect results different from those obtained under constant returns. To help identify the source of changes, we report the welfare results in three sets of experiments: one incorporating imperfect competition and imposition of quotas in the steel sector only, one incorporating imperfect competition and removal of quotas in autos only, and one incorporating imperfect competition in both autos and steel and the joint removal of quotas.

For the case of steel, table 7.2 contrasts the results with three pricing rules under increasing returns with the results for constant returns presented in chapter 5. The welfare costs of rationing steel are less under all three pricing rules than under constant returns with marginal cost pricing because of the dominating effect of the reduction in unit costs from expanding output when there are increasing returns. Not surprisingly, the least costly of the three pricing rules is contestable market pricing because there is no firm entry to increase average costs and no monopolistic price increases.

Under our version of monopolistic competition, protection gives rise to some profits in the absence of firm entry. In turn, profits raise the cost of protection (the second term in equation 7.14) relative to the costs with contestable markets. Firm entry to eliminate the small profit rate (0.2 percent) further increases the welfare cost of the VER because firms are less able to exploit economies of scale. This effect dominates the effect of the elimination of monopoly profits, increasing the costs of protection.

In the aggregate the estimates of the welfare cost of rationing steel are little affected by the introduction of imperfect competition. This is so for

Table 7.2
Welfare costs of quotas on steel under different pricing rules: central elasticity case (billions of 1984 US dollars)

Item	CRTS[a] (1)	Contestable markets (2)	Monopolistic competition: Short-run (no entry/exit) (3)	Monopolistic competition: Long-run (entry/exit) (4)
Welfare costs[b]	0.86	0.75	0.78	0.82
Rent costs	0.74	0.72	0.74	0.73
Distortion costs	0.12	0.03	0.04	0.09
Fixed costs		2.30	2.30	2.35
Profit rate[c] (%)			0.02	
Number of firms[d] (ratio to base)				1.02

a. CRTS is constant returns to scale. Results are from table 5.5 in chapter 5.
b. Welfare is the equivalent variation measure defined in appendix 3A in chapter 3. Distortion costs are calculated as the difference between total costs and the rent.
c. Results are for cases with no firm entry/exit.
d. Results are for cases with firm entry/exit (i.e., $N_i/\bar{N}_i$ is reported).

two reasons, the main one being that rent transfers to foreign exporters account for between 86 and 96 percent of the total costs of rationing steel, and these are largely invariant to market structure. In addition the estimated cost disadvantage ratio in steel is low, so the benefits from exploiting economies of scale are small and our estimate of pure profit is zero.

In comparing estimates of the distortionary cost component only, however, we find that introducing imperfect competition substantially changes the estimated value. Under contestable market pricing, which is probably the most plausible pricing rule for the steel industry, the estimate of the distortionary cost component drops to $30 million from a level of $120 million under competitive pricing with constant returns to scale. Even under monopolistic competition with firm entry, the estimates of the distortionary cost component drops to $90 million.

For autos the results are also affected by whether initial profits were induced by the VER. We start with the case of no initial profits, depicted in columns 2, 4, and 5 of table 7.3. As in the case of steel (columns 2, 3, and 4 in table 7.2), the welfare effects of protection are less under imperfect competition than under constant returns to scale. This is so for the same reason, namely, the dominating effect of the third term in expression 7.14 which states that for a fixed number of firms, production should be expanded whenever there are unexploited economies of scale. Likewise the gains from removing protection are greater with exit to reduce the losses

Table 7.3
Welfare costs of voluntary export restraints on Japanese automobiles under different pricing rules: central elasticity case (billions of 1984 US dollars)

		Contestable market		Monopolistic competition			
Item	CRTS[a] (1)	No initial profit (2)	Initial profit (3)	No initial profit short-run (no entry/exit) (4)	No initial profit long-run (entry/exit) (5)	Initial profit long-run (entry/exit) (6)	Endogenous conjectures, initial profit, long-run (entry/exit) (7)
Welfare cost[b]	9.82	8.75	10.31	8.97	9.51	12.21 (3.17 + 9.04)[c]	9.97 (1.26 + 8.71)[c]
Rent costs[d]	7.88	7.89	7.89	7.88	7.89	7.16	7.08
Distortion costs[a]	1.94	0.86	2.42	1.09	1.62	5.07	2.89
Fixed costs		13.3	13.3	13.3	12.7	17.0	15.7
Profit rate[f] (%)				−0.01			
Number of firms[g] (ratio to base)					0.95	1.28	1.18

a. CRTS is constant returns to scale. Results are from table 5.4 in chapter 5.
b. Welfare is the equivalent variation measure defined in appendix 3A in chapter 3. Distortion costs are the difference between total costs and rents.
c. Costs of the VER are the sum of the costs of inefficient entry to eliminate VER-induced profits (first term in parenthesis) plus the estimate of the remaining distortion and rent costs from a zero-profit equilibrium (second term in parenthesis). With international capital mobility, the costs increase to 12.30 (3.25 + 9.05) for column 6 and to 10.05 (1.33 + 8.72) for column 7.
d. Rent capture estimates in the case of initial profits are assumed not to alter market structure, so profits are not affected by rent capture.
e. Defined as total costs less rent costs.
f. Results are for cases with no firm entry/exit.
g. Results are for cases with firm entry/exit (i.e., $N_i/\bar{N}_i$ is reported).

induced by removing the VER (column 5) than with contestable market pricing (column 2) because the remaining firms can produce at lower average cost. As a result the estimated welfare costs of the VER on autos is almost the same under monopolistic competition with entry as under constant returns to scale.

Next we allow for VER-induced profits under three scenarios (columns 3, 6, and 7). First, removing the VER may force firms to price more competitively, which we model by assuming contestable market pricing after removal of the VER. This scenario (column 3) yields about $500 million more in benefits than with constant returns to scale. The reason is obvious: When price exceeds average costs, there are additional welfare gains from increasing quantity (the second term in equation 7.14), which in the case of contestable markets are not dampened by firm entry.

In the other two scenarios with monopolistic competition, which is our preferred market structure, firm entry is required to eliminate profits. In one case conjectures remain fixed, as calibrated from equation 7.7; in the other they are endogenous, as calibrated from equation 7.8. As discussed in section 7.1, we believe that over $9 billion of the industry's profits in 1984 were pure profits generated by the VER. Profits will induce entry; in fact we believe that the massive entry into US auto manufacturing by Japanese firms after the imposition of the VER (detailed in appendix B) was causally related to the VER-induced pure profits. Consequently we simulate the costs of the VER in these scenarios by decomposing the welfare costs into two components. First, in response to the positive profits created by the VER, we assume that entry would continue until a zero profit equilibrium is reached. This gives us the first component of the welfare cost. Second, we evaluate the remaining costs of the VER from the zero-profit equilibrium. The total welfare costs of the VER is then calculated as the sum of the welfare costs of VER-induced entry to create a zero-profit equilibrium plus the welfare costs of retaining the VER. In addition we estimate the VER rents accruing to foreigners after entry has created a zero-profit equilibrium. The rents are reduced because domestic entry lowers the relative price of domestically produced autos which reduces demand for imported autos. We define the distortion costs as the total costs less the rents to foreigners.

Of all the scenarios the welfare costs of the VER are highest with initial profits, firm entry, and fixed conjectures (column 6 of table 7.3). Entry to eliminate pure profits imposes a welfare cost of $3.17 billion. This is because the loss of scale efficiency from entry (the third term in equation 7.14) dominates the benefits from the reduction in monopoly profits. Reaching the zero-profit equilibrium requires 33 percent more firms in the market (not reported in table 7.3). Starting from this counterfactually created zero-profit equilibrium, simulating the removal of the VER results in an additional $9.04 billion cost. Since removing the auto VER from a zero-profit equilibrium induces exit, the adverse impact of the VER on scale efficiency is reduced to an estimated 28 percent increase in the number of firms (reported in table 7.3). The key reason for the higher total costs of the VER in column 6 is that the industry ends up with 28 percent more firms than before the VER. In this formulation VERs are considerably more costly than under perfect competition because entry results in a loss of scale efficiency as firms move up their average cost curve, along the lines described by Horstman and Markusen (1986).[21]

With endogenous conjectures the costs of the VER are less (column 7) because the price reduction needed to eliminate profits is achieved after fewer firms have entered the market than in the case of fixed conjectures. So the entry of inefficient firms imposes considerably lower costs (only $1.26 billion). The total costs of the VER, however, remain higher than under constant returns to scale, but only slightly.[22]

We also assess the benefits of trade liberalization in autos under the assumption of international capital mobility since the evidence (section 7.1.2) suggests that the firms entering the US auto industry were foreign firms, which usually repatriate their profits. With international capital mobility along the lines described in section 6.5, the costs of inefficient entry to eliminate profits increase to $3.25 billion for the fixed conjecture case (column 6) and to $1.33 billion for the endogenous conjectures case (column 7) without any increase in the number of firms. The subsequent removal of the VER from the zero-profit equilibrium results in a very small increase in benefits relative to the case without international capital mobility. The reason that entry by foreign firms results in greater costs than entry by domestic firms is another application of the Brecher and Díaz-Alejandro theorem explained in section 6.5. Because of the VER the marginal social product of capital in autos is less than the marginal private product of capital. Imported capital, which receives the rental rate on capital (i.e., the marginal private product), consequently obtains more than its marginal social product. (See de Melo and Tarr 1991 for an elaboration of these pure profit and international capital mobility scenarios under alternative closures.)

Which of the scenarios we estimated for autos is the most relevant? Given the evidence of pure profits in autos in 1984 (section 7.1), the most plausible scenarios are those summarized in columns 3, 6, and 7 of table 7.3.

Of these, estimates somewhere between those of columns 6 and 7, modified to accommodate international capital mobility, are probably most representative, given the substantial firm entry into auto production in the United States through foreign direct investment by Japanese companies.

Estimates close to those of the scenario with endogenous conjectures have the further advantage that they partly remedy our model's neglect of product differentiation at the firm or product level. (We model product differentiation only at the national level.) In our formulation firm entry results in market fragmentation that generally leads to welfare losses, with no compensating benefit for greater product variety. But firm entry will be considerably less inefficient to the extent that new varieties of products desired by consumers are supplied to the market.[23] Consequently the monopolistic competition model with fixed conjectures is likely to overestimate the costs of inefficient entry to the extent that new varieties are introduced. With endogenous conjectures, however, the costs are considerably reduced, as would occur in a model with product variety at the firm level. Although varying conjectures is controversial, the welfare value of increased product variety is generally accepted. We obtain a proxy for the impact of product variety on lowering the costs of entry by our closure with endogenous conjectures.[24] Note, however, that in all three cases with initial profits (columns 3, 6, and 7), estimates of the costs of the auto VER exceed those under constant returns to scale.

As was the case with steel, the effect of market structure on our results is dampened by the large share of the rent transfer component in total costs since this cost remains virtually unchanged in all our scenarios. The magnitude of the distortionary cost component, however, is strongly affected by our assumptions about market structure and initial profits in the equilibrium under the VER. The distortion costs of the VER range from \$2.9 and \$5.1 billion in the case of initial profits to \$1.9 billion under an assumption of constant returns to scale and no initial profits.

Finally, we consider interactions between the auto and steel industries when both sectors have imperfectly competitive behavior (table 7.4). To simulate the costs of VERs in both sectors, we counterfactually create an equilibrium in which steel is rationed and then remove the VERs in both sectors. Since this involves assessing the gains of removing the VERs from different initial solutions, the estimates are not strictly comparable across experiments. As a benchmark we report the results under constant returns to scale (not reported in chapter 5).

As one would expect, the results follow the same pattern as those for steel and autos alone (tables 7.2 and 7.3). The results for joint costs are

Table 7.4
Combined welfare costs of quotas in automobiles and steel under imperfectly competitive behavior in both industries: central elasticity case (billions of 1984 US dollars)

				Monopolistic competition			
		Contestable market					Endogenous conjectures
	CRTS[a]	No initial profit	Initial profit[b]	No initial profit short-run (no entry/ exit)	No initial profit long-run (entry/exit) in steel only)	Initial profit[b] long-run (entry/exit)	Initial profit[b] long-run (entry/exit)
Item	(1)	(2)	(3)	(4)	(5)	(6)	(7)
Ration steel	−0.86	−0.77	−0.77	−0.79	−0.83	−0.84	−0.82
Remove quotas from autos and steel	10.68	9.52	11.09	9.75	10.33	13.07 (3.19 + 9.88)[c]	10.83 (1.29 + 9.54)[c]
Fixed costs[d]							
Autos	0.0	13.3	13.3	13.3	12.7	17.0	15.7
Steel	0.0	2.3	2.3	2.3	2.3	2.3	2.3
Profit rate[e] (%)							
Autos				−0.01			
Steel				0.0			
Number of firms[f] (ratio to base)							
Autos					0.95	1.28	1.18
Steel					1.00	1.00	1.00

Note: Welfare is the equivalent variation measure defined in appendix 3A in chapter 3. The estimates are not strictly comparable across experiments because the estimate is from a counterfactually created equilibrium with rationed steel. Rent capture estimates are not reported separately (see tables 7.2 and 7.3).

a. CRTS is constant returns to scale. These results for the combined sectors are presented here as a benchmark, although they were not reported in chapter 5.

b. In autos only.

c. Costs of the quotas are the sum of the costs of inefficient entry to eliminate quota-induced profits (first term in parenthesis) plus the estimate of the remaining distortion and rent costs (second term in parenthesis).

d. After removing quotas.

e. Results are for cases with no firm entry/exit.

f. Results are for cases with firm entry/exit (i.e., $N_i/\bar{N}_i$ is reported).

mostly additive of the separate results. This is explained by the fact that both the separate and the joint results were derived in a general equilibrium model that incorporated interactions between the two sectors as well as economywide constraints. In particular, the economywide balance-of-trade constraint and the constraints on the use of capital and labor have been incorporated in the estimates for the individual sectors.

7.4 Conclusion

In this chapter we examined the sensitivity of the estimates of the welfare costs of VERs in autos and steel to the assumption of constant returns to scale and marginal cost pricing made in chapter 5. For steel the results suggest that the welfare costs of VERs would be between 5 and 13 percent less under assumptions of increasing returns to scale and noncompetitive pricing than under constant returns and marginal cost pricing. The difference is relatively small for three reasons: The estimate of unexploited economies of scale in steel is quite small, our estimate of pure profits in the base year is zero, and the rent transfer component is such a large share (between 86 percent and 96 percent) of the total welfare cost of VERs in steel. Since the rent transfer component of the welfare cost of VERs is insensitive to assumptions about domestic market behavior, it is not surprising that total welfare costs are not very sensitive to the introduction of economies of scale and imperfectly competitive behavior. For the distortionary cost component of VERs in steel, exploitation of economies of scale under a contestable market pricing rule reduces the costs from $120 million to $30 million. The reduction is somewhat less ($90 million) under monopolistic competition with firm entry because firm entry to remove profits created by protection leads to a loss of the benefits of scale economies.

The welfare costs of VERs in autos, however, are more strongly affected by imperfect competition. The distortionary cost of the auto VER under constant returns to scale and zero profits was estimated at $1.94 billion. The presence of profits in autos, made possible in part by the VER, affects the results in another dimension. In the case where the removal of the VER induces contestable market pricing, the distortionary costs of the VER are 25 percent greater ($2.42 million) than under constant returns. This results because removing the VER eliminates monopoly profits, which would not have been dampened by firm entry under the contestable market assumption.

Under assumptions of monopolistic competition, fixed conjectures, firm entry, and international capital mobility, the distortionary cost of the VER increases to $5.22 billion. (These results are not reported in table 7.3, which refers to the case with immobile international capital.) This represents a 169 percent increase over the constant returns estimate. This result is dominated by the higher production costs that arise because of substantial firm entry to eliminate the VER-induced profits. With endogenous conjectures and international capital mobility, the distortionary costs are lower at $3.05 billion, which is 57 percent greater than the constant returns estimate. Since fewer firms need to enter the market before profits are eliminated, there is less fragmentation of production with endogenous conjectures.

For reasons explained in section 7.3, we have argued that the monopolistic competition model with pure profits in the initial equilibrium and international capital mobility best characterizes the auto industry. Moreover, also for reasons discussed in section 7.3, we think the most appropriate results are from the closure with endogenous conjectures. Nonetheless, since the estimates of the distortionary costs vary significantly depending on model closure, we have also presented the results from other model closures. This method has the additional benefit of making it easier to isolate the relative importance of various effects.

Appendix 7A: Derivation of the Price Elasticity of Demand

We seek an expression for the elasticity of demand for the domestic good in sector i with respect to its price (ε_i^d). Total demand for the domestic output of sector i is given by equation 24 of table 3.1:

$$D_i = CD_i + VTD_i. \tag{7A.1}$$

Define

$$\varepsilon_i^d \equiv -\frac{PD_i}{D_i}\frac{\partial D}{\partial PD_i},$$

$$\varepsilon_i^F = -\frac{PD_i}{CD_i}\frac{\partial CD_i}{\partial PD_i},$$

and

$$\varepsilon_i^v \equiv -\frac{PD_i}{VTD_i}\frac{\partial VTD_i}{\partial PD_i}$$

as the elasticities of demand, final demand, and intermediate demand, respectively. Denote by

$$S_i^F \equiv \frac{CD_i}{D_i} \quad \text{and} \quad S_i^v \equiv \frac{VTD_i}{D_i}$$

the shares of final and intermediate demand in sector i, respectively. Differentiate equation 7A.1 with respect to PD_i, multiply both sides by PD_i/D_i, and multiply the terms on the right side by CD_i/CD_i and VTD_i/VTD_i to get an expression for the price elasticity of demand in terms of its components:

$$\varepsilon_i^d = \varepsilon_i^F S_i^F + \varepsilon_i^v S_i^v. \tag{7A.2}$$

Equation 7A.2 shows that the total elasticity is a share-weighted average of the final and intermediate elasticities. We now derive each component of equation 7A.2.

7A.1 The Elasticity of Final Demand (ε_i^F)

To derive the elasticity of final demand ε_i^F rewrite the first-order condition (equation 22) of table 3.1 as follows:

$$CD_i = \overline{AC}_i^{\sigma c_i - 1}(1 - v_i)^{\sigma c_i}\left(\frac{PD_i}{PC_i}\right)^{-\sigma c_i} C_i, \tag{7A.3}$$

where we have substituted PC_i for the inverse of the Lagrangian multiplier.[25] Rewrite equation 7A.3 in the following form:

$$CD_i = H[PD_i, PC_i, C_i; \Omega_i], \tag{7A.4}$$

where the Ω_i terms are the parameters of the problem and the subscripts on the function H have been suppressed. Differentiate equation 7A.4, and apply the chain rule:

$$\frac{\partial CD_i}{\partial PD_i} = \frac{\partial H}{\partial PD_i} + \frac{\partial H}{\partial PC_i}\frac{\partial PC_i}{\partial PD_i} + \frac{\partial H}{\partial C_i}\frac{\partial C_i}{\partial PD_i}. \tag{7A.5}$$

Evaluate the five partial derivatives on the right side of 7A.5.

From equation 7A.3 we have

$$\frac{\partial H}{\partial PD_i} = -\sigma c_i\left(\frac{CD_i}{PD_i}\right), \tag{7A.6}$$

$$\frac{\partial H}{\partial PC_i} = \sigma c_i\left(\frac{CD_i}{PC_i}\right), \tag{7A.7}$$

and

$$\frac{\partial H}{\partial C_i} = \frac{CD_i}{C_i}. \tag{7A.8}$$

Use equation 13 to derive

$$\frac{\partial PC_i}{\partial PD_i} = (1 - v_i)^{\sigma c_i}\left(\frac{PC_i}{PD_i}\right)^{\sigma c_i}. \tag{7A.9}$$

Finally, we require $\partial C_i/\partial PD_i$. The demand for composite final consumption of sector i is given by equation 20 of table 3.1. PD_i influences this demand through its impact on the composite price PC_i. We have

$$\frac{\partial C_i}{\partial PD_i} = \frac{\partial C_i}{\partial PC_i}\frac{\partial PC_i}{\partial PD_i} = \frac{\partial PC_i}{\partial PD_i}\left[\frac{-\beta_i}{PC_i^2}(Y - COMIT) - \frac{\beta_i}{PC_i}\lambda_i\right]. \tag{7A.10}$$

Substitute from equation 7A.9 into equation 7A.10, and rearrange to obtain

$$\frac{\partial C_i}{\partial PD_i} = -(1 - v_i)^{\sigma c_i}\frac{\beta_i}{PC_i}\left(\frac{PC_i}{PD_i}\right)^{\sigma c_i}\left(\lambda_i + \frac{Y - COMIT}{PC_i}\right). \tag{7A.11}$$

Substitute equations 7A.6, 7A.7, 7A.8, 7A.10, and 7A.11 into equation 7A.5, multiply both sides of equation 7A.5 by $-PD_i/CD_i$, and substitute $C_i - \lambda_i$ for $\beta_i(Y - \text{COMIT})/PC_i$ from equation 20. This yields

$$\varepsilon_i^F = \sigma c_i + (1 - v_i)^{\sigma c_i}\left(\frac{PC_i}{PD_i}\right)^{\sigma c_i - 1}\left[-\sigma c_i + 1 + \frac{\lambda_i(\beta_i - 1)}{C_i}\right]. \tag{7A.12}$$

7A.2 The Elasticity of Intermediate Demand (ε_i^v)

Total intermediate demand is defined by equation 23 of table 3.1. Define

$$\varepsilon_{ij}^v = -\frac{\partial VD_{ij}}{\partial PD_i}\frac{PD_i}{VD_i}$$

and

$$S_{ij}^v = \frac{VD_{ij}}{VTD_i},$$

where ε_{ij}^v is the elasticity of intermediate demand for the output of sector i by sector j with respect to a change in the price of the domestic variety of sector i, and S_{ij}^v is the quantity-weighted share of sector j in total domestic intermediate demand for the output of sector i.

Differentiate VTD_i of equation 23 with respect to PD_i, and multiply both sides by PD_i/VTD_i. After a little algebra this yields

$$\varepsilon_i^v = \sum_{j \in N} \varepsilon_{ij}^v S_{ij}^v. \tag{7A.13}$$

The elasticity of total domestic intermediate demand in sector i is a share-weighted average of the elasticities (ε_{ij}^v) from each of the sectors that demand domestic intermediate output from sector i.

Analogous to the derivation of equation 7A.3, cost minimization by firms in sector j implies that

$$VD_{ij} = \overline{AV}_{ij}^{\sigma v_i - 1}(1 - \delta_i)^{\sigma v_i}\left(\frac{PD_i}{PV_{ij}}\right)^{-\sigma v_i} V_{ij}. \tag{7A.14}$$

Rewrite the right side of equation 7A.14 as

$$VD_{ij} = G[PD_i, PV_{ij}, V_{ij}; \mathbf{\Omega}_{ij}], \tag{7A.15}$$

where the $\mathbf{\Omega}_{ij}$ terms are the parameters and the subscripts on the function G have been suppressed. Differentiate equation 7A.15 by PD_i, and apply the chain rule to obtain

$$\frac{\partial VD_{ij}}{\partial PD_i} = \frac{\partial G}{\partial PD_i} + \frac{\partial G}{\partial PV_{ij}}\frac{\partial PV_{ij}}{\partial PD_i} + \frac{\partial G}{\partial V_{ij}}\frac{\partial V_{ij}}{\partial PD_i}. \tag{7A.16}$$

Unlike the final demand elasticity, the composite demand for the output of sector i (domestic and imported) does not depend on PD_i (compare equation 8 and equation 20 in table 3.1). Thus $\partial V_{ij}/\partial PD_i = 0$, and the third term on the right side of equation 7A.16 vanishes. Differentiate equations 7A.14 and 12, which yields

$$\frac{\partial G}{\partial PD_i} = -\frac{\sigma v_i VD_{ij}}{PD_i}, \tag{7A.17}$$

$$\frac{\partial G}{\partial PV_{ij}} = \frac{\sigma v_i VD_{ij}}{PV_{ij}}, \tag{7A.18}$$

and

$$\frac{\partial PV_{ij}}{\partial PD_i} = (1 - \delta_i)^{\sigma v_i}\left(\frac{PV_{ij}}{PD_i}\right)^{\sigma v_i}. \tag{7A.19}$$

Substitute equations 7A.17, 7A.18, and 7A.19 into the right side of equation 7A.16, and multiply both sides by PD_i/VD_{ij} to obtain

$$\varepsilon_{ij}^v = \sigma v_i - \sigma v_i(1 - \delta_i)^{\sigma v_i}\left(\frac{PV_{ij}}{PD_i}\right)^{\sigma v_i - 1}. \tag{7A.20}$$

7A.3 The Price Elasticity of Demand (ε_i^d)

Substitute equation 7A.13 into equation 7A.2:

$$\varepsilon_i^d = \varepsilon_i^F S_i^F + \left(\sum_{j \in N} \varepsilon_{ij}^v S_{ij}^v \right) S_i^v. \tag{7A.21}$$

This elasticity can now be calculated from equations 7A.12 and 7A.20 and the share data and equals

$$\varepsilon_i^d = S_i^F \left\{ \sigma c_i + (1 - v_i)^{\sigma c_i} \left(\frac{PC_i}{PD_i} \right)^{\sigma c_i - 1} \left[-\sigma c_i + 1 + \frac{\lambda_i(\beta_i - 1)}{C_i} \right] \right\}$$
$$+ S_i^v \left\{ \sum_{j \in N} S_{ij}^v \left[\sigma v_i - \sigma v_i (1 - \delta_i)^{\sigma v_i} \left(\frac{PV_{ij}}{PD_i} \right)^{\sigma v_i - 1} \right] \right\}. \tag{7A.22}$$

8 Revenue-Raising Taxes: Evaluation of Alternative Strategies for Taxing Petroleum Industries

In chapter 6 we analyzed the welfare implications of removing protection in a second-best situation with distortions in the labor market. In this chapter we further modify the basic model of chapter 3 and examine the welfare implications of using trade taxes to raise revenue. We add two energy sectors, expanding the model to twelve sectors. As in chapter 6 we are dealing with a second-best situation because we limit our analysis to the use of trade and excise taxes in two energy sectors to raise government revenue.

The exercises in this chapter illustrate several propositions from the theory of optimal taxation: that excise taxes are more efficient than tariffs, that a given revenue objective can be achieved at a lower cost with additional tax instruments, and that the least burdensome way to impose excise taxes is to vary their rates inversely with the elasticity of final demand. Also, to partially offset the production distortion induced by limiting excise taxes to two sectors, a small amount of protection should accompany the excise taxes. Furthermore we show that because of the vertically integrated structure of the two energy sectors, it is efficient to impose the higher excise tax on the upstream sector and the higher tariff on the downstream sector.

This chapter is organized as follows: Section 8.1 recalls the events that led to the recent proposals to raise energy taxes and evaluates the proposals. Section 8.2 presents the changes needed in the basic model of chapter 3 to analyze the welfare implications of using trade taxes to raise revenue, along with the aggregation scheme and elasticity specifications for the crude oil and petroleum products sectors. Section 8.3 reports on the welfare and government revenue estimates for the proposed taxes. Section 8.4 reports results on the set of least costly taxes in the crude oil and petroleum products sectors that would raise $20 billion in government revenue.

8.1 Recent Proposals for Taxing Petroleum Industries

During the 1970s proposals to increase the import tariffs on crude oil were commonly offered as a means of counteracting the power of the OPEC cartel. Domestic petroleum product refiners have also sought an import tariff on refined petroleum products (see Anderson and Metzger 1987). By the late 1980s, however, the most prominent proposals to increase taxation of energy sectors were being offered as a means of reducing the large US federal budget deficit and its twin trade deficit. In addition some tax proponents argue that such taxation will help the United States become energy independent in a relatively painless way because of the decline in energy prices in the late 1980s.[1] Opponents argue that such taxes would be very costly to the US economy in terms of lost welfare and adverse impacts on other sectors.

Because of these conflicting concerns President Reagan asked the Department of Energy to study the issue to determine whether any policy changes were warranted. Without proposing specific policies, that study drew the vague conclusion that the challenge to policymakers is to use the market where possible and to otherwise find appropriate cost-effective solutions to the nation's energy problems (US Department of Energy 1987, 3).

In this chapter we start with a reexamination of the welfare, fiscal, and employment implications of the two most prominent recent proposals to increase taxes or tariffs in the energy sector. One proposal suggests an increase in tariffs on crude oil imports of $5 to $10 a barrel (roughly 25 to 50 percent of the value of the imported oil).[2] Another recommends an increase in taxes on final petroleum products of 5 cents to 25 cents a gallon (roughly 5 to 25 percent of the value of a gallon of gasoline).[3] More specifically we take the cases of a 25 percent import tax on imported crude oil and a 15 percent excise tax on petroleum products.

The estimates are derived from a slightly modified version of the basic model presented in chapter 3. The modified model has twelve sectors but remains calibrated to 1984. Thus our estimates are derived under the assumption that the quantitative restrictions (QRs) prevailing in 1984 in the textile and apparel and automobile sectors would remain in effect.[4] Next we go beyond the existing literature to determine the least costly combination (in terms of US welfare) of taxes and tariffs on the crude oil and petroleum product sectors for generating a given amount ($20 billion) of revenue.

8.2 Adaptation of the Basic Model to the Energy Sector

8.2.1 Modifications to the Basic Model

For the petroleum industries we allow for the possibility of an upward-sloping supply curve of imports for crude oil, as suggested by Anderson and Metzger (1987).[5] Positive excise taxes tx_i apply only to the two petroleum industries—oil and gas and petroleum products. The excise tax is imposed on top of the existing tariff rates (0.2 percent for oil and gas and 3.1 percent for petroleum products).

These changes imply the following minor modifications to the basic model presented in table 3.1 of chapter 3. For the crude oil and petroleum products sectors, the sales-tax-inclusive domestic price is now defined as

$$PD_i = \tilde{PD}_i(1 + tx_i), \qquad i \in E,$$

where $\tilde{PD}_i$ is the domestic price of crude oil and petroleum products exclusive of the tax and E is the set of crude oil and petroleum products sectors. Likewise, for imported crude oil and petroleum products, equation 17 of table 3.1 is replaced by

$$PM_k^v = PWM_k(1 + tm_k)(1 + prc_k)(1 + tx_k)ER. \tag{17'}$$

In this chapter $tx_k = 0$ unless $k \in E$, and $prc_k > 0$ for autos and textiles. Equation 16 for intermediate imports is similarly modified.

We also distinguish two components of government revenue: that from trade taxes GR_1, defined by equation 29 in table 3.1, and that from the sales tax on crude oil and petroleum products, defined as follows:

$$GR_2 = \sum_{i \in E} (\tilde{PD}_i D_i tx_i) + \sum_{i \in E} VTM_i ER\, PWI_i^v tx_i + \sum_{i \in E} CM_i ER\, PWM_i^v tx_i. \tag{29'}$$

In the experiments reported in section 8.3, we take the domestic sales tax tx_i and tariffs on the oil and gas and petroleum products sectors as exogenous policy instruments. We ask what are the revenue and welfare effects of imposing taxes and tariffs at the proposed levels. We measure the change in government revenue from the application of an excise tax using GR_2 and the change from the joint application of an excise tax and an import fee using $\Delta GR \equiv GR^1 - GR^0$, where $GR \equiv GR_1 + GR_2$ and superscripts 0 and 1 refer to the situation before and after the policy change, respectively.

In the experiments reported in section 8.4, we seek instead the values of tx_i and tm_i (for the oil and gas and the petroleum products sectors) that would maximize welfare (given by the Stone-Geary utility indicator) subject to the constraint that government revenue must increase by $20 billion. Thus in section 8.4 we solve the following problem:

$$\text{Max}\, U = \prod_{i=1}^{m} (C_i - \lambda_i)^{\beta_i}, \tag{8.1}$$

where U is the Stone-Geary welfare indicator described in section 3.4, subject to the following constraint:

$$GR \geqslant GR^0 + 20, \tag{8.2}$$

where GR^0 is government revenue before the tax. Now tariff and excise tax rates in the crude oil and petroleum products sectors are endogenous variables. Computations are done with the MINOS5 algorithm available from Brooke, Kendrick, and Meeraus (1988).

8.2.2 Elasticity Specifications for the Energy Sector

The twelve sectors of the model are the ten sectors from the basic model of chapter 3 (agriculture, food, mining, textiles and apparel, automobiles, steel, other consumer goods, other manufactures, traded services, construction, and nontraded services) and the two energy sectors, crude oil and natural gas and petroleum products. Mining and manufacturing are disaggregated to permit analysis of five important policy sectors: automobiles, textiles and apparel, steel, crude oil and natural gas, and petroleum products. Unlike the case in previous chapters, mining is disaggregated into crude oil and natural gas and other mining, and other manufactures is further disaggregated into petroleum products and a residual other manufactures. Because the model is calibrated to 1984, we assume that existing import quotas on textiles and apparel and automobiles remain in effect under the alternative taxation schemes analyzed here.

The structure of demand, the level of output and employment, and the selected elasticities for the two energy sectors appear in table 8.1. Imports are a larger share of domestic supply in the oil and gas sector than in the petroleum products sector. The oil and gas sector is also the more labor intensive. All sales from the oil and gas sector are sales to other sectors. Thus an increase in that sector's relative price will have a negative supply effect on sectors that use oil and gas intensively as an intermediate input,

Table 8.1
Production and demand structure and elasticities in US petroleum industries

Item	Oil and gas	Petroleum products
Production and demand (billions of 1984 US$)		
Gross output (XD)	157.3	217.2[a]
Employment (L)	619.0	204.0
Domestic final demand sales (CD)	0.07	45.7
Intermediate sales (VD)	156.4	167.3
Imports		
Intermediates (VM)	43.6	16.6
Final demand (CM)	0.02	4.5
Substitution elasticities (central elasticity case)		
Capital-labor (σ_i)	0.8	0.8
Final demand (σc_i)	2.36	2.36
Intermediate demand (σv_i)	2.36	2.36
Export supply (σt_i)	2.9	2.9
Price elasticity of composite final demand	−0.82	−0.82

a. Intermediate purchases from the oil and gas sector account for 56.3 percent of (direct) total costs.

in particular, the petroleum products sector for which such purchases constitute 56.3 percent of its total costs.

For our elasticity estimates we use Caddy's (1976) estimate of 0.8 for the elasticity of substitution between capital and labor for both sectors and the 2.36 estimate reported in Shiells, Stern, and Deardorff (1986, table 4) for the elasticity of substitution in both final and intermediate demand for the two sectors. A compensated price elasticity of supply of US exports of 2.9 is assumed for both sectors. (We show in appendix B that results are insensitive to a wide range of values for this parameter.) The composite price elasticity of final demand for domestic and imported petroleum products is assumed to be −0.82, which is within the range bounded by the estimates of −0.79, reported in Shiells, Stern, and Deardorff (1986), and −0.96, reported in Stern, Francis, and Schumacher (1976).

In most simulations we rely on these values for elasticities (referred to as the central elasticity case). However, to check on the sensitivity of results, we also carried out experiments for low elasticity and high elasticity cases. (The low and high elasticity cases are obtained by increasing or decreasing by one standard deviation the values of the central elasticities of all twelve sectors in the manner described in chapter 5.) For the high and low elasticities of substitution in intermediate and in final demand in the oil and gas and petroleum products sectors, the central elasticity values were doubled or halved. Finally, we also experiment with values of 1 and 3 for the foreign elasticity of supply of imported crude oil, which are in the range suggested by Anderson and Metzger (1987).

8.3 Revenue and Welfare Effects of Tax Proposals

We report first on the revenue, welfare, and employment effects of tariffs on imports of oil and gas products and of a domestic sales tax on petroleum products for the central elasticity case. Next we establish the likely upper and lower bounds of the welfare costs per dollar of government revenue generated. We also estimate the welfare cost of additional percentage increases in the tax and tariff rates.

8.3.1 Revenue, Employment, and Welfare Estimates

Almost five times more revenue would be generated by the proposed 15 percent excise tax on petroleum products than by the 25 percent import tariff on oil and gas (table 8.2).[6] This outcome is to be expected since the excise tax would apply to all domestic sales (imports and domestic production, amounting to $234 billion), whereas the import tariff has a much smaller base ($43.6 billion). Since the excise tax applies to all sales and is therefore nondiscriminatory by source (see section 8.4), it is also much less distortionary than the import tariff on oil and gas products. Thus an excise tax on petroleum products raises about five times more revenue at 37 percent of the welfare cost of an import tariff on oil and gas products.

The import tariff on oil and gas products would also have employment effects across the entire economy, requiring the relocation of 142,500 workers (table 8.2). The tariff's interindustry employment effects are strong, with only 65,300 of the 142,500 workers relocating in the energy industries. The interindustry effects on employment are weaker for the proposed excise tax on petroleum products, with 18,500 of the 38,900 dislocated workers changing jobs within the energy industries. These effects are weaker because an excise sales tax does not discriminate between domestic production and imports. In addition 77 percent of petroleum product sales go to other sectors, and our model allows no substitution of intermediate inputs from other sectors, so purchasers of petroleum products cannot shift to other inputs. Such an assumption is of course a simplification that is likely to hold only for the short to medium run. If this assumption is lifted, both the estimated gain in government revenue and

Table 8.2
Revenue, welfare, and employment effects of tariffs and excise taxes in the petroleum industry: central elasticity case

Experiment	Increase in government revenue (billion $ 1984)	Change in welfare[a] (billion $ 1984)	Employment change (thousand work-years)		Economywide employment relocation[b] (thousand work-years)
			Oil and gas	Petroleum products	
(E-1): 25% import tariff on oil and gas	7.29	−1.37	62.3	−3.0	142.5
(E-2): 15% excise tax on domestic sales of petroleum products	34.63	−0.47	−11.8	−6.7	38.9
(E-1) + (E-2)	42.30	−2.29	49.5	−9.4	170.7

a. Welfare is the equivalent variation measure defined in appendix 3A and expressed in billions of 1984 dollars.
b. Computed as half the sum of the absolute value of the employment changes (expressed in thousand work-years).

the welfare cost would decline as users shift out of petroleum products and into other sources of energy in response to the increase in the relative price of oil and gas or petroleum products.

8.3.2 Relative Efficiency of Proposed Taxes

In evaluating the relative efficiency of the proposed revenue-raising tax schemes, we consider the welfare cost per dollar of government revenue raised and the increase in government revenue for each percentage point increase in the tax rate. These efficiency indicators are reported for simulations under low and high elasticities in table 8.3. In the following section we also compare our results with previous estimates.

Low elasticities result in more government revenue and less welfare cost for each tax scheme than do high elasticities. Why this is so is shown in figure 8.1, which illustrates in partial equilibrium the effect of high and low import demand elasticities on the welfare and revenue effect of an import tariff. Initially equilibrium is at PM_0, VM_0, with an infinitely elastic import supply of intermediates. After the imposition of an import tariff (we ignore shifts in the derived demand for imported intermediates), the new equilibrium shifts to PM_1, VM_1^L in the low elasticity case and to PM_1, VM_1^H in the high elasticity case. It is clear that the welfare costs, given by $W = \frac{1}{2}(PM_1 - PM_0)(VM_0 - VM_1)$, are higher in the high elasticity case and that the government revenue, given by $(PM_1 - PM_0)VM_1$, is higher in the low elasticity case. This observation corresponds to the prescription of Pigou (1947, 105) based on partial equilibrium analysis:[7]

> the best way of raising a given revenue ... is by a system of taxes, under which the rates become progressively higher as we pass from uses of very elastic demand or supply to uses where demand or supply are progressively less elastic.

It is also clear from the results in table 8.3 that raising revenue through taxes that do not discriminate between domestic and foreign production is more efficient when the United States does not have monopsony power in trade. This is clearly seen by comparing an import tariff on oil and gas with an excise tax of equivalent size on domestic sales of oil and gas (rows 1 and 3). Not only does the excise tax raise far more revenue than the import tariff because it applies to all domestic sales, but it also generates revenue at a much lower welfare cost per dollar of revenue raised (column 4). When the United States has significant monopsony power in importing, however, the tariff improves the US terms of trade and thereby generates a substantial increase in welfare and in the welfare cost–efficiency ratio.

Table 8.3
Relative efficiency of tariffs and excise taxes in the petroleum industry: low and high elasticity cases (billions of 1984 US dollars)

Tax proposal	Elasticity[a] (1)	Increase in government revenue (2)	Change in welfare[b] (3)	Welfare/revenue (3) ÷ (2) (4)	Increase in revenue per percentage point increase in tax (5)
25% import tariff on oil and gas	Low	8.7	−0.8	−0.09	0.35
	High	5.0	−2.1	−0.42	0.20
25% import tariff on oil and gas: US has monopsony power in oil and gas	Low[c]	8.6	3.6	+0.41	0.34
	High[c]	6.9	3.1	+0.45	0.28
25% excise tax on domestic sales of oil and gas	Low	50.5	−0.5	−0.01	2.02
	High	48.3	−1.5	−0.03	1.93
15% excise tax on domestic sales of petroleum products	Low	35.1	−0.2	−0.01	2.34
	High	33.6	−1.0	−0.03	2.24

a. Low (high) elasticities are obtained by decreasing (increasing) central elasticities by one standard deviation (see chapter 5).
b. Welfare is the equivalent variation measure defined in appendix 3A.
c. Central elasticity case for all parameters except the import supply elasticity (ε_s^m) of oil-gas imports (low: $\varepsilon_s^m = 1.0$; high: $\varepsilon_s^m = 3.0$).

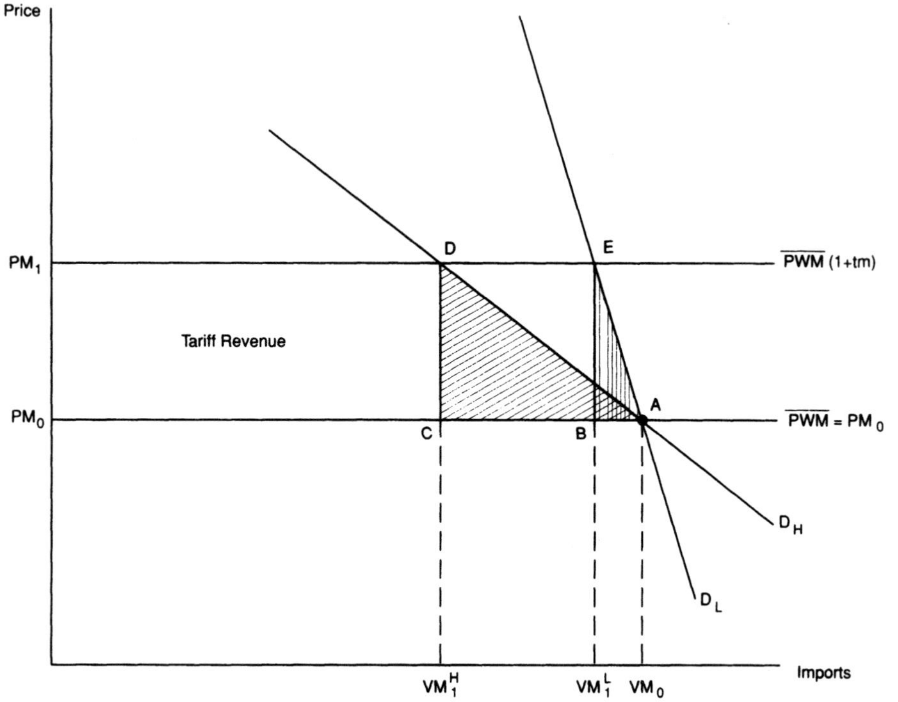

Note: ABE = Welfare loss (low elasticity)
ACD = Welfare loss (high elasticity)

Figure 8.1
Import demand elasticity and welfare loss

8.3.3 Comparison with Earlier Studies

An earlier version of the results of this chapter appeared in de Melo, Stanton and Tarr (1989), where a nonseparable linear expenditure system for the final demand structure implied that for low price elasticities, imported and domestic petroleum products were complements in final demand. In the present formulation, with separable utility for the composite of imported and domestic products in all sectors (as discussed in chapter 3), imported and domestic petroleum products are gross substitutes. The differences in the two formulations can have strong effects for results on resource allocation in the domestic import competing industry (see section 2.6), but weak effects on welfare calculations because (absent second-best distortions in the domestic industry) the magnitude of the welfare effect is influenced primarily by the own elasticity of demand in the import sector. Indeed, welfare results from table 8.3 are very close to the corresponding ones in table 4 of de Melo, Stanton, and Tarr.

In their partial equilibrium study for the US Federal Trade Commission, Anderson and Metzger (1987) estimated that a $5 per barrel import tariff on both crude oil and petroleum products will generate $6.7 billion a year for the government but at a cost of $3.8 billion in deadweight losses. Since the bulk of the government revenues generated by tariffs in our model derive from the crude oil tariff, our estimate of revenue generation may be compared with theirs. Their implied estimate of the welfare costs per dollar of revenue generated (57 cents) is on the high side compared with those we present in table 8.3, but close to our range.[8]

Only Boyd and Uri (1988a, b) have conducted general equilibrium experiments similar to ours.[9] They estimate the effects of a $5 per barrel import fee on crude oil (1988a) and a 15 cent per gallon tax on gasoline (1988b). These taxes are about equal to our 25 percent import fee on crude oil and 15 percent tax on petroleum products. They estimate that the $5 a barrel import fee on crude oil will raise $3.4 billion in government revenue at a cost of $208 million in lost social welfare. The welfare to government revenue ratio (−0.06) is about two-thirds the value of our low elasticity estimate (see table 8.3, column 4).

For the 15 cents a gallon excise tax on gasoline, Boyd and Uri (1988b) find a gain of $8 billion in government revenue at a cost of $15 billion in welfare. So each dollar of government revenue comes at a welfare cost of almost $2 compared with a welfare cost of less than 2 cents in our case. In terms of our other efficiency indicator, for each 1 percent of tax on gasoline they find that the government receives about $0.5 billion in revenue, compared with about $2.3 billion in our case. However, Boyd and Uri apply the tax only on final demand, whereas our experiments apply the tax on both intermediate and final demand, which makes our tax base 4.7 times larger. When adjusted for the size of the tax base, our results on dollars of revenue obtained per percentage of tax are very close. We chose to include intermediate demand because arbitrage would make it difficult, if not impossible, to tax only final demand for gasoline and because the proposals to tax gasoline do not envision excluding intermediate usage. However, we find it difficult to reconcile our estimate of the ratio of welfare costs per dollar of tax revenues raised from excise taxes with the unusually high estimate of Boyd and Uri.[10]

8.4 Efficient Taxation of Petroleum Industries

Partial equilibrium analysis suggests that the least burdensome way to impose excise taxes to raise a given amount of revenue is to levy a set of excise taxes that vary inversely with the elasticity of final demand of the sector. When general equilibrium interactions are taken into account, rules are more difficult to derive and numerical calculations are computationally difficult to obtain. Consequently little empirical work has been done on the subject. Harris and MacKinnon (1979) developed an algorithm for calculating optimal taxes and provide largely illustrative examples. Dahl, Devarajan, and van Wijnbergen (1986) calculated optimal tariffs for Cameroon and investigate the conditions under which departures from a uniform tariff structure are optimal. They do not, however, consider the interaction of taxes with tariffs in numerical terms.

We now ask, What is the least costly way, in terms of foregone welfare, to raise a specified amount of government revenue? As explained in section 8.2, this is a difficult computational problem. It involves solving for the tariff (*tm*) and excise tax rate (*tx*) in the oil and gas and petroleum products industries that maximize welfare, subject to the additional constraint that these taxes increase government revenue by $20 billion.[11]

In our computation of optimal tax rates, several results stand out (table 8.4). First, the welfare cost of raising $20 billion is less when taxation is allowed in both energy sectors than when it is allowed in only one sector. This is an illustration of the principle that a given revenue objective can be achieved at a lower cost using more than one tax instrument, since the additional tax instruments can be used to reduce the price wedge created by taxing a single sector. With additional tax instruments the distortion does not fall on one sector, which would cause resources to flow out of that sector. If all sectors could be taxed, distortion-induced resource movements would be minimized, and one would reach the first-best optimum.[12]

Second, when only one sector is taxed, combining an excise tax with an import tariff is less costly than a tariff alone because of the second-best situation created by a tariff. Since an excise tax does not discriminate by source, we are in the situation described by Dixit (1985), namely, that domestic taxes or subsidies on goods and factors are superior to tariffs for raising revenue. This is so because a tariff induces domestic resources to flow into the protected industry when the product could be obtained at a lower relative price through international trade, but the excise tax does not discriminate by source. Why then, if excise taxes are preferable to tariffs, are tariffs (albeit small ones) included in the optimum revenue-raising

Table 8.4
Optimal excise tax and tariff rates for raising $20 billion in government revenue: central elasticity case

Industry instrument(s)	Oil and gas Excise tax (1)	Oil and gas Tax plus Tariff[a] (2)	Petroleum products Excise tax (3)	Petroleum products Tax plus tariff[a] (4)	Oil and gas and petroleum products Excise tax (5)	Oil and gas and petroleum products Tax plus tariff[a] (6)	Oil and gas and petroleum products, ε^s_m(oil) = 3.0, Tax plus tariff[a] (7)
Oil and gas							
Tariff rate (%)		2.5				3.3	36.6
Tax rate (%)	10.1	9.6			4.6	14.6	6.7
Petroleum products							
Tariff rate (%)				2.4		11.7	6.5
Tax rate (%)			8.7	8.6	4.6	−4.9	−1.9
Change in welfare[b] (billions of 1984 $)	−0.176	−0.157	−0.165	−0.164	−0.141	−0.086	+2.33

a. Initial tariff rates are 0.2 percent in oil and gas and 3.1 percent in petroleum products. Unless otherwise indicated, tax and tariff rates are held at their initial values.
b. Welfare is the equivalent variation measure defined in appendix 3A.

strategy? The answer is that we have limited the use of excise taxes to one or two sectors. When the energy sectors are taxed but others are not, resources flow out of the energy sectors and into the rest of the economy. This production distortion is reduced through the use of a tariff. But while a tariff reduces the production distortion, it increases the consumption distortion. The optimum is a mix of the two, which has been explained by Corden (1974, 82–84) (and derived by Dahl, Devarajan, and van Wijnbergen 1986 for the case of zero cross-elasticity of demand) is illustrated in figure 8.2.[13]

In addition the base tariff structure is nonuniform, especially for textiles and apparel, whose high tariff rate results in excessive resources being devoted to that sector. When we allow the tariffs in the energy sectors to seek optimal levels, the optimal values will partly offset the distortions of the base tariff structure.

A third interesting result is that when both energy sectors are taxed simultaneously, the pattern of optimal taxation is strongly influenced by the interdependence between the two sectors. The results shown in the last two columns of table 8.4 indicate a subsidy to petroleum products, which is explained by the fact that a tax on crude oil is, in effect, a tax on petroleum products. This results in a second-best situation wherein output in the petroleum sector is too low because it is being taxed indirectly while the nonenergy sectors are not being taxed. The reason for a gross subsidy to petroleum products is the same as the rationale for a tariff: to reduce distortion-induced resource movements created by high excise taxes.

Figure 8.2 illustrates this principle in partial equilibrium for the case of an excise tax on crude oil (tx_c). A tax on crude oil shifts up the supply curve for the petroleum industry from S to $S(1 + tx_c)$, creating a distortion (equal to area ABC) in the market for domestic petroleum products.[14] This results in a second-best situation, since output in the petroleum sector is too low because the nonenergy sectors are not being taxed. A tariff on imported petroleum products (tm) or even a subsidy for domestic producers of petroleum products will reduce this distortion. Figure 8.2 illustrates this distortion reduction for the case of a tariff on imported petroleum products, which induces an increase in demand for their principal substitute, domestic petroleum products, from D^0 to D^1. This will reduce the distortion costs in the domestic petroleum products industry (caused by the tax on crude oil) from ABC to ADE.

The results of the exercise on optimal revenue-raising tax rates presented in table 8.4 support this interpretation. When a combination tax plus tariff is imposed on both sectors (column 6), the rates are roughly propor-

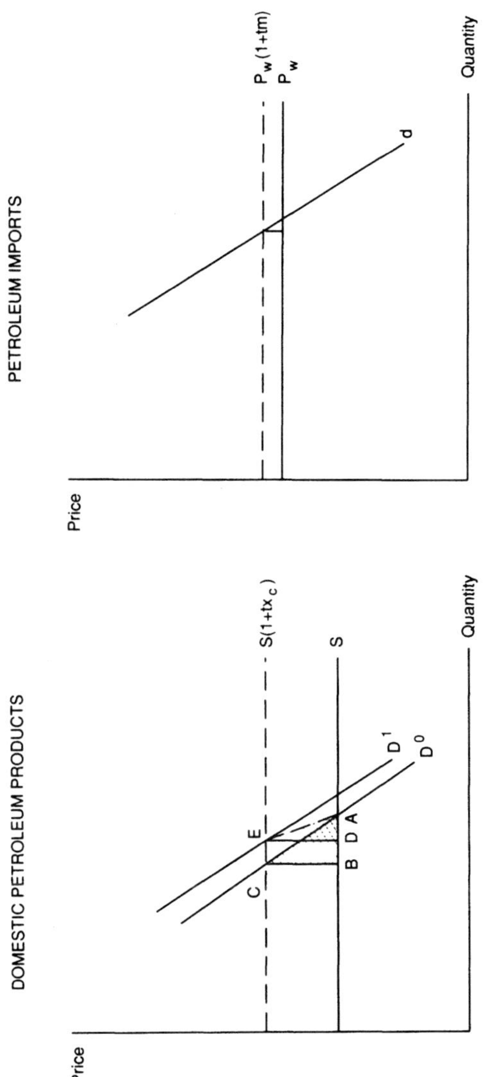

tx_c is the excise tax on crude oil products

Figure 8.2
Welfare impact on domestic petroleum products of a tariff on imported petroleum products given an excise tax on crude oil

tional to those for the case in which the combination tax and tariff is imposed only on the oil and gas sector (column 2) but result in a small subsidy to the domestic petroleum products sector compared to the case in which only that sector receives the tax plus tariff (column 4). Of course there is a net effective tax on petroleum production equal to about 3.3 percent [−4.9 + 0.563(14.6)], since purchases from the oil and gas sector constitute 56.3 percent of the total costs of the petroleum products sector.

A fourth noteworthy result is that the excise tax and tariff rates are not uniform in the two sectors. Atkinson and Stiglitz (1980) have shown that in our case of perfectly inelastic labor supply, a uniform excise tax is optimal for revenue-raising purposes. Since a uniform tax on all goods is equivalent to a tax on labor alone, a uniform tax will minimize distortion-induced resource movements if labor supply is perfectly inelastic. (With nonconstant labor supply, it is optimal to tax products that are good substitutes for leisure at a lower rate to minimize a distortion-induced increase in leisure.)

The key to understanding the pattern of optimal taxation is to recognize that the demand for crude oil is a derived demand from the petroleum products industry. A fully uniform tax is not possible in our case because we have not allowed taxation of the nonenergy sectors. Thus, as discussed above, a production distortion results, with too few resources going to the two energy sectors, which can be reduced by a tariff. A tariff on crude oil is inefficient, however, because it raises the cost of production of petroleum products. A higher tariff on the final good, petroleum products, is optimal because it increases the demand for the output of both sectors. Analogously the higher excise tax is on the intermediate product because a tax on petroleum products would reduce the demand for crude oil, aggravating the problem of too few resources in crude oil. Although a tax on crude oil aggravates the problem of too few resources in petroleum products, that problem can be more efficiently attacked by a tariff.

As a final illustration we take the case in which the United States is assumed to have monopsony power on world oil markets (column 7 of table 8.4). We examine the effect of an upward-sloping supply curve of oil and gas imports on the optimal taxation of both industries. A 30 percent decline in US demand for imported oil is assumed to result in a 10 percent decline in world oil prices. Not surprisingly the optimal taxation is now dominated by the optimal tariff on oil and gas imports, which is set close to the value predicted by the rule-of-thumb welfare maximizing value ($1/\varepsilon_m^s$).[15] The welfare gains from improved terms of trade now dominate the calculations, and welfare actually increases by $2.33 billion. Since revenue can be raised in a welfare-enhancing manner through a tariff on crude oil, all other taxes (which are welfare reducing) are scaled down accordingly. Of course this last simulation is only illustrative since it ignores both the possibility of retaliation and the case of a nonconstant import supply elasticity. Both considerations would lead to a lower optimal tariff rate than the one presented in table 8.4.

8.5 Conclusion

The estimates in this chapter suggest that a tariff on crude oil imports would be a very inefficient way to reduce the US trade deficit. A tariff would cause much labor dislocation (an estimated 143,000 workers would have to find new jobs) because sectors using crude oil would have to adjust to the 25 percent tariff. The welfare cost would be large as well, resulting in an estimated welfare loss of 19 cents for every dollar of raised revenue. Our estimates show that an excise tax would raise revenue more efficiently, resulting in both higher revenue for each additional percentage increase in tax (because of a larger tax base) and a much lower welfare cost of about 1 to 3 cents per dollar of increased revenue.

Besides being an inefficient instrument for raising revenue, an import tariff on crude oil would pose several problematic trade policy issues for the United States. To begin with, since US tariff rates on crude oil are "bound" in the GATT, any rate increase would require compensation on other products—and in any case the GATT specifically prohibits the imposition of import fees for fiscal purposes (Article VIII: 1a). In addition an oil import fee would complicate US trade relations with Canada, Mexico, and Venezuela.

In estimating the least costly combination of excise taxes and import tariffs for raising a predetermined amount of government revenue, we restricted taxation to the two energy sectors. This meant that taxation could not be uniform and that a production distortion would result, with too few resources going to the energy sectors. Under these conditions the least costly combination of tariffs and excise taxes in the two sectors is an excise tax on crude oil and a tariff on petroleum products. This combination results in a small subsidy on petroleum products, which counteracts the distortionary costs induced by the taxation of crude oil, a substantial input (nearly two-thirds of the value of intermediate purchases) to the petroleum products sector. Setting the higher tariff on the final good, petroleum products, increases the demand for both sectors, while imposing a higher excise tax on the intermediate product avoids the reduction in the demand for crude oil that would result from a tax on petroleum products.

9 Conclusions

We began this book with the observation that in popular discussions of US foreign trade policy, the claim is often made that barriers to trade are now almost insignificant because of successive rounds of multilateral negotiations. We also noted that many observers have been alarmed by the recent increase in nontariff barriers, arguing that they have canceled out many of the gains achieved through painstaking efforts during thirty years of multilateral negotiations. In this book we have evaluated the costs of these nontariff barriers under a number of alternative institutional and behavioral assumptions. Now, in this chapter, we summarize these results and put the costs of protection in a broader perspective by taking into account the adjustment costs of displaced workers were protection to be removed. We also address the erosion of the gains from multilateral tariff reductions caused by the rise in nontariff barriers.

In section 9.1 we summarize our estimates of the welfare costs to the US economy of quantitative restrictions (QRs) on imports of textiles and apparel, autos, and steel products. We first summarize the results of the basic model, and then we review how these results are affected by wage distortions, which are themselves influenced by protection; by economies of scale in the steel and auto sectors; and by abnormal profits in the auto sector because of the voluntary export restraints (VERs). We also discuss the inefficacy of trade policy for reducing the fiscal deficit.

In section 9.2 we calculate the cost to the economy of each job protected by QRs, taking into account the time it would take displaced workers to relocate if protection were removed. Our calculations of the benefit–cost ratio indicates that the QRs in these three sectors exact a high cost. In section 9.3 we provide an indicative estimate of the costs of quotas in all sectors of the US economy. The high costs of protection through QRs receives further confirmation in section 9.4, where we ask the question: What tariff structure would yield the same economic costs as those result-

Table 9.1
Welfare cost comparisons with earlier studies (billions of current dollars)

Study	Year of estimate	Textiles and apparel	Autos	Steel[a]
Hufbauer, Berliner, and Elliot (1986)	1984	6.65	1.4	1.3
Cline (1987)	1986	8.13		
Winston and Associates (1987)	1984		5.0	
Dinopoulos and Kreinin (1988)	1984		5.86	
Tarr and Morkre (1984)	1985			0.80
de Melo and Tarr[b]	1984	6.9–14.95 (10.4)	7.3–10.3 (9.82)	0.54–2.43 (0.86)
de Melo and Tarr[c]	1984		9.62–9.74	0.78–0.99
de Melo and Tarr[d]	1984		8.75–12.19	0.75–0.82

Note: Except where indicated, estimates are from computations presented in table 1.1 of chapter 1.
a. All estimates for steel are for the year 1985.
b. From tables 5.3, 5.4, and 5.5 in chapter 5. Estimates for central elasticity (small-country assumption) are in parentheses.
c. From table 6.8 in chapter 6.
d. From tables 7.2 and 7.3 in chapter 7.

ing from the quotas in the three sectors we have examined? Finally, in section 9.5 we suggest some directions for future research.

9.1 Summary of Results

In this section we reflect on the main lessons from our modeling exercise on the costs of QRs. Before doing so, however, we briefly compare our estimates with those of previous studies.

Table 9.1 summarizes the welfare cost estimates of this study and those of earlier studies for the same or comparable years. For steel previous estimates fall within the range of our estimates (which depend on elasticities) and are close to our central elasticity estimate. For textiles and apparel and even more so for autos, our estimates are higher than previous estimates.[1] One reason is that we have benefited from more accurate estimates of the premia occasioned by the QRs. Another reason, which applies only in autos, is that we modeled the impact of imperfect competition and economies of scale, which resulted in larger estimates of the costs of protection in our preferred scenario. Different modeling assumptions also account for lower estimates in earlier studies. General equilibrium estimates derived from multicountry models usually assume unrealistically large terms-of-trade effects due to the modeling assumption of imperfect substitutability in foreign trade. As a result multicountry models often yield losses from unilateral tariff reductions.

Welfare costs. We distinguished two components of the welfare costs of QRs, rent transfer costs and distortionary costs, and estimated the contribution of each component to the total welfare cost of QRs. While in the aggregate about two-thirds of welfare costs are due to the rent transfer component, there is much variation across the three sectors. Variations in the share of the distortionary cost component are due largely to the different quota premium rates in the three sectors; distortion costs increase more than proportionately with the level of the distortion. Thus the distortionary cost component of QRs is lower in steel than in textiles and apparel, even though the elasticity of substitution in use between domestic and foreign products is higher in steel than in textiles (see table 5.1).

Our calculations suggest that the United States could achieve the same degree of protection as under the current system of QRs at about one-third the cost by shifting to a system that transfers the quota rights to domestic firms. For political economy reasons, however, such a shift would be quite difficult. Quota rents are a means of compensating foreigners for US protection against their exports, so US capture of the quota rents could lead to retaliation. Since the benefits of capturing quota rents depend on the nature of such repercussions, the political economy of auctioning quota rents is complex and should be taken into account when assessing a system of auction quotas.

Employment. If the supply of work is inversely related to income, elimination of QR protection would lead to a small reduction in the supply of work, taking into account general equilibrium repercussions through changes in the real wage (a reduction of about 20,000 work-years).

Abstracting from the small effect of QR protection on the supply of work, we find that removal of QR protection would lead to a relocation of workers from the textile and apparel and steel industries to the rest of the economy. The revealed pattern of comparative advantage at the ten-sector level of disaggregation suggests that the two service sectors and the other manufactures sector would expand the most with removal of QRs. We found that removal of tariff protection would lead to job losses in textiles and nontraded services. The textile sector loses because it has the highest tariff protection. The nontraded services sector loses because the real exchange rate depreciates when tariffs are eliminated. Because of the elimination of quota rents when QRs are removed, there is much less real exchange rate depreciation than when tariffs are eliminated. Hence nontraded services are affected differently by the two types of trade liberalization.

Terms of trade. Estimating the magnitude of the terms-of-trade loss induced by elimination of protection by the United States is a controversial issue. Some analysts believe that the United States is large enough in the world economy that it is likely to suffer a substantial income loss from a unilateral reduction in protection. Others disagree, arguing that US shares in world trade volumes at the sectoral level are small enough that the terms-of-trade-induced income losses resulting from policy changes of the magnitude considered here are likely to be small.

Although we share the latter view, we systematically investigated the terms-of-trade issue by modeling foreign trade in a way that makes it easy to explore the sensitivity of welfare results to different values of foreign import supply elasticities and foreign export demand elasticities. (Our best guess is that only about 25 percent of the recovered distortionary costs of QRs would be "dissipated" abroad in unavoidable terms-of-trade losses.) As detailed in chapter 5, it appears that with generalized monopoly and monopsony power (i.e., with across-the-board import supply and export demand elasticities of 3 to 4), the removal of the distortionary costs of QRs would be offset by the induced terms-of-trade losses. However, because of the rent transfer component, there would still be a welfare gain of about $15 billion with QR removal.

Disaggregation. Because of our focus on QR protection, we used a fairly aggregated model (ten or twelve sectors) for our simulations. However, there is a noticeable downward bias in the estimate of the distortionary cost component of QR protection when aggregation reduces the variance in dispersion.[2] To minimize the reduction in the variance of the distortion caused by aggregation, we have been careful to isolate the sectors subject to distortions. In fact, as previously mentioned, a six-sector version of our model that preserves steel, autos, and textiles as separate sectors closely replicates our results. In general, however, if aggregation occurs across distorted sectors, the consistency advantages of general equilibrium-based estimates over partial equilibrium-based estimates must be traded off against the disadvantages of insufficient disaggregation.

The institutional characteristics of the auto and steel industries (economies of scale and strong labor unions) could also alter the estimation of the costs of QR protection in these industries. For this reason we considered three different types of interactions between market structure and QRs: (1) second-best effects, (2) QR-influenced (endogenous) wage distortions, and (3) imperfect competition.

Second-best effects. The costs of QRs under two kinds of second-best effects were considered: (1) that auto and steel workers received a wage exceeding the value marginal product of homogeneous workers in other sectors, and (2) that increased foreign direct investment, as occurred because of the VER in autos, might reduce welfare. Unlike the potentially strong second-best effects often considered in the theoretical literature on the normative aspects of protection, however, we found second-best effects to have a very negligible impact on the welfare costs of QRs in autos and steel.[3] In the case of a distortionary wage, the protection-induced cost was small for diverting workers from sectors to which they should be attracted because their marginal value product is higher. And while protection increased the costs of the VER in autos because it induced increased foreign entry into a sector where the private marginal product of capital exceeded its social marginal product, here too the effect was small.

QR-influenced wage distortions. We also considered a formulation in which wages are set by the auto and steel workers unions instead of being determined exogenously. In this formulation unions had a trade-off between employment and wages, and a change in trade policy affected the wages chosen by the unions. The distortionary and employment effects of QRs in steel were found to be quite sensitive to the modeling of this trade-off, especially if the union places a greater premium on wages than on employment. In this case the welfare benefits of removing the QRs may be greater than in the case of no wage distortion because the unions chose a lower wage premium with the removal of the QR, thereby reducing the wage distortion.

Imperfect competition. Allowing for the presence of increasing returns to scale in steel does not significantly alter the estimation results because steel producers do not price monopolistically and have little scope for exploiting economies of scale. Thus whether firms' pricing behavior is represented by contestable-market pricing with the price set equal to average cost or by monopolistic competition with free entry/exit, the welfare cost estimates under increasing returns to scale are close to those under constant returns.

The auto sector has greater scope for exploiting economies of scale, and it is likely that the VER allowed US auto producers to make abnormally high profits in 1984. Under a scenario of monopolistic competition with fixed conjectures, initial profits, and increasing returns to scale, firm entry to eliminate the VER-induced profits leads to a distortionary cost two times that under constant returns because of the loss of scale efficiency. We argued, however, that the welfare costs of the auto VER are best characterized in a monopolistic competition model with free entry and exit, international capital mobility, endogenous conjectures, and initial pure profits. With endogenous conjectures, less inefficient entry occurs, so the distortionary cost component of QR protection is lower, but it is still 10 percent higher than under constant returns ($2.13 billion vs. $1.94).

Protection and government revenue. Trade policy has been invoked not only for protecting jobs but also for raising revenue to reduce the US budget deficit. With a disaggregation of the energy sector into oil and gas and petroleum products, we illustrated numerically several propositions from the literature on tax incidence and on optimal taxation. Excise taxes that do not discriminate by source (imports versus domestic production) were found to be a far more efficient means to raise revenue than a tariff on imports of crude oil. With taxation limited to the two vertically related energy sectors, it becomes optimal for second-best reasons to impose a relatively low tariff on petroleum products to reduce the flow of resources out of these sectors. It is less burdensome to impose higher excise taxes on crude oil, the intermediate sector, than on petroleum products because a tax on petroleum products would reduce demand for crude oil. This combination of excise tax and tariff policy would result in a small subsidy to petroleum products to compensate for the indirect tax that the sector would pay because of the tax on crude oil. We show that a given amount of tax revenue could be collected from both energy sectors at a welfare cost of less than 0.05 percent of the tax revenue by selecting an optimal combination of excise taxes, tariffs, and subsidies.

9.2 Costs per Job Protected by Quota Protection

Considering that protection is obtained through the political process, some might argue that Congress has decided to value a job in the protected sectors more highly than jobs elsewhere in the economy. In that case, however, we should ask: What is the cost per job protected in the quota-protected sectors, given that overall employment is not increased?

We consider the case of joint quota protection in textiles and apparel, autos, and steel, using the central elasticities of the basic model presented in chapter 5. In chapter 5 we estimated that these quotas cost the US economy \$21.1 billion (in 1984 dollars) while preventing about 294,000 workers from having to relocate to other sectors. Thus the annual cost per job protected in these three sectors is about \$72,000 a year, or 5 times the annual total compensation of workers in the textile and apparel sector and 1.7 times the annual compensation of workers in autos and steel.

If quotas are removed, some workers in previously protected domestic industries will lose their jobs and have to look for jobs in other industries. Economists studying the effects of trade liberalization have traditionally considered labor adjustment to involve costs to the economy that need to be subtracted from the gross benefits of liberalization to obtain the net benefits (Baldwin 1984b). Adjustment of displaced workers takes time and often involves a number of activities including job search, relocation, and training (e.g., see Mussa 1978, 1984). This adjustment is a complex process that raises many factual questions. What are the characteristics of the displaced workers (e.g., their age and skills), how long does it take them to find new jobs, what wage do they receive in their new jobs, how far do they have to move to find new jobs?

Good information on these issues is lacking, so measures of labor adjustment costs are not fully satisfactory. A proxy for these adjustment costs is the discounted value of a displaced worker's earnings losses over a lifetime, obtained by comparing the lifetime earnings stream of displaced workers with the earnings stream of workers who were not displaced.[4] This measure has the advantage that it allows us to estimate how much the gainers from a trade liberalization measure will have left after compensating displaced workers for their earnings losses.

Estimated earnings losses are significant in the first two years after displacement and then decline considerably over the next four years, reaching almost zero after six years. Workers in high-wage industries lose more than workers in low-wage industries (Jacobson 1978). To estimate the net benefits of removing protection, we take the present value of the displaced workers' earnings losses over six years and subtract it from the present value of the benefits over six years.[5] This calculation yields a conservative estimate of the net benefits because after six years earnings losses are zero, whereas benefits do not decay. This measure of net benefits takes the form

$$NB = \frac{\sum_{t=0}^{5} (EV - C_t)}{(1 + r)^t}, \tag{9.1}$$

where $EV = 20.9$ is the equivalent variation measure of gross benefits, $r = 7$ percent is the discount rate, and C_t is the estimated earnings loss in year t.

Table 9.2
Net benefits from quota removal: central elasticity case (billions of 1984 dollars)

	Textiles	Autos	Steel	All three
Earnings loss (*C*)[a]	1.2	2.1	1.1	3.9
Net benefits (*NB*)[b]	53.0	50.1	4.4	107.4
Benefit–cost ratio[c]	44.0	24.0	4.0	28.0

a. Present value of earnings loss (or adjustment costs).
b. As defined in equation 9.1.
c. *NB*/*C*, or the economywide gain per dollar of displaced workers' earnings losses.
Calculation: As an example, to derive the earnings loss of $3.9 billion for all three sectors, we first considered steelworkers. We took the average hourly compensation (AHC) of $20.65 per hour from unpublished data provided by the Bureau of Labor Statistics, Office of Productivity and Technology. We obtained the average number of hours worked (AHW) per week of 40.4 from *Employment and Earnings*, February 1985, using the ratio of average weekly earnings to average hourly earnings in November 1984. We then computed average yearly compensation (AYC) of a steelworker of $42,563 by multiplying AHC times AHW times 52 weeks.

Jacobson's (1978) data reveal that a displaced steelworker earns 46.6 percent less in the first two years after displacement and 12.6 percent less in the subsequent four years. For all industries, Jacobson finds that earning losses are approximately zero after six years. Using a discount factor of 7 percent implies that the present value of a representative steelworker's earnings losses is $55,347.

The same data sources were used for similar calculations for workers in the textile and apparel and auto sectors and to compute an average for manufacturing workers. The present value of the average earnings losses of representative displaced workers by industry are $57,206 in autos, $4,697 in textiles and apparel, and $16,680 for all manufacturing workers. (For textiles and apparel, the separately reported textile and apparel categories were weighted.)

For the experiment in which we remove QRs in all three sectors (see table 5.7 in chapter 5), we obtain the following pattern of displaced workers: 245,000 textile and apparel workers, 16,700 steelworkers, and 31,800 autos workers. The present value of the earnings losses is 245,000 × $4,697 + 16,700 × $55,347 + 31,800 × $57,206 = $3.9 billion.

The results of the calculations of the costs per job saved by QR protection in the three sectors individually and jointly appear in table 9.2. If we take as an example the cost of QR protection in all three sectors, we find that the benefit–cost ratio of quota removal is 28—that is, the present value of the benefits of quota removal of $111.3 billion divided by the present value of the earnings losses (or adjustment costs of workers) of $3.9 billion. Thus the net benefit from removal of the quotas in these three industries is $107.4 billion. So for every dollar of earnings losses of displaced workers, the economy gains $28 from quota removal in the three industries. The calculations for individual sectors show that the benefit–cost ratio of removing QRs is highest in textiles, a sector with low wages and a high-quota premium rate.

9.3 Estimated Costs of All Quantitative Restrictions

Because of the growing interest in the aggregate costs to the US economy of all protection (US Department of Commerce 1987), we provide an estimate in this section of the aggregate costs of QRs using our general equilibrium model.

The United States imposes QRs in other sectors as well as in textiles and apparel, autos, and steel. For example, Hufbauer, Berliner, and Elliot (1986) report QRs in book manufacturing, motorcycles, shipbuilding and maritime industries, sugar and food products containing sugar, cheese and other dairy products, peanuts, and meat. Morkre (1990) has estimated the quota premium rate (in 1987) at 31 percent in cheese[6] and dairy products and 56 to 166 percent in sugar. Using this and other information, and assuming that the quota rents accrue entirely to foreigners, we simulated the effects of removing all QRs in the economy under the following sets of high and low quota premium rates: 5 and 2.5 percent in agriculture; 3 and 1.5 percent in other manufactures, other consumer goods, and food; and zero in the remaining sectors. The result of removing all QRs (including those in textiles, autos, and steel) is a welfare gain of $28.5 billion in the case of the high premium rates and $24.8 billion in the case of the low premium rates. Since the quota premium rates are best guesses, these estimates of the benefits of removing all QRs are only suggestive.

9.4 Computation of Tariffs with a Welfare Cost Equivalent to That of Quotas

Another way of evaluating the costs of the quotas is to estimate the tariff structure required to generate the same welfare costs as those resulting from the quotas in the three sectors—that is, a tariff structure that is "welfare equivalent" to the quotas. Estimated total welfare costs in our central elasticity case (chapter 5) were $21.05 billion, of which $6.4 billion is distortion costs and $14.65 billion is rent transfers to foreigners. Here we ask what tariff structures would yield the same distortionary costs and the same total welfare costs as those resulting from the QRs in the three sectors.

We calculate the welfare-equivalent tariff structure in two different ways (table 9.3). In one set of calculations, we compute the uniform tariff rates that would result in the same distortionary costs and the same total welfare costs as those estimated for QRs in textiles and apparel, autos, and steel. We find that a uniform tariff of 23.7 percent (column 1) would yield the

Table 9.3
Tariff structures yielding costs equal to those of quotas: central elasticity estimates

	Uniform protection		Linear tariff increase	
	Distortionary cost (1)	Total cost (2)	Distortionary cost (3)	Total cost (4)
Welfare cost[a]	6.4	21.0	6.4	21.0
Average tariff ($\bar{t}$)[b]	23.7	49.0	13.1	23.4
Variance in tariffs (σ_t)	0.0	0.0	16.0	28.7

a. Welfare is the equivalent variation measure in billions of 1984 dollars defined in appendix 3A of chapter 3. It is measured from a quota-free uniform protection level for the uniform tariff measure and from a quota-free solution with actual tariffs for the linear tariff increase measure.
b. Average tariff weighted by import shares.

same distortion cost and that a uniform tariff of 49.0 percent (column 2) would yield the same total welfare cost.

The multilateral tariff negotiations, however, have not resulted in a uniform tariff structure but rather have lowered tariffs proportionately. So in an alternative set of estimates, we calculate radial across-the-board tariff increases for all sectors, starting from tariff rates at their 1984 levels: $tm_i^1 = tm_i^0 \alpha$, where tm_i^1 is the new tariff rate and tm_i^0 is the 1984 rate. To yield an average tariff rate that has the same distortion costs as the QRs in the three sectors (column 3), all initial tariff rates must be multiplied by 3.9; the result is an average tariff rate of 13.1 percent, with a variance of 16.0. To yield a tariff rate with the same total welfare cost as the QRs in the three sectors, all tariff rates must be multiplied by 8.58 (column 4); the result is an average tariff level of 23.4 percent with variance of 28.7.

By comparison the average tariff rates on manufactured goods were 10 percent before the Kennedy Round, 7 percent after the Kennedy Round, and 5 percent after the Tokyo Round (Balassa and Balassa 1984). The tariff structure presented in table 9.3 as the welfare equivalent of the costs of quotas covers only three sectors and so underestimates the total costs of US quotas. But even in terms of the welfare costs only in textiles and apparel, autos, and steel, it is no exaggeration to conclude that QRs have taken us back to pre-World War II levels.[7]

9.5 Directions for Future Research

This study has discussed a number of trade policy issues traditionally referred to as "strategic." There are several areas in which greater attention to strategic interactions could provide useful insights. One such case is the evaluation of industrial policy in the presence of wage distortions. We incorporated union behavior into our model, which made wage distortions endogenous and showed that protection increases the wage distortion. If in addition, however, the government employs industrial policy (such as subsidies or protection) to correct for wage distortions, unions might try to influence the level of the tariff or the level of wage subsidies received by the industry by altering its wage demands. The costs of industrial policy to correct for wage distortions would likely be higher than we have estimated, but that estimation would require the modeling of the strategic interactions between the government and the union.[8]

Another area of strategic interaction relates to optimal tariffs. We modeled the exploitation of monopoly and monopsony power under the assumption that foreign governments do not retaliate, which would overestimate the benefits of protection for exploiting such power. To properly address these issues, however, would require a model that incorporates other regions in the world as agents—preferably in a dynamic context since that is how strategic interactions are properly modeled.[9]

Recent advances in economic theory indicate that the benefits of trade liberalization are considerably greater than has previously been estimated for two reasons: (1) specialization is magnified by increasing returns to scale, as firms move up or down their average cost curve, and (2) previously unestimated dynamic gains are likely to be greater than the static gains. Results from static CGE models with increasing returns to scale have supported the first hypothesis.[10] The failure to realize economies of scale in many developing countries implies that additional empirical applications of models of the type developed in chapter 7 would be useful for assessing the benefits of trade liberalization in developing countries, as well as the resulting pattern of specialization.

The second hypothesis also has important repercussions. With constant returns to scale, factor returns exhaust the product, and it is unprofitable to invest in research and development for new products or production processes. But with constant returns to scale, per capita growth is zero in the Solow-type (1956) growth model. Thus the traditional growth model could explain long-run per capita growth only in terms of exogenous technological change.

The new growth theory, however, has explained that the introduction of new technologies temporarily creates increasing returns to scale and thereby explains endogenous technological change (see Romer 1986, 1989; Grossman and Helpman 1989, 1990). However, since new technology is subject to the law of diminishing returns (like all factors), increasing returns to scale will revert to constant returns (with no per capita growth) unless there is continued introduction of new technologies. An open economy can import technologies from the rest of the world instead of relying on its own limited research and development effort. For a small economy the greatest cost of protection may be a significant reduction in its growth rate because of a lack of imported modern technology.[11] The challenge is to get firmer evidence of the likely magnitude of these effects so that they may be credibly incorporated into forward-looking policy models.

Appendix A: Data Set Construction and Model Calibration

This appendix describes the data manipulations and calibration calculations used to obtain the benchmark equilibrium for counterfactual simulations. The steps are summarized in figure A.1. Some data assembly and manipulation were required because the most recent input-output table available was for 1982. And some reconciliations were necessary because we used data from other sources. Data sources and manipulations are described in section A.1. Section A.2 presents the Social Accounting Matrix (SAM) that resulted from these manipulations. The SAM for 1984 describes the flows between the agents included in the model. This brief description of the SAM introduces the discussion of how the model was fitted (or calibrated) to the base year flows embodied in the SAM, which is covered in section A.3.

A.1 Data Set Construction and Data Sources

In applied general equilibrium modeling, the most consuming task in the data set construction typically involves manipulation of the interindustry table to make it consistent with the data coming from the National Income and Product Accounts (NIPA). For our study, we had to start with an input-output table for 1982 and update it to 1984. The steps involved are described below.

A.1.1 Input-Output Updating

We started with the 80 by 80 matrix of interindustry flows constructed by the US Forest Service for 1982, which is an update of the 500 by 500 table of the US Department of Commerce built from the 1977 census data. The 1982 update draws on data from the 1982 census. The mapping from eighty sectors to twelve sectors is shown in table A.1.[1]

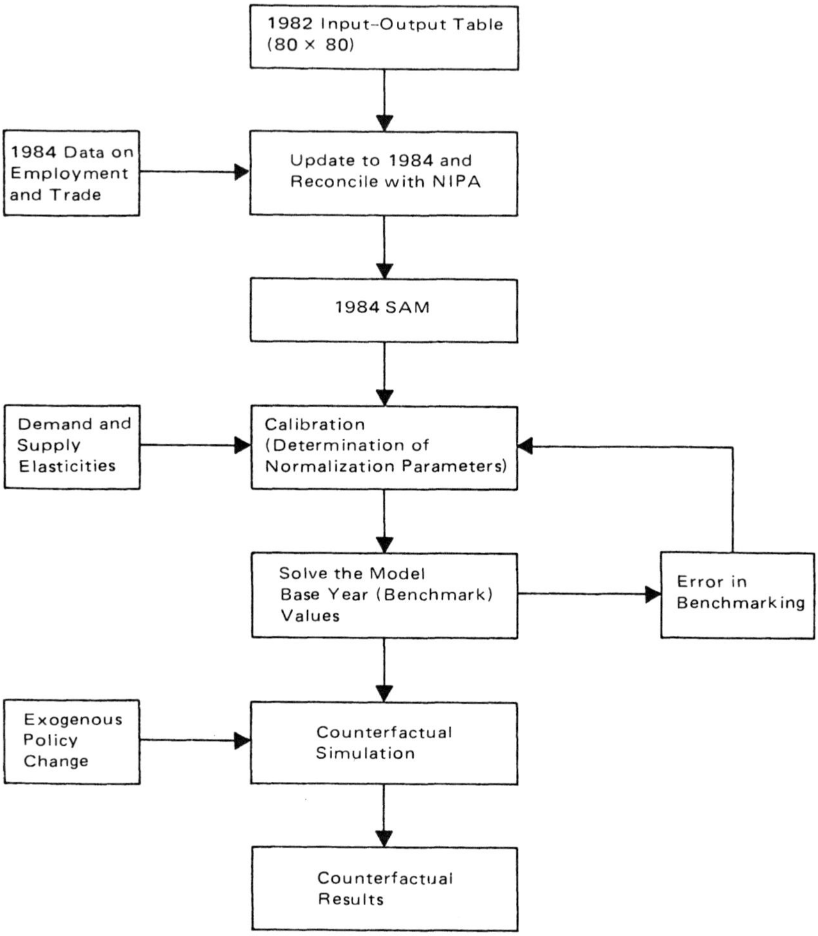

Figure A.1
Benchmarking

Table A.1
Mapping of eighty-sector input-output (I/O) matrix into twelve sectors

Sectors in 80 industry I/O tables	Map into
1. Dairy; livestock; foodgrains; feedgrains; cotton oil; fruits; vegetables; tobacco, sugar	Agriculture
2. Food, tobacco products	Food
3. Mining	Mining
4. Oil and gas extraction	Crude oil and natural gas
5. Apparel; fabric—yarn; textiles—miscellaneous; textiles—fabricated	Textiles and apparel
6. Motor vehicles	Motor vehicles
7. Iron and steel	Iron and steel
8. Petroleum-related products	Petroleum-related products
9. Furniture—household; furniture—other; drugs; leather goods; household applicances; radios, televisions and phonographs; footwear	Other consumer goods
10. Munitions; lumber and wood; trucks and buses; wood containers; paper and allied products; paper containers; printing; chemicals; plastics; paints; rubber; glass and stone; nonferrous metals; metal containers; heating and plumbing products; screw-threading machines; other fabricated metals; engines and turbines; farm machinery; construction machinery; materials and machinery; metalwork machinery; special industrial machinery; general industrial machinery; miscellaneous machinery; computing equipment; other office equipment; service machinery; electrical equipment; electric wiring; electronic tubes; semiconductors; other electronic components; electronics—miscellaneous; parts—motor, aircraft; other transportation equipment; professional science equipment; optical and photographic equipment; noncomparable imports; other industry	Other manufacturing
11. Telephone-telegraph; communications—radio and television; transportation—communication; trade—wholesale and retail; banking and insurance; business services; rest of world industry	Traded services
12. Construction—nongovernment; construction—government; real estate; health and education services; personal services; government business; electricity, gas, and water	Nontraded services

The US Department of Commerce publishes NIPA data, including value added by sector, annually. These data were taken from the July 1986 issue of the *Survey of Current Business* (table 6.1). NIPA data were not sufficiently disaggregated for three of our twelve sectors. NIPA data are for motor vehicles and equipment, rather than for motor vehicles, and primary metal products, rather than for iron and steel. And NIPA data for electric and electronic equipment contain both consumer goods and part of our other manufactured goods. Using data from the Federal Reserve Board's industrial production indexes published in the *Federal Reserve Bulletin*, we were able to allocate the value added of these three aggregated sectors into the appropriate sectors of our model.[2] The mapping of the NIPA value added data into the twelve sectors is shown in table A.2.

The first step was to update the gross output vector of the 1982 table. Given data on value added for 1984, we calculated gross output by sector (X_i):

$$X_i^{84} = \frac{VA_i^{84}}{1 - \sum_{j=1}^{n} a_{ji}^{82}}, \qquad i = 1, \ldots, n, \tag{A.1}$$

where VA_i is value added in sector i, superscripts denote observations of the variables in the respective year, and (as described below) base-year prices are set equal to unity by choice of units.

Assuming Leontief technology, interindustry flows for 1984 are given by

$$V_{ji}^{84} = a_{ji} X_i^{84}, \qquad i, j = 1, \ldots, n, \tag{A.2}$$

where no superscript on the a_{ji} indicates the assumption of constant input-output coefficients over the time period.

A.1.2 Balance of Payments and Transfers

Data on foreign transactions in the NIPA accounts are from the *Survey of Current Business* (June 1986, table A.1). We defined the category "other service" exports and imports in this table as the exports and imports of our traded services sector. As explained below, factor income exports and imports were treated as exogenous remittances.

Total exports and imports of goods and services for 1984 were calculated from merchandise exports and imports plus other services exports and imports. Total exports were \$283 billion (\$224.1 + \$58.9), and total imports were \$390.3 billion (\$336 + \$54.3). The difference of −\$107.3 is the deficit in the US balance of trade on goods and services.

Table A.2
Mapping of National Income and Product Accounts (NIPA) value-added data into the twelve-sector aggregation (numbers in parentheses are value added in billions of 1984 US dollars)

Sectors in NIPA accounts	Map into
1. Farms (79.0); agricultural services (15.0)	Agriculture (94.0)
2. Food (67.7); tobacco (12.4)	Food (80.1)
3. Metal mining (3.1); coal mining (17.3); nonmetallic minerals (5.6)	Mining (26.0)
4. Oil and gas extraction (99.1)	Oil and gas extraction (99.1)
5. Textiles mill products (17.3); apparel and other textile products (21.3)	Textiles and apparel (38.6)
6. Motor vehicles and equipment (50.3 × 0.529)[a]	Motor vehicles (26.62)
7. Primary metal products (35.7 × 0.652)[a]	Iron and steel (23.28)
8. Petroleum and coal products (29.6)	Petroleum and coal products (29.61)
9. Rubber and plastic products (24.7); leather and leather products (3.5); furniture and fixtures (12.8); electric and electronic equipment (76.1 × 0.108)[a]	Other consumer goods (49.2)
10. Lumber and wood products (23.6); stone, clay, and glass products (23.4); fabricated metal products (53.6); machinery, except electrical (88.9); other transportation equipment (45.4); instruments and related products (24.9); miscellaneous manufacturing industries (11.9); electric and electronic equipment (76.1 × 0.892);[a] paper products (32.1); printing and publishing (47.5); chemicals and allied products (64.3); motor vehicles and equipment (50.3 × 0.471);[a] primary metals (35.7 × 0.348)[a]	Other manufacturing goods (519.6)
11. Railroad transportation (24.0); local transit (7.5); trucking (56.7); water transportation (7.9); transportation by air (26.2); pipelines (4.9); transportation services (8.5); telephone and telegraph (92.2); radio and television broadcasting (10.4); wholesale trade (262.1); retail trade (348.3); banking (72.3); credit agency (10.2); security and commodity brokers (21.0); insurance carriers (34.7); insurance agents (20.7); holding companies (8.2); business services (125.7); legal services (41.7); miscellaneous professional services (57.3); statistical discrepancy (−1.9); rest of the world (47.5)	Traded services (1,286.1)

Table A.2 (continued)

Sectors in NIPA accounts	Map into
12. Electric, gas, and sanitary services (112.6); construction (171.1); federal government (132.0); federal government enterprises (27.9); real estate (409.9); hotels (27.4); personal services (24.8); auto repair (29.9); miscellaneous repair service (12.5); movies (7.5) recreation services (18.4); health services (168.8); educational services (22.6); social services (35.7); private households (9.1); state and local government (258.9); state and local enterprises (23.5)	Nontraded services (1492.6)

Source: US Department of Commerce, *Survey of Current Business*, July 1986.
Note: Because of rounding, the value of the aggregate category may not always equal the sum of the parts.
a. See text and text note 2 for an explanation of how NIPA sectors were disaggregated for allocation to our twelve-sector aggregation.

Remittances are defined as net factor income plus net transfer payments for interest paid by government to foreigners. In 1984 US resident factors received \$101.6 billion from foreigners, and factors resident in foreign countries received \$53.6 billion from the United States, for a net US factor income of \$48 billion. The United States paid out \$12 billion to foreigners in net transfer payments and \$19.8 billion in government interest to foreigners, so net remittances to the United States were \$16.2 billion (\$48 − \$12 − \$19.8). These net remittances reduced the deficit on goods and services, yielding a current account deficit of −\$91.1 billion (\$283 − \$390.3 + \$16.2), which of course was exactly offset by foreign capital inflow.

A.1.3 Import and Export Data

Table A.3 defines the mapping from the Standard International Trade Classification (SITC) used by the US Customs Service into our twelve-sector model. The SITC data required three types of manipulation. First, data on traded services were taken from the balance of payments part of the NIPA (*Survey of Current Business*, June 1986, table A.1), which reports service exports and imports under both factor income and other services income. Factor income exports refers to labor and capital services of US factors abroad for which US residents receive payments. Factor income imports are defined analogously for foreign factors. The bulk of factor income exports are interest payments on US capital loaned abroad. We

Table A.3
Mapping of Standard International Trade Classification (SITC) data into the twelve-sector model

SITC categories	Map into
1. 00, 01, 031, 041, 042, 043, 045, 046, 047, 051, 052, 054, 061, 071, 072, 08, 21, 22, 29, 42, 42	Agriculture
2. 02, 032, 048, 053, 055, 062, 073, 09, 11, 12, 43	Food
3. 2311, 241, 27, 283, 284, 285, 286	Mining
4. 331, 3411	Crude oil and natural gas extraction
5. 26, 65, 84	Textile and apparel products
6. 7321	Motor vehicles
7. 281, 282, 67	Iron and steel
8. 332, 3412	Petroleum-related products
9. 54, 55, 6291, 7241, 7242, 7292, 7294, 7331, 7334, 82, 83, 85, 86, 94, 96	Other consumer goods
10. 2312, 2313, 2314, 242, 243, 244, 25, 32, 35, 51, 52, 53, 56, 57, 58, 59, 61, 6210, 6293, 6294, 6299, 63, 64, 66, 68, 69, 71, 7221, 7222, 7231, 7232, 7249, 7250, 7261, 7262, 7291, 7293, 7295, 7296, 7297, 7299, 7324, 7325, 7326, 7327, 7328, 7329, 7333, 734, 735, 81, 89, 95, 7322, 7323	Other manufactured goods

Source: Authors' definition.

treat factor income exports and imports as exogenous remittances. The "other services income" from the NIPA is then included in our model as exports (receipts) and imports (payments) of the traded services sector.

Second, we scaled the sectoral import and export data of customs by aggregate imports and exports from the NIPA data. To do this, we took aggregate data on merchandise imports ($336 billion) and exports ($224.1 billion) from the NIPA accounts and calculated each sector's share of aggregate imports and exports using the customs' data:

$$s_i = \frac{E_i^C}{\sum_{j=1}^{n} E_j^C}$$

and

$$s_i^* = \frac{M_i^C}{\sum_{j=1}^{n} M_j^C},$$

where E_i^C and M_i^C are exports and imports of sector i taken from the customs' data. Then, to get import and export vectors scaled by the NIPA data, we defined each sector's total imports (exports) as each sector's share (defined above) times total imports (exports) from the NIPA data.

Third, we converted the data to US producer prices. This manipulation was necessary because customs data on exports reports the price of the product at the port of export. The producer receives something less than this amount because the transportation and the wholesale and retail trade sectors receive part of this value. Because these sectors constitute the traded services sector of our twelve-sector model, we needed to adjust the export data of each sector for the share of traded services embodied in the value of the item at the port of export.

To do this, we used US Department of Commerce data on the share of transportation and wholesale and retail trade embodied in exports (*Survey of Current Business*, May 1984, table A). We mapped these data into our twelve-sector classification. Except for traded services, the export data of each sector were then reduced to $E_i = (1 - \hat{s}_i)E_i^N$, where $\hat{s}_i$ is the share of traded services embodied in the value of exports and E_i^N are sectoral exports from the customs service data, adjusted for consistency with the NIPA data as described above. Traded services exports were correspondingly increased to $\sum_{i \neq TS}(1 - \hat{s}_i)E_i^N + E_{TS}^N = E_{TS}$, where TS is the index for traded services.[3]

Import data were collected on a c.i.f. rather than an f.a.s. basis (the value at the US port of entry rather than the value at the foreign port of origin). Since interindustry flows already include wholesale and retail trade and transportation margins in the use of inputs, no further adjustments of the import data were required. These calculations yield imports in US producer prices of appropriate categories.

Data on tariffs were obtained from US Department of Commerce publication *FT-990* (December 1984, p. A-17). These data were mapped into the twelve-sector classification. The ad valorem tariff rates t_i were then calculated as the ratio of the calculated duty to general imports (c.i.f. value).

A.1.4 Final Demand

Sectoral final demand expressed in composite goods and inclusive of investment demand and changes in inventories C_i was calculated residually using the following sectoral material balance equation under the assumption that prices (inclusive of tariffs and tariff equivalents) are set equal to unity:

$$C_i = -\sum_{j=1}^{n} V_{ij} - E_i + M_i + X_i, \qquad i = 1, \ldots, n. \tag{A.3}$$

Two sectors, steel, and oil and gas extraction, had slightly negative values for C_i. These negative values partly reflect a reduction of inventories, which are not included as a separate component of final demand. These negative values may also have resulted because of changes in the value of input-output coefficients between 1982 and 1984.

Take steel as an example. Assuming that the import and export data are accurate, a negative value for C_i means that more steel was shipped for intermediate use than was produced. Barring a decumulation of inventories, this means that the values of the input-output coefficients reflecting steel use are too large. Recall that 1982 was a recession year, so firms probably added to their inventories of steel. Thus, in 1984, when firms were not adding to their inventories of steel, simply multiplying the 1982 input-output coefficient a_{ij} by the gross output value of sector i in 1984 will overestimate steel usage in sector i. Accordingly we deflated the input-output coefficients across the steel and crude oil and natural gas rows as follows:

$$a_{ij}^{84} = \frac{a_{ij}^{82}}{1.264} \qquad \text{for } i = \text{steel}, j = 1, \ldots, n,$$

and

$$a_{ij}^{84} = \frac{a_{ij}^{82}}{1.0625} \qquad \text{for } i = \text{crude oil}, j = 1, \ldots, n,$$

where the deflation was carried out to eliminate negative values of consumption for steel and for crude oil and natural gas extraction. Since the adjustment coefficients were calculated to obtain positive but small values of final consumption, these sectors can be regarded as pure intermediate sectors.

The results of all these manipulations are summarized in the interindustry flows reported in table A.4.

A.1.5 Employment Data

Data on employed civilians by industry for 1984 were taken from the US Department of Labor, *Employment and Earnings* (January 1985, pp. 186–189). Aggregation to the twelve-sector classification was straightforward, with the exception of motor vehicles, since data were reported as motor vehicles and equipment. From other issues of *Employment and Earnings*, we determined that the proportion of employees in motor vehicles and equipment (SIC 371) accounted for by employees in motor vehicles (SIC 3711)

Table A.4
Twelve-sector interindustry flow matrix for the United States for 1984: intermediate flows (billions of 1984 US dollars)

	Agriculture	Food	Mining	Oil and gas	Textiles	Motor vehicles	Steel	Petroleum products
Agriculture	69.73	88.58	0.01	0.01	3.32	0.00	0.00	0.00
Food	19.96	52.83	0.01	0.02	0.05	0.01	0.03	0.09
Mining	0.27	0.24	7.06	0.02	0.08	0.04	5.00	0.43
Oil and gas	0.51	0.17	0.10	16.73	0.05	0.02	0.16	122.24
Textiles	0.55	0.14	0.10	0.04	47.16	4.22	0.04	0.02
Vehicles	0.01	0.00	0.01	0.00	0.00	8.45	0.03	0.01
Steel	0.09	0.02	0.29	0.62	0.02	1.38	7.28	0.07
Petroleum products	12.03	2.21	1.80	1.42	1.23	0.37	1.38	24.11
Nontraded services	27.07	11.39	4.79	27.38	5.16	1.61	5.64	11.29
Trade services	26.53	37.65	4.69	5.98	11.42	10.43	7.42	19.33
Consumer goods	0.82	1.58	0.02	0.04	0.74	1.49	0.06	0.65
Other manufactures	21.88	41.44	6.65	5.98	14.98	69.55	7.19	9.34
Total intermediate use	179.45	236.25	25.53	58.24	84.20	97.58	34.23	187.58
Value added	94.00	80.10	26.00	99.10	38.60	26.62	23.28	29.60
Total expenditures	273.45	316.35	51.53	157.34	122.80	124.20	57.51	217.18

	Nontraded services	Traded services	Consumer goods	Other manufactures	Total intermediate demand	Imports plus duties	Exports	Final demand	Total receipts
Agriculture	12.22	1.36	0.25	8.19	183.66	17.26	29.41	77.64	273.45
Food	56.20	1.17	1.88	1.36	133.61	8.75	4.70	186.78	316.35
Mining	17.10	0.02	0.13	13.65	44.05	3.53	2.17	8.83	51.53
Oil and gas	52.89	1.88	0.08	5.14	199.98	43.59	0.86	0.0818	157.34
Textiles	7.33	1.27	2.26	6.82	69.96	23.62	6.76	69.71	122.80
Vehicles	0.73	0.13	0.00	1.24	10.62	32.61	4.86	141.34	124.20
Steel	7.73	0.59	2.19	48.59	68.85	12.71	1.36	0.0057	57.51
Petroleum products	53.75	51.85	2.39	31.39	183.93	21.19	4.23	50.21	217.18
Nontraded services	271.21	201.43	7.41	95.53	669.91	0.00	0.00	1,773.41	2,443.32
Traded services	251.66	343.03	19.46	181.51	919.10	54.30	88.03	1,041.52	1,994.35
Consumer	14.66	1.80	8.16	4.09	34.12	29.01	10.44	109.98	125.54
Manufactures	205.24	103.71	32.14	447.64	965.73	156.70	130.18	425.56	1,364.77
Total intermediate use	950.72	708.25	76.33	845.17	3,483.54	403.27	283.00	3,885.07	7,248.34
Value added	1,492.00	1,286.00	49.20	519.60	3,764.80[a]				
Total expenditure	2,443.32	1,994.35	125.54	1,364.77	7,248.34				

Source: Authors' calculations based on data sources explained in the text.

a. The sum of value added for all sectors.

Table A.5
US civilian employment by sector in 1984 (thousands of employees)

Sector	Number of employees
Agriculture	3,321
Food	1,752
Mining	338
Oil and gas extraction	619
Textiles and apparel	1,969
Motor vehicles	536
Iron and steel	531
Petroleum products	204
Other consumer goods	2,599
Other manufactured	13,404
Traded services	42,043
Nontraded services	37,689
Total employment	105,005

Sources: Authors' calculations based on data obtained from the US Department of Labor, Bureau of Labor Statistics, *Employment and Earnings* (January 1985, pp. 186–189).

was 0.452. Thus we allocated 0.452 of the employees in motor vehicles and equipment to motor vehicles and the remainder to "other manufacturing." The results of these tabulations are presented in table A.5.

A.1.6 Rental Rate on Capital

The value of the net stock of fixed private residential plus nonresidential capital for 1984 is $6,936 billion (*Survey of Current Business*, August 1986, p. 36). To obtain the return to capital R (defined as the annual return to capital divided by the capital stock), we subtract from national income ($3028.6 billion) that share not received by capital (*Survey of Current Business*, July 1987, p. 25), which includes employee compensation ($2213.9 billion), depreciation, or the capital consumption allowance ($254.5), and labor's estimated share of proprietors' income ($157.1 billion).[4] This yields a value of the return to capital in 1984 of $403.085 billion,[5] or $R = 5.8$ percent (403.085/6,936).

A.2 A Social Accounting Matrix for 1984

Here we lay out the Social Accounting Matrix (SAM) underlying the model. The SAM provides insight into the model and can be used to derive the economywide income-expenditure identity (Walras' law) from the underlying budget constraints faced by each institution. Algebraically a SAM is represented as a square matrix with elements

$$T = t_{ij}, \tag{A.4}$$

where t_{ij} is the value of the transaction with income accruing to account (institution) i from expenditure by account (institution) j.[6] Each row sum must equal the corresponding column sum, reflecting the fact that each institution exactly satisfies its budget constraint—its receipts must equal its expenditures. Algebraically

$$\sum_j t_{kj} = \sum_i t_{ik} \qquad \text{for all } k. \tag{A.5}$$

Thus the data set is consistent if equation A.5 is satisfied. The data manipulations described in section A.1 ensure that the data set is consistent.

Table A.6 outlines in schematic form the SAM underlying the model, and table A.7 presents the accounting identities underlying the SAM. Six accounts are distinguished.[7] The first two accounts are the activities and commodities accounts. The activities account buys intermediate inputs (domestic and imported) and hires factor services to produce commodities, generating value added in the process. The commodities account combines domestic supply with imports.[8] Interindustry flows are aggregated into one cell. Note also that activities receipts are at producer prices (a "make table" in input-output terminology), while expenditures by activities are in purchasers' prices (a "use table" in the same terminology). Hence we have the steps described in section A.1.3 to bring both receipts and expenditures into the same valuation (here producer prices).

The next two accounts are factor and household accounts. A distinction is made here between these two accounts to show the mapping from value added to household expenditure along the lines of the model description in chapter 3 (table 3.1).[9] Households receive net factor income transfers from the government account (here tariff revenue) and—when the United States is assumed to capture part of the quota rents—rents from the quantitative restrictions in autos and textiles and apparel (see the experiments presented in chapter 5).

The last two accounts are the government account and the rest-of-the-world account. It is clear from the layout that the government's role is purely redistributive, since there are no government expenditures in this model. The rest-of-the-world account includes exogenous foreign exchange expenditures and transfers to foreigners arising out of the system of quantitative restrictions in place in 1984.

Table A.6
A Social Accounting Matrix

Receipts \ Expenditures	1. Activities	2. Commodities	3. Factors	4. Households	5. Government	6. Rest-of-the-world	7. Total
1. Activities		Gross outputs					Total sales
2. Commodities	Intermediate demand			Consumption		Exports	Aggregate demand
3. Factors	Value added					Net factor income and other foreign exchange expenditures	Net factor income
4. Households			Net factor income		Government transfer	QR rents to domestic residents	Household income
5. Government						Tariffs	Government income
6. Rest-of-the-world		Imports					Foreign exchange expenditures
7. Total	Total costs	Aggregate supply	Factors expenditure	Household expenditure	Government expenditure	Foreign exchange receipts	

Table A.7
Accounting identities underlying table A.6 (notation as in table 3.1)

Receipts	Expenditures
1. Activities	
$\sum_i (VTD_i + CD_i)PD_i + \left(\sum_k PWE_k E_k\right)ER$	$= W\overline{LS} + R\overline{KS} + \sum_i \sum_k V_{ik} PC_{ik}$
2. Commodities	
$\sum_i \sum_k V_{ik} PC_{ik}$	$= \sum_i VTD_i PD_i + \sum_k VTM_k PMI_k^v$
3. Factors	
$W\overline{LS} + R\overline{KS} - \overline{B} \times ER$	$= NFY$
4. Households	
$NFY + GR + \sum_k (1 - \theta_k)(\mathrm{RENT}C_k + \mathrm{RENT}I_k)$	$= \sum_i CD_i PD_i + \sum_i CM_k PM_k^v$
5. Government	
$\sum_k \left(1 - \frac{1}{1 + tm_k}\right)\left(PM_k^v CM_k + \sum_j PMI_k^v VM_{kj}\right)$	$= GR$
6. Rest-of-the-world	
$\sum_k (PWM_k CM_k + PWI_k VTM_k)ER + \theta_k(\mathrm{RENT}C_k + \mathrm{RENT}I_k)$	$= \left(\sum_k PWE_k E_k\right)ER - \overline{B} \times ER$

Table A.8 presents the resulting SAM underlying the model. In the reported flows, there are no quantitative restrictions on steel and foreigners are assumed to capture all quota rents.

A.3 Model Calibration

The calibration[10] determines the values of the normalizing (or free) parameters so as to replicate the observed flow values incorporated in the SAM. Except where we have evidence to the contrary, we have assumed that factors earn equal rewards in different activities. As discussed below in section A.3.3, this implies that calibration also involves determining the value of capital stocks that is consistent with the assumed rate of return on capital described in section A.1.6.

The calibration starts with choice of units. We set prices inclusive of premia and tariffs equal to unity:

$$\begin{aligned} &PD_i = 1.0, \qquad i \in N, \\ &PE_k = PM_k^v = PMI_k^v = 1.0, \qquad k \in T, \\ &PMI_{kj}^v = 1.0, \qquad k \in T, j \in N, \\ &ER = 1.0. \end{aligned} \tag{A.6}$$

From this choice of units, given tariff rates tm_k and premia rates in textiles and autos $PRI_k = PRC_k$, one can solve for the world price of traded goods PWE_k, PWI_k, and PWM_k from equations 15, 16, and 17 in table 3.1 of chapter 3.

A.3.1 Interindustry Flows

The United States does not publish data distinguishing domestic and foreign sources of intermediates. Thus the interindustry flow matrix V_{ij} is a matrix of composite domestic and foreign intermediate input use by each sector. This implies that we are forced to assume that all sectors j use domestic and intermediate inputs of sector i in the same proportion. We reconstruct the domestic and imported interindustry flows by defining the domestic-use ratio d_i for each sector:

$$d_i = \frac{X_i - E_i}{X_i + M_i - E_i}, \qquad i = 1, \ldots, n, \tag{A.7}$$

where, by choice of units, prices of unity have been omitted. For any sector

Table A.8
A US Social Accounting Matrix for 1984 (billions of 1984 US dollars)

Receipts \ Expenditures	1. Activities	2. Commodities	3. Factors	4. Households	5. Government	6. Rest-of-the-world	7. Total
1. Activities		7,248.336					7,248.336
2. Commodities	3,483.536			3,885.069		283.000	7,651.605
3. Factors	3,764.800					107.299	3,872.099
4. Households			3,872.099		12.970		3,885.069
5. Government						12.970	12.970
6. Rest-of-the-world		403.269					403.269
7. Total	7,248.336	7,651.605	3,872.099	3,885.069	12.970	403.269	

i, domestic interindustry flows are defined by

$$VD_{ij} = d_i V_{ij}, \qquad j = 1, \ldots, n. \tag{A.8}$$

The imported component of interindustry flows is determined residually by

$$VM_{ij} = V_{ij} - VD_{ij}, \tag{A.9}$$

which takes into account prices of unity, the linear homogeneity of the CES aggregator function (see equation 5 in table 3.1), and Euler's theorem (see Tarr 1989, A-17, for details).

This and later applications of Euler's theorem in the calibration implies that the observed flows correspond to equilibria in which the first-order conditions for profit maximization or cost minimization hold. In fact calibration or benchmarking consists of determining parameter values under the assumption that all equations describing the equilibrium values in the model are met in the base year.

The same calibration steps are followed to obtain domestic and imported final demand consumption flows:

$$CD_i = d_i C_i, \quad CM_i = C_i - CD_i, \qquad i = 1, \ldots, n, \tag{A.10}$$

so the same domestic-use ratio is applied to consumption and intermediate demand.[11]

The remainder of the calibration depends upon whether technology is described by constant returns to scale (*CRTS*) or increasing returns to scale (*IRTS*). Under *IRTS* it also depends on whether we assume that the quota-ridden solution in autos includes supernormal profits. We start with *CRTS*.

A.3.2 Constant Returns to Scale (*CRTS*)

In calibrating the CES and CET functions (equations 6, 10, and 22 in table 3.1), we define the general form as follows, since all three functions are calibrated analogously:

$$X = \bar{A}(\gamma X_1^\rho + (1 - \gamma)X_2^\rho)^{1/\rho}, \tag{A.11}$$

where we drop sector subscripts. Then we may rewrite the first-order condition 6, 10, or 22 as

$$\gamma = \left[1 + \left(\frac{X_1}{X_2}\right)^{\rho-1} \frac{P_2}{P_1}\right]^{-1}, \tag{A.12}$$

where P_1 and P_2 are the prices corresponding to X_1 and X_2, and the value of ρ is given by the elasticity of substitution or transformation (discussed in appendix B). Under *CRTS* the prices are unity by choice of units, and the values of X_1, X_2, and X are those of the initial data. Consequently the solution of equation A.12 for γ guarantees that the first-order conditions 6, 10, and 22 hold in the initial equilibrium. Given the value of γ, the solution of equation A.11 for $\bar{A}$, guarantees that equations 5, 9, and 21 in table 3.1 hold in the initial equilibrium. Then unit prices for the CES (CET) aggregator functions are determined from equations 11, 12, and 13 in table 3.1.[12] Likewise the value added (net price) is determined from equation 14 of table 3.1.

The λ_i parameters of equation 20 have been interpreted as the minimum subsistence requirements. Define Frisch $= -Y/(Y - \text{COMIT})$. Then

$$\lambda_i = C_i + \left(\frac{\beta_i}{PC_i}\right)\left(\frac{Y}{\text{Frisch}}\right), \qquad i \in N. \tag{A.13}$$

As discussed in appendix B, the values of the β_i parameters are derived from the elasticities. It has been shown that Frisch is the marginal utility of income with respect to income (see Frisch 1959; Brown and Deaton 1972). To calibrate demand functions to be consistent with separate estimates of the own-price elasticities of demand, we choose Frisch equal to -1.09 in the central elasticity case, to -0.39 in the high elasticity case, and to -3.55 in the low elasticity case. Since estimates of Frisch tend to become smaller in absolute value as income rises, these estimates are roughly consistent with the estimates of Lluch, Powell, and Williams (1977) of the Frisch parameter for the United States. They find a value of the Frisch parameter of between -1.4 and -1.8. Given the β_i values, the Frisch values, $PC_i \equiv 1$ by choice of units, and initial data for C_i, we calculate λ_i from equation A.13.

With labor-leisure choice the elasticities of demand for goods do not change. The elasticities derived above are subject to $\sum_{i \in N} \beta_i = 1$. With labor-leisure choice, however, we have $\sum_{i=0}^{n} \beta_i = 1$, where good 0 is leisure. We scale β_i such that $\beta_i = \beta_i^*(1 - \beta_0)$, $i = 1, \ldots, n$, where the β_i^* values are the values with no labor-leisure choice. From equation 20′ of section 6.1.1, it follows that the demand functions and elasticities for commodities are unchanged.

The calibration of the labor supply equation is discussed in appendix 6A.

A.3.3 Capital Stock, Efficiency Units, and Distortions in Factor Markets

In equation 2 of table 3.1, capital is measured in units of comparable productivity ("efficiency units"). In any sector the capital stock comprises many different kinds of capital—machinery, vehicles, and buildings. We assume that these different types of capital can be aggregated *for each sector* into a measure of the capital stock. The US Department of Commerce statistics report the dollar value of the capital stock by sector; the capital stock of each sector is aggregated, using a measure of the value of each of its components.

A dollar of capital does not necessarily produce the same value of output in all sectors. But because of the extreme difficulty of measuring capital accurately, the US Department of Commerce statistics do not fully adjust for differences in productivity of capital across sectors. Also because of various measurement problems the value of capital may not be correctly measured. The following example illustrates how this measurement error affects rate-of-return calculations:

Let

$$K_i = RD_i \times \tilde{K}_i, \tag{A.14}$$

where K_i is an accurate measure of the quantity of the capital stock in use in sector i, RD_i is a scalar that converts a dollar of capital in sector i (as measured by the official statistics) into capital in efficiency units in sector i, and $\tilde{K}_i$ is the capital reported in official statistics.

Take the case of a Cobb-Douglas production function. According to equation A.14, the first-order condition for capital use is

$$R \times RD_i = \frac{(1 - \alpha_i)X_i PN_i}{\tilde{K}_i}, \tag{A.15}$$

where $PN_i = PVC_i/X_i$. The numerator of equation A.15 is the return to capital. Since the denominator is the measured capital stock, the ratio is the return to measured capital. Here R is the economywide average return to capital (explained in section A.1.6). The more productive a dollar of capital in sector i (higher RD_i), the higher will be the rate of return to measured capital $\tilde{K}_i$, $R \times RD_i$.

We argue that differences in observed rates of return result from a failure to measure capital accurately. Divide both sides of equation A.15 by RD_i:

$$R = \frac{(1 - \alpha_i)X_i PN_i}{RD_i \times \tilde{K}_i}. \tag{A.16}$$

The denominator of equation A.16 is the "true" capital stock in sector i, and R is the return to appropriately measured capital. We assume perfect capital mobility across sectors. Then in equilibrium the rate of return to capital will be the same across sectors (as in equation A.16). This interpretation attributes observed differences in rates of return to error in the measurement of capital across sectors.

An analogous heterogeneity exists for labor. Depending on the skill level of labor in different sectors, the same amount of labor would result in varying amounts of output and so in different wages. For example, a surgeon is more productive than an unskilled worker, but both are measured as one unit of labor (one person year).

There is, however, an alternative interpretation of equation A.15. Suppose, instead, that we believe that the official statistics of the US Department of Commerce accurately measure the capital stock of different sectors in terms of their relative efficiency. In this case, given $K_i = \tilde{K}_i$, the right side of equation A.15 is the rate of return on K_i, and the rates of return would differ across sectors. One could then attribute these different rates of return to factor market distortions, after accounting for differences in the composition of capital and adjusting for risk (de Melo 1977 is an example of such an interpretation). Now we would let RD_i equal the relative distortion in the capital market of sector i so that $R \times RD_i$ equals the rate of return on capital in sector i. Then equation A.15 holds, and RD_i would be interpreted as a measure of the distortion in the capital market in sector i.

As a practical matter we will observe different rates of return on the measured capital stock across sectors. The question is whether these rates of return reflect measurement error or limitations on the flow of capital due to a disequilibrium situation or to capital market distortions. Our calibration approach reflects primarily the former view. We would defend it on the grounds that unlike in the case of labor heterogeneity (discussed below), there is little evidence against this view.

We do, however, have a short-run version of the model in which capital is fixed in each sector so that the rate of return varies across sectors. It is also clear that it is easy to depart from the equal-returns-to-factors assumption. In our model we limit this interpretation to wage distortions in the automobile and steel markets where there is strong evidence that labor receives above-normal wages after adjusting for skill variations.

Primary variable costs PVC_i are the sum of labor and capital costs, $W\phi_i L_i + RK_i = PVC_i$, where we have allowed for the possibility of a wage distortion ϕ_i in sector i. Using equations 1, 14, and 32 from table 3.1, it may be verified that $PVC_i = PN_i X_i$. Consequently we calibrate K_i from the following equation:

$$K_i = \frac{PN_i X_i - W\phi_i L_i}{R}, \qquad i \in N. \tag{A.17}$$

The capital stock for sector i computed from equation A.17 will have a rate of return of R for all sectors. Given K_i for all sectors, we calibrate the share parameter for the CES function describing technology for value added as in equation A.11, and $\overline{AX}_i$ from the equation corresponding to equation A.12.[13]

A.3.4 Increasing Returns to Scale (*IRTS*)

In the *CRTS* case marginal costs are constant, so equation 32 implies that price equals marginal costs. Under *IRTS* total costs exceed variable costs by the fixed-cost component:

$$TC_i = FC_i + CV_i \tag{A.18}$$

and

$$CV_i = INTC_i + P\tilde{V}C_i, \tag{A.19}$$

where the $P\tilde{V}C_i$ values are primary variable costs under *IRTS* and are calibrated from

$$P\tilde{V}C_i = PVC_i - CDR_i \times TC_i, \tag{A.20}$$

where CDR_i (defined as $CDR_i = FC_i/TC_i$) is the cost-disadvantage ratio and PVC_i is primary variable cost under *CRTS*. We assume that the labor share in fixed costs (*LSFC*) is given by the labor share in value added:

$$LSFC_i = \frac{WL_i}{PN_iX_i}. \tag{A.21}$$

Then the allocation of fixed costs between labor and capital is given by

$$\overline{LF}_i = LSFC_i\frac{FC_i}{W}, \quad \overline{KF}_i = (1 - LSFC_i)\frac{FC_i}{R}. \tag{A.22}$$

The same initial solution as under *CRTS* is replicated by rescaling $\overline{AX}_i$, L_i, K_i by $(1 - CDR_i)^{-1}$.

With a contestable market pricing rule we impose the average cost pricing rule of $PX_i = AC_i$. With monopolistic competition we first calculate the market price elasticity of demand ε_i^d implied by the demand system (see appendix 7A of chapter 7). Then, as explained in the text, for a given number of firms we determine the conjecture by inverting the pricing rule (equation 7.7 in chapter 7):

$$\Omega_i = N_i \varepsilon_i^d \left[1 - \left(\frac{CV_i}{PD_i X_i} \right) \right]. \tag{A.23}$$

Given the elasticity ε_i^d, equation 7.7 identifies only the ratio Ω_i / N_i.

Thus, as discussed in chapter 7, some authors fix $\Omega_i = 1$ (Cournot conjectures) and calibrate N_i from equation 7.7, the Cournot equivalent number of firms. The equivalent approach, which we adopt, is to fix $N_i = 1$ and calibrate Ω_i from equation A.23. For assessing industry competitiveness in autos and steel, however, we estimate $N_i = 3$ in autos and $N_i = 7$ in steel and calibrate Ω_i.

In the case with initial profits, after rescaling primary variable costs to take into account fixed costs, we solve for the vector of domestic prices $P\hat{D}_i$ which satisfies the firm's budget constraint:

$$PE_i E_i + P\hat{D}_i D_i = P\tilde{V}C_i + FC_i + \sum_j VM_{ji} PMI_{ji}^v + \sum_j P\hat{D}_j VD_{ji} + PROF_i, \quad i = 1, \ldots, n, \tag{A.24}$$

where all other variables in equation A.24, including profits, are exogenous. It is clear from equation A.24 that one could scale each term of the equation to express all quantities and profits in unit terms. Hence this calibration can be used to calculate the vector of domestic prices consistent with any arbitrary exogenous vector of sectoral profit rates. Since $P\hat{D}_i \neq 1.0$, all the steps determining the parameters for the CES and CET functions with the new vector of domestic prices, starting with equation A.12, must be redone with the new set of prices.

A.3.5 The Cost Disadvantage Ratio (CDR)

We suppress sector subscripts and divide equation A.17 by TC to obtain

$$1 = \frac{FC}{TC} + \frac{CV/X}{TC/X} = \frac{FC}{TC} + \frac{MC}{AC}, \tag{A.25}$$

where we have substituted $MC = CV/X$ because of our assumption of constant marginal costs. Then define CDR by

$$CDR \equiv 1 - \frac{MC(X)}{AC(X)} = \frac{FC}{TC(X)}.$$

For an industry with $IRTS$, $AC > MC$ and AC declines as output increases. With constant marginal costs, CDR decreases toward zero as output increases.

For the sole purpose of calibrating the *CDR*, we assume that *AC* declines according to a constant elasticity curve until it reaches the minimum efficient scale (*MES*) output, Q_m, that is,

$$AC = \bar{K}Q^{\varepsilon}, \qquad Q \leq Q_m,$$
$$AC = MC, \qquad Q \geq Q_m, \tag{A.26}$$

where ε is a negative constant and *MC* is a positive constant.

From econometric studies we obtain a pair of values α and s, where

$$AC(\alpha Q_m) = AC(Q_m)(1 + s) \tag{A.27}$$

and where $0 < \alpha < 1$, and s is the percentage increase in average total costs due to loss of scale efficiency at output level αQ_m.

From equation A.26 we have

$$\ln AC(\alpha Q_m) - \ln AC(Q_m) = \beta \ln(\alpha). \tag{A.28}$$

But from equation A.27, the left side of equation A.28 equals $\ln(1 + s)$. Consequently, given α and s, we calibrate the elasticity of the *AC* curve as

$$\varepsilon \equiv \frac{\ln(1 + s)}{\ln(\alpha)}. \tag{A.29}$$

Given any average plant size Q_1, it follows from equation A.26 that

$$\ln AC(Q_1) - \ln AC(Q_m) = \varepsilon \ln\left(\frac{Q_1}{Q_m}\right). \tag{A.30}$$

Let s_1 be the proportionate increase in costs at output Q_1,

$$AC(Q_1) = AC(Q_m)(1 + s_1) = MC(1 + s_1). \tag{A.31}$$

From equations A.30 and A.31,

$$1 + s_1 = \exp\left[\varepsilon \ln\left(\frac{Q_1}{Q_m}\right)\right]. \tag{A.32}$$

From equations A.29, A.31 and A.32, we have

$$CDR = 1 - \frac{MC}{AC(Q_1)} = 1 - \frac{1}{1 + s_1} = 1 - \exp\left[-\varepsilon \ln\left(\frac{Q_1}{Q_m}\right)\right]$$

or

$$CDR = 1 - \exp\left[-\frac{\ln(1 + s)}{\ln(\alpha)} \ln\left(\frac{Q_1}{Q_m}\right)\right]. \tag{A.33}$$

In the case of steel, we calibrate *CDR* from equation A.33. As mentioned in chapter 7, drawing on Tarr (1984), we estimate the *MES* steel plant (Q_m) at 6 million tons per year.

Our *MES* estimate falls between Cockerill's (1974) estimate of 10 million tons per year and Barnett's and Schorsch's (1982) estimate of 4 million tons per year. Given Barnett's and Schorsch's estimate of 4 million tons as the average integrated US plant size, $Q_1/Q_m = 2/3$. Scherer et al. (1975) estimated that average costs increase by 11 percent at (1/3) Q_m; that is, $s = 0.11$ and $\alpha = 1/3$. Substituting in equation A.33 and rounding yields $CDR = 0.04$.

For automobiles we use the estimate of *MC/AC* from Friedlaender, Winston, and Wang (1984).

A.3.6 The Quota Premium Rate When Domestic Agents Receive Rents

Rents are defined from equations 27 and 28 of table 3.1. To simplify notation, we suppress sector subscripts, let $M =$ total initial imports, $PWM = PWI = PW$, and $PM^v = PMI^v = P$. Then total rents in sector i are

$$\text{RENTS} = R = \left(\frac{P}{1 + tm} - PW \times ER\right)M. \tag{A.34}$$

From equations 16 and 17 in table 3.1 and our assumptions above, with preexisting quotas, the premium rate satisfies

$$P = PW \times ER(1 + tm)(1 + p), \tag{A.35}$$

where $p =$ the premium rate. Equation A.35 can be rearranged to yield

$$\left(\frac{P}{1 + tm}\right) - PW \times ER = PW \times ER \times P. \tag{A.36}$$

Substituting from equation A.36 into equation A.34 yields

$$R = PW \times ER \times p \times M. \tag{A.37}$$

The methodology discussed in chapter 4 yielded a premium rate p earned by foreigners. Equation A.37 expresses the relationship between the premium rate earned by foreigners and total rents earned by foreigners. If domestic residents also earn rents, this implies that total rents R^* satisfy

$$\theta R^* = R, \tag{A.38}$$

where θ is the share of rents earned by foreigners. In addition the premium rate p^* inclusive of domestic rents satisfies

$$R^* = PW^* \times ER \times p^* \times M, \tag{A.39}$$

where PW^* is the calibrated relative price of imports with the higher premium rate.

Dividing equation A.37 by equation A.39 yields

$$\frac{R}{R^*} = \frac{PWp}{PW^*p^*}. \tag{A.40}$$

Substituting from A.38 yields

$$p^* = \frac{PWp}{PW^*\theta}. \tag{A.41}$$

Solving for PW and PW^* from equation A.35 and dividing yields

$$\frac{PW}{PW^*} = \frac{1 + p^*}{1 + p}. \tag{A.42}$$

Substituting equation A.42 into equation A.41 and rearranging yields

$$p^* = \frac{k}{1 - k} \qquad \text{if } k < 1, \tag{A.43}$$

where $k = p/[(1 + p)\theta]$.

First, consider the case of textiles and apparel. We estimated that the premium rate that accrues to foreigners is $p = 0.405$. If we counterfactually assume that domestic agents receive 25 percent of the total rents, then $\theta = 0.75$. It follows from equation A.43 that the premium rate on textiles and apparel that reflects all rents is $p^* = 0.624$.

Now consider automobiles. From the discussion in section 4.3.5, we have $p = 31.8$ and $p^* = 36.4$. That is, US auto dealers captured \$500 per vehicle of rents on Japanese autos but no rents on European autos, yielding an increase in the weighted average premia from 31.8 to 36.4 percent. Then, solving equation A.43 for θ,

$$\theta = \left(\frac{1 + p^*}{1 + p}\right)\left(\frac{p}{p^*}\right), \tag{A.44}$$

we have $\theta = 0.90$, and foreigners captured 90 percent of the rents.

Appendix B: Elasticity Specification and Data Sources

This appendix describes the elasticities used in the model and their sources. Since the values selected for these elasticities affect our results, we specified a range of elasticities. We discuss in some detail how we settled on that range and what data sources we used. Each set of elasticity estimates is described separately in sections B.1–B.6. Section B.7 provides evidence of foreign direct investment in the auto industry.

B.1 Elasticity of Substitution between Imported and Domestic Intermediates (σv_i)

The elasticity of substitution σv_i appears in equation 6 of chapter 3, which is rewritten here as

$$\frac{VD_{ji}}{VM_{ji}} = \left(\frac{1-\delta_j}{\delta_j}\right)^{\sigma v_j} \left(\frac{PD_j}{PMI_j^v}\right)^{-\sigma v_j}, \qquad j \in T, i \in N. \tag{B.1}$$

Note that equation B.1 assumes that there is one elasticity of substitution regardless of the sector of destination. For example, the elasticity of substitution between domestic and imported steel is the same whether steel is used in automobiles, agriculture, or some other sector.

Multiplying both sides of equation B.1 by VM_{ji}, and denoting dZ/Z by $\hat{Z}$ for any variable Z, we have

$$\widehat{VD}_{ji} = -\sigma v_i(\widehat{PD}_j - \widehat{PMI}_j^v) + \widehat{VM}_{ji}, \qquad i = 1, \ldots, n, j \in T. \tag{B.2}$$

If we hold all other variables constant, then $\sigma v_i = \widehat{VD}_{ji}/\widehat{PD}_j$, and similarly, $\sigma v_i = \widehat{VD}_{ji}/\widehat{PMI}_j^v$. The elasticity of substitution is the own-elasticity of demand for domestic goods or, analogously, the cross-elasticity of demand for domestic goods with respect to a change in the price of imported goods. However, σv_i is not an ordinary uncompensated own-elasticity of demand because in the derivation of equation B.1, we minimized the cost of producing a fixed output level. So σv_i is similar to a compensated elasticity of demand because the firm stays on the same isoquant in response to the price change.[1]

Estimates of σv_i are available from Shiells, Stern, and Deardorff (1986) and Stern, Francis, and Schumacher (1976). Stern, Francis, and Schumacher summarize estimates from the literature and report best guesses; these estimates have been used widely in applied economic models. Shiells, Stern, and Deardorff estimate these elasticities econometrically, provide an upper bound on the weighted average standard error of the estimates, and compare the results of the two approaches.

For the central elasticity (or best-estimate) case, we used the Shiells, Stern, and Deardorff estimates (table 4). There is a close concordance between the aggregation they define and the sectors in our model, especially for steel, vehicles, textiles, and food. We used their estimate of σv_i for textiles but not for apparel because the σv_i elasticity relates to intermediate production, whereas for apparel we need a final demand elasticity. Where there is no close concordance between their classification and the sectors in our model, we selected elasticities from representative sectors in their tables (grain for agriculture and footwear for consumer goods). For traded services and mining, we relied on the elasticity estimates for the Australian ORANI model, as reported in Dixon et al. (1982). For our expanded twelve-sector model in chapter 8, we used the best-guess estimate of Stern, Francis, and Schumacher on petroleum refineries for both crude oil and petroleum products.

For steel, textiles and apparel, agriculture, and other manufactures, the high and low estimates are equal to the best estimate plus or minus one times the standard error of the estimate as reported in Shiells, Stern, and Deardorff. For food and motor vehicles, their estimate of the standard error exceeded the best estimate, so we subtracted a value less than the standard error to avoid a negative elasticity. For the remaining five sectors, the high and low estimates are approximately double or one-half of the best estimate. Results are reported in table B.1.

B.2 Elasticity of Substitution of Capital for Labor (σ_i)

Caddy (1976) has surveyed estimates of the elasticity of substitution between capital and labor, and these elasticities are reproduced in Whalley (1985). The elasticities generally fall between 0.5 and 1, with time-series estimates generally around 0.5, and cross section estimates generally

Table B.1
Elasticities of substitution: imports for domestic goods in intermediate production

	Elasticities (σv_i)		
Sector	Low estimate	Central estimate	High estimate
Agriculture	0.85	1.42	1.99
Food	0.15	0.31	3.51
Mining	0.25	0.50	1.10
Iron and steel	1.10	3.05	5.00
Motor vehicles	0.50	2.01	8.39
Textiles and apparel	0.60	2.58	4.56
Other consumer goods	1.58	3.15	6.30
Other manufactures	0.13	3.55	6.97
Traded services	0.90	2.00	4.00
Crude oil[a]	1.18	2.36	4.72
Petroleum products[a]	1.18	2.36	4.72

Source: Interpolated from data in Shiells, Stern, and Deardorff (1986), Stern, Francis, and Schumacher (1976), and Dixon et al. (1982).
a. Elasticity estimates for these sectors are used only in chapter 8.

around 1. For agriculture, motor vehicles, food, and textiles and apparel, we used Caddy for our central estimate.[2] For the high and low estimates for these industries, we added or subtracted one times the variance of the estimates. For steel we used Hekman's (1978) estimate. For the remaining industries (nontraded services, mining, other manufactures, other consumer goods, and the energy sectors) data are not directly available from Caddy. Since Caddy finds it difficult to rationalize the assignment of different elasticities to different industries, we assigned a central elasticity of 0.8 to all these industries. To obtain high and low estimates, we added or subtracted 0.2, a value representative of the variances listed in Whalley (1985). The results are reported in table 5.2. The values for the best-estimate case are similar to those of Whalley (1985) and Ballard et al. (1985). Our results are reported in table B.2.

B.3 Elasticities of Transformation (σt_i)

Multiplying both sides of equation 10 by E_i yields

$$D_i = \left(\frac{1 - \gamma_i}{\gamma_i}\right)^{-\sigma t_i} \left(\frac{PD_i}{PE_i}\right)^{\sigma t_i} E_i, \qquad i \in T. \tag{B.3}$$

Holding all other variables constant, the own-elasticity of supply to the domestic market (or to the export market) equals the elasticity of

Table B.2
Elasticities of substitution: capital for labor in production

	Elasticities (σ_i)		
Sector	Low estimate	Central estimate	High estimate
Agriculture	0.48	0.61	0.74
Food	0.62	0.79	0.96
Mining	0.60	0.80	1.00
Iron and steel	0.84	1.00	1.16
Motor vehicles	0.50	0.81	1.12
Textiles and apparel	0.83	1.00	1.17
Other consumer goods	0.60	0.80	1.00
Other manufactures	0.60	0.80	1.00
Traded services	0.60	0.80	1.00
Crude oil[a]	0.60	0.80	1.00
Petroleum products[a]	0.60	0.80	1.00

Source: Interpolated from data in Caddy (1976), as reported in Whalley (1985), Hekman (1978), and Dixon et al. (1982).
a. Elasticity estimates for these chapters are used only in chapter 8.

transformation:

$$\frac{\hat{D}_i}{\widehat{PD}_i} = \sigma t_i = \hat{E}_i / \widehat{PE}_i. \tag{B.4}$$

In the derivation of equation B.3, we assume that the firm allocates any fixed level of composite output between domestic and foreign sales to maximize revenue. Since the output level is fixed, σt_i is not an ordinary elasticity of supply but an elasticity of transformation. This elasticity reflects the ease with which the firm can shift its factors of production to substitute domestic for foreign output, given the change in the relative price of output sold to the domestic and foreign markets. The elasticity is related to the production function, not to sales.

Econometricians generally have had more success estimating elasticities of import demand than elasticities of export supply, and estimates of the elasticity of transformation are scarce. For most sectors we take 2.9 as our central elasticity estimate, with 4.2 and 1.3 as the high and low estimates. These should be regarded as our interpolations. We find some basis for these estimates in Faini (1988), who estimates that the long-run elasticity of transformation for an aggregate of manufactured goods for Turkey is 2.9, with a standard error of 1.3. We have found, however, that our welfare estimates are rather insensitive to significant changes in their values.[3]

Table B.3
Elasticities of transformation in production: domestic goods and exports

	Elasticities (σt_i)		
Sector	Low estimate	Central estimate	High estimate
Agriculture	2.6	3.9	5.2
Food	1.6	2.9	4.2
Mining	1.6	2.9	4.2
Iron and steel	1.6	2.9	4.2
Motor vehicles	1.6	2.9	4.2
Textiles and apparel	1.6	2.9	4.2
Other manufactured goods	1.6	2.9	4.2
Other consumer goods	1.6	2.9	4.2
Traded services	0.3	0.7	1.1
Crude oil[a]	1.6	2.9	4.2
Petroleum products[a]	1.6	2.9	4.2

Source: Authors' interpolations (see text).
a. Elasticity estimates for these sectors are used only in chapter 8.

In principle, the more homogeneous the product, the larger the value of the elasticity of transformation. If the export and domestic products are identical, the manufacturer does not need to alter the production process to switch between domestic and export markets, and the elasticity of substitution between domestic and export products approaches infinity. We assume that traded services are much less homogeneous than average and that agricultural products are more homogeneous than average, and adjust our estimates accordingly. The results are in table B.3.

B.4 Elasticities of Demand for Composite Final Goods

Equation 20 has ten β_i and ten λ_i parameters. All other values in the equation are data in the initial equilibrium. As discussed in appendix A, once the β_i values are given, the λ_i values are determined by the assumption of initial equilibrium. Thus we need only specify ten elasticities and one parameter, known as the Frisch parameter, to obtain the β_i value.

In terms of the parameters of the demand functions, the own-elasticities of demand can be written as

$$e_{ii} = -1 + (1 - \beta_i)\frac{\lambda_i}{C_i}, \qquad i \in N. \tag{B.5}$$

Given the restrictions on the parameters, this means that good i will be price inelastic if λ_i is positive, and price elastic if λ_i is negative. The cross-elasticities of demand are

$$e_{ij} = -\frac{\lambda_j \beta_i PC_j}{C_i PC_i}, \qquad i \neq j,\ i, j \in N. \tag{B.6}$$

Thus the cross-elasticity is positive (i.e., the jth good is a gross substitute for the ith) if, and only if, λ_j is negative. In view of the discussion in section B.5, this means that we can have gross substitutes only if we have price elastic goods. If any good is price elastic with respect to its own demand, then it will be a gross substitute for all other goods in the system. Conversely, if it is price inelastic with respect to its own demand, then it will be a gross complement for all other goods in the system.

Finally, the elasticity of demand for composite final commodity i with respect to income is

$$e_i^Y = \frac{\beta_i Y}{PC_i C_i}, \qquad i \in N. \tag{B.7}$$

In calibrating the β_i parameters, one can choose a value for β_i so that the implied own-price elasticities are consistent with literature estimates of either price elasticities or income elasticities. We chose to base our elasticities on income elasticities on the work of Lluch, Powell, and Williams (1977, ch. 3). They estimated an LES consumption function of composite consumption across seventeen countries including the United States, and their structure is identical to our top-level consumption structure. For income elasticities, they found a pattern across countries (with the exception of Jamaica) that was consistent with restrictions imposed by utility theory. We normalized all income elasticities so that their weighted averages satisfied the Engel aggregation condition. (Otherwise, Walras' law will fail to hold in general equilibrium.) Since consumption shares have changed since the work of Lluch, Powell, and Williams, notably because of an increase in the shares of the various service sectors, normalization lowered our income elasticities for the services sectors.

For sectors in our model that are not explicitly estimated in Lluch, Powell, and Williams, we selected the closest substitute estimates. In addition for autos we benefited from Levinsohn's (1988) careful estimates of demand elasticities. We chose a value of β_i to yield a *price* elasticity of composite autos equal to Levinsohn's estimate (about -0.82).[4] We selected an elasticity twice that of the price elasticity of the central elasticity case for our high elasticity of composite final demand and half that for our

Table B.4
Elasticity of final demand for composite goods: price and income

	Central elasticity	
Sector	Normalized income elasticity	Own price elasticity[a]
Agriculture	0.30	−0.28
Food	0.30	−0.29
Mining	0.89	−0.81
Iron and steel	0.89	−0.81
Motor vehicles	0.89	−0.82
Textiles and apparel	1.15	−1.06
Other consumer goods	1.29	−1.17
Other manufactures	1.06	−0.98
Traded services	1.05	−0.97
Nontraded services	1.05	−0.98
Crude oil[b]	0.89	−0.82
Petroleum products[b]	0.89	−0.82

Source: Interpolated from Lluch, Powell, and Williams (1977), and Levinsohn (1988).
a. The high elasticity estimate is approximately twice the values of the central elasticity estimate and the low elasticity estimate is about half the central elasticity estimate.
b. Elasticities for these sectors are used only in chapter 8.

low elasticity of composite final demand. The results for the income and price elasticities of demand in the central case are shown in table B.4.

B.5 Elasticities of Substitution between Imported and Domestic Final Products (σc_i)

With the exception of the auto sector, we used the estimates reported in table B.1 for our estimated elasticities of substitution between imported and domestic final demand. For autos, we drew on Levinsohn's estimates of own- and cross-elasticities of demand, since he did not explicitly estimate an elasticity of substitution. Given our nesting assumptions, we can obtain a value for σc_i from his estimates. In particular, for our assumed CES composite good, Armington (1969, app. eq. 26, and R. G. D. Allen 1938, 373) have shown (dropping subscripts)

$$\frac{\partial D}{\partial PD}\frac{PD}{D} = -(S_D e + S_M \sigma c), \tag{B.7}$$

$$\frac{\partial M}{\partial PD}\frac{PM}{M} = -(S_M e + S_D \sigma c), \tag{B.8}$$

$$\frac{\partial M}{\partial PD}\frac{PD}{M} = S_D(\sigma c - e), \tag{B.9}$$

$$\frac{\partial D}{\partial PM}\frac{PM}{D} = S_M(\sigma c - e), \tag{B.10}$$

where $S_D = PD \times D/[PD \times D + PM \times M]$, $S_M = 1 - S_D$, and e is the elasticity of demand of the composite commodity (taken to be positive in the derivation of equations B.7–B.10). Levinsohn (1988, table 2.4) has estimated each of the values on the left side of equations B.7–B.10 as well as $e = 0.82$. Since the shares are data, we have four equations to solve for one parameter, σc; that is, we have an overdetermined system. We take the mean of the four solutions, $\sigma c = 1.88$, as our central elasticity estimate, and the largest and smallest solution values, 2.56 and 1.08, as our high and low estimates for σc.

B.6 Elasticity of Labor Supply

Analogous to the case of demand functions for commodities, we can choose a value of β_0 that is consistent with an estimated value of the elasticity of labor supply with respect to either income or the real wage. Once a value is chosen for β_0, both elasticities will be determined, as can be seen from the following relationships.

From equation 6.2, the elasticity of labor supply with respect to the real wage is

$$e_{LW} = \left[\frac{(1 - \beta_0)\overline{\text{MAXHOURS}}}{\text{LS}}\right] - 1, \tag{B.11}$$

and the elasticity of labor supply with respect to income is

$$e_{LY} = \frac{-\beta_0 Y}{(1 - \beta_0) W \times LS}. \tag{B.12}$$

As discussed in appendix 6A, $\overline{\text{MAXHOURS}}$ is determined from the initial data and from β_0. Hence, once a value is chosen for β_0, both elasticities will be determined in the initial equilibrium since data on the initial values of labor supply, wage rate, and income level are also known.

It turns out in our experiments that the real wage changes by very small amounts, generally less than 0.1 percent, while income changes are sometimes much more significant, reaching as much as 0.5 percent. Thus we choose a value of β_0 consistent with the estimates of the elasticity of labor supply with respect to income. We discuss estimates of labor supply elasticity with respect to the real wage as well, and conclude that the implied value of this elasticity is consistent with the new econometric estimates.

Estimates of the elasticity of US labor supply with respect to income have been surveyed by Killingsworth (1983, table 3.5). The Abbott and Ashenfelter (1976, 1979) estimates for a model like ours are about −0.12. Almost all other estimates for the United States fall between −0.12 and −0.24. Thus we take −0.12 as the central elasticity estimate and −0.24 as the high elasticity estimate of the elasticity of labor supply with respect to income.

Most studies of the elasticity of the labor supply to the real wage separate men and women. Estimates in Pencavel's survey of the uncompensated elasticity of labor supply of men, based on nonexperimental data, range from −0.29 to +0.14, with a median of −0.11. Pencavel takes −0.10 as the best-point estimate of the elasticity of labor supply for US men with respect to the real wage.

The evidence for women is more controversial. Until recently it was generally accepted that the labor supply of women is more sensitive to the real wage than that of men (see Killingsworth 1983, 432). Killingsworth and Heckman's (1986, ch. 2, especially pp. 189, 190) survey of labor supply elasticity estimates for women shows a much larger range (from approximately 0 to 15) than for men. Work by Mroz (1987), however, argues for dramatically lower estimates. Using the same data set, Mroz is able to replicate most of the range of elasticities found in previous studies, but statistical tests reject the economic and statistical assumptions needed to obtain the larger estimates. He concludes that his tests indicate that the elasticity of labor supply for women should be close to that of men.[5] For this reason we believe that the appropriate elasticity is much lower than the median of the estimates surveyed by Killingsworth and Heckman and is not very far from zero.

Since the overall elasticity of labor supply to the real wage is a weighted average of the elasticities of labor supply for men and women (women constituted 43.7 percent of the work force in 1984; US Department of Labor, *Employment and Earnings*, January 1985), the overall elasticity cannot be significantly greater than zero. We choose a value of β_0 consistent with the estimates of the elasticity of labor supply with respect to income discussed above; then the implied elasticity of labor supply with respect to the real wage is +0.049 in the central case and +0.093 in the high elasticity case.

Table B.5
Foreign direct investment in the US automobile industry, 1982–88 (millions of current US dollars)

	Assembly		Parts	
	Plant	Other	Plant	Other
1982		65.0	4.0	
1983	1.4	100.0	32.0	
1984	485.0	2.5	48.0	
1985	628.0		62.0	9.0
1986	850.8		234.8	
1987	435.5		743.7	
1988	402.1	17.4	700.8	130.0

Source: Compiled from US Department of Commerce, *Foreign Direct Investment in the United States*, various issues.
Note: "Plant" consists of new plant, plant expansion, and joint venture; "other" consists of equity increase, acquisition or merger, other, and real estate.

B.7 Foreign Direct Investment in the Automobile Industry during the VER

Since the VER on autos was negotiated with Japan, Japanese-owned auto companies have invested substantially in the US auto industry. Here we report US Department of Commerce data on foreign direct investment (FDI) in the US auto industry decomposed into (1) FDI in auto *assembly* (SIC 3711) and (2) FDI in auto *parts* manufacture (SIC 3714). Within each standard industrial classification (SIC), FDI is classified by type: new plant, plant expansion, joint venture, equity acquisition or increase, merger or acquisition, real estate purchase, and miscellaneous other types.

We aggregate the Commerce Department data into two groups: plant—composed of new plants, plant expansions, and joint ventures; and other—composed of all other types of FDI. The "plant" category represents an addition to real productive capacity, whereas the "other" category represents primarily financial transactions. The FDI in plant most directly influences the behavior of US auto producers, although investment in the "other" category is also relevant since it is a form of capital mobility.

B.7.1 FDI in Plant

Table B.5 summarizes available data. Although no published data are available prior to 1982, we were able to obtain information on the most

Table B.6
Foreign direct investment above $50 million in US automobile assembly plants, 1979–88 (millions of current US dollars)

Year	Foreign owner	Facility	Value of investment
1979	Volkswagen	Car plant, Pennsylvania	200
1980	Honda	Car plant, Ohio	200
1981	Nissan	Truck plant, Tennessee	500
1984	Honda	New car line, Ohio	240
	Toyota[a]	Small cars, California	150
	Nissan	Small cars, Tennessee	85
1985	Mazda[b]	Cars, Michigan	450
	Mitsubishi[c]	Cars, Illinois	340
1986	Toyota	Cars, Kentucky	800
1987	Fuji Heavy Industries and Isuzu[d]	Cars and light trucks, Indiana	405
1988	Honda	Cars and plant, Ohio	380

Source: US Department of Commerce, *Foreign Direct Investment in the United States*, various issues; and unpublished data of the Office of Trade and Investment, US Department of Commerce.
a. Fifty percent joint venture with General Motors; each company invested $150 million.
b. Twenty-five percent owned by Ford Motor Company.
c. Fifty percent joint venture with Chrysler; each company invested $340 million. (Chrysler also runs 15 percent of Mitsubishi.)
d. Joint venture between the two Japanese companies.

significant FDI (FDIs above $50 million) in plant for 1979 to 1988.[6] These data (listed in table B.6) indicate that in 1987,[7] Fuji Heavy Industries and Isuzu (a joint venture) became the sixth Japanese company to locate a plant in the United States.[8] Thus between 1980 and 1987 the traditional Big Three US automakers, who had seen virtually no entry of new competitors in the previous 30 years, were suddenly confronted by six new Japanese companies producing in the United States.

B.7.2 FDI in Parts

By 1987 the largest share of FDI in the auto industry had switched from assembly to parts manufacture (table B.5). FDIs in plants for parts manufacture are almost always under $100 million.[9] Japanese investments in parts reflect two economic phenomena: lower inventory costs when parts suppliers are located in the United States, and the traditional pattern of vertical business organization in Japanese auto companies, which establish long-term relationships with only two or three suppliers of a part, often with interlocking ownership (see Fung 1990). By contrast, the traditional US auto industry model relied on competition among several parts producers. The Japanese contend that product development, which is crucial in the modern market, requires substantial investment in research and development and is fostered by long-term relationships with the auto assembler. Such relationships reduce uncertainty for the parts supplier and consequently should increase upstream investment in new product development.[10] Thus Japanese investment in parts companies followed naturally from the earlier investment in assembly plants.

The Big Three US auto firms are also beginning to establish longer-term relationships with fewer suppliers, apparently in response to competition from Japanese-owned firms in the United States and the potential efficiencies to be gained from a more vertically integrated structure. As a result parts suppliers based in Japan are experiencing increasing difficulty penetrating the US market, leading to complaints of monopolistic relationships and domestic favoritism similar to those lodged by US businesses attempting to sell in Japan.[11]

Notes

Chapter 1

1. The balance on the US current account has shifted from a surplus of $7 billion in 1981 to a deficit of $141 billion in 1986 *Economic Report of the President*, February 1988, p. 364.).

2. See, for example, the polls reported in *The Washington Post* (March 6, 1988, pp. H1, H8).

3. The Smoot-Hawley Act was passed into law in June 1930 in the middle of the depression. As a result, between 1929 and 1931, the average rate of import taxation rose by 13 percentage points, or nearly 33 percent of 1929 levels. The intention was to reduce unemployment through the increase in protection. Since other countries were following similar policies (known as "beggar-thy-neighbor" policies), the increase in protection was largely ineffective. For an evaluation of the economic consequences of the Smoot-Hawley tariff, see Eichengreen (1986).

4. See Balassa and Balassa (1984) for an assessment of protection in developed countries.

5. Anderson (1988) is another contribution to this literature, with a greater emphasis on theoretical aspects of the costs of quotas.

6. See Morkre and Tarr (1980, ch. 3) and Bergsten et al. (1987) for a general discussion of auction quotas.

7. See Takacs (1987) for a description of auction quotas in Australia and New Zealand.

8. Tarr and Morkre (1984) attempted an aggregation based, in part, on general equilibrium estimates.

Chapter 2

1. Samuelson (1953) was the first to show that the law of one price implies extreme specialization in an economy where goods are produced under constant returns to

scale and the number of commodities exceeds the number of factors of production. Specialization, following the law of comparative advantage, will generally result in only as many goods being produced under free trade as there are factors. Melvin (1968) and Pearce (1970) explored further the indeterminacy of production in the standard trade-theoretic model; Johnson (1965) showed that the production possibility frontier is not likely to be as concave in practice as drawn in textbooks, although Vanek (1963) showed that the presence of intermediate inputs in fixed proportions along the lines adopted by most CGE modelers introduces extra curvature to the net production possibility surface. Though useful, the introduction of nontraded goods—whose classification implies that their prices are always determined entirely in domestic markets—is only a partial palliative to the problem of extreme specialization.

2. Empirical evidence by Aspe and Gavazzi (1982) also suggests that producers of German machinery face different prices for domestic and foreign sales. Thus the empirical evidence suggests that there are degrees of tradability, with corresponding relative autonomy of the domestic price system.

3. This section draws on de Melo and Robinson (1989).

4. The CET formulation was first suggested by Powell and Gruen (1968). Though more elegant and easier to work with than the logistic supply curve proposed by Dervis, de Melo, and Robinson (1982), it can be shown that the two specifications are empirically very close for local changes around equilibrium.

5. Under appropriate numéraire selection, r becomes the real exchange rate, in which case it should be referred to as such. An increase (decrease) in this price of tradables relative to nontradables is referred to as a real depreciation (appreciation).

6. For the analysis here, we could assume that equation 1 is a utility function that consumers seek to maximize.

7. If we replace equation 1 with an explicit utility function, the "iso-goods" curves can be interpreted as indifference curves. Nothing changes in the analysis.

8. This result can be derived from the maximization of equation 1 subject to equations 2 and 9 and is derived in the appendix to de Melo and Robinson (1989).

9. See Caves and Jones (1985, ch. 5) for a graphical treatment of the homogeneous product case, which elaborates the different possibilities for specialization and relative price determination.

10. Note that for $0 < \zeta < 1$, the external constraint slopes downward.

11. For an analysis of trade wars in applied general equilibrium, see Harrison, Rutstrom, and Wigle (1989).

12. Despite product differentiation our definition of the offer curve is almost identical to the Mill-Marshall offer curve; it is the locus of combinations of import demand and export supply corresponding to various price ratios of imports to exports. This definition differs from Marshall's only in that, with product differ-

entiation, import demand and export supply are not excess demand or excess supply of a homogeneous product.

13. Also note that the real exchange rate will depreciate.

14. For example, suppose $P^d = 1.5$ in the new equilibrium and that the tariff rate is 100 percent. Then $-\text{MRS} = 0.75 < -\text{MRT} = 1.5$. Suppose producers are induced to produce one less unit of the domestic good. The economy is capable of transforming the freed resources into the production of 1.5 additional units of the export good (MRT $= -1.5$). The extra 1.5 units of the export good may be exchanged, at world prices, for 1.5 units of the import good (FRT $= -1$). Since MRS $= -0.75$, consumers value the 1.5 units of the import good equal to two units of the domestic good (-1.5/MRS), but the economy only sacrificed one unit of the domestic good. Thus, this feasible reallocation of resources is welfare improving, and we have drawn C_1C_1 below C_0C_0 in figure 2.5.

15. Calibration, by which is meant the determination of normalizing constants in the CET and CES functions and other parameters, is discussed in appendix A at the end of this book.

16. Another problem relates to the choice of weights used to proxy the domestic price index in computations of real exchange rate indices, in cases where a full-fledged model is unavailable. Typically the domestic price index is proxied by some published price index such as the CPI or the GDP deflator, both of which include traded goods. As shown by the values in the last two columns of table 2.2, when values of σ and Ω are low, the choice of proxy for the domestic price index can make a great deal of difference in the computed value of the real exchange rate. For example, with $\sigma = \Omega = 0.5$, the real exchange rate index with CPI (P^q) or GDP (P^x) weights used as proxy has a value of 0.75 (0.74), whereas the correct value is 0.68.

17. The presentation in this section extends the material in de Melo and Robinson (1985).

18. Note that the import ratio also changes as σ changes. In taking this limit, we assume a fixed import ratio as we change the shape of the curve. Since $M/D = [\beta/(1-\beta)]^\sigma(P^d/P^m)^\sigma$, it is convenient to pick units so that $M/D = 1$; hence $P^m/P^d = \beta(1-\beta)$.

19. With the large-country assumption, import and export prices are no longer fixed, and the expressions for E^e and E^m carry terms in their denominators that feature the relevant export demand and import supply elasticities.

Chapter 3

1. Two applications of the basic model have verified that a six-sector aggregation that preserves autos, steel, and textiles as separate sectors replicates closely our welfare results for policy simulations affecting these sectors (see de Melo and Roland-Holst 1990; Morkre 1989). Also see the discussion in chapter 2, section 2.5.

2. Peronni and Rutherford (1989) show that with sufficient nesting, the CES aggregator is a flexible functional form. The required nesting structure, however, may violate separability.

3. The primary variable cost (PVC_i) component of the cost function (equation 1 in table 3.1) is the cost function that is dual to a CES value-added function of the form

$$VA_i = \overline{AX}_i(\alpha_i L_i^{\rho_i} + (1 - \alpha_i)K_i^{\rho_i})^{1/\rho_i}, \qquad \rho_i < 1, \qquad i \in N,$$

where $\sigma_i = 1/(1 - \rho_i)$. See Varian (1984) for a derivation of the cost function for a CES function.

4. For an econometric estimation of the CET function between several export markets of Korean footwear, see de Melo and Winters (1990). For a discussion of the implications of the separability assumptions embodied in the CET, see de Melo and Winters (1989).

5. As is customary in single country open economy models, the rest of the world is treated parametrically rather than as an agent. Although this formulation allows us to vary the shape of the foreign offer curve, and hence control the degree of terms-of-trade effects, we do not model the foreign country's domestic behavior that gives rise to its foreign offer curve. Since foreigners are not treated as agents in our model, one may easily verify that the behavior of domestic agents satisfies homogeneity of degree zero in prices. However, an interpretation is required of the foreign offer curve. In tracing out the import supply curve, for example, we assume that prices in the foreigner's home market (not explicitly incorporated in equations 18 and 19) are held constant, while the price for the foreigner's export variety changes. Then the import supply curve also depends on relative rather than absolute prices.

6. The Stone-Geary utility function is strongly separable in the composite commodities, which may easily be seen by employing the natural log transformation of equation 3A.1.

7. See Phlips (1974), Blackorby, Primont and Russell (1978), or Deaton and Muellbauer (1980, ch. 5) for derivations of the results on weakly separable utility and two-stage budgeting.

8. If rationing existed in the base equilibrium but further restrictions were exogenously imposed, we would use equations 25 and 26 with the addition of the preexisting premium terms entered multiplicatively.

9. This derivation appeared in Condon, Corbo, and de Melo (1989).

Chapter 4

1. The situation regarding Japanese restraint of exports after March 31, 1985 is less clear. In March 1985 the Reagan administration announced that it would not seek an extension of the VER. The Japanese, apparently unilaterally, then announced a willingness to extend their limitation on auto exports to the United States but at a

less restrictive level than that negotiated under the VER. Two explanations for this action are possible. One is that the Japanese learned from their experience with the VER that they could increase their profits in the United States by limiting supply and increasing price. That is, they believed they had market power in autos and chose to exploit it in classic monopoly restriction fashion. Another is that the Japanese may have been concerned that the US Congress would impose stiff sanctions against them if they did not place some limits on auto exports to the United States. We have no information for deciding which explanation is the more likely.

2. The United States did have some restraints on steel imports in 1984, as mentioned in section 4.4.

3. See Hamilton (1986) and Bark and de Melo (1987) for a description of how quota rights are allocated among exporters. We note that we utilize the term quantitative restriction (QR) in a broad sense so that it encompasses any quantitative restriction of imports regardless of the method by which the quota rights are allocated. The three QRs examined in detail in this study, however, are administered by the exporting countries, that is, they are export restraint agreements.

4. This is directly analogous to the oligopolist's cartel cheating problem. See Stigler (1968) and Rotemberg and Saloner (1988).

5. This is explained in the new work on the theory of contestable markets by Baumol, Panzar, and Willig (1982).

6. Krishna (1989a) and Tan (1990) establish conditions under which a tariff need not be superior to giving away some of the licenses to producers and auctioning off the remainder.

7. The "Short-Term Agreement" was in place from October 1, 1962, to September 30, 1963.

8. As of 1984, forty-one countries were participants in the MFA (USITC 1985, xi).

9. The reader should consult Keesing and Wolf (1980) for a more detailed history of the MFA.

10. By May 1987 the United States had negotiated bilateral agreements with thirty-nine countries to control imports of textiles and apparel (USITC 1987).

11. Since we do not know the wholesale price, we cannot conclude from the Cline data that retailers take comparable profit margins on imports and domestic apparel products.

12. See Morkre (1979) for a description of this market.

13. If there is insufficient competition to force the price of the quota rights up to their full value, our measure of the premium rate will underestimate the true cost of the quotas. In other words, the costs of the quotas will be higher than we estimate because of this bias. As described in Takacs (1987), this could happen if

the exporter and the producer are different firms and the exporter has monopoly power. Analogous to the case of monopsony power in US importing, exporting firms could then capture some of the rents from their producers. From the perspective of US residents and welfare, however, the allocation of rents between foreign exporting and producing firms is irrelevant.

14. Hamilton obtained the data from the US Chamber of Commerce in Hong Kong.

15. This average quota premium is a weighted average over all the apparel products surveyed by Hamilton and exported to the United States in 1984. We take this to be reflective of all exports. Quota premia vary considerably among apparel products, reflecting the relative severity of their quotas. Some products may have no quota premium. (This occurs when the quota is not binding.) Since we are examining the effects of quotas on all apparel imports, it is appropriate to use the average quota premium discussed in the text. This procedure is analogous to using the weighted average tariff rate for a class of products when assessing the effects of tariffs on imports.

Note also that though we are estimating the effects of quotas in 1984, we recognize that the average quota premium for Hong Kong changes from year to year. In 1982, for example, the average quota premium reported by Hamilton was only 10 percent. Unfortunately, information on quota premia are not available after 1984. However, as discussed in the text, the recently extended MFA expands quota coverage to previously uncontrolled products and therefore is more restrictive. Thus, the average quota premium under the new MFA may be higher than that reported in 1984.

16. We prefer the term "premium rate" over "import tariff equivalent" because the quota rents from textiles and apparels and autos are captured by foreigners and so their economic effects are not the same as those implied by the term "import tariff equivalent." See Bhagwati (1965) and Takacs (1977).

17. See Morkre and Tarr (1980) and Cline (1987, 26) for a description of the relative capital intensity of the two sectors of the industry.

18. These labor cost estimates are obtained from the Office of Productivity and Technology, Bureau of Labor Statistics, US Department of Labor, as reproduced in Hamilton. The data are an average of the compensation costs for 1981–83. In the case of Thailand and China, the compensation costs are for the textile industry.

19. Calculated from data in USITC (1987a, A-12).

20. The USITC study notes that the MFA imposes quotas on groups of product categories that, in general, are less than the sum of the quota amounts of the individual categories within the group. Therefore quotas for a subcategory may be binding, even if the quota for that category is less than 100 percent filled.

21. This was calculated from data in USITC (1987a, B-1, C-1, D-1). We classified categories 300–329, 400–429 and 600–629 as textile products, and the remainder as apparel. A number of the items, such as quilts and pillows, classified under

apparel are not items of wearing apparel. But these are final products and contain more labor value added than do the yarns and fabrics in the textile category. Thus they more appropriately go in the apparel category.

22. The conclusion is unaltered in the case of the Hong Kong supplier who is allocated quota rights by the government and chooses to use them to supply the US market rather than sell them. By using the quota rights to supply the US market, the producer incurs a cost (opportunity cost) equal to the value of the quota rights on the market. So the producer's own cost of production, including the opportunity cost of the quota rights, must be less than or equal to the price received from the US importer; otherwise, the producer would offer the quota rights for sale on the Hong Kong market. The opportunity cost of the quota rights are this producer's quota rents.

23. See Tarr and Morkre (1984) for details of the VER limitations as it related to vans and to Puerto Rico.

24. See Feenstra (1984) for a description of the legislative efforts to curb imports.

25. The conclusions will follow even if the products can substitute for each other in demand.

26. This presentation follows Bark and de Melo (1987).

27. This condition was shown by Falvey (1979); see also Rodriguez (1979).

28. For conditions in terms of elasticities, see Bark and de Melo (1987).

29. See Boorstein and Feenstra (1987) and Aw and Roberts (1986) for analyses of quality upgrading in steel and footwear, respectively. However, de Melo and Winters (1989) found an example of quality downgrading in footwear.

30. See Krishna (1985) for a discussion of welfare maximization with quality upgrading under VERs.

31. The supply function technique appropriately adjusts for the appreciating value of the US dollar over this period and would therefore be expected to yield higher estimates.

32. For example, Consumers Union, publisher of *Consumer Reports,* reported that when the quota was implemented, many dealers charged more than the sticker price, often by charging high prices for such "mandatory options" as decal stripes, rustproofing, and undercoating. *Consumer Reports* readers indicate that this practice was especially common among Toyota, Honda, and Mazda dealers (*Consumer Reports,* August 1983, p. 391). See also the statement by Senator John Chafee (*Congressional Record,* February 29, 1984, S.1996); *Fortune* ("Can Detroit Live without Quotas?" June 25, 1984, p. 20); and *Washington Post* ("Car Dealer Markups Raise Questions," Washington Business, November 19, 1984, pp. 1, 34, 35).

33. A separate quota was prescribed for semifinished steel, which was excluded from these calculations. See Tarr and Morkre (1984, ch. 6) for details of the

restraints. Some quotas were in effect before negotiation of the VERs. Most notable was the United States–European Community (EC) Arrangement that settled the antidumping and countervailing dispute of 1982. In return for the withdrawal of antidumping and countervailing complaints by US steel companies, the EC agreed to limit its exports of certain steel products to the United States to specified percentages of US consumption. (See Tarr 1988a for details of the negotiation of this agreement.) In addition, in July 1983, President Reagan granted four years of global quotas on imports of stainless steel bar and rod and alloy tool steel. The estimates in this study are for the additional costs and effects of the new VERs, given that these other restraints were in effect in 1984.

34. See *Steel Industry: Quarterly Industry Review* (Merrill Lynch, January 1988, p. 33).

35. The Korean Pipe and Tube Association issues certificates for pipe and tube products, and the Korean Iron and Steel Association issues certificates for other steel products.

Chapter 5

1. An earlier version of most of the results in this chapter appears in de Melo and Tarr (1990b). In the earlier version there was no nesting in consumer demand, which implies less demand responsiveness to trade policy changes.

2. As mentioned in chapter 4, we assume that the welfare value to the consumer of any quality upgrading is equal to the monetary value of the upgrading. This means that estimates of the cost of QRs are biased downward.

3. Because the input-output table for the United States does not distinguish between domestic and imported intermediate purchases, we had to assume that all users of, say, steel, use domestic and imported steel in the same proportion. See appendix A.

4. In addition the government collects tariff revenues on the additional purchases of the formerly QR-restrained product. The additional tariff revenue equals

$ER \times \overline{PWM_1} \times tm_i[CM_i^1 - CM_i^0]$.

The tariff revenues also increase with the elasticity of demand. These revenues are part of the distortion costs of the quota because they are captured on what was deadweight losses under the quota.

5. Our estimate would be different had we benchmarked the premium rate accruing to foreigners rather than the dollar value of the rents. In that case the initial premium rate would have been 54 percent, with resulting total costs of $15.0 billion, of which $8.5 billion is the distortionary cost.

6. The constraint on steel imports covers aggregate imports of steel. Appendix 5A treats the case when the quota is user specific.

7. Steel imports are restrained by fixing the quantity of steel imports and solving for the premium-inclusive price at which the restrained amount of steel is actually demanded. Conversely, removing QRs on steel while simultaneously removing premia on textiles and apparel and autos is done by fixing the premium rates in autos and textiles and apparel to zero, and freeing the quantity of steel imported.

8. Assessment of the quantity impact of removing a QR would have to incorporate elasticity assumptions.

9. The real wage is the wage rate deflated by the numéraire. Our numéraire, equation 33, is not an exact measure of the real consumption wage since it uses gross output (rather than consumption inclusive of imports) as its weight.

10. Rent-seeking behavior under QRs has been analyzed by Krueger (1974), but accurately estimating the costs of rent-seeking is a difficult task that has yet to be done.

11. This point was first made by Jones and Berglas (1977).

12. Our individual sector estimates have been adjusted for balance of trade and other general equilibrium effects.

13. The estimates of Dinopolous and Kreinin, who use comparable premium estimates, are comparable to ours.

14. An appropriate distinction would be between the consumption and production cost components of the distortionary cost, which would be possible to estimate in our model.

15. Deardorff and Stern (1986, 41), de Melo (1986), and Brown (1987) have questioned the theoretical assumptions that result in such large terms-of-trade effects for small countries. In particular, Brown has shown that the Armington assumption in multiregional models necessarily results in terms-of-trade effects for even the smallest countries that cannot be overcome by increasing the elasticity of substitution between imports and domestic products in consumption. With adequate nesting of the import structure, however, parameter choices can be made that would overcome these unrealistic implications.

Chapter 6

1. See, however, Ballard et al. (1985) for an approach that selects the central Stone-Geary utility function with labor-leisure choice.

2. It is well known, however, that labor-leisure choice is crucial for some policy questions, such as assessing the impact of a tax on labor income on government revenue (see Ballard et al. 1985, ch. 10).

3. One exception are the steelworkers at "minimills," who are not generally represented by the United Steelworkers. The proportion of output produced by the minimills has grown from about 3 percent in 1960 to over 20 percent. See

Barnett and Crandall (1987) for a discussion of the minimill sector of the steel industry.

4. Several "efficiency wage" theories, based on differences in technology across industries, explain these wage premia. Shapiro and Stiglitz (1984) suggest that in industries where shirking is difficult or costly to detect, it may be efficient for firms to pay premium wages. Similarly an industry that faces relatively high costs from labor turnover will find it optimal to pay premium wages (Stiglitz 1985, Weiss 1980). Akerlof (1984) argues that if the firm is perceived to be earning rents, productivity may suffer if workers do not also receive rents. A particularly appealing theory is developed by Thaler (1989), who argues that it may be desirable in some industries to pay high (nondistortionary) wages to attract highly qualified workers in particular skill categories. As a result the productivity of workers in skill categories where premia are not desirable to the firm may decline, unless they also receive a premium that is distortionary.

5. Corden (1974) and Magee (1973) discuss factor market distortions in open economies. An early empirical estimate of the costs of factor market distortions in a developing country is given by de Melo (1977). See Ethier (1988) for a detailed explanation of the model underlying figure 6.2.

6. See section 6.3 for a discussion of endogenous wage distortions. Katz and Summers discount union rent-seeking activity based on their observation that unions spend little on political activity. But if the government became more activist, it would be optimal to increase rent-seeking expenditure; moreover subsidies to a sector can be appropriated by increasing wage demands without lobbying. See Fernandez (1989) for a discussion of strategic behavior by unions in response to industrial policy.

7. For example, deregulation in the airline and trucking industries led to a considerable reduction in the rents captured by the unions in these industries. See Kahn (1980) and Levinson (1980).

8. We sketch an intuitive proof as follows: Profit is a function of W and L. Isoprofit curves must be concave, as depicted in figure 6.5, for the following reason. Consider a point on an isoprofit curve to the left of $L(W)$. Hold W constant, and increase L by a small amount. Profits must increase because the firm is moving toward $L(W)$, which is by definition the maximum profit level of L for a given W. Thus, to remain on the isoprofit curve, it is necessary to raise W (profits are monotonically decreasing in W). Converse reasoning applies to the right of $L(W)$. Since the sign of the slope of the isoprofit curve changes at $L(W)$, $L(W)$ must go through the isoprofit curves where the tangent to the isoprofit curves is zero. Due to quasi-concavity the indifference curves of the union slope downward. Thus tangencies between the indifference curves of the union and the isoprofit curves must occur on the downward sloping portion of the isoprofit curves. The locus of these tangencies is the contract curve. Since the labor demand curve is the locus of points going through the isoprofit curves where the isoprofit curves have zero slope, the contract curve must lie to the right of the labor demand curve.

9. The union might accept a "low" wage in return for guarantees by the firm that it would employ more workers than given by its demand curve. But asymmetric information about product demand shifts (for which the firm must be permitted to adjust employment, or it would not agree to the contract) will allow the firm to cheat on the agreement. Alternatively, an incentive-compatible contract that pays the union a lump-sum amount independent of employment in return for a "low" wage will present problems for the union in allocating the lump-sum payments to the members of its choosing. See Farber (1986).

10. As was shown in figure 5.2, the value of capturing the quota rents is significantly affected by elasticity values when QRs are imposed. For this reason the value of quota rent capture in the case of imposition of QRs in steel increases monotonically from case 0 to case 3. By contrast, in autos the value of capturing quota rents is unchanged at $7.87 billion in the four cases of table 6.8.

11. The parameter for which we have the least amount of information is the weight unions place on wages relative to employment. Thus in a qualitative sense we have an Eaton-Grossman (1986) style result because the logic of which sectors should be targeted for industrial policy is reversed depending on an essentially unknown parameter. Quantitatively, however, the argument against protection because of wage distortions is stronger than the Eaton-Grossman uncertainty of which industry to target, because the impact of endogenous (compared to exogenous) wage distortions is to increase the estimated costs of protection back to (or above) the estimated costs of protection in the absence of wage distortions. In other words, estimates of the costs of QRs that ignore wage distortions (such as those in chapter 5) are not necessarily biased. See de Melo and Tarr (1990b) for a treatment of the impact of wage distortions under different market structure assumptions.

12. Consequently these results would also apply to a model with fixed labor and variable capital, as might occur where laws restrict the firm's employment options.

13. There is symmetry in the tariff imposition case where the costs of imposing tariffs are greater in the high supply elasticity case.

14. The welfare measure follows from the methodology of Burns (1973). See Morkre and Tarr (1980) for an explanation.

15. As shown in de Melo and Roland-Holst (1990a) in simulations with a six-sector version of this model, allowing for initial foreign holdings of the capital stock does not fundamentally affect the results reported below.

16. The reason for the capital inflow is the high labor intensity of textiles and apparel. When the quota is removed, the resources that flow out of textiles and apparel cannot be absorbed without increasing the rental rate of capital relative to the wage rate of labor. With international capital mobility, the increased demand for capital will be manifested in capital imports rather than a rise in the rental rate of capital.

17. A similar result of welfare-reducing capital inflow occurs in an experiment reported in chapter 7.

18. We may also solve for $\overline{\text{MAXHOURS}}$ in terms of equation 6.2. In that case β_0 is a parameter determined by the elasticity of labor supply. When $\beta_0 = 0$, labor supply is fixed and $\overline{\text{MAXHOURS}}$ equals initial labor supply LS_0. For $\beta_0 > 0$, the maximum work force is determined by the elasticities and initial data:

$$\overline{\text{MAXHOURS}} = LS^0 + \left(\frac{\beta_0}{WG^0}\right)\left(\frac{Y^0 - \sum_{j=1}^{n} PC_j^0 \lambda_j}{1 - \beta_0}\right),$$

where a superscript on a variable denotes values in the initial equilibrium. Thus the value for $\overline{\text{MAXHOURS}}$ is determined by initial income, prices and wages, the form of the utility function, and parameters derived from econometrically estimated elasticities.

Chapter 7

1. It should, however, be kept in mind that the US steel industry could have realized considerable cost savings from higher capacity utilization rates.

2. Adams and Dirlam (1964) also characterize US steel pricing of the late 1950s as oligopolistic.

3. For a similar view, see Scherer (1980, 178–180). He concludes that "what was once [pre-1960] a clear example of collusive price leadership had evolved into something more closely matching the barometric model." By the barometric model, Scherer means that prices cannot exceed marginal costs for extended periods of time.

4. While this estimate is for additional profits due to the VER, the industry may have earned some pure profits that were not due to the VER. On the basis of their cost function estimates, Winston and Associates (1987) conclude that the VER on Japanese autos resulted in an additional $8.9 billion of profits to the US auto industry.

5. For developing countries, studies by de Melo and Urata for Chile (1986) and Harrison for Côte d'Ivoire (1989) have shown that trade liberalizations reduce price-cost margins in highly protected sectors.

6. Dixit (1988) finds pricing to be less competitive than Bertrand. Both Dixit and Krishna, Hogan, and Swagel (1989) find that the Japanese companies acted more collusively during the VER period. Note, however, that Saloner (1989) has argued that observed pricing that is more competitive than Bertrand is probably due to inaccurate calibration of costs; in particular, a larger share of costs is fixed, so price–marginal cost margins are higher than calibrated.

7. Our approach to modeling fixed costs follows Harris (1984) and Cox and Harris (1985).

8. In assessing competitive behavior, $\bar{N}_i$ will be taken to equal 3 and 7 in the domestic auto and steel industries, respectively. Otherwise, without affecting results, our choice of $\bar{N}_i$ may be arbitrarily set at 1.

9. Fixed costs are obtained from the relation $FC_i = CDR_i \times TC_i$, which implies that when we calibrate the model to the same initial data set, we reduce primary variable costs (PVC_i in equation 1) by the amount that goes into fixed costs.

10. Goto (1988) developed a theoretical model along these lines to analyze the effect of Japanese VERs on auto exports to the United States. In his model of Chamberlinian competition à la Krugman (1979), the number of autos available to the US consumer is endogenously determined, so there is an extra gain from trade liberalization because of the increased number of varieties. Cox and Harris (1985) also assume a constant elasticity of substitution across varieties but do not determine endogenously the number of varieties, as does Goto. In his empirical estimates, however, in which he determines the number of cars produced in the United States and in Japan, Goto simulated a change from US autarky to integration into a single economy with Japan, rather than the effects of the VER in autos. Also see Smith and Venables (1988) and Krishna, Hogan, and Swagel (1989) for applications where utility is an increasing function of the number of varieties.

11. It is well known that except under very limited circumstances, an equilibrium fails to exist in the Bertrand price adjusting homogeneous product oligopoly model once increasing returns to scale are introduced. Moreover its prediction of marginal cost pricing, independent of the number of firms or the elasticity of demand, is not regarded as realistic. See Shapiro (1989) and Bresnahan (1989).

12. Since the model is static, true dynamic reactions are impossible, so the proper interpretation of an equilibrium is a point from which no firm would want to deviate unilaterally. An appropriate theory of conjectures should be formulated in a dynamic framework. See Fudenberg and Tirole (1986) for a treatment of expectations in a dynamic framework and Tarr (1972, 1975) for stability implications.

13. We have assumed that domestic firms form conjectures only about domestic rivals. It would, however, be simple to extend the model to include a conjectural variation parameter with respect to imports. In that case the additional term $PD \times Q_i \times \Omega^m / M\varepsilon^m$ would be added to the right side of equation 7.6, where M is imports of sector i, Ω^m is the conjectural variation parameter of domestic firms for imports (i.e., $\partial M / \partial Q_i = \Omega^m$), and ε^m is a cross-elasticity of demand (i.e., $\varepsilon^m = (\partial M / \partial PD)(PD/M)$. With Cournot conjectures with respect to imports $\Omega^m = 0$, our first-order condition is unchanged from equation 7.6.

14. Novshek (1980) points out that simply adding more firms drives Cournot output to zero in the limit, which is different from the competitive result. He shows, however, that if the minimum efficient scale becomes small in relation to demand as firms enter, then Cournot equilibria with free entry exist as $n \to \infty$, and firms approach perfect competition. We do not address the issue of enforceability that arises in the case of collusive behavior. For a discussion of the sustainability of a cartel, see Rotemberg and Saloner (1988) or Stigler (1968).

15. Our approach is taken by Krugman (1987), Krishna, Hogan, and Swagel (1989), Dixit (1988), and Devarajan and Rodrik (1989). The last two studies calibrate for the Cournot equivalent number of firms. Alternate views are taken by Smith and Venables (1988), who adjust elasticities to be consistent with Cournot conjectures, and Saloner (1989), who argues that it is appropriate to adjust marginal costs.

16. See appendix A, equation A.24 for a discussion of this part of the calibration.

17. The elasticity is calculated based on read-in elasticities of substitution, share data, and final demand based on the methodology described in appendix 7A. The conjecture Ω_i is calibrated in two steps. As discussed in appendix A, the difference between price and average cost is computed based on initial profits for autos. Next the difference between average and marginal costs are calibrated based on the cost disadvantage ratio discussed in section 7.1, which in the case of autos yields marginal costs that are 89 percent of average costs. Thus, given our choice of units, in the case of autos the left side of equation 7.7 equals $1.08 - 0.89/1.08 = 0.176$.

18. Seventeen corporations produced raw steel in 1984. However, the top seven produced 87 percent of the total and were the only "integrated" producers; the remaining producers were minimills. See *Iron Age*, May 3, 1985, pp. 36–37. Thus our calculation is based on seven steel firms.

19. The right side of equation 7.13 is a slight simplification of equation 7.10.

20. In the case of autos and steel, export sales are a very small fraction of total sales. Therefore the induced shift in the demand curve for domestic sales is small when a greater share of domestic production is directed toward export sales as a result of a removal of protection.

21. The phenomenon of many firms operating at an inefficient level is often observed in highly protected (often by quantitative restraints) sectors in developing countries. This scale inefficiency effect adds considerably to the high costs of trade barriers.

22. Removing the VER from a zero-profit equilibrium results in lower benefits with endogenous conjectures ($8.69 billion) than with fixed conjectures ($9.03 billion). This is because removal of the VER causes losses and exit. With endogenous conjectures it takes fewer exiting firms to restore a zero-profit equilibrium because conjectures become more collusive as exit occurs. Since the beneficial effect of exit on scale efficiency dominates the losses from greater monopoly distortion, the scenario with more exit yields greater estimated gains.

23. See Corden (1974, 210–215) for an early discussion of these issues.

24. Another criticism concerns the elasticity of demand. With firm-level product differentiation, the firm's perceived elasticity of demand will be dependent on all the firms in the world (Brown and Stern 1989). Entry into the US market then will have less of an effect on the firm's elasticity of demand than in our model with national product differentiation.

25. At the point of optimum consumption, the inverse of the Lagrangian multiplier is the minimum expenditure required for an additional unit of composite consumption. Since we have derived PC_i from the expenditure function, this value is PC_i.

Chapter 8

1. The energy independence issue is not an argument for taxation. With an exhaustible resource such as oil, the faster it is used in the present, the less of it that will be available in the future. Moreover, if we take the energy independence argument seriously and apply the principle of using the most direct instrument to achieve a noneconomic objective (see Bhagwati and Srinivasan 1969; Bhagwati 1971), stockpiling is a less costly alternative. See Anderson and Metzger (1987) for further details.

2. See the US General Accounting Office (1986) for a survey of these results.

3. See US House of Representatives Committee of Ways and Means (1987), Congressional Budget Office (1988), Greenspan (1988), and US Department of Energy (1987).

4. Thus we start with the same base solution as in chapter 5.

5. Anderson and Metzger (1987) also consider the case of an upward-sloping import supply curve for imported crude oil and for gasoline. But they have competing terms-of-trade effects that neutralize each other because they assume that a tariff on crude oil has the effect not only of lowering the import supply price of crude oil but also of raising the price of imported gasoline.

6. We assume that the import tariff totals 25 percent, that is, a 24.8 percent increase.

7. See Atkinson and Stiglitz (1980, 366–370) for a detailed discussion.

8. The only significant difference between our results and those of Anderson and Metzger (1987, 1991) is that because of their assumption of perfect substitutability between domestic and foreign crude oil as well as petroleum products, a tariff on crude oil in their model yields zero revenue because all imports of crude oil would cease and the import tariff leads to a large increase in petroleum products imports. As we elaborated at length in chapter two, the extreme specialization prediction of the perfect substitutes-perfect competition model is strongly contradicted by the evidence on trade flows and by the absence of the law of one price. Even for products which appear similar physically, considerations such as security of supply and inventory costs would result in product differentiation. Thus, we choose to model imported and domestic products in the two petroleum sectors as less than perfect substitutes. Note, however, that by combining crude oil and natural gas the revenue and welfare results from our simulations are overstated by the share of natural gas in sectoral imports (5–6 percent); but ratios of welfare to revenue would remain unchanged.

9. Policy issues relating to the energy sector have previously been addressed in a general equilibrium framework, but these studies generally focused on long-run alternatives to petroleum as an energy input. Examples of earlier efforts include Hudson and Jorgenson (1974), Manne (1976) and Borges and Goulder (1984). These studies, however, do not specifically address the issue of taxation. Manne (1984) provides a critical survey of these earlier studies.

10. As we discuss later in this chapter, both theory and our estimates indicate that excise taxes impose lower welfare costs per dollar of revenue raised than do tariffs. This also makes it difficult to explain the welfare results of Boyd and Uri since their results imply dramatically higher welfare costs per dollar of revenue raised using excise taxes compared to using tariffs.

11. To simplify the computation and interpretation of results in this section, we assume that quotas are not binding. However, we maintain the existing tariffs in other sectors.

12. For a numerical application of this principle in a model with externalities instead of a government revenue constraint, see de Melo and Robinson (1990).

13. The 2.4 percent optimal tariff in column 4 under petroleum products represents a 0.7 percentage point reduction in the tariff level.

14. We assume in figure 8.2 that foreign suppliers of petroleum products purchase their crude oil on world markets so that their supply curve is unaffected by the domestic tax on crude oil.

15. See Markusen and Melvin (1988) for a derivation of the optimal tariff.

Chapter 9

1. On the other hand, many partial equilibrium studies of the costs of quotas to consumers yield higher estimates than ours. For example, estimates by Hufbauer, Berliner, and Elliot (1986) and Cline (1987) of the costs to consumers of textile and apparel restraints are 107 percent and 56 percent higher than our estimates, respectively (compare table 1.1 in chapter 1 and table 5.3 in chapter 5). Winston and Associates (1987) estimate a cost to consumers for the auto VERs about 50 percent higher than our estimate (compare table 1.1 in chapter 1 and table 7.3 in chapter 7). The reason for the difference is that partial equilibrium assessments of costs to consumers interpret increases in the producers surplus as losses to consumers, whereas we model the gains to producers from QRs as part of consumer income through factor returns. Thus it is inappropriate from an economywide perspective to distinguish consumer and producer gains.

2. There is another bias from aggregation due to the effect of elasticities on the distortionary cost.

3. In all fairness it should be recognized that the theoretical writings on the subject (e.g., Corden 1974; Bhagwati and Srinivasan 1983) often have in mind developing countries where distortions in goods and factor markets are pervasive.

4. See Morkre and Tarr (1980, ch. 3) for a discussion of the merits of this measure versus the alternative unemployment cost measure.

5. To be conservative, we measure total compensation losses, which exceed earnings losses by the amount of fringe benefits.

6. Cheese quotas are allocated by giving licenses to US importers, thus capturing rents and imposing lower costs domestically. On the other hand, quotas are allocated by country, which raises costs by preventing supply from the low-cost supplier (see Anderson 1985).

7. See USITC (1988) for detailed calculations of the average duties paid in the United States since 1900.

8. See Fernandez (1989) for a description of other strategic situations where unions or industry would frustrate the achievement of "optimal" industrial policy.

9. The model of Goulder and Eichengreen (1989) is one that incorporates these two features. See Harrison, Rutstrom, and Wigle (1989), however, for an applied trade war model.

10. The path-breaking article is by Harris (1984) for Canada. Similar results have been found for Cameroon by Devarajan and Rodrik (1989) and (using the model and computer program developed for chapter 7) for Korea by de Melo and Roland-Holst (1990b). See also Condon and de Melo (1990).

11. An early effort at quantifying these effects in a Solow-type model is that of Baldwin (1989) who finds that the dynamic effects of EC 1992 may be three to four times the static benefits.

Appendix A

1. We thank Sherman Robinson for providing us with the input-output table and for helping us reconcile it with the NIPA.

2. Allocating the more aggregated value-added data into component parts was done by a three-step procedure that maintained consistency with our original industry classification scheme. First, we obtained the value added of each of the component parts from the 1982 input-output table. For example, in the case of motor vehicles and equipment, the value added of motor vehicles was $15.087 billion in 1982, and the combined value added of trucks and buses with motor vehicle parts and accessories was $18.054 billion. Second, we used data from the Federal Reserve Board's indexes of industrial production (which allowed us to determine the percentage increase in production of each of these categories between 1982 and 1984) to obtain interim updated value added. (Recall that from the Leontief assumption, value added is a constant multiple of output, so the percentage increase in production is equal to the percentage increase in value added.) We calculated the value added of motor vehicles in 1984 at $23.571 billion and the value added of motor vehicle parts and trucks and buses at $20.966 billion. The

share of motor vehicles value added of the total is thus 0.529 (23.571/[23.571 + 20.966]). Third, we used the shares obtained in step two to allocate the value added of the more aggregated category in the NIPA data. Thus we calculated motor vehicle value added as $26.621 billion (0.529 × $50.3 billion) and value added for motor vehicle parts and trucks and buses to be as $23.679 billion ($50.3 − $26.621 billion).

For the primary metal category, iron and steel was determined to be 65.2 percent of the value added of the category. In the case of electric and electronic equipment, radio, television and phonograph, and household appliances were classified as consumer goods; electrical equipment, electrical wiring, electronic tubes, miscellaneous electrical equipment, radio and television communication equipment, semiconductors, and other electronic components were classified as other manufactured goods. The share of electric and electronic equipment value added accounted for by the consumer category was 10.8 percent.

3. According to US Department of Commerce officials who produce the data, the value added numbers are adjusted analogously. That is, lumber value added, for example, does not include transportation or wholesale and retail trade margins. Thus by this adjustment we are treating the export data and the domestic data symmetrically.

4. Labor's share of overall income in our base data is $\frac{2}{3}$. Proprietors' income in 1984 is $234.5 billion, but some portion of this income results from the labor services of the proprietor. We assume this share is also $\frac{2}{3}$, so labor's share of proprietors' income is $157.1 billion.

5. It would, of course, have been equivalent to add up the return to capital items in the *Survey of Current Business* table directly, and then subtract depreciation.

6. The convention in a SAM is to list receipts of an account (institution) along a row and its expenditures down the corresponding column.

7. We could have used a classification along functional lines (e.g., capital and labor), but this was not necessary since the model has only one representative consumer.

8. The convention follows the definitions provided in the United Nations' System of National Accounts (SNA)—see United Nations Statistical Office (1968, 230–231).

9. Net factor income from abroad and other exogenous foreign exchange transactions are placed here rather than in the household account to separate it from transfers associated with quotas.

10. For a more detailed discussion of calibration in the primal version of the basic model, see Tarr (1989). Other detailed discussions of calibration of CGE models include Dervis, de Melo, and Robinson (1982, app. B), Ballard, et al. (1985), and Mansur and Whalley (1984).

11. The reader may wonder why we did not simplify the model because of these data constraints, since the resulting model has a demand structure similar to the

one in Dervis, de Melo, and Robinson (1982, chs. 5 and 6). The more detailed formulation is required for the simulations reported in the appendix to chapter 5.

12. Using Euler's equation, it can be verified that for the choice of units in equation A.6, the unit cost (revenue) prices in equations 11–13 of table 3.1 are equal to unity.

13. Given total employment and the overall wage share in GNP, we determine W as $W = \alpha \, GNP/L$. This is approximately $18,000 per worker per year. In the context of our discussion, α_i should be regarded as an efficiency unit's adjusted share. That is, we reserve ϕ_i for a distortion measure. Let

$$L_i = \tilde{L}_i \times WD_i, \tag{A.3.9'}$$

where $\tilde{L}_i$ is hours worked, L_i is skill-adjusted or efficiency units of labor, and WD_i is the scalar that converts unadjusted hours worked into efficiency units. Substituting equation A.3.9′ into equation A.3.7 yields

$$\alpha_i = \left[1 + \left(\frac{\tilde{L}_i WD_i}{K_i}\right)^{\rho_i - 1} \frac{R}{W}\right]^{-1}.$$

Since $\rho_i < 1$, the more productive is labor in sector i (higher WD_i), the larger will be the calibrated share α_i.

Appendix B

1. We thank Clint Shiells for helpful discussions on this point.

2. The textiles and apparel elasticity is a weighted average of the separate elasticities for textiles and apparel.

3. For example, in the medium elasticity case the estimated welfare benefits of removing VERs in autos, steel, and textiles are $21.05 billion (table 5.6). If we double (halve) all the elasticities of transformation (holding all other elasticities constant), the welfare benefits increase (decrease) to $21.19 ($20.94) billion—a change of less than 1 percent.

4. One can obtain an elasticity of demand for composite autos from Levinsohn's regressions (1988, table 2.3) by assuming an equiproportionate increase in the price of imported and domestic autos. We thank James Levinsohn for helpful discussion regarding his estimates.

5. Killingsworth and Heckman (1986, 193–196) accept that Mroz has made a significant contribution regarding the formal testing of a variety of previously untested propositions.

6. We thank Eleanor Uzzelle of the Office of Trade and Investment Analysis, US Department of Commerce, for providing unpublished information.

7. Two other investments are also worth noting. In 1980 Renault acquired 46 percent equity interest in American Motors for $167.5 million, and in 1982 and

1983 the government of France acquired an equity interest in Mack trucks for a combined investment of $165 million.

8. In the same year, however, Volkswagen announced it would close its facility in Pennsylvania.

9. Two notable exceptions were that in 1987 Honda undertook a $450 million expansion of its Anna, Ohio, engine facility to include drive trains, suspensions, and brake assembly and that in 1988 Toyota undertook a $300 million expansion of its facility in Georgetown, Kentucky, to produce engines.

10. Polls indicate that the Japanese believe there is substantial merit in some of the US complaints regarding the US trade deficit with Japan; for example, the Japanese distribution system is in need of reform and is partly responsible for the high prices Japanese consumers pay for many products. However, there is widespread support in Japan for the "Keretsu" system of long-term relationships. See *The Washington Post*, April 2, 1990, p. 1.

11. For a similar view, see Lawrence (1990).

References

Abbott, M., and O. Ashenfelter. 1976. Labour supply, commodity demand and the allocation of time. *Review of Economic Studies* 43: 389–411.

Adams, W., and J. Dirlam. 1964. Steel, imports and vertical oligopoly power. *American Economic Review* 54: 626–655.

Akerlof, G. 1984. Gift exchange and efficiency wages: Four views. *American Economic Review* 74: 79–83.

Allen, R. G. D. 1938. *Mathematical Analysis for Economists*. London: Macmillan.

Anderson, J. E. 1985. The relative inefficiency of quotas: The cheese case. *American Economic Review* 75: 178–190.

Anderson, J. E. 1988. *The Relative Inefficiency of Quotas*. Cambridge: MIT Press.

Anderson, K., and M. Metzger. 1987. *A Critical Evaluation of Petroleum Import Tariffs: Analytical and Historical Perspectives*. Washington: US Federal Trade Commission.

Anderson, K., and M. Metzger. 1991. *Petroleum Tariffs as a Source of Government Revenue*. Washington: US Federal Trade Commission.

Armington, P. 1969. A theory of demand for products distinguished by place of production. *IMF Staff Papers* 16: 159–178.

Arrow, K., and G. Debreu. 1954. Existence of an equilibrium for a competitive process. *Econometrica* 22: 265–290.

Arrow, K., and F. Hahn. 1971. *General Competitive Analysis*. San Francisco: Holden Day.

Ashenfelter, O., and R. Layard, eds. 1986. *Handbook of Labor Economics*. Amsterdam: North-Holland.

Aspe, P., and F. Giavazzi. 1982. The short-run behaviour of prices and output in the exportables sector: The case of German machinery. *Journal of International Economics* 12: 83–89.

Atkinson, A., and J. Stiglitz. 1980. *Public Economics*. New York: McGraw-Hill.

Aw, B. Y., and M. J. Roberts. 1986. Measuring quality change in quota-constrained markets: The case of US footwear. *Journal of International Economics* 21: 45–60.

Balassa, B., and C. Balassa. 1984. Industrial protection in the developed countries. *The World Economy* 7: 179–196.

Baldwin, R. E. 1982. *The Inefficacy of Trade Policy*. Essays in International Finance 150. Princeton: Princeton University Press.

Baldwin, R. E. 1984a. The changing nature of US trade policy since World War II. In R. E. Baldwin and A. Krueger, eds., *The Structure and Evolution of Recent US Trade Policy*. Chicago: University of Chicago Press for NBER.

Baldwin, R. E. 1984b. Trade policies in developed countries. In R. Jones and P. Kenen, eds., *Handbook of International Economics*, vol. 1. Amsterdam: North-Holland.

Baldwin, R. 1989. The growth effects of 1992. *Economic Policy* 9: 248–281.

Ballard, C., D. Fullerton, J. Shoven, and J. Whalley. 1985. *A General Equilibrium Model for Tax Policy Evaluation*. Chicago: University of Chicago Press for NBER.

Bark, T., and J. de Melo. 1987. Export mix adjustment to the imposition of VERs: Alternative allocation schemes. *Weltwirtschaftliches Archiv* 123: 668–678.

Bark, T., and J. de Melo. 1989. Efficiency and export earnings implications of two-tier quota allocation rules. *International Economic Journal* 3: 31–42.

Barnett, D., and R. Crandall. 1987. *Up from the Ashes: The Rise of the Steel Minimill in the United States*. Washington: Brookings Institution.

Barnett, D., and L. Schorsch. 1982. *Steel: Upheaval in a Basic Industry*. Cambridge, MA: Ballinger.

Baumol, W., J. Panzar, and R. Willig. 1982. *Contestable Markets and the Theory of Market Structure*. New York: Harcourt Brace Jovanovich.

Bergsten, C. F., K. A. Elliot, J. J. Schott, and W. Takacs. 1987. *Auction Quotas and United States Trade Policy*. Washington: Institute for International Economics.

Bhagwati, J. 1965. On the equivalence of tariffs and quotas. In R. E. Baldwin, ed., *Trade, growth and the balance of payments*. Chicago: Rand McNally.

Bhagwati, J. 1971. The generalized theory of distortions and welfare. In C. Kindleberger and J. Bhagwati, eds., *Trade, Balance of Payments, and Growth: Papers in International Economics in Honor of Charles P. Kindleberger*. Amsterdam: North-Holland.

Bhagwati, J., and T. N. Srinivasan. 1969. Optimal intervention to achieve non-economic objectives. *Review of Economic Studies* 36: 27–38.

Bhagwati, J., and T. N. Srinivasan. 1983. *Lectures on International Trade*. Cambridge: MIT Press.

Blackorby, C., D. Primont, and R. Russell. 1978. *Duality, Separability and Functional Structure: Theory and Economic Applications*. Amsterdam: North-Holland.

Bluestone, B., and B. Harrison. 1988. The growth of low-wage employment: 1963–86. *American Economic Review* 78: 124–128.

Bohi D., and M. Russell. 1978. *Limiting Oil Imports: An Economic History and Analysis*. Baltimore: Johns Hopkins University Press.

Boorstein, R., and R. Feenstra. 1987. Quality upgrading and its welfare cost on US steel imports, 1969–74. NBER Working Paper 2452. Cambridge, MA: National Bureau of Economic Research.

Borges, A. M., and L. H. Goulder. 1984. Decomposing the impact of higher energy prices on long-term growth. In H. E. Scarf and J. B. Shoven, eds., *Applied General Equilibrium Analysis*. Cambridge: Cambridge University Press.

Boyd, R., and N. Uri. 1989a. Assessing the impact of an oil import fee. *Energy: The International Journal* 14: 29–44.

Boyd, R., and N. Uri. 1989b. Potential benefits and costs of an increase in US gasoline tax. *Energy Policy* 17: 356–369.

Brander, J. A., and B. J. Spencer. 1983. International R&D rivalry and industrial strategy. *Review of Economic Studies* 50: 707–722.

Brander, J. A., and B. J. Spencer. 1984. Tariff protection and imperfect competition. In H. Kierkowski, ed., *Monopolistic Competition and International Trade*. Oxford: Oxford University Press.

Brecher, R. A., and C. F. Díaz-Alejandro. 1977. Tariffs, foreign capital, and immiserizing growth. *Journal of International Economics* 7: 317–322.

Bresnahan, T. 1981. Duopoly models with consistent conjectures. *American Economic Review* 71: 934–945.

Bresnahan, T. 1989. Empirical studies of industries with market power. In R. Schmalensee and R. Willig, eds., *Handbook of Industrial Organization*, vol. 2. Amsterdam: North-Holland.

Brooke, A., D. Kendrick, and A. Meeraus. 1988. *GAMS: A User's Guide*. Palo Alto, CA.: The Scientific Press.

Brown, D. 1987. Tariffs, the terms of trade and national product differentiation. *Journal of Policy Modelling* 9: 503–526.

Brown, D., and R. Stern. 1989. US–Canada bilateral tariff elimination: The role of product differentiation and market structure. In R. Feenstra, ed., *Trade Policies for International Competitiveness*. Chicago: University of Chicago Press.

Brown, J., and A. Deaton. 1972. Models of consumer behavior: A survey. *Economic Journal* 82: 1145–1236.

Burns, M. 1973. A note on the concept and measure of consumers' surplus. *American Economic Review* 63: 335–344.

Caddy, V. 1976. Empirical estimation of the elasticity of substitution: A review. Preliminary Working Paper OP-09. IMPACT Project, Industries Assistance Commission. Melbourne, Australia.

Caves, R., and R. Jones. 1985. *World Trade and Payments.* Boston: Little, Brown.

Cline, W. 1979. Imports and consumer prices: A survey analysis. *Journal of Retailing* 5: 3–24.

Cline, W. 1987. *The Future of World Trade in Textiles.* Washington: Institute for International Economics.

Cockerill, A., with A. Silbertson. 1974. *The Steel Industry: International Comparisons of Industrial Structure and Performance.* Cambridge: Cambridge University Press.

Collyns, C., and S. Dunaway. 1987. The cost of trade restraints: The case of Japanese automobile exports to the United States. *IMF Staff Papers* 34: 150–175.

Condon, T., V. Corbo, and J. de Melo. 1989. Exchange rate based disinflation, wage rigidity and capital inflows: Tradeoffs for Chile, 1977–81. *Journal of Development Economics* 32: 113–132.

Condon, T., and J. de Melo. 1990. Industrial organization implications of QR trade regimes: Evidence and welfare costs. *Empirical Economics,* forthcoming.

Congressional Budget Office. 1984. *The Effects of Import Quotas on the Steel Industry.* Washington: US Government Printing Office.

Congressional Budget Office. January 1987. *Reducing the Deficit: Spending and Revenue Options.* Washington: US Government Printing Office.

Corden, W. M. 1974. *Trade Policy and Economic Welfare.* Oxford: Clarendon Press.

Cox, D., and R. Harris. 1985. Trade liberalization and industrial organization: Some estimates for Canada. *Journal of Political Economy* 93: 115–145.

Crandall, R. 1981. *The US Steel Industry in Recurrent Crisis.* Washington: Brookings Institution.

Crandall, R. 1984. Import quotas and the automobile industry: The costs of protectionism. *The Brookings Review* 2: 8–16.

Crandall, R. 1985. Assessing the impacts of the automobile voluntary export restraints upon US automobile prices. Washington: Brookings Institution. Photocopy.

Crandall, R. 1987. The effects of US trade protection for autos and steel. *Brookings Papers on Economic Activity* 1: 271–288.

Dahl, H., S. Devarajan, and S. van Wijnbergen. 1986. Revenue neutral tariff reform: theory and an application to Cameroon. CPD Discussion Paper 1986–26. Washington: World Bank.

Deardorff, A., and R. Stern. 1986. *The Michigan Model of World Production and Trade*. Cambridge: MIT Press.

Deaton, A., and J. Muellbauer. 1980. *Economics and Consumer Behaviour*. Cambridge: Cambridge University Press.

De Rosa, D., and M. Goldstein. 1981. Import discipline in the US manufacturing sector. *IMF Staff Papers* 28: 600–634.

Dervis, K., J. de Melo, and S. Robinson. 1982. *General Equilibrium Models for Development Policy*. Cambridge: Cambridge University Press.

Devarajan, S., and D. Rodrik. 1989. Pro-competitive effects of trade reform: Results from a CGE model of Cameroon. *European Economic Review*, forthcoming.

Dinopoulos, E., and M. Kreinin. 1988. Effects of the US–Japan auto VER on European prices and US welfare. *Review of Economics and Statistics* 70: 484–491.

Dixit, A. 1985. Tax policy in open economies. In A. Auerbach and M. Feldstein, eds., *Handbook of Public Economics*. Amsterdam: North-Holland.

Dixit, A. 1988. Optimal trade and industrial policies for the US automobile industry. In R. Feenstra, ed., *Empirical Methods in International Trade*. Cambridge: MIT Press.

Dixit, A., and J. Stiglitz. 1977. Monopolistic competition and optimum product diversity. *American Economic Review* 67: 297–308.

Dixon, P. 1978. Economies of scale, commodity disaggregation, and the costs of protection. *Australian Economic Papers* 90: 312–326.

Dixon, P., B. Parmenter, J. Sutton, and D. Vincent. 1982. *ORANI: A Multisectoral Model of the Australian Economy*. Amsterdam: North-Holland.

Domowitz, I., R. G. Hubbard, and B. Petersen. 1986. Business cycles and the relationship between concentration and price-cost margins. *Rand Journal of Economics* 17: 1–17.

Dornbusch, R. 1987. Exchange rates and prices. *American Economic Review* 77: 93–106.

Dornbusch, R., and F. L. H. Helmers, eds. 1988. *The Open Economy*. Oxford: Oxford University Press.

Eastman, H., and S. Stykolt. 1960. A model for the study of protected oligopolies. *Economic Journal* 70: 336–347.

Eaton, J., and G. Grossman. 1986. Optimal trade and industrial policy under oligopoly. *Quarterly Journal of Economics* 101: 383–406.

Eichengreen, B. 1986. The political economy of the Smoot-Hawley tariff. NBER Working Paper 2001. Cambridge, MA: National Bureau of Economic Research.

Ethier, W. 1988. *Modern International Economics.* New York: Norton.

Faini, R. 1988. Elasticities of supply: some estimates for Morocco and Turkey. Washington: World Bank. Photocopy.

Farber, H. 1986. The analysis of union behavior. In O. Ashenfelter and R. Layard, eds., *Handbook of labor economics.* Amsterdam: North-Holland.

Falvey, R. 1979. The composition of trade within import restricted product categories. *Journal of Political Economy* 87: 1105–1114.

Feenstra, R. 1984. Voluntary export restraints in US autos, 1980–81: Quality, employment and welfare effects. In R. E. Baldwin and A. Krueger, eds., *The Structure and Evolution of Recent US Trade Policy.* Chicago: University of Chicago Press for NBER.

Feenstra, R. 1985. Automobile prices and protection: the US–Japan trade restraint. *Journal of Policy Modeling* 7: 49–68.

Feenstra, R. 1988. Quality Change under Trade Restraints: theory and evidence from Japanese autos. *Quarterly Journal of Economics* 102: 131–146.

Fernandez, R. 1989. Comment. (On Katz and Summers 1989a). In R. Feenstra, ed., *Trade Policies for International Competitiveness.* Chicago: University of Chicago Press.

Finger, M. 1990. The meaning of "unfair" in United States import policy. Washington: World Bank. Photocopy.

Friedlaender, A., C. Winston, and K. Wang. 1984. Costs, technology, and productivity in the US automobile industry. *Bell Journal of Economics* 14: 1–20.

Frisch, R. 1933. Monopole-polypole: La Notion de force dans l'economie. Festschrift til Harald Westergaard. Supplement to *Nationalekonomick Tidsskrift.* English translation in E. Henderson, ed., 1951, *International Economic Papers 1.* London: Macmillan.

Frisch, R. 1959. A complete scheme for computing all direct and cross demand elasticities in a model with many sectors. *Econometrica* 27: 177–196.

Fudenberg, D., and J. Tirole. 1986. Dynamic models of oligopoly. In A. Jacquemin, ed., *Fundamentals of Pure and Applied Economics,* vol. 3. New York: Harwood.

Fung, K. C. 1990. Characteristics of Japanese industrial groups and their potential impact on US–Japan trade. In R. E. Baldwin, ed., *Empirical Studies of Commercial Policy.* Chicago: University of Chicago Press, forthcoming.

Goto, J. 1986. A general equilibrium analysis of international trade and imperfect competition in both product and labor markets—theory and evidence from the automobile trade. Ph.D. dissertation. Yale University, New Haven.

Goto, J. 1988. International trade and imperfect competition: Theory and application to the automobile trade. PPR Working Paper 95. Washington: World Bank.

Goulder, L., and B. Eichengreen. 1989. Savings promotion, investment promotion, and international competitiveness. In R. Feenstra, ed., *Trade Policies for International Competitiveness*. Chicago: University of Chicago Press.

Grais, W., J. de Melo, and S. Urata. 1986. A general equilibrium estimation of the effects of reductions in tariffs and quantitative restrictions in Turkey in 1978. In T. N. Srinivasan and J. Whalley, eds., *General Equilibrium Trade Policy Modeling*. Cambridge: MIT Press.

Green, H. A. J. 1964. *Aggregation in Economic Analysis*. Princeton: Princeton University Press.

Greenspan, A. 1988. Statement before the Committee on the Budget, United States Senate. March 2. Washington: Federal Reserve System.

Grossman, G. 1986. Imports as a cause of injury: The case of the US steel industry. *Journal of International Economics* 20: 201–223.

Grossman, G., and E. Helpman. 1989. Quality ladders in the theory of growth. Cambridge, MA: National Bureau of Economic Research. Photocopy.

Grossman, G., and E. Helpman. 1990. Comparative advantage and long-run growth. *American Economic Review* 80: 796–815.

Hamilton, C. 1986. An assessment of voluntary export restraints on Hong Kong exports to Europe and the USA. *Economica* 53: 339–350.

Hamilton, C. 1988. Restrictiveness and international transmission of the "new" protectionism. In R. E. Baldwin, C. Hamilton, and A. Sapir, eds., *Issues in US-EC Trade Relations*. Chicago: University of Chicago Press for NBER.

Harberger, A. 1988. Trade policy and the real exchange rate. Washington: Economic Development Institute, World Bank. Photocopy.

Harris, R. 1984. Applied general equilibrium analysis of small open economies with scale economies and imperfect competition. *American Economic Review* 74: 1016–1032.

Harris, R., and J. G. MacKinnon. 1979. Computing optimal tax equilibria. *Journal of Public Economics* 11: 197–212.

Harrison, A. 1988. Exchange rate pass-through and imperfect competition: The case of the U.S. steel industry. Washington: World Bank. Photocopy.

Harrison, A. 1989. Productivity, imperfect competition and trade liberalization in Côte d'Ivoire. Washington: World Bank. Photocopy.

Harrison, G., E. E. Rutstrom, and R. Wigle. 1989. Costs of agricultural trade wars. In A. Stoeckel, D. Vincent, and S. Cuthbertson, eds; *Macroeconomic Effects of Farm Support Policies*. Durham, NC: Duke University Press.

Hekman, J. 1978. An analysis of the changing pattern of iron and steel production in the twentieth century. *American Economic Review* 68: 123–133.

Hickock, S. 1985. The consumer costs of US trade restraints. *Quarterly Review* 2: 1–12. New York: Federal Reserve Bank.

Horstman, I., and J. Markusen. 1986. Up the average cost curve: Inefficient entry and the new protectionism. *Journal of International Economics* 20: 225–248.

Houthakker, H., and L. Taylor. 1970. *Consumer demand in the United States: Analyses and Projections*. Cambridge: Harvard University Press.

Hudson, E., and D. Jorgenson. 1974. US energy policy and economic growth 1975–2000. Discussion Paper 372. Cambridge: Harvard Institute of Economic Research.

Hufbauer, G., D. Berliner, and K. Elliot. 1986. *Trade Protection in the United States: 31 Case Studies*. Washington: Institute for International Economics.

Isard, P. 1977. How far can we push the law of one price? *American Economic Review* 67: 942–948.

Jacobson, L. 1978. Earnings losses of workers displaced from manufacturing industries. In W. De Wald, ed., *The Impact of International Trade and Investment on Employment*. Washington: US Department of Labor.

Johnson, H. 1960. The cost of protection and the scientific tariff. *Journal of Political Economy* 68: 327–345.

Johnson, H. 1965. Factor market distortions and the shape of the transformation curve. *Econometrica* 34: 686–698.

Jondrow, J., D. Chase, and C. Gamble. 1982. The price differential between imported and domestic steel. *Journal of Business* 55: 383–399.

Jones, R., and E. Berglas. 1977. Import demand and export supply: An aggregation theorem. *American Economic Review* 67: 183–187.

Kahn, M. 1980. Airlines. In G. Somers, ed., *Collective bargaining: Contemporary American Experience*. Chicago: University of Chicago Press.

Katz, L., and L. Summers. 1989a. Can interindustry wage differentials justify strategic trade policy? In R. Feenstra, ed., *Trade Policies for International Competitiveness*. Chicago: University of Chicago Press.

Katz, L., and L. Summers. 1989b. Industry rents: Evidence and implications. *Brookings Papers on Economic Activity*: 209–290. Special issue on microeconomics.

Keesing, D., and M. Wolf. 1980. *Textile Quotas against Developing Countries*. London: Trade Policy Research Centre.

Killingsworth, M. 1983. *Labor Supply*. Cambridge: Cambridge University Press.

Killingsworth, M., and J. Heckman. 1986. Female labor supply: a survey. In O. Ashenfelter and R. Layard, eds., *Handbook of Labor Economics*. Amsterdam: North–Holland.

Kravis, I., and R. Lipsey. 1971. *Price Competitiveness in World Trade*. New York: National Bureau of Economic Research.

Kreinin, M. 1984. Wage competitiveness in the US auto and steel industries. *Contemporary Policy Issues* 1: 39–50.

Krishna, K. 1985. Trade restrictions as facilitating practices. NBER Working Paper 1546. Cambridge, MA: National Bureau of Economic Research. Reprinted in *Journal of International Economics* 26: 251–270.

Krishna, K. 1989a. The case of vanishing revenues: Auction quotas with oligopoly. NBER Working Paper 2723. Cambridge, MA: National Bureau of Economic Research.

Krishna, K. 1989b. Making altruism pay in auction quotas. NBER Working Paper 3230. Cambridge, MA: National Bureau of Economic Research.

Krishna, K. 1990. The case of vanishing revenues: Auction quotas with monopoly. *American Economic Review* 80: 828–836.

Krishna, K., K. Hogan, and P. Swagel. 1989. The non-optimality of optimal trade policies: the US automobile industry revisited, 1979–1985. In P. Krugman and A. Smith, eds., *Empirical Studies of Strategic Trade Policy*. Chicago: University of Chicago Press.

Krueger, A. 1969. Balance of payments theory. *Journal of Economic Literature* 7: 1–26.

Krueger, A. 1974. The political economy of the rent seeking society. *American Economic Review* 64: 291–303.

Krueger, A. B., and L. H. Summers. 1988. Efficiency wages and the inter-industry wage structure. *Econometrica* 56: 259–293.

Krugman, P. 1979. Increasing returns, monopolistic competition, and international trade. *Journal of International Economics* 9: 469–479.

Krugman, P. 1987. Market access and competition in high technology industries. In H. Kierzkowski, ed., *Protection and Competition in International Trade*. Oxford: Basil Blackwell.

Krugman, P., and A. Smith, eds. 1991. *Empirical Studies of Strategic Trade Policy*. Chicago: University of Chicago Press, forthcoming.

Lawrence, R. 1990. Comment on Fung. In R. E. Baldwin, ed., *Empirical Studies of Commercial Policy*. Chicago: University of Chicago Press.

Lerner, A. 1936. The symmetry between import and export taxes. *Economica* 3: 306–313.

Levinsohn, J. 1988. Empirics of taxes on differentiated products: the case of tariffs in the US automobile industry. In R. E. Baldwin, ed., *Trade Policy Issues and Empirical Analysis*. Chicago: University of Chicago Press.

Levinson, H. 1980. Trucking. In G. Somers, ed., *Collective Bargaining: Contemporary American Enterprise*. Madison, WI: Industrial Relations Research Association.

Lluch, C., A. Powell, and R. Williams. 1977. *Patterns in Household Demand and Savings*. Oxford: Oxford University Press.

Magee, S. 1973. Factor market distortions, production and trade: a survey. *Oxford Economic Papers* 25: 1–43.

Mancke, R. 1968. The determinants of steel prices in the US: 1947–65. *Journal of Industrial Economics* 16: 147–160.

Manne, A. S. 1976. ETA: A model for energy technology assessment. *Bell Journal of Economics and Management Science* 7: 379–406.

Manne, A. S. 1984. Comments. In H. E. Scarf and J. B. Shoven, eds., *Applied General Equilibrium Analysis*. Cambridge: Cambridge University Press.

Mansur, A., and J. Whalley. 1984. Numerical specifications of applied general equilibrium models: Estimation, calibration, and data. In H. Scarf and John Shoven, eds., *Applied General Equilibrium Analysis*. Cambridge: Cambridge University Press.

Markusen, J., and J. Melvin. 1988. *The Theory of International Trade*. New York: Harper and Row.

Marvel, H. 1980. Foreign trade and domestic competition. *Economic Inquiry* 18: 103–122.

McDonald, I. M., and R. M. Solow. 1981. Wage bargaining and employment. *American Economic Review* 71: 896–908.

Melo, J. de. 1977. Distortions in factor markets: Some general equilibrium estimates. *Review of Economics and Statistics* 59: 398–405.

Melo, J. de. 1986. A comparison of 50% multilateral tariff reductions in two global trade models. In T. N. Srinivasan and J. Whalley, eds., *General Equilibrium Trade Policy Modeling*. Cambridge: MIT Press.

Melo, J. de. 1988. Computable general equilibrium models for trade policy analysis in developing countries: A survey. *Journal of Policy Modeling* 10: 469–503.

Melo, J. de, and P. Messerlin. 1988. Price, quality and welfare effects of European VERs on Japanese autos. *European Economic Review* 32: 1527–1546.

Melo, J. de, and S. Robinson. 1985. Product differentiation and trade dependence of the domestic price system in computable general equilibrium trade models. In T. Peeters, P. Praet, and P. Reding, eds., *International Trade and Exchange Rates in the Late Eighties*. Amsterdam: North-Holland.

Melo, J. de, and S. Robinson. 1989. Product differentiation and the treatment of foreign trade in computable general equilibrium models of small economies. *Journal of International Economics* 27: 47–67.

Melo, J. de, and S. Robinson. 1990. Productivity and externalities: Models of export led growth. PRE Working Paper 387. Washington: World Bank.

Melo, J. de, and D. Roland-Holst. 1990a. International capital mobility and the costs of US import restraints. PRE Working Paper No. 516. Washington: World Bank.

Melo, J. de, and D. Roland-Holst. 1990b. Industrial organization and trade liberalization: Evidence from Korea. In R. E. Baldwin, ed., *Empirical Studies of Commercial Policy*. Chicago: University of Chicago Press.

Melo, J. de, and D. Tarr. 1990a. Do wage distortions justify protection in the US auto and steel industries. PRE Working Paper No. 517. Washington: World Bank.

Melo, J. de, and D. Tarr. 1990b. The welfare costs of US quotas in textiles, autos, and steel. *Review of Economics and Statistics* 77: 489–497.

Melo, J. de, and D. Tarr. 1991. VERs under imperfect competition and foreign direct investment: A case study of the US-Japan auto VER. PRE Working Paper No. 667. Washington: World Bank. Photocopy.

Melo, J. de, and S. Urata. 1986. The influence of increased foreign competition on industrial concentration and profitability. *International Journal of Industrial Organization* 4: 287–304.

Melo, J. de, and A. Winters. 1989. Do exporters gain from VERs? PPR Working Paper 326. Washington: World Bank.

Melo, J. de, and A. Winters. 1990. Voluntary export restraints and resource allocation in exporting countries. *World Bank Economic Review*. 4: 209–233.

Melo, J. de, J. Stanton, and D. Tarr. 1989. Revenue raising taxes: General equilibrium evaluation of alternative taxation in US petroleum industries. *Journal of Policy Modeling* 11: 425–449.

Melvin, J. 1968. Production and trade with two factors and three goods. *American Economic Review* 58: 1249–1268.

Morkre, M. 1979. Rent-seeking and Hong Kong's textile quota system. *The Developing Economies* 18: 100–118.

Morkre, M. 1984. Import quotas on textiles: the welfare effects of United States restrictions on Hong Kong. Report by the Bureau of Economics to the US Federal Trade Commission, Washington, DC.

Morkre, M. 1989. Effects of US import restraints on manufactured products: General equilibrium results. Submission by the US Federal Trade Commission Staff to the US International Trade Commission in Investigation No. 332-262, March 31. Washington, DC.

Morkre, M. 1990. Effects of US import restraints on agricultural and other products: General equilibrium results. Submission by the US Federal Trade Commission Staff to the US International Trade Commission in Investigation No. 332-262, February 21. Washington, DC.

Morkre, M., and D. Tarr. 1980. The effects of restrictions on US imports: Five case studies and theory. Report by the Bureau of Economics to the US Federal Trade Commission, Washington, DC.

Mroz, T. 1987. The sensitivity of an empirical model of married women's hours of work to economic and statistical assumptions. *Econometrica* 55: 765–799.

Munger, M. 1985. A time series investigation into factors influencing US auto assembly employment. Report by the Bureau of Economics to the US Federal Trade Commission, Washington, DC.

Mussa, M. 1978. Dynamic adjustment in a Heckscher-Ohlin-Samuelson model. *Journal of Political Economy* 86: 775–791.

Mussa, M. 1984. The adjustment process and the timing of trade liberalization. NBER Working Paper 1458. Cambridge, MA: National Bureau of Economic Research.

Neary, J. P. 1988. Tariffs, quotas, and voluntary export restraints with and without internationally mobile capital. *Canadian Journal of Economics* 11: 714–735.

Neary, J. P., and K. Roberts. 1980. The theory of household behavior under rationing. *European Economic Review* 13: 25–42.

Neary, J. P., and F. Ruane. 1988. International capital mobility, shadow prices, and the cost of protection. *International Economic Review* 29: 571–585.

Oswald, A. 1982. The microeconomic theory of the trade union. *Economic Journal* 92: 576–596.

Novshek, W. 1980. Cournot equilibrium with free entry. *Review of Economic Studies* 47: 473–486.

Panzar, J. C., and R. Willig. 1977. Economies of scale in multi-output production. *Quarterly Journal of Economics* 91: 481–494.

Parsons, D., and E. Ray. 1975. The United States steel consolidation: The creation of market control. *Journal of Law and Economics* 18: 181–219.

Pearce, I. F. 1970. *International Trade*. New York: Norton.

Pencavel, J. 1986. Labor supply of men: A survey. In O. Ashenfelter and R. Layard, eds., *Handbook of labor economics*, vol. 1. Amsterdam: North-Holland.

Perroni, C., and T. Rutherford. 1989. Regularly flexible functional forms for applied general equilibrium analysis. Working Paper 8906c. Center for the Study of International Economic Relations, London, Canada.

Phlips, L. 1974. *Applied Consumption Analysis*. Amsterdam: North-Holland.

Pigou, A. C. 1947. *A Study in Public Finance*, 3d ed. London: Macmillan.

Powell, A., and F. Gruen. 1968. The constant elasticity of transformation production frontier and linear supply system. *International Economic Review* 9: 315–328.

Pugel, T. 1978. *International market linkages and US manufacturing: prices, profits, and patterns*. Cambridge, MA: Ballinger.

Pyatt, G., and J. Round, eds. 1985. *Social Accounting Matrices: A Basis for Planning*. Washington: World Bank.

Riedel, J. 1986. Trade policy in the United States: from multilateralism to bilateralism. Washington: Johns Hopkins, School for Advanced International Studies. Photocopy.

Rippe, R. 1970. Wages, prices and imports in the American steel industry. *Review of Economics and Statistics* 47: 34–46.

Robinson, S. 1988. Multisector models of developing countries: A survey. In H. B. Chenery and T. N. Srinivasan, eds., *Handbook of Development Economics*. Amsterdam: North-Holland.

Rodriguez, C. A. 1979. The quality of imports and the differential welfare effects of tariffs, quotas, and quality controls as protective devices. *Canadian Journal of Economics* 12: 439–449.

Rodrik, D. 1988. Imperfect competition, scale economies and trade policy in developing countries. In R. E. Baldwin, ed., *Trade Policy Issues and Empirical Analysis*. Chicago: University of Chicago Press.

Romer, P. 1986. Increasing returns and long-run growth. *Journal of Political Economy* 94: 1002–1037.

Romer, P. 1989. What determines the rate of growth of technological change? PRE Working Paper 279. Washington: World Bank.

Rotemberg, J., and G. Saloner. 1988. Tariffs vs. quotas with implicit collusion. *Canadian Journal of Agricultural Economics* 22: 237–244.

Saloner, G. 1989. Comments on Krishna et al. In P. Krugman and A. Smith, eds., *Empirical Studies of Strategic Trade Policy*. Chicago: University of Chicago Press.

Samuelson, P. 1947. Some implications of linearity. *Review of Economic Studies* 15: 88–90.

Samuelson, P. 1953. Prices of factors and goods in general equilibrium. *Review of Economic Studies* 22: 1–21.

Scherer, F. M. 1980. *Industrial Market Structure and Economic Performance*. Boston: Rand McNally.

Scherer, F. M., A. Beckenstein, E. Kaufer, and R. D. Murphy. 1975. *The Economies of Multi-plant Operations*. Cambridge: Harvard University Press.

Shapiro, C. 1989. Theories of oligopoly behavior. In R. Schmalansee and R. Willig, eds., *Handbook of Industrial Organization*. Amsterdam: North-Holland.

Shapiro, C., and J. Stiglitz. 1984. Equilibrium unemployment as a worker discipline device. *American Economic Review* 74: 433–444.

Shiells, C., R. Stern, and A. Deardorff. 1986. Estimates of the elasticities of substitution between imports and home goods for the United States. *Weltwirtschaftliches Archiv* 122: 497–519.

Shoven, J., and J. Whalley. 1984. Applied general equilibrium models of taxation and international trade. *Journal of Economic Literature* 22: 1007–1051.

Smith, A., and A. J. Venables. 1988. Completing the internal market in the European Community: some industry simulations. *European Economic Review* 32: 1501–1525.

Solow, R. 1956. A contribution to the theory of economic growth. *Quarterly Journal of Economics* 70: 65–94.

Spence, M. 1976. Product selection, fixed costs, and monopolistic competition. *Review of Economic Studies* 43: 217–236.

Srinivasan, T. N., and J. Whalley, eds. 1986. *General Equilibrium Trade Policy Modeling*. Cambridge: MIT Press.

Stern, R., J. Francis, and B. Schumacher. 1976. *Price Elasticities in International Trade: An Annotated Bibliography*. London: Macmillan for the Trade Policy Research Centre.

Stigler, G. 1968. A theory of oligopoly. In G. Stigler, ed., *The Organization of Industry*. Chicago: Irwin.

Stone, J. 1979. Price elasticities of demand for imports and exports: Industry estimates for the US, EEC and Japan. *Review of Economics and Statistics* 61: 306–312.

Takacs, W. 1977. The nonequivalence of tariffs, import quotas and voluntary export restraints. *Journal of International Economics* 8: 565–573.

Takacs, W. 1987. Auctioning import quota licenses: an economic analysis. Seminar Paper 390. Stockholm: Institute for International Economic Studies.

Takacs, W. 1990. Options for dismantling trade restrictions in developing countries. *World Bank Research Observer* 5: 25–46.

Tan, L. H. 1990. Some notes on the implementation of auction quotas. Cambridge: Harvard University. Photocopy.

Tarr, D. 1972. Stability in a Cournot market characterized by uncertainty. *Western Economic Journal* 10: 330–336.

Tarr, D. 1975. On the stability of oligopoly with nondogmatic conjectures. *Metroeconomica* 27: 184–190.

Tarr, D. 1984. The minimum efficient size steel plant. *Atlantic Economic Journal* 12: 122.

Tarr, D. 1985. Does protection really protect? *Regulation* 9: 29–34.

Tarr, D. 1987. Effects of restraining steel exports from the Republic of Korea and other countries to the United States and the European Economic Community. *The World Bank Economic Review* 1: 397–418.

Tarr, D. 1988a. Costs and benefits to the United States of the 1985 steel import quota program. In R. Sato and P. Wachtel, eds., *Trade Friction: Problems and Prospects for Japan and the United States.* Cambridge: Cambridge University Press.

Tarr, D. 1988b. The steel crisis in the United States and the European Community: Causes and adjustments. In R. E. Baldwin, C. Hamilton, and A. Sapir, eds., *Issues in US-EC Trade Relations.* Chicago: University of Chicago Press for NBER.

Tarr, D. 1989. A general equilibrium analysis of quotas on US imports. Washington: US Federal Trade Commission.

Tarr, D., and M. Morkre. 1984. Aggregate costs to the United States of tariffs and quotas on imports. Report by the Bureau of Economics to the US Federal Trade Commission. Washington, DC.

Thaler, R. H. 1989. Anomalies: Interindustry wage differentials. *Journal of Economic Perspectives* 3: 181–193.

Trella, I., and J. Whalley. 1988. Global effects of developed country trade restrictions on textiles and apparel. London, Ontario: Center for the Study of International Economic Relations, University of Western Ontario. Photocopy.

Tumlir, J. 1985. *Protectionism: Trade Policy in Democratic Societies.* Washington: American Enterprise Institute for Public Policy Research.

United Nations Statistical Office. 1968. *A System of National Accounts.* New York: United Nations.

US Department of Agriculture. 1984. *Dairy: Background for 1984 Farm Legislation.* Washington: USDA.

US Department of Commerce, International Trade Administration. 1987. *Development of a Protection Cost Index: Issues and Challenges.* Proceedings of a conference held August 6, 1987, Washington, DC.

US Department of Energy. 1987. *Energy Security.* Washington: USDOE.

US Federal Trade Commission. 1977. The United States steel industry and its international rivals. Staff report by D. Tarr and others. Washington: US Government Printing Office.

US General Accounting Office. 1986. *Petroleum Products: Effects of Imports on US Oil Refineries and US Energy Security*. Washington, DC.

US House of Representatives, Committee on Ways and Means. June 25, 1987. *Description of Possible Options to Increase Revenue*. Washington: US Government Printing Office.

US International Trade Commission. 1985. *The Multifiber Arrangement, 1980–84*, Publication no. 1693. Washington, DC. USITC.

US International Trade Commission. 1987a. *US Imports of Textiles and Apparel under the Multifiber Arrangement: Statistical Report through 1986*. Publication no. 1986. Washington, DC. USITC.

US International Trade Commission. 1987b. *US Global Competitiveness: The US Textile Mill Industry*. Publication no. 2048. Washington, DC. USITC.

US International Trade Commission. 1988. Value of US imports for consumption, duties collected and ratio of duties to values. Washington: Statistical Services Division. USITC.

Vanek. J. 1963. Variable factor proportions and interindustry flows in the theory of international trade. *Quarterly Journal of Economics* 77: 129–142.

Varian, H. 1984. *Microeconomic Analysis*. New York: Norton.

Webbink, D. 1985. Factors affecting steel employment besides steel imports. Bureau of Economics Working Paper 128. Washington: Federal Trade Commission. Photocopy.

Weiss, A. 1980. Job queues and layoffs in labor markets with flexible wages. *Journal of Political Economy* 88: 526–538.

Whalley, J. 1985. *Trade Liberalization among Major World Trading Areas*. Cambridge: MIT Press.

Willig, R. 1976. Consumer surplus without apology. *American Economic Review* 66: 589–597.

Winston, C., and Associates. 1987. *Blind Intersection? Policy and the Automobile Industry*. Washington: Brookings Institution.

Name Index

Abbott, M., 140, 237
Adams, W., 252
Akerlof, G., 250
Anderson, J., 241, 257
Anderson, K, 174, 175, 178, 183, 255
Armington, P., 16, 18
Arrow, K., 42, 43
Ashenfelter, O., 140, 237
Aspe, P., 242
Atkinson, A., 188, 255
Aw, B., 247

Balassa, B., 200, 241
Balassa, C., 241
Baldwin, Richard, 257
Baldwin, Robert, 42, 197
Ballard, C., 141, 231, 249, 258
Bark, T., 245, 247
Barnett, D., 146, 227, 250
Baumol, W., 245
Berglas, E., 249
Bergsten, C., 78, 102, 241
Berliner, D., 7, 8, 9, 192, 199, 256
Bhagwati, J., 120, 246, 255, 256
Blackorby, C., 50, 244
Boorstein, R., 247
Borges, A., 256
Boyd, R., 183, 256
Brander, J., 120
Brecher, R., 137
Bresnahan, T., 253
Brooke, A., 176
Brown, D., 17, 249, 254
Brown, J., 221
Burns, M., 251

Caddy, V., 177, 230, 231
Caves, R., 242
Chase, D., 17
Cline, W., 7, 9, 70, 76, 78, 192, 245, 246, 256
Cockerill, A., 227
Condon, T., 244, 257
Corbo, V., 244
Corden, W., 186, 250, 254
Cox, D., 151, 252, 253
Crandall, R., 78, 116, 250

Dahl, H., 184, 186
De Rosa, D., 149
Deardorff, A., 10, 106, 177, 230, 249
Deaton, A., 140, 221, 244
Debreu, G., 42
Dervis, K., 242, 258, 259
Devarajan, S., 184, 186, 254, 257
Díaz-Alejandro, C., 137
Dinopolous, E., 8, 9, 81, 82, 105, 192, 249
Dirlam, J., 252
Dixit, A., 149, 150, 152, 156, 184, 252, 254
Dixon, P., 230
Domowitz, I., 149
Dornbusch, R., 17

Easton, J., 251
Eichengreen, B., 257
Elliot, J., 7, 8, 9
Elliot, K., 192, 199, 256
Ethier, W., 250

Faini, R., 231
Falvey, R., 247
Farber, H., 125, 251
Feenstra, R., 8, 9, 78, 80, 81, 82, 105, 247
Fernandez, R., 250, 257
Finger, M., 1
Francis, J., 177, 230

Friedlaender, A., 147, 227
Frisch, R., 152, 221
Fudenberg, D., 253
Fung, K., 240

Gamble, C., 17
Giavazzi, F., 242
Goldstein, M., 149
Goto, J., 253
Goulder, L., 256, 257
Greenspan, A., 255
Grossman, G., 201, 251
Gruen, F., 52, 242

Hahn, F., 43
Hamilton, C., 71, 72. 76, 105, 245, 246
Harris, R., 151, 184, 252, 253, 257
Harrison, A., 147, 252
Harrison, G., 242, 257
Heckman, J. 237, 259
Hekman, J., 231
Helpman, E., 201
Hickock, S., 7, 8, 9
Hogan, K., 150, 252, 253, 254
Horstman, I., 162
Hubbard, R., 149
Hudson, E., 256
Hufbauer, G., 7, 8, 9, 192, 199, 256

Isard, P., 17

Jacobson, L., 197, 198
Johnson, H., 242
Jondrow, J., 17
Jones, R., 242, 249
Jorgenson, D., 256

Kahn, M., 250
Katz, L., 119, 120, 250
Keesing, D., 245
Kendrick, D., 176
Killingsworth, M., 237, 259
Kravis, I., 17
Kreinin, M., 8, 9, 81, 82, 105, 116, 192, 249
Krishna, K., 4, 69, 148, 150, 245, 247, 252, 253, 254
Krueger, A., 42, 249
Krueger, A. B., 118
Krugman, P., 17, 253, 254

Lawrence, R., 260
Leontief, W., 17, 35
Lerner, A., 29
Levinsohn, J., 234, 236, 259
Levinson, H., 250
Lipsey, R., 17
Lluch, C., 221, 234

MacKinnon, G., 184
Magee, S., 250
Mancke, R., 147
Manne, A., 256
Mansur, A., 258
Markusen, J., 162, 256
Marvel, H., 149
McDonald, I., 126
Meeraus, A., 176
Melo, J. de, 162, 182, 183, 192, 242, 243, 244, 245, 247, 248, 249, 250, 251, 252, 256, 257, 258, 259
Melvin, J., 242, 256
Metzger, M., 174, 175, 178, 183, 255
Morkre, M., 7, 8, 9, 71, 76, 77, 78, 192, 199, 241, 243, 245, 246, 247, 251, 257
Mroz, T., 237, 259
Muellbauer, J., 140, 244
Mussa, M., 197

Neary, J., 53, 132, 135
Novshek, W., 253

Oswald, A., 126

Panzar, J., 148, 245
Parsons, D., 146
Pearce, I., 242
Pencavel, J., 237
Peronni, C., 244
Petersen, B., 149
Phlips, L., 50, 244
Powell, A., 52, 221, 234, 242
Primont, D., 50, 244
Pugel, T., 149

Ray, E., 146
Rippe, R., 147
Roberts, M., 53, 247
Robinson, S., 242, 243, 256, 258, 259
Rodriguez, C., 247
Rodrik, D., 157, 254, 257
Roland-Holst, D., 243, 251, 257
Romer, P., 201
Rotemberg, J., 245, 253

Ruane, F., 135
Russell, R., 50, 244
Rutherford, T., 244
Rutstrom, E., 242, 257

Saloner, G., 245, 252, 253, 254
Samuelson, P., 241
Scherer, F., 252
Schorsch, L., 146, 227
Schumacher, B., 177, 230
Shapiro, C., 250, 253
Shiells, C., 177, 230
Smith, A., 253, 254
Solow, R., 126
Spence, M., 152
Spencer, B., 120
Srinivasan, T., 120, 255, 256
Stanton, J., 182, 183
Stern, R., 10, 17, 106, 177, 230, 249, 254
Stigler, G., 146, 245, 253
Stiglitz, J., 152, 188, 250, 255
Summers, L., 118, 119, 120, 250
Swagel, P., 150, 252, 253, 254

Takacs, W., 241, 245, 246
Tan, L., 245
Tarr, D., 7, 8, 9, 77, 78, 112, 116, 146, 162, 182, 183, 192, 220, 227, 241, 246, 247, 248, 251, 253, 257, 258
Thaler, R., 250
Tirole, J., 253
Trella, I., 72

Urata, S., 252
Uri, N., 183, 256

van Wijnbergen, S., 184, 186
Vanek, J., 242
Varian, H., 61, 131, 244
Venables, A., 253, 254

Wang, K., 147, 227
Weiss, A., 250
Whalley, J., 10, 72, 106, 230, 231, 258
Wigle, R., 242, 257
Williams, R., 221, 234
Willig, R., 148, 245
Winston, C., 8, 9, 147, 148, 192, 227
Winston, C., and Associates, 252, 256
Winters, A., 244, 247
Wolf, M., 245

Subject Index

Aggregate index of commodities, 112
Aggregation, general equilibrium model and, 43–44
Agriculture, 7
elasticity specifications, 88, 232, 233, 235
employment, joint removal of quotas and, 100–101, 115, 132
exports and imports, joint removal of quotas and, 101
joint quota removal, 100–101, 115
quotas with sectorally fixed capital stocks, 132
Apparel. *See* Textiles and apparel. *See also* Multifiber Arrangement (MFA)
Armington assumption, 16, 18
Auction quota, 95
Automobile(s), 5, 85, 151, 159, 176
conjectures, Cournot, 155, 156
conjectures, endogenous, 158, 162, 163
costs of VER protection under *CRTS*, 93–96
costs of VER protection under *IRTS*, 160
costs of wage distortions in, 118–120
costs of VERs with exogenous wage distortions, 121
economies of scale, 147–148
elasticity specifications, 88, 232, 233, 235, 236
employment, 100, 115, 132
endogenous wage distortions, 128–130, 139
European, 81–82, 95
exports and imports, joint removal of quotas and, 101
foreign direct investment and the VER, 162, 238–240
imperfect competition and costs of VERs, 158–163
interactions with steel, 163
interindustry wage differences, 121
labor unions, modeling of, 123–130
price elasticity of demand in general equilibrium, 167–171
pricing, 148–150
production and demand structure, 87, 89
profits and the VER, 149, 155, 160
quality upgrading under VERs, 78–80
quantitative restrictions, 65, 87, 121
quota removal, with sectorally fixed capital stock, 131
quota removal, with internationally mobile capital, 136–138
quota rent capture by foreigners, 82–83
quota rent estimates, 78–83
terms-of-trade effects, impact on costs of VERs, 96
wage distortions in, 116–118
welfare cost comparisons, 192
Autonomy of domestic prices, 38

Balance of payments and transfers, 206–208
Balance of trade constraints, 7, 54
partial equilibrium bias from ignoring, 105
Barriers to trade, 191
Benchmarking, 43, 204
under constant returns to scale, 220–224
under increasing returns to scale, 224–227
Bertrand, 150
Bilateral protectionism, 3
Binding quotas, 76

Calibration of model. *See* Benchmarking
Capital market mobility, integration of, 4, 134–138

Capital stock measurement, and distortions in factor markets, 221–224
Capture of quota rents, 8, 65–69, 93, 95
competition in importing and, 68
contestable markets in importing and, 67–68
monopoly in exporting and, 68–69
monopsony and, 67–68
oligopsony and, 67–68
political economy considerations and, 102
theory of, 65–67
CDR (cost disadvantage ratio), 146, 225–227
CES. *See* Constant elasticity of substitution
CET (constant elasticity of transformation), 18, 30, 220–221
Chamberlinian monopolistic competition, 147, 155
Cobb-Douglas function, 50, 222
Compensating variation, 58–62, 86, 141–142
Competition in importing, capture of quota rents and, 68
Conjectures, endogenous, 158, 162, 163
Constant elasticity of substitution (CES), 18, 30, 36, 44, 50, 54, 112, 220–221
aggregator function, 50, 220
trade-aggregation functions, 37
Constant elasticity of transformation (CET), 18, 30, 52, 220–221
Constant returns to scale (*CRTS*), 16, 42, 159, 162, 220–221, 224
Consumer demand functions, 54
Consumer goods, elasticity specification, 232, 235
Consumer income, 55
Contestable market pricing, 153, 155, 159, 161, 166
Contestable markets in importing, capture of quota rents and, 67–68
Cost disadvantage ratio (*CDR*), 146, 225–227
Cost equation, 47
Cost minimization, in intermediate demand, 51
Cost of quotas in textiles, apparel, and steel, evaluation of the welfare tariff equivalent, 199, 200
Costs of protection
aggregation and, 43
previous studies, 7–10
Costs per job protected by quota protection, 196–198
Counterfactual simulation analysis, 2
Cournot conjectures, 150, 152, 155, 156
Cross-hauling, 17
CRTS. *See* Constant returns to scale
Crude oil, 176, 183, 186
elasticities specifications, 232–233, 235
excise taxes and tariffs, relative efficiency of, 179–189
modification of model to include excise taxes, 175–176
production and demand structure, 177

Degree of trade dependence, 35, 36–37
Direct compensation function, 61
Direct utility function, 61
Disaggregation, 43–44, 193, 194–195
Distortionary costs of protection, 26, 32, 85, 159
elasticities on, 90–91, 96–97
in production, 24, 85–86
of quantitative restrictions, removal of, 194
of quotas, 106–107
of tariff protection, 33–34
of voluntary export restraints, 166–167
welfare costs of QRs and, 193
Domestic price response elasticity to import prices, 35–39
Domestic pricing hypothesis, 152–153
Domestic-use ratio, 218
Dual vs. primal model specification, 55–56

Eastman-Stykolt hypothesis, 151
Economies of scale, 5, 145, 166, 195
automobile industry, 147–148
in steel industry, 146
Efficiency units, in factor markets, 221–224
Elasticity, 36
of domestic price with respect to import price, 35–39
of final demand, 168–169, 233–235
impact on costs (asymmetric) of imposing quotas, 97–98
impact on costs of removing quotas, 90–91
of intermediate demand, 169–170
of labor supply, 236–237
market, general equilibrium derivation of, 167–171

specifications, 44–46, 87–89, 105, 176–178, 229–240
of substitution, 51, 95, 229–230, 230–231, 235–236
of transformation, 231–233
Employment, 4
data, 211, 214
import tariff on oil and gas products and, 178
imposing VERs on steel and, 96–98
joint quota removal, 92–92, 100–101, 115
labor unions and wage premium, 124–128
quota removal, in textiles and apparel and, 89–90
quota removal, with internationally mobile capital and, 136–138
quota removal, with wage distortions, 120–121, 128–130
quotas, with fixed capital stocks, 132
removal of VER on autos and, 93–95
by sector, 214
welfare costs of QRs and, 193–194
Endogenous conjectures, 154
Endogenous variables, definitions of, 49
Endogenous wage distortion, 124–130
Energy sectors
elasticity specifications for, 176–178
general equilibrium model modifications for, 175–176
optimal taxation of, 184–189
relative efficiency of excise taxes and tariffs, 179–189
taxation proposals for, 174
Equivalent variation (*EV*), 58–62, 86, 141–142
European automobiles, 81–82, 95
Exchange rates, 17, 20, 62–63
Excise taxes, 173
on gasoline, 183
government revenues and, 196
in petroleum industry, relative efficiency of, 175, 180–181, 184–188
Exogenous variables, definitions of, 50
Expenditure function, 61–62, 141–142
Export data, 208–210
Export demand, elasticities, 7, 103
Export licenses, 80
Export quotas, of textiles and apparel, 70
Export restraint agreements, 65. *See also* Quantitative restrictions; Voluntary export restraint

Factor accounts, 215
Factor markets (basic model), 47, 51
Factor market distortions, 116–121, 221–224
costs of QRs with endogenous wage distortions, 128–130
costs of QRs with exogenous wage distortions, 121–123
Final demand, 54, 210–211
Fiscal deficits, reduction, 6
Food
elasticity specifications, 88, 232, 233, 235
employment, joint removal of quotas and, 100–101, 115, 132
employment, quota removal with sectorally fixed capital stocks, 132
exports and imports, joint removal of quotas and, 101
joint quota removal, 100–101, 115
Foreign demand elasticity, equilibrium with, 23–24
monopoly and monopsony power, 54, 103–104
Foreign direct investment, 4, 195
costs of quotas with, 134–138, 162–165
in automobile assembly plants, 238–239
in automobile industry during VER, 238–240
in automobile parts, 239–240
in US automobiles by Japanese automakers, 6
Foreign rate of transformation through trade (FRT), 26
Foreign transfers, 27, 32
Frisch parameter, 221, 233

GATT (General Agreement on Tariffs and Trade), 1, 102, 189
GDP, 33–34
GDP deflator, 30
General Agreement on Tariffs and Trade. *See* GATT
General equilibrium model
accommodation of imperfect competition, 150–156
adaptation to energy sector, 175–178
aggregation and, 43–44
allocation of production, 44–45
consumer demand, 44–45
costs of QRs with imperfect competition, 158–163

General equilibrium model (cont.)
  data set construction and data sources, 203–214
  elasticity specification and, 44–46
  equations, 46–58
  labor-leisure choice modification, 112–113, 139–142
  model structure, 44–45
  one-sector (*see* One-sector general equilibrium model)
  overview, 41–43
  rationale for, 6–7
  total domestic demand for output, 41–42
  welfare costs of US quotas in, 85–110
  welfare measure, 58–59, 139, 141–142
Government accounts, 215
Government revenues, 42, 48, 196
  excise taxes and, 175

Hedonic regression, 80–81
Hicksian compensating variation, 62, 86, 141–142
Hicksian equivalent variation, 58–60, 62, 86, 141, 142
Hong Kong, 8, 67, 71–74, 76, 77
Household accounts, 215

Imperfect competition, 17, 195–196
  calibration under, 224–227
  general equilibrium model modifications for, 150–156
  welfare costs of quantitative restrictions, 156–166
Import data, 208–210
Import supply, 7, 47–48
Import tariffs, 180, 189
Import tax, vs. excise tax, 6–7, 179–189
Imposing a tariff, in one–sector general equilibrium model, 26–29
Income, elasticity of labor supply and, 236–237
Income definition, 48
Increasing returns to scale (*IRTS*), 146–148, 220, 224–225. *See also* Economies of scale
Indirect compensation function, 61
Indirect utility function (*IU*), 61
  with labor-leisure choice, 141
Input-output updating, 203–206
Interactions between product and factor market distortions, 5
Interindustry flows, 211, 212–213, 218, 220–221
Interindustry linkages, 6, 7
Interindustry wage differentials, distortions from, 119–121
Intermediate demand, 47, 51
Internal prices of traded goods, 47
International capital mobility, 139, 166–167
  trade liberalization in autos and, 162
  welfare costs of quotas and, 134–138
International comparisons, of hourly compensation costs for steel and automobile workers, 117
Iron and steel. *See* Steel
IRTS (increasing returns to scale), 145–148, 220, 224–225
IU (indirect utility function), 61

Japan, 73, 74, 83–84
  direct foreign investments of, 163
Japanese automobiles, 4, 95. *See also* Automobiles
  direct foreign investment in the US by producers of, 163, 238–240
  quota rent estimates and price of, 80–81
  removal of voluntary export restraints, 93–96
  US imports of, value of, 82
  voluntary export restraints, 5, 8
Japan Iron and Steel Exporters Association-USA, 84

Kennedy Round, 200
Korean Ministry of Trade and Industry, 83–84

Labor adjustment, 6
  trade liberalization and estimated costs of, 196–198
Labor displacement, 7
Labor-leisure choice, 112–115, 138
Labor relocation, from QR removal, 93
Labor supply
  elasticity of, 236–237
  leisure demand and, 140–141
Labor union(s)
  employment determination and, 124–128
  modeling of, in automobile and steel sectors, 123–130
  wage determination and, 124–128
  wage differential, derivation of, 142–143

Large-country case, one-sector model, 22–24
Law of one price, 16
Le Chatelier principle, 131
Leontief production function, 50
Leontief production function, 17, 35, 50–51
Lerner symmetry theorem, 29
LES (linear expenditure system), 44, 113, 140, 182
Liberalization, with endogenous quota premia, 107–109
Linear expenditure system. *See* LES
Long-Term Agreement on Cotton Textiles, 69, 76

Marginal rate of substitution, 26
Marginal rate of transformation, 26
MES (minimum efficient scale), 146, 226–227
MFA. *See* Multifiber Arrangement
Minimum efficient scale (MES), 146, 226–227
Mining, 176
  elasticity specifications, 88, 232, 233, 235
  employment, joint removal of quotas and, 100–101, 115, 132
  employment, quota removal with sectorally fixed capital stocks, 132
  exports and imports, joint removal of quotas and, 101
  joint quota removal, 100–101, 115
Money metric utility function, 61
Monopolistic competition 149–150, 155, 158, 161, 163, 166–167
Monopoly in exporting, capture of quota rents and, 68–69
Monopoly power, 104
  in agriculture, 103
  in exports, 18
  facilitating practice for, 4
  foreign offer curve and, 29
  United States, 54
  welfare costs and, 24, 103–104
Monopsony power, 77–78, 93, 96, 104
  capture of quota rents and, 67–68
  foreign offer curve and, 29
  United States, 54
Motor vehicles. *See* Automobile(s)
MRS (marginal rate of substitution), 26
Multifiber Arrangement (MFA), 66–70, 76, 92. *See also* Textiles and apparel
Multilateral negotiations, 1, 3, 6, 191, 200
Multisector general equilibrium trade model. *See* General equilibrium model

National income, 157
National Income and Product Accounts (NIPA), 203, 206
National product differentiation, 17–18
Natural gas, 176
Neoclassical general equilibrium specification, 11
Nested CES, 32
NIPA (National Income and Product Accounts), 203, 206
Nominal exchange rate, 20, 31
Nontariff barriers, 1, 3, 6
Nontraded services, 193–194
  elasticity specifications, 88, 232, 233, 235
  employment, joint removal of quotas and, 100–101, 115, 132
  employment, quota removal with sectorally fixed capital stocks, 132
  exports and imports, joint removal of quotas and, 101
  joint quota removal, 100–101, 115
Numéraire, 16, 29–31, 48

Oil and gas products, revenue, employment and welfare estimates, 178–180. *See also* Petroleum products industry
Oil import quota system, 67
Oligopsony, capture of quota rents and, 67–68
One-sector general equilibrium model, 15, 31
  costs of protection, 31–34
  with differentiated trade, 18–24
  equations, 18–20
  equilibrium in, 20–22
  imposing a tariff, 26–29
  introduction of exports, 38–39
  large-country case, 22–24
  numéraire and the real exchange rate, 29–31
  terms-of-trade effects in, 24–26
  with product differentiation, graphical presentation, 21–22
OPEC, 174
Optimal taxation, 173, 184–186, 188
Optimization algorithm, 176

Partial equilibrium analysis, 8, 10, 15, 105–106, 180, 184
of costs of protection in textile, apparel, automobile and steel, 9
estimates, comparison with general equilibrium, 105–106
Passive firm and wage determination, 124–125, 127
Petroleum products industry, 176
demand from, 188
optimal taxation of, 184–189
elasticities specification, 176–178, 232–233, 235
modification of general equilibrium model for excise taxes, 175
production and demand structure, 177
relative efficiency of excise taxes and tariffs, 179–189
taxation proposals for, 174
Policy issues, 1–5
Premium rate, overall, quota rent estimates and, 82
estimate in automobiles, 78–83
estimate in textiles and apparel, 69–78
Price elasticity of demand, general equilibrium derivation of, 167–171
Price elasticity of supply, 131
Price indexes, 53–54
Pricing, imperfect competition and, 152
in automobiles, 148–150
in steel, 146–147
Product differentiation, 76
firm level, 17
and imperfect substitution on import side, 35–38
justification for, 17
national, 17–18
specialization and, 16–18
Protection. *See also* Quantitative restrictions; Tariff removal
endogenous wage distortions and, 130
government revenue and, 196
instruments of, 2
monopolistic competition and, 158
pressure for, 1
removal of, in steel and auto sectors, 6
terms-of-trade loss and, 194
unilateral removal, in multiregion model, 10
in US, rise of, 3
using CGE model, consequences of, 6
Quality upgrading, voluntary export restraints and, 78–80
Quantitative restrictions (QR), 3, 32, 115, 135, 138, 139, 174
on apparel, 87 (*see also* Textiles and apparel)
on autos, 87 (*see also* Automobiles)
on steel (*see* Steel)
costs, with rationing by sector, 109–110
distortionary costs of, 85–86, 91–92, 121
elasticities, impact on costs (asymmetric) of imposing quotas, 97–98
elasticities, impact on costs of removing quotas, 90–91
with endogenous quota premia, 107–109
as facilitating practices, 4
under imperfect competition, 156–166
joint removal, 100–101, 103
with labor-leisure choice, costs of, 113–115
protection, 194–195
removal, 85, 87, 104
removal, with endogenous wage distortions, 128–130, 195
removal, with exogenous wage distortions, 121–122
removal, with international capital mobility, 130–132
size of premiums, 65
as tariff equivalents, 108–109
as tariff equivalence in welfare, computation of, 199–200
welfare costs, 191
welfare costs, with imperfect competition, 156–166
Quota premium rate, 73, 199, 227–228. *See also* Premium rate
Quota removal. *See* Quantitative restrictions
Quota rent capture, 3–4, 65
in automobiles, 82–83
benefits from, 101–102
by exporters, lower-bound estimate, 77–78
by foreigners, 24, 26
in Hong Kong, 77
Quota rent estimates
in textiles and apparel, 69–78
for automobiles from Japan and Europe, 78–83
Quota rents, 42, 85, 193
capture of (*see* Quota rent capture)

Quotas. *See* Quantitative restrictions

Rationing, 48
of steel by sector, welfare costs of, 109–110
Real exchange rate, 15–16, 20, 30, 42, 62–63
choice of numéraire and, 29–31
fixing, 105
QR removal and, 100
welfare and, 30–31
Real wage
elasticity of labor supply and, 236–237
joint removal of quotas and, 98–101
Relative price of traded to nontraded goods, 16
Relocation of workers, with protection removal, 7
Rental rate on capital, 214
Rents in rationed sectors, 48
Rent transfer component of QRs, 32, 85–87, 193. *See also* Capture of quota rents
Rest-of-the-world account, 215
Revenue-raising protection, 5, 179–189
Ricardian case, 22, 30

SAM. *See* Social Accounting Matrix
Second-best effects, cost of QRs under, 195
Sectors. *See also specific sectors*
aggregation and, 43
gross output calculation, 206
input-output updating, 203–206
Shephard's lemma, 51, 127
SITC. *See* Standard International Trade Classification
Smoot-Hawley tariff, 1
Social Accounting Matrix (SAM)
description, 214–218
model calibration, 218–228
Solow-type growth model, 201
Standard International Trade Classification (SITC), 17, 208–209
Steel, 17, 34, 44, 85, 151, 166, 176, 195
costs of QR protection, 6, 8, 96–98
distortionary costs of QRs, 121, 128, 130, 166–167
economies of scale, 146
elasticities, effects on costs of imposing QRs, 96–98
elasticities specification, 88, 232–233, 235
employment, change in quotas and, 100–101, 115, 132
endogenous wage distortions and costs of QRs, 128–130, 139
exogenous wage distortions and costs of QRs, 138
exports and imports, change in QRs and, 101
imperfect competition and costs of quotas, 158–160
imperfect competition in, 146–147, 158
imposition of quantitative restrictions, 128
interactions with automobile sector under imperfect competition, 163–166
interindustry wage differences, 117–121
joint quota removal, 100–101, 115
labor unions and wage distortions, 123–130
production and demand structure, 87, 89
quantitative restrictions, 121, 128, 130
quota removal, with sectorally fixed capital stock, 130–134
quota removal, with internationally mobile capital, 136–138
quotas with fixed capital stocks, 132
rationing by sector, welfare costs of, 109–110
removal of protection, 6
short-run welfare costs of quotas, 130–134
voluntary export restraints, 83–84, 96–98, 166–167
wage distortions, 5, 116–118
welfare cost comparisons, 192
Stone-Geary utility function, 32, 54, 59, 61, 76, 112–113, 124
extended, 139, 141

Tariff removal, gains from, 102
with fixed capital stock, 131
with internationally mobile capital, 136, 138
joint removal of quotas and, 98–101
effect of supply elasticity on, 132–133
Tariffs, 6, 8, 34, 42, 72, 92 95, 138, 139, 173, 174, 184–186, 196, 210
computation of, with welfare cost equivalent to quotas, 199–200
imposing, in one-sector general equilibrium model, 26–29
optimal, in energy industries, 178–181

Tariffs (cont.)
protection, elimination of, 85
rates of, 188
Taxes, 42, 174, 196. *See also* Excise taxes
on final petroleum products, 5
Terms-of-trade, 46, 93, 96, 103–104, 194
graphical analysis of, 24–26
Textiles, 85, 176, 193–194. *See also* Multifiber Arrangement (MFA)
capture of quota rents, 66–67
capture of quota rents by foreigners, 92
costs of protection in, 89, 90
costs of QR protection in, 7–8
elasticities, effect on costs of VERs, 90–92
elasticity specifications, 88, 232, 233, 235
employment, quota removal and, 100–101, 115, 132
estimating the quota premium rate, 69–78
exports and imports, joint quota removal, 100–101, 115
production and demand structure, 87, 89
quantitative restrictions, 65, 87
quota premium rates, and estimation of, 69–78
quota removal, 89–93, 131
quota removal, with internationally mobile capital, 136–137
quota removal, with sectorally fixed capital stock, 131
welfare cost comparisons, 192
Tokyo Round, 10, 200
Trade balance constraint, 48
Trade deficit, reduction, 6, 174
Trade dependence, product differentiation and degree of, 36
Trade distortions, 30
Traded services
elasticity specifications, 88, 232, 233, 235
employment, joint removal of quotas and, 100–101, 115, 132
employment, quota removal with sectorally fixed capital stocks, 132
exports and imports, joint removal of quotas and, 101
joint quota removal, 100–101, 115
Trade elasticities, 32
Trade policy issues, 3–5, 191–202
Trade protection. *See* Protection
Two-way trade, 17

Union-firm contract curve, 126–127
Unit cost and revenue prices, 47
United Autoworkers Union, 5, 116, 123
United States International Trade Commission, 4
United Steelworkers Union, 5, 116, 123
Uruguay Round, 10

Virtual price, 53
Voluntary export restraint (VER), 2, 3, 42, 80, 81, 96, 145, 163, 191, 195
in automobiles (*see* Automobiles)
distortionary cost component, 85–87, 166–167
joint removal in three sectors, 98–101
quality upgrading and, 78–80
removal of, on Japanese autos, 93–96
in steel (*see* Steel)
on textiles and apparel (*see* Textiles and apparel)
welfare costs of, tariff equivalence, 96, 199–200

Wage determination, labor unions and, 124–128
Wage distortions, 4, 6, 115–116, 201
in automobiles, 116–118
endogenous, 128–130, 138, 139
estimation methods, 118
exogenous, 118–121, 138
quantitative restrictions and, 195
quota removal with endogenous, 128–130,
quota removal with exogenous, 121–123
removal, employment effects of, 120–121
removal, welfare effects of, 120
in steel, 116–118
Walras' law, 20, 43, 55, 214–215
Welfare, 6. *See also* Equivalent variation
analysis, with labor-leisure trade off, 141–142
benefits, of quota removals, 106–107
impact, of tariff on imported petroleum products, 186–187
real exchange rate and, 30–31
Welfare costs comparisons, 9, 192
to equivalent tariff, 199–200
Welfare costs of quantitative restrictions, 65, 85, 191
in automobiles (*see* Automobiles)
comparison with earlier estimates, 9, 105–107

conjectures, impact of, under imperfect competition, 162–163
distortionary costs and, 193
with endogenous wage distortions, 128–130
with exogenous wage distortions, 128–130
with imperfect competition, 156–166
with international capital mobility, 134–138
with labor-leisure choice, 113–114
with sectorally fixed capital stocks, 130–134
with rationing by sector, 109–110
in steel (*see* Steel)
in textiles and apparel (*see* Textiles and apparel)
Welfare-equivalent tariff structure, calculation of, 199–200
Welfare estimates, for taxes and tariffs on oil and gas products, 178–180
Welfare measure, definition of, 59–63
Welfare-reducing capital import, 6, 137
Women, elasticity of labor supply, 237

Breinigsville, PA USA
08 February 2011
255102BV00004B/119/P